The Resilience of Multiculturalism

The Resilience of Multiculturalism

Ideas, Politics and Practice

Essays in honour of Tariq Modood

Edited by

THOMAS SEALY, VARUN UBEROI,
NASAR MEER

EDINBURGH
University Press

Edinburgh University Press is one of the leading university presses in the UK. We publish academic books and journals in our selected subject areas across the humanities and social sciences, combining cutting-edge scholarship with high editorial and production values to produce academic works of lasting importance. For more information visit our website: edinburghuniversitypress.com

Edinburgh University Press Ltd
13 Infirmary Street
Edinburgh EH1 1LT

Typeset in 10.5/13 ITC Giovanni Std by
IDSUK (DataConnection) Ltd

A CIP record for this book is available from the British Library

ISBN 978 1 3995 3725 4 (hardback)
ISBN 978 1 3995 3726 1 (paperback)
ISBN 978 1 3995 3727 8 (webready PDF)
ISBN 978 1 3995 3728 5 (epub)

CONTENTS

FIGURES

ACKNOWLEDGEMENTS

This volume would not have been possible without funding from the Zutshi-Smith Fund. They allowed the 'Who do we think we are?' Symposium at the University of Bristol in September 2022 to occur, at which the chapters in this volume were first discussed. We would like to thank Judith Squires, Julian Rivers and Therese O'Toole for their support and contributions to the event. We are extremely grateful to John Denham, Zara Mohammed and Gary Younge for the public event panel discussion that got the conference off to such a thought-provoking start. As well as those contributors to this volume, the conference benefited immensely from the presence and contributions of Anne Phillips, Anthony Heath, Adrian Favell, Michèle Lamont, James Nazroo, Nadia Fadil, Colin Tyler, Salman Sayyid, Jan Dobbernack, Erdem Dikici and Samir Sweida-Metwally. We are grateful to our editorial team at EUP for their enthusiasm for the book and seeing it through from start to finish, as well as to the anonymous reviewers, who made useful suggestions that helped to improve the volume. But without Tariq Modood's political, philosophical and sociological scholarship and public interventions, such a book would not have been necessary. We thus dedicate this book to him in recognition of how he has influenced his fellow academics in different disciplines and public debate while stimulating our own scholarship and that of so many others.

NOTES ON THE CONTRIBUTORS

Rajeev Bhargava is Director of the Parekh Institute of Indian Thought at the Centre for the Study of Developing Societies in New Delhi, where he has worked since 2005. His writings include *What is Political Theory and Why Do We Need It?* (2010) and *The Promise of India's Secular Democracy* (2010). His latest book is *Reimagining Indian Secularism* (Seagull Books, 2023).

David Boucher is Professor of Political Philosophy and International Relations. He has held visiting fellowships and professorships at the Australian National University; Canterbury University, Christchurch, New Zealand; The National Sun Yat Sen University, Taiwan; and Oxford University. He is also Distinguished Visiting Professor, Department of Political Science, University of Johannesburg, South Africa 2016–26. His most recent books are *Bob Dylan and Leonard Cohen: Deaths and Entrances* (2021, with Lucy Boucher); *Language, Culture and Decolonisation* (ed. 2022); and *Decolonisation: Revolution and Evolution* (ed. with Aysha Omar 2023).

Riva Kastoryano is a research director at the CNRS (National Centre for Scientific Research) and Professor at SciencesPo Paris. Her work focuses on identity and minority issues and more specifically on their relations to states in France, Germany and the United States. She was a lecturer at Harvard University 1984–7, has been teaching at the Institute for Political Studies in Paris (Sciences Po) since 1988, and a Visiting Professor at the New School for Social Research since 2005. Her books include *Negotiating Identities: States and Immigrants in France and Germany* (Princeton University Press, 2002); *Les codes de la différence: Religion, Origine, Race en France, Allemagne et Etats-Unis* (Codes of Otherness: Religion, Ancestors and Race in France, Germany and the United States) (Presses de Sciences

Po, 2005); *Turkey Between Nationalism and Globalization* (Routledge, 2013). Her most recent books are *Que faire des corps des djihadistes? Territoire et identité* (Fayard, 2015) and *Burying Jihadis: Bodies between State, Territory and Identity* (OUP and Hurst, 2018).

Will Kymlicka is Professor and Canada Research Chair in Political Philosophy at Queen's University, Canada. His books include: *Contemporary Political Philosophy* (OUP, 1990); *Multicultural Citizenship* (OUP, 1995), which was awarded the Macpherson Prize by the Canadian Political Science Association and the Bunche Award by the American Political Science Association; *Multicultural Odysseys: Navigating the New International Politics of Diversity* (OUP, 2007), which was awarded the North American Society for Social Philosophy's 2007 Book Award; and *Zoopolis: A Political Theory of Animal Rights* (OUP, 2011), co-authored with Sue Donaldson, which was awarded the Canadian Philosophical Association's Best Book Prize in 2013.

Cécile Laborde holds the Nuffield Chair of Political Theory at the University of Oxford and is a Fellow of the British Academy. She is the author of *Pluralist Thought and the State* (2000), *Critical Republicanism* (2008) and *Liberalism's Religion* (2017), which was published by Harvard University Press and won the 2018 Spitz Prize. Her work on republicanism, non-domination, secularism and religion has appeared in *Journal of Political Philosophy, American Political Science Review, American Journal of Political Science, Law and Philosophy, Legal Theory, British Journal of Political Science, European Journal of Political Theory, Oxford Studies in Political Philosophy*.

Sune Lægaard, PhD, is Associate Dean for Education at the Department for Communication and Arts at Roskilde University, Denmark. He works in political philosophy on issues related to multiculturalism, including politics and religion, toleration and recognition, and free speech, and on the methodology of political philosophy. He is Editor-in-Chief of the journal *Res Publica* (published by Springer), a member of the board of the Danish Institute of Human Rights, and a member of the steering committee of the ECPR standing group on Methods of Normative Political Theory.

Geoffrey Brahm Levey is Associate Professor of Political Science at the University of New South Wales, Sydney. He is editor of *The Research Handbook on Multiculturalism* (Edward Elgar, forthcoming) and co-edited, with Tariq Modood, *Secularism, Religion and Multicultural Citizenship* (Cambridge University Press, 2008).

Gurpreet Mahajan was, prior to retirement, Professor at the Centre for Political Studies, School of Social Sciences, Jawaharlal Nehru University. She has written extensively on issues of multiculturalism, minority rights, secularism and civil society. She is the author of *Explanation and Understanding in the Human Sciences* (OUP, 1992, 1997, 2011), *Identities and Rights: Aspects of Liberal Democracy in India* (OUP, 1998), *The Multicultural Path: Issues of Diversity and Discrimination in Democracy* (Sage, 2002) and *India: Political Ideas and the Making of a Democratic Discourse* (Zed Books, 2013). Her other recent publications include *Religion, Community and Development: Changing Contours of Politics and Policy in India* (Routledge, 2010) and *Accommodating Diversity: Ideas and Institutional Practices* (OUP, 2011).

Maleiha Malik is Professor of Law at King's College, London. Her teaching and research interests include UK, EU and comparative discrimination law; feminism; the relationship between race, culture and law; legal pluralism. She is the co-author of a leading text titled *Discrimination Law: Theory and Context*. She was part of the steering committee of the AHRC-ESCRC Religion and Society programme and on the advisory board of the Max Planck Institute in Halle, Germany. Her research has been supported by, inter alia: UK Arts and Humanities Research Council; Leverhulme Trust; British Council; Open Society Institute. She has held a number of Visiting Professor roles, including at the Université Libre de Bruxelles in Belgium and Vietnam National University in Hanoi.

Nasar Meer is Professor in Social and Political Sciences at the University of Glasgow, Scotland. He was previously Professor of Sociology and Director of RACE.ED at the University of Edinburgh, and Professor of Comparative Social Policy at the University of Strathclyde. He is a Fellow of the Royal Society of Edinburgh (FRSE) and Fellow of the Academy of Social Sciences (FAcSS) and his books include *The Cruel Optimism of Racial Justice* (2022) and *Citizenship, Identity and the Politics of Multiculturalism: The Rise of Muslim Consciousness* (2015 2nd edition).

Tariq Modood is Professor of Sociology, Politics and Public Policy and the founding Director of the Centre for the Study of Ethnicity and Citizenship at the University of Bristol. He was awarded a MBE for services to social sciences and ethnic relations in 2001, made a Fellow of the Academy of Social Sciences (UK) in 2004 and elected a Fellow of the British Academy in 2017. In 2022 he was ranked in the top twenty UK-cited scholars in Politics, Law, Sociology and Social Policy.

His latest book, with Thomas Sealy, is *The New Governance of Religious Diversity* (Polity, 2024). His website is tariqmodood.com

Lord Bhikhu Parekh is Emeritus Professor of Political Philosophy, University of Westminster and Emeritus Professor, University of Hull. He is a Fellow of the British Academy and served as President of the Academy of Social Sciences from 2003 to 2008. He was appointed a life peer of the House of Lords in 2000.

Thomas Sealy is Lecturer in Ethnicity and Race at the University of Bristol and a member of the Centre for the Study of Ethnicity and Citizenship. He researches and teaches on multiculturalism, ethnicity and racism, and religion and politics. He has published journal articles and book chapters in these areas, including co-editing special issues of *The Political Quarterly* and *Religion, State and Society*. His latest book (with Tariq Modood) is *The New Governance of Religious Diversity* (Polity, 2024).

Charles Taylor is Emeritus Professor of Philosophy at McGill University, Montreal. His books include *Sources of the Self* (1989) and *A Secular Age* (2007).

Simon Thompson is Associate Professor in Political Theory at the University of the West of England, Bristol. He is also an Affiliated Member of the Centre for the Study of Ethnicity and Citizenship, University of Bristol. He is author of *The Political Theory of Recognition* (2006) and co-editor of *Global Justice and the Politics of Recognition* (2013), *The Politics of Misrecognition* (2012), *Politics and the Emotions* (2012), *Emotions, Politics and Society* (2006) and *Richard Rorty: Critical Dialogues* (2001). He has co-edited special issues of *Ethnicities* (2012, 2022) and *Res Publica* (2012). He has also published articles in a wide range of journals, including *Contemporary Political Theory*, *Ethnicities*, *European Journal of Political Theory*, *Philosophy and Social Criticism*, *Political Studies* and *Res Publica*.

Anna Triandafyllidou holds the Canada Excellence Research Chair in Migration and Integration at Toronto Metropolitan University. She is also the Scientific Director of a new Canada First Research Excellence Fund Research Programme entitled Bridging Divides. Prior to joining TMU in August 2019, she held a Robert Schuman Chair at the European University Institute in Florence, Italy. She is Editor of the *Journal of Immigrant and Refugee Studies*. In 2021 the University of Liège awarded her a doctorate *honoris causa* in recognition of her contribution to migration scholarship. Her recent work has appeared in *Journal of Ethnic and Migration Studies*

(2022), *Environment and Planning A: Economy and Society* (2022), *Journal of Immigrant and Refugee Studies* (2023), *Ethnicities* (2023, 2022), *Comparative Migration Studies* (2021, 2022), *International Migration* (2022, 2019) and *Nations and Nationalism* (2020).

Varun Uberoi is Reader in Political Theory and Public Policy at Loughborough University. He and Tariq Modood published *Multiculturalism Rethought* and he has published widely on multiculturalism in journals such as *History of Political Thought, Political Studies, Critical Review of International, Social and Political Philosophy, Ethnicities* and *Journal of Ethnic and Migration Studies*.

Modoodian Multiculturalism

Thomas Sealy, Varun Uberoi, Nasar Meer

The Resilience of Multiculturalism

Since the turn of the millennium, a range of voices have questioned the suitability of multicultural ideas, including those sympathetic to cultural diversity more broadly. For its detractors, multiculturalism has been blamed for all manner of social ills, including community segregation, a lack of shared identity and belonging, and even extremism (Meer and Modood 2009; Vertovec and Wessendorf 2010). It has come under fierce critique across Europe, South America, and in countries as distinct as Canada and India. It was famously pronounced a failure by David Cameron, Nicolas Sarkozy and Angela Merkel over a decade ago, something routinely repeated by successive politicians in Western European states. Some scholars have referred to it as a zombie category; 'the living dead' and no longer fit for purpose (Beck 2002; Cantle 2012; Uberoi and Modood 2013; Meer and Modood 2014; Sealy 2018). Such assertions of failure persist in recent debates around populism and the so-called 'culture wars', and recent scholarly work has addressed multiculturalism's supposed inability to pay sufficient attention to majority groups (Orgad and Koopmans 2023).

Despite its death knell having been sounded by scholars and politicians alike over some two decades, multiculturalism has proven to be remarkably resilient and continues to be immensely salient on issues of citizenship, diversity and identity, and its insights and ideas remain extremely influential. As a political idea and intellectual orientation, multiculturalism has proven to be enduring as well as contested, with wide-ranging and multidimensional implications for how we imagine national identities (Uberoi 2018, 2023; Modood 2020; Chin 2020), conceive the role and status of cultural groupings (Parekh 2000; Banting 2021) and configure membership and citizenship (Kymlicka 1995; Modood 2013). Moreover, multiculturalism and issues of citizenship, identity and belonging have been prominent on political and media agendas and broader public debates as part of recent significant political events. For example, as social movements such as the protests under the banner of Black Lives Matter spread around the world in 2020, have brought issues of ethnic and racial justice to the foreground; current and former politicians in Britain continue to pronounce on multiculturalism's futility or benefits (see, for example, Braverman 2023; Denham 2023); Australia held a referendum to recognise indigenous people in the constitution (which failed to pass) (Maguire 2023); and recent debates in India around the prospect of a Uniform Civil Code pose serious questions for Indian multiculturalism and secularism (BBC 2022, 2023; Reuters 2023).

Multiculturalism is also healthier in policy than the rhetoric would have it seem. Analysis of policies in twenty-one countries between 1980 and 2020 shows that only three countries had a lower score on multicultural policies in 2020 than they did in 2000 (Multiculturalism Policy Index n.d.). Canada and Australia have celebrated more than fifty years of official policies of multiculturalism (Kymlicka 2021; Banting 2022; May 2022). Despite the 'majoritarian turn', Indian policies for minorities 'remain an important lever of inclusion' (De Souza, Ahmed and Alam 2019: 155). In Britain, behind repeated political rhetoric to the contrary, multiculturalism remains a central feature of the policy landscape (Mathieu 2017; Dupont, Sealy and Modood 2023; Sealy, Dupont and Modood 2024), and social trust among different groups, recognition of the importance of addressing discrimination, and the valuing of diversity are at an all-time high (World Values Survey 2023).

Britain provides a good example of how the endurance we describe is also characterised by a consistency in the advocacy of multiculturalism, something illustrated by setting contemporary obituaries of multiculturalism alongside others at the turn of the millennium in Britain (Meer 2022: 50). This was a long overdue opening to rethink the national story alongside the election of a Labour government that came to office with a large electoral mandate and reforming agenda. As the government declared a commitment to creating a country where racial diversity was 'celebrated' (Home Office 2000: 1), activists, commentators and academics were labouring on a state-of-the-nation-type report published by the *Commission on the Future of Multi-Ethnic Britain* (CMEB 2000). The report, led by the political philosopher Bhikhu Parekh, made the case to better align the formal representation of Britain so as to reflect the identifications of its people – shifting from a laissez-faire 'multicultural drift' (Hall 1996) to a concerted, policy-based recognition of how postcolonial Britons had remade Britain. The clue was in the title: *the Future of Multi-Ethnic Britain*. Revisiting the report today, it is a strikingly measured and sophisticated attempt to reconcile a changing national identity with an honest and necessary account of its origins; to forge a country that did not disenfranchise its Black and ethnic minorities (Meer 2020; Sealy 2020; Uberoi 2015; Uberoi 2020). This is why the commission recommended that central government take steps in formally declaring Britain 'a multicultural society' (CMEB 2000: 296) – it was hoped that such an approach would begin to invalidate the social and political inequalities derived from postcolonial migration and settlement.

A question that then arises is: how can we understand this resilience of multiculturalism and its expression in politics, policy and culture today? This is the question at the centre of this volume. This book brings together contributions from scholars who have been deeply attentive to these debates and to the global relevance of multiculturalism. It does so in relation to one of the most respected and influential thinkers of multiculturalism engaged with the issues identified above and who has done much to show how a political multiculturalism is not just very much alive, but has continued to develop it and bear relevance for contemporary issues and debates: Tariq Modood. Modood's thought has had a demonstrable impact through cutting-edge contributions across disciplinary traditions in politics, sociology and social policy, and thematically spanned citizenship, ethnicity and racism, religion and secularism, diversity and integration, and nationalism and migration.

Modood was an active commissioner on the CMEB, but his first book-length statement on multiculturalism (2007) came after the backlash had begun. Modood argued, 'Contrary to those who think that the time to speak of multiculturalism is over, I think it is most timely and necessary, and that we need more not less' (2007: 14). Modood's book and subsequent work across the fields identified above has elaborated why this is the case. Modood's contributions to these debates have provided the point of orientation for other scholars, those who might call themselves multiculturalists, those who are extremely critical of multiculturalism, as well as others in between who are engaged with multiculturalism's core areas of concern. In these ways, Modood's thought has played a key role in maintaining and demonstrating the continued relevance of multiculturalism as a theoretical endeavour, as part of the policy landscape, and as a significant voice in live debates about how we can and should live together. Modood's contribution is not only scholarly, therefore, as it is also found in significant contributions as a public intellectual (on which, see Modood 2017), in policy oriented work, and media appearances and writings.

Bringing together leading scholars from the Global North and Global South, this book interrogates ideas of multiculturalism and their resilience in politics, policy and culture, contributing to debates on citizenship and diversity, identity and belonging, and nationalism and migration. To do so, the chapters are centrally engaged with Modood's thought and work as one of the foremost thinkers and proponents in the field; critically treating different areas of Modood's thought in ways generative of novel concerns.

The chapters themselves arise out of papers presented at a Festschrift conference held at the University of Bristol in September 2022. The chapters are organised into four thematic sections, each reflecting related but distinct concerns of multicultural thinking. The first addresses core principles. The second section addresses the most central concern of multiculturalism, the inclusion of ethnic and cultural diversity. The third section turns to a key aspect of multicultural inclusion: nationalism, and includes transnational perspectives on this issue. The fourth section turns to a more specific form of diversity that has been important for multicultural thinking, religious diversity and secularism. The volume concludes with a response from Modood to the contributions and their engagement with the idea of multiculturalism.

In the sections that follow for this introduction to the volume, we introduce key components of Modood's multiculturalism, highlighting its distinctiveness, and point to how the contributions of this volume relate to various aspects of it.

Modoodian Multiculturalism

A recent development in what we might call the meta-literature has been to more clearly identify 'schools' of multiculturalism, how they relate to each other, what unites and differentiates them. In an article in the journal *Ethnicities*, Levey (2019) interpellated the Bristol School of Multiculturalism (BSM). Identifying key figures and collaborations, Levey notes in particular the significance of the institutional association of the Centre for the Study of Ethnicity and Citizenship at the University of Bristol, which Tariq Modood co-founded and has directed since 1997, and of which Modood 'has been the driving force, intellectually and organisationally' (Levey 2019: 201). Levey's article and accompanying symposium pieces get at some of the fundamental aspects of the distinctiveness of the BSM.[1] What we want to go on to do in the following sections of this introduction, however, is outline the main features of what we are referring to as a distinctive *Modoodian multiculturalism*, which underpins the BSM more broadly.

As mentioned above, Modood's output and contributions have straddled and combined different disciplinary areas, and this in many ways is what makes Modood's thought distinctive. A particularly instructive way to begin here is more biographical. The following section sketches a brief biographical trajectory, which subsequent sections will use to flesh out in relation to the development and key features of a Modoodian multiculturalism.

Karachi to Kilburn to Kingsdown

Born in Karachi, Pakistan, Modood came to Britain when he was eight years old (in 1961) with very little English. His own school life hints at some of the changes taking place in Britain at the time that would come to put multiculturalism firmly on the landscape, in particular a shift from his school being majority white British when he started to being majority made up of national ethnic minority pupils when he left, and during which time he experienced racism and ethnic tensions. It was during Modood's school years in Kilburn, London that Britain moved to an understanding of integration conceived, in the words of Roy Jenkins, 'not as a flattening process of assimilation but as equal opportunity, accompanied by cultural diversity, in an atmosphere of mutual tolerance' (1967: 267).

Having gained a GCSE in Sociology (his only formal qualification in the subject), Modood studied philosophy and politics at Durham, before a Master's in political theory, then a PhD in philosophy at Swansea. While he did have a couple of temporary lectureships in political theory, the contraction in employment opportunities in this field in the 1980s pushed him out of academia. After a hiatus at the tax inspectorate, he moved into local government equal opportunities policy work, working on the labour market and racial inequality. It was here that Modood encountered and came to question the dominant ways of thinking about racism and anti-racism at the time oriented around political blackness, and how he did not fit into the political categories ascribed to him by those to whom he was 'other' or offered to him by those opposing racism in Britain. This was to gain greater significance following the Satanic Verses Affair, which proved something of a crossroads for Modood as well as Muslims more generally, creating a political and sociological sense of Muslim identity and agency, and a matter into which Modood would make notable interventions. Not only did Modood view as too simple the oppositional approach of the anti-racisms of the time, and out of which he wanted to build something positive, but also the ethical obligation to correct distortions of the British Muslim complaints (Modood 1990: 155).

Modood would go on to lead a team of sociologists to produce the Fourth National Survey of Ethnic Minorities (1993–7; see report: Modood et al. 1997), where he would further develop the position he had begun through his early publications (scholarly and media) on ethnic minority experiences and identities in Britain, particularly for South Asians (see, for example, Modood 1988, 1989, 1992).

Reflecting significant aspects of this biographical trajectory, when taking up his professorship at the University of Bristol in 1997, Modood took the title Professor of Sociology, Politics and Public Policy, and has described himself as 'an exile from political theory' coming into sociology. Modood has remained at Bristol, and the Centre for the Study of Ethnicity and Citizenship recently celebrated its twentieth anniversary.[2]

Modoodian multiculturalism

Modood, then, would establish his form of multiculturalism through a bringing together of political theory and sociology. Yet, as Boucher outlines in his chapter in this volume, the foundational philosophical orientations from Modood's doctoral thesis and engagement with British idealism are clearly discernible in his multiculturalism. Boucher argues that it is from his encounters with Oakeshott and Collingwood, on whom Modood wrote his doctoral thesis, where his rejection of the distinction between, and subsequent rapprochement between theory and practice that would come to underpin his approach to multiculturalism intellectually derives.

It is, nevertheless, equally impossible to understand Modood's political multiculturalism without his sociology of ethnicity and racism. Modood himself has said that it was considerations in relation to the latter that led to the 'bigger questions' of the former. While Levey's calling into being the BSM outlines with some clarity its distinctiveness in relation to other multiculturalisms, its focus on the political theory of multiculturalism overlooks the vital sociology that provides so much of the impetus and energy, as well as distinctiveness, of Modood's thought. Modood's time leading the Fourth National Survey and engagement with the Satanic Verses Affair had provided grounded empirical sociological research that underpinned his theoretical political thinking. This combination of sociology and political theory continued to shape Modood's work; not just in the sense of an empirically informed political theory, but in how an engaged empirical sociology would also become central to Modood's way of doing political theory itself. This is one of the key distinguishing features between Modood and Parekh, for instance, despite the mutual influence, intellectual indebtedness and friendship they share. Whereas they share a position which sees people as deeply culturally embedded, an understanding of human beings as formed in socio-cultural webs of meaning (Parekh 2000), Modood's work would add sociological thickness to this, principally through considering the case of South Asians in Britain (as does Parekh), and Muslims in particular.

Prompted by the Satanic Verses Affair, Modood pointed to how neither the Race Relations Act 1976 (the main anti-racism legislation in the UK at the time of the SV Affair), nor accommodations made for other minority groups on the basis of ethnicity (and seen therefore as concomitant with 'race'), such as those for Jews and Sikhs, offered protection for Muslims qua Muslims (1994). Muslims were not an ethnic or national group, covering several such, and thus could not be politically or legally recognised as one, a point also made by the courts (Modood 2016). Significant, also, was that prevailing anti-racism movements at the time of the Satanic Verses Affair went missing, being more cautious when religion is on the agenda, meaning that Muslims lacked social solidarity from these groups. Added to this was a further factor Modood highlighted: most Muslims did not see themselves as either ethnically or politically 'black', and therefore prevailing understandings of racism based *only* on 'colour racism', and anti-racisms that relied on 'political blackness' to combat them, were unable to capture both the discrimination Muslims faced on the basis of being an ethno-religious group as well as the types of claims Muslims wanted to make on this basis.

As a result, Modood argued for a shift to a more plural anti-racism that focused on ethnicity and different experiences of racism as well as different senses that groups had of themselves (2015 [1997]), a feature that also subsequently emerged out of his work leading the Fourth National Survey of Ethnic Minorities (1997). Here he contrasted with one of his predecessors at Bristol: the pioneering and pivotal figure in race and ethnic relations studies, Michael Banton. Like Banton, Modood challenged the suitability of 'political blackness' that had prevailed in the 1970s and 1980s for anti-racism, concerned foremost that if this was the only vehicle for anti-racism, it would not capture nor serve the interests of, and indeed might be harmful to, South Asian communities. Unlike Banton, however, Modood (2015 [1997]) also sought to expand the concept of racism to include 'cultural racism', and more recently that cultural racism, as a form of racialisation, does not simply point to how discourses on culture can reflect those of 'race' and operate in similar ways, but that it is a form of racism in its own right (Modood and Sealy 2022). Although the idea that racialisation can traverse categories of 'race', ethnicity, culture, nationality and religion has become more widely accepted, this was not the case in the 1990s when Modood started making these arguments (Meer 2019). Bringing these concerns together, much of Modood's own work here has been focused on Muslims, and he has made major contributions on Islamophobia as a particular form of cultural racism, and the position of Muslims in areas such as the labour market, identifying in work with Nabil Khattab (2015) an ethnic as well as religious penalty faced by Muslims. In relation to entry into higher education, he was one of the first to note that ethnic minorities were on a trajectory to overtake, sometimes quite significantly, the higher education participation rates of white peers, and complementing work on the ethnic penalty, he created a concept of 'ethnic capital' to explain how (some) disadvantaged minorities have resources to overcome obstacles in ways not picked up by sociology to date (Modood 2004). This important stream of quantitative sociology, working with quantitativist collaborators, founded in the Fourth Survey but going well beyond it was reflected in the presentations of Anthony Heath, James Nazroo (a colleague of Modood's on the Fourth Survey) and Samir Sweida-Metwally at the Festschrift conference but could not be included in this book.

In relation to questions of ethnicity and cultural racism, a key conceptual innovation Modood made was that of ethno-religious identities to capture how Muslims constructed a political identity with two complementary dynamics. On the one hand, a particular group in society might come to be racialised as 'other' and face discrimination as a result. On the other hand, a group might relate to each other as a community in a political sense, to combat discrimination and/or as a positive identity category which is meaningful and the basis for claims for recognition. While then beginning with negativised difference, this view goes beyond simple de-othering and adds that positive identity making and assertiveness, held and led by minorities themselves, can challenge inferiorised negative minority identities. It is this that underpins Modood's, and by extension the BSM's, view of equality, and the idea that we become equals when minorities make progress in a struggle for recognition and shaping of shared identities (Modood 2013 [2007]). The concept of recognition is foundational to Modood's multiculturalism. While recognition has been theorised by philosophers as distinct as Honneth and Ricouer, Modood follows Charles Taylor's (1994) rendering of the term. It is Modood's use of the concept of recognition that Thompson explores in detail. He shows how ideas of equality, identity, struggle and inclusion orient around the idea of recognition, and raises some critical questions of Modood's application of the term suggestive of new avenues of thought.

The issue of race-religion is picked up in two contributions. In her chapter, Malik traces the development of UK race relations legislation from the early race relations acts to the Brexit referendum result. She does so though by linking it to a 'bigger' historical question, that of empire. Malik's chapter thus locates Modood's interventions in a story that he himself has not said much about, in the sociology of race and Islamophobia in relation to the legacy of the British Empire. The drawing together of political theory and sociology, and of 'race' and religion, is the focus of Laborde's chapter. In her contribution, Laborde juxtaposes Rawls's bifurcated treatment of religion and 'race', noting its 'Americanness', with Modood's more integrated approach reflecting the British context, and ultimately uses the two to suggest her own way of navigating the two terms and managing freedoms and equalities in relation to them.

What both Malik and Laborde's chapters also help highlight, in different ways, are two further key distinguishing features of Modood's multiculturalism. The first is the significance of context and contextualism, in relation to which both Malik and Laborde's chapters highlight the significance of the British context for Modood's thought. Contextualism has though been not just an empirical matter, but a key theoretical and methodological feature and principle of Modood's work, and his sociologically grounded political theory. While it is possible to trace the significance of such an orientation through Modood's oeuvre, it is also something that he has elaborated and developed explicitly in recent publications with Simon Thompson (2018), where they have outlined what they call 'iterative contextualism'. It is Modood's contextual political theory that Lægaard's chapter interrogates. He looks at Modood's interventions in relation to the Danish cartoon affair, drawing out notable challenges in the application of contextualism as a methodology in political theory building.

The second, and more direct, feature relevant here is that sometimes the important minority identities are not national, linguistic or indigenous, as for Canadian multicultural theorists, but concerned with ethno-religious minorities, and which may be shaped by racism, centred on religious community membership, or both, as in the case of anti-Muslim racism (Modood and Sealy forthcoming; see also Sealy 2021). The concern with religious minorities, however, has not been limited to the racialisation of ethno-religious minorities, and this is where we can turn to a further aspect of Modoodian multiculturalism that is distinctive, his writings on political secularism and the governance of religious diversity.

Modood's engagement with issues of religious diversity is traceable to his concern with Muslim minorities, and their experiences and claims on ethno-religious grounds. Modood has also brought the principle of recognition to more directly bear on questions of political secularism and state–religion relations (Modood 2019; Thompson and Modood 2022; Modood and Sealy 2024). Modood's work in this area has several strands and has included thinking on what it means to be a secular state, identifying particular forms of secularism (2010, 2017; Modood and Sealy 2022), and normative arguments for a particular, multiculturalised, form of secularism (Modood and Sealy 2024).

Gurpreet Mahajan's chapter offers an assessment of multiculturalism with a particular eye on religion and secularism. After highlighting some of multiculturalism's key ideas and challenges to them, she identifies four 'unfinished tasks' for multiculturalism and secularism, and in so doing helps to point to future areas in which multicultural theorising may fruitfully develop and make necessary contributions to scholarly and public debates on public religion.

In his chapter in this volume, Bhikhu Parekh picks up the question of the importance of secularism, but also of its limits. He highlights the importance of considering secularisms in the multiple and of the purposes of secularism; that it is not for its own sake (or it risks becoming secular*ist*) but whose value lies in in its capacity to help the realisation of freedoms and equalities in multicultural polities. Rajeev Bhargava, a long-term interlocutor of Modood's on these issues and questions, also picks up the point of multiple secularisms. Bhargava traces the points of agreement and mutual critique between his own and Modood's thinking, and also offers a critical view of moderate – as well as what he refers to as 'modest' – European secularisms. He contrasts these with Indian secularism, before also assessing current trends in India against its own idealised mode of political secularism.

A final area of Modood's multiculturalism we highlight here is related to national belonging. Indeed, questions of belonging and citizenship are at the very centre of Modood's multiculturalism, and issues to which multicultural recognition is central in his thought. Modood's first book (a collection of essays) bore the title *Not Easy Being British* (1992) and questions of what it means to be British and how, in particular, minorities are and can be British has been a constant concern through his writings. It is also one which has had more recent, focused elaboration. In contrast to those who, from a variety of positions, seek to do away with the idea of national identity and purposefully avoid or disavow 'methodological nationalism' (Cantle 2012; Zapata-Barrero 2019; Valluvan 2019), or those who advocate and defend liberal forms of nationalism, Modood has developed a particular conception of 'multicultural nationalism' as a key mode of citizenship and belonging (2018). Multicultural nationalism, for Modood, involves remaking the national story and national identity in a way which includes minorities such that all have a sense of belonging to it (something we can see stemming from his involvement with the Commission on the Future of Multi-Ethnic Britain). At its heart are the combating of exclusionary racisms, the positive recognition and accommodation of minorities, and respect for difference. For Modood, it is a form of multicultural nationalism that is best able to overcome political polarisation (2023).

These questions of belonging, of nationalism and of unity in diversity orient several of the chapters in this volume. Charles Taylor's contribution takes up the rise of exclusionary and politically fragmenting populisms. He addresses the question of 'what is to be done?' to reunite people and makes an urgent call for this to be addressed not just for sense of identification and belonging but also to deal with rising inequalities and other challenges such as the environmental crisis. Kymlicka takes up how multiculturalism and nationalism are seen by many as incompatible. Drawing on data from several different countries, and using this to develop T. H. Marshall's citizenship framework, he explores perceptions of membership. He focuses on how ethnic majority citizens view the contributions, commitments and deservingness of ethnic minorities and how this affects how they view minorities' membership of a state. Levey brings Modood into critical conversation with Kymlicka. He rejects both Kymlicka's claim that Modood's multicultural nationalism is largely the same as his own liberal nationalism, and Modood's claim that his multicultural nationalism is better suited as distinct from Kymlicka's liberal nationalism on the question of post-immigrant diversity and inclusion. Levey instead graces the intersections of the two positions to argue for a mode of nationalism that includes the best of both.

Two chapters in this volume take up an issue of multiculturalism and nationalism that has remained outside of Modood's own purview, but one which is of vital importance for a globalised world: transnationalism. In her chapter, Anna Triandafyllidou traces major shifts in migration and nationalism over the last decade, and considers these at different levels. In particular she asks what forms of nationalism might prove enduring in an age so constituted by digital technologies, communications, and their impact on identity formation. Riva Kastoryano focuses on how transnational belonging necessarily reconfigures forms of nationalism in ways not bounded by the nation-state and is productive of distinct forms of nationalism, and one that presents challenges for multicultural nationalisms conceived within national borders.

An introduction of this sort cannot hope to do justice to the full breadth and depth of three decades of Modood's writing, and certainly cannot do equal justice to its constitutive elements, but we hope to provide a statement on foundational elements and orientations of what we refer to as Modoodian multiculturalism. Likewise, the contributions included here do show something of the range and influence of Modood's thinking and writing on multiculturalism. What we can see even from this brief overview is how some use different aspects of Modood's work to help them construct their own positions and develop novel concerns, paths of thought, and significant contributions to ongoing debates oriented around the salience, resilience and future of multiculturalism. They, and many others, have done so both in areas in which Modood himself has centrally engaged as well as used aspects of Modood's thought in areas in which Modood himself has not directly contributed. Indeed, Modood's contributions have been fundamental to the editors' own trajectories, and we have all co-researched, thought and authored with him on different aspects of multiculturalism.

Notes

1. While some welcomed Levey's 'Schoolification' of multiculturalisms, especially among some key members of the BSM (see Uberoi and Modood 2019), others remain unconvinced as to what extent the distinctions are not more simply contextual (Kymlicka 2019).
2. On moving to the University of Bristol – Modood's first and only permanent academic position – he and his family settled in the Kingsdown area of Bristol in 1998, where he has been a resident since, completing a journey started in Karachi and progressing via Kilburn.

References

Banting, K. (2021), 'Multiculturalism: Maximum Misunderstandings', in R. Zapata-Barrero, J. Dirks and R. Kastoryano (eds), *Contested Concepts in Migration Studies*. Abingdon and New York: Routledge.

Banting, K. (2022), 'Multiculturalism Policy in Canada', in E. Lindquist et al. (eds), *Policy Success in Canada*. Oxford: Oxford University Press.

BBC (2022), 'UCC: The Coming Storm over a Single Common Law in India', 30 May. Accessed at: https://www.bbc.co.uk/news/world-asia-india-61589491

BBC (2023), 'Uniform Civil Code: India Tribes Fear for Identity Over Proposed Law', 7 August. Accessed at: <https://www.bbc.co.uk/news/world-asia-india-66358035>

Beck, U. (2002), 'The Cosmopolitan Society and Its Enemies', *Theory, Culture & Society*, 19 (1–2), 17–44.

Braverman, S. (2023), 'The Value of Conservatism', Speech at NatCon UK, May 2023. Accessed at: <https://www.youtube.com/watch?v=NS5nh1aD-qM>

Cantle, T. (2012), *Interculturalism: The New Era of Cohesion and Diversity*. Basingstoke: Palgrave Macmillan.

Chin, C. (2021), 'Multiculturalism and Nationalism: Models of Belonging to Diverse Political Community', *Nations and Nationalism*, 26 (1), 112–29.

Commission on the Future of Multi-Ethnic Britain (CMEB) (2000), *The Future of Multi-Ethnic Britain*. London: Profile Books.

de Souza, P. R., H. Ahmed and M. S. Alam (2019), *Democratic Accommodations: The Minority Question in India*. New Delhi: Bloomsbury.

Denham, J. (2023), 'To Tackle Hate and Division, Labour Must Reflect on What Multiculturalism Means'. Accessed at: <https://labourlist.org/2023/11/to-tackle-hate-and-division-labour-must-reflect-on-what-multiculturalism-means/>

Dupont, P.-L., T. Sealy and T. Modood (2023), 'The Relation between Multicultural-ism, Interculturalism and Cosmopolitanism in UK Diversity Politics', *Identities*, 30 (6), 785–804.

Hall, S. (1996), 'New Ethnicities', in H. A. Baker Jr, M. Diawara and R. H. Lindeborg (eds), *Black British Cultural Studies: A Reader*. Chicago, IL: University of Chicago Press, 163–72.

Home Office (2000), *Race Equality in Public Services: Driving Up Standards and Accounting for Progress*. London: HMSO.

Jenkins, R. (1967), *Essays and Speeches*, edited by A. Lester. London: Collins.

Khattab, N. and T. Modood (2015), 'Both Ethnic and Religious: Explaining Employ-ment Penalties across 14 Ethno-religious Groups in the United Kingdom', *Journal for the Scientific Study of Religion*, 54 (3), 501–22.

Kymlicka, W. (1995), *Multicultural Citizenship: A Liberal Theory of Minority Rights*. Oxford: Clarendon Press.

Kymlicka, W. (2019), 'Deschooling Multiculturalism', *Ethnicities* 19 (6), 971–82.

Kymlicka, W. (2021), 'The Precarious Resilience on Multiculturalism in Canada', *American Review of Canadian Studies*, 51 (1), 122–42.

Levey, G. B. (2019), 'The Bristol School of Multiculturalism', *Ethnicities*, 19 (1), 200–26.

Maguire, A. (2023), 'Explainer: Australia Has Voted against an Indigenous Voice to Parliament. Here's What Happened', *The Conversation*. Accessed at: <https://the-conversation.com/explainer-australia-has-voted-against-an-indigenous-voice-to-parliament-heres-what-happened-215155>

Martínez, D. O. (2013), 'Intellectual Biography, Empirical Sociology and Normative Political Theory: An Interview with Tariq Modood', *Journal of Intercultural Studies*, 34 (6), 729–41.

Mathieu, F. (2017), 'The Failure of State Multiculturalism in the UK? An Analysis of the UK's Multicultural Policy for 2000–2015', *Ethnicities*, 18 (1), 43–69.

May, P. (2022), 'Canada: The Standard Bearer of Multiculturalism in the World? An Analysis of the Canadian Public Debate on Multiculturalism (2010–2020)', *Ethnic and Racial Studies*, 45 (10), 1939–60.

Meer, N. (2019), 'The Bristol School of Multiculturalism, and the Political Sociology of Identity', *Ethnicities*, 19 (6), 991–8.

Meer, N. (2020) 'Britain had a chance to talk about race 20 years ago. Let's get it right this time', *The Guardian*, 12 July 2020.

Meer, N. (2022), *The Cruel Optimism of Racial Justice*. Bristol: Bristol University Press.

Meer, N. and T. Modood (2009), 'The Multicultural State We're in: Muslims, "Multi-culture" and the "Civic Re-Balancing" of British Multiculturalism', *Political Studies*, 57, 473–97.

Meer, N. and T. Modood (2014), 'Cosmopolitanism and Integrationism: Is Multiculturalism in Britain a "Zombie category"?', *Identities: Global Studies in Culture and Power*, 21 (6), 658–74.

Modood, T. (1988), '"Black", racial equality and Asian identity', *Journal of Ethnic and Migration Studies*, 14 (3), 397–404.

Modood, T. (1989), 'Religious Anger and Minority Rights', *The Political Quarterly*, (60) 3, 80–4.

Modood, T. (1990), 'British Asian Muslims and The Rushdie Affair', *The Political Quarterly*, 61 (2), 143–60.

Modood, T. (1992), *Not Easy Being British: Colour, Culture and Citizenship*, Runnymede Trust and Trentham Books.

Modood, T. (1994), 'Political Blackness and British Asians', *Sociology*, 28 (4), 859–76.

Modood, T. (2004), 'Capitals, Ethnic Identity and Educational Qualifications', *Cultural Trends*, 13 (2), 87–105.

Modood, T. (2013 [2007]), *Multiculturalism: A Civic Idea*, 2nd edn. Cambridge: Polity.

Modood, T. (2015 [1997]), '"Difference", Cultural Racism and Anti-Racism', in T. Modood and P. Werbner (eds), *Debating Cultural Hybridity: Multicultural Identities and the Politics of Anti-Racism*. London: Zed Books, 154–72.

Modood, T. (2016), 'Ethno-Religious Assertiveness out of Racial Equality', in D. Llewellyn and S. Sharma (eds), *Religion, Equalities, and Inequalities*. Farnham: Ashgate, 38–48.

Modood, T. (2017), 'Intercultural Public Intellectual Engagement', *Journal of Citizenship and Globalisation Studies*, 1 (1), 36–47.

Modood, T. (2018), 'A Multicultural Nationalism', *Brown Journal of World Affairs*, 25, 233–46.

Modood, T. (2019), *Essays on Secularism and Multiculturalism*. London: European Consortium of Political Research, and Rowman and Littlefield International.

Modood, T. (2023), 'Multiculturalism: How it Can Contribute to Depolarising the Current Political Polarisation', *Progressive Review*, 30 (2), 77–83.

Modood, T., R. Berthoud, J. Lakey, J. Nazroo, P. Smith, S. Virdee and S. Beishon (1997), *Ethnic Minorities in Britain: Diversity and Disadvantage – The Fourth National Survey of Ethnic Minorities*. London: Policy Studies Institute.

Modood, T. and T. Sealy (2024), *The New Governance of Religious Diversity*. Cambridge: Polity.

Modood, T. and T. Sealy (2022), 'Beyond Euro-Americancentric Forms of Racism and Anti-racism', *The Political Quarterly*, 93 (3), 433–41.

Modood, T. and T. Sealy (forthcoming), 'Muslims and Multiculturalism', in G. B. Levey (ed.), *Research Handbook on Multiculturalism*, Edward Elgar.

Modood, T. and S. Thompson (2018), 'Revisiting Contextualism in Political Theory: Putting Principles into Context', *Res Publica*, 24, 339–57.

Multiculturalism Policy Index (n.d.). Accessed at: <https://www.queensu.ca/mcp/>

Orgad, L. and R. Koopmans (2023), *Majorities, Minorities and the Future of Nationhood*. Cambridge: Cambridge University Press.

Parekh, B. (2000), *Rethinking Multiculturalism: Cultural Diversity and Political Theory*. London: Macmillan.

Reuters (2023), 'India's Modi Sparks Political Storm with Pitch for Common Civil Code', 7 August. Accessed at: <https://www.reuters.com/world/india/indias-modi-sparks-political-storm-with-pitch-civil-code-2023-07-14/>

Sealy, T. (2018), 'Multiculturalism, Interculturalism, "Multiculture" and Super-Diversity: Of Zombies, Shadows and other Ways of Being', *Ethnicities*, 18 (5), 692–716.

Sealy, T. (2020), 'Back to the Future of Multi-Ethnic Britain', 20 November. Accessed at: <https://www.opendemocracy.net/en/global-extremes/what-can-multiculturalism-offer-fight-against-racism-britain/>

Sealy, T. (2021), 'Islamophobia: With or Without Islam?', *Religions*, 12 (6): 369.

Sealy, T., P.-L Dupont and T. Modood (2024), 'Difference and Diversity: Combining Multiculturalist and Interculturalist Approaches to Integration', *The Sociological Review*, Online First: <https://doi.org/10.1177/00380261241238585>

Taylor, C. (1994), 'The Politics of Recognition', in A. Gutmann (ed.), *Multiculturalism and the Politics of Recognition*. Princeton, NJ: Princeton University Press, 25–73.

Thompson, S. and T. Modood (2022), 'The Multidimensional Recognition of Religion', *Critical Review of International Social and Political Philosophy*, 70 (3), 780–96.

Uberoi, V. (2015), 'The Parekh Report – National Identity without Nations and Nationalism, *Ethnicities*, 15:4.

Uberoi, V. (2018), 'National Identity – A Multiculturalist's Approach', *Critical Review of International Social and Political Philosophy*, 21 (1), 46–64.

Uberoi, V. (2020), 'Can Black Lives Really Matter in the UK before Addressing Britishness?', 9 July. Accessed at: <https://www.opendemocracy.net/en/global-extremes/can-black-lives-really-matter-uk-addressing-britishness/>

Uberoi, V. (2023), 'Bhikhu Parekh', in M. Ramgotra and S. Choat (eds), *Reconsidering Political Thinkers*. Oxford: Oxford University Press.

Uberoi, V. and T. Modood (2013), 'Has Multiculturalism in Britain Retreated?', *Soundings*, 53, 129–42.

Uberoi, V. and T. Modood (2019), 'The Emergence of the Bristol School of Multiculturalism', *Ethnicities*, 19 (6), 955–70.

Valluvan, S. (2019), *The Clamour of Nationalism*. Manchester: Manchester University Press.

Vertovec, S. and S. Wessendorf (2010), *The Multiculturalism Backlash*. London: Routledge.

World Values Survey (2023), *UK Public among Most Trusting in World*. Policy Institute, King's College London.

Zapata-Barrero, R. (2019), *Intercultural Citizenship in the Post-Multicultural Era*. London: Sage.

Part One

Orientations and Underpinnings

ONE

Invoking the Idealist World of Ideas

David Boucher

'The social profit that would accrue from bringing the philosopher down to facts is altogether insignificant when compared to the good that would ensue from bringing the practical man to consider principles' (Jones 1910: x).

Introduction

Modood's background is in political philosophy, but he says that he has not brought it to bear on the study of race and ethnicity (2005: 1). I want to argue that he employed philosophy implicitly, and also for a different purpose, to clear the way for, and justify, his role as a public intellectual. He is quite explicit that since he developed his interests in issues of equality and multiculturalism his aim has been to change perceptions and to influence policy debates (Martínez 2013: 735). Varun Uberoi has perceptively noticed some of the idealist influences on Modood in his article dealing more explicitly with the idealist influence on Bhikhu Parekh (2021: 752). My exploration goes deeper and broader, by suggesting that the idealist world view to which Modood was exposed as a PhD student at University College, Swansea, is subsequently presupposed in his work on multiculturalism, even though those principles formulated in his early years are not always argued for or explicitly referred to in his later writings (Modood 1984). Hence the appropriateness of the concept of invoking a world of ideas.

The idea of invoking a world of ideas entails implicating a conceptual framework, capable of change, within limits, while tolerating a diversity of conclusions which rely upon a common frame of reference for their efficacy. Multiple worlds of ideas may be invoked by a single thinker. They are not mutually exclusive, and their relation may be character-ised as historical populations of ideas in Toulmin's sense, who him-self draws upon the work of Collingwood (Toulmin 1972). This paper will focus upon the philosophical idealist world of ideas that informs Modood's work, while not denying that there are others. Invoking a world of ideas does not entail fully articulating its contours. It is the background that gives a certain intelligibility to a concept, phrase or argument (Bouche 2016). We see from Modood's early encounters with Oakeshott and Collingwood, in particular, that through their influence, the idealist world of ideas that they inherited and inhabited is brought to bear on problems of multicultural citizenship. We see, for example, a desire to attain a rapprochement between theory and practice; a distaste for abstraction; an anti-rationalism manifest in Oakeshott's distaste for ideologies; the characterisation of changing groups of actors in terms of identity in difference, unity in diversity and continuity through change. Similarly, there is a degree of pragmatism in Modood's conceptualisa-tion of multiculturalism, a tendency found in idealism, especially in Bradley and Oakeshott, and developed by the American Pragmatists.

If we were to take the Hegelian approach to considering Modood's career from the vantage point of the present by imposing a rational coherence on his trajectory, we may credibly argue that he spent his early years developing the justification for his engagement in practical politics as a public intellectual. The chapter will first explore the nature of his justification. The principal philosophers he chose to study, Oake-shott and Collingwood, represented the two alternative answers.

First, Michael J. Oakeshott, the disinterested philosopher, disdainful of politics and politicians, dismissive of any connection between philos-ophy and practical politics. Philosophy, as far as he was concerned, made no difference to the activities it investigated. He is famously reported to have said, in answer to the question what he thought of Britain's entry into the European Union, that he found it unnecessary to hold opinions on such matters. Similarly, poetry or aesthetics could have no practical purpose because poetry does not conform to propositional logic. In this respect he echoes Sir Philip Sydney's contention: 'the poet nothing affir-meth and therefore never lieth' (cited in Aristotle 2013: xxix). Oakeshott does not ask of poetic images whether they are right or wrong, true or false, we merely delight in them.

Secondly, the other philosopher was R. G. Collingwood, who con-sidered it the role of the philosopher to change, not only how we think about a subject-matter, but also how an activity is conducted (Collingwood 1938: vi–vii). Collingwood's explicit political intent is increasingly more pronounced in his later work, *The Principles of Art*, *An Autobiography*, *An Essay of Metaphysics* and *The New Leviathan*, as he becomes increasingly attuned to various threats against civilisation posed by a variety of forms of irrationalism.

Modood's PhD betrays a sympathy for Collingwood's idea of philosophy as the unifier of a fragmented cultural life. The idea of overlap, which Oakeshott denied, Collingwood theorised in *An Autobiography* as a rapprochement between theory and practice, and particularly between philosophy and history (2013: 57). Tariq argues in his thesis that Collingwood's *Speculum Mentis* (Collingwood 1924) enables us to sustain the conclusion that philosophy at the very least, in relation to the forms of experience, makes them aware of their distinctive characters, in terms of their unique rationalities, removing scepticism and clearing the way for perceiving the possibilities for what they may attain. Collingwood identified five forms of experience: art, religion, science, history and philosophy, all of which he related in a hierarchical, overlapping scale, each more adequate than the one it succeeds, resolving the contradictions inherent in it, but nevertheless, giving rise to contradictions of its own, with the exception of philosophy. Philosophy makes positive interventions into cultural forms by criticising their presuppositions, and constructing conceptual frameworks as contributions towards the development of the forms of experience. By making the forms aware of their limitations, philosophy is able to demonstrate their relation to the whole of which each is a part (1984: 351).

I want to examine Modood's case for rejecting Oakeshott's separation of theory and practice, which he bases on Collingwood's theory of overlapping forms. This requires exploring Oakeshott's understanding of the limits of philosophical enquiry, which I contend Modood misunderstood, by attributing to him assumptions which he did not hold. Philosophically identifying an identity, such as culture, is logically different from recommending ways in which that culture may improve. Getting at the heart of what Oakeshott and Modood are engaged in are their views on anti-essentialism, and where and when it may be appropriate, and here there are respects in which they agree and differ. For example, especially in terms of their anti-rationalist positions on ideology, and their alternative characterisation of politics as the pursuit of intimations.

Oakeshott's View of Philosophy

Oakeshott's conception of philosophy has three prominent features. First, it is not eristic. It doesn't purport to persuade. Second, it is parasitic on the other modes of experience, or voices in the conversation of mankind, a term Oakeshott came to adopt to indicate the nature of the relationship in which such modes as history, science and poetry stood in relation to each other, and to the whole (Oakeshott 1962: 197–247). And, third, it is not a body of knowledge. Oakeshott was consistent throughout his life on these principles. Philosophy, he contended in his first book, *Experience and Its Modes* (1933), does not consist in 'persuading others, but in making our own minds clear'. 'It is', he argued, 'something we may engage in without putting ourselves in competition. It is something independent of the futile attempt to convince or persuade' (1933: 7). He always remained faithful to the view that experience, or what he came to refer to as what is 'going-on', is one undifferentiated whole, and that our attempts to understand it involve identifying them in terms of characteristics that presuppose certain postulates. This is defended in all his major books: *Experience and Its Modes, Rationalism in Politics, On Human Conduct* and *On History*. Identifying and questioning the postulates that differentiate each mode is the activity of philosophy, and therefore necessarily parasitical.

The metaphor of a conversational relationship, which he introduced in *Rationalism in Politics* (1962), between the variety of voices is not a proposition about the terms on which each voice tolerates the others. It is instead an 'appropriate image' in terms of which to comprehend the 'manifold' which constitutes the 'meeting-place' of 'diverse idioms of utterance which make up current human intercourse' (Oakeshott 1962: 198–9). Philosophy is one voice in the conversation, reflecting upon the other voices and their relation to one another, but having no 'specific contribution' to make. In other words, philosophy has no practical relevance to the other voices.

In his attitude to practical life, Oakeshott was in fact at variance with many of his fellow British Idealists. For most of them philosophy was a weapon in the social and political debates of late-Victorian and early Edwardian Britain. Philosophy's purpose was, at least in part, to provide a practical guide to life. The very title of Henry Jones's book, for example, *Idealism as a Practical Creed* (1909: 38), betrayed the relation in which, for him, philosophy and practical life stood.

On the other hand, J. M. E. McTaggart, Oakeshott's philosophy teacher at Cambridge, maintained that people's views on practical matters were largely unaffected by their metaphysical beliefs (McTaggart 1934: 38). For Oakeshott, practice was a distinct mode of experience that admitted of no theoretical intrusions from science, history or philosophy (1933). Both Bradley, from whom Oakeshott partially derived his scepticism, and Oakeshott argued that it is the business of philosophy to understand what is. Philosophy has no positive contribution to make to any other categorially distinct activity, including practical life. 'Moral philosophy', for example, Bradley argued, 'has to understand morals, and has no business to manufacture them or offer a blueprint for manufacturing them' (Bradley 1928: 193). For Oakeshott, philosophy was something undertaken for its own sake. Indeed, to him, most of the British Idealists, with the possible exception of Bradley, were what he pejoratively called *Savants, philosophes, preachers* and *theoreticians*. Whereas Oakeshott himself consistently denied that the philosopher has anything of practical advice to offer, many of his disciples, including Parekh and Modood, have wanted to draw practical implications, which for him are simply *ignorentio elenchi*, category errors (Oakeshott 1933: 153–5).

Modood's main concern in his early career was to examine and refute the tendency in twentieth-century British philosophy, which Oakeshott exemplified, to make a categorial distinction between theory and practice, which was also evident in Russell's logical atomism; Ayer's Logical Positivism; and Wittgenstein's linguistic philosophy (Hall and Modood 1982: 157; cf. 1979, 1982a, 1982b). W. H. Greenleaf had written on this tendency approvingly in his contribution to Oakeshott's Festschrift in 1968, when he compared the philosophies of Oakeshott, Wittgenstein and Ryle (Greenleaf 1968b). Dale Hall and Tariq Modood rejected this tendency, taking first Gordon Graham (Hall and Modood 1979) as their target, and then Oakeshott, as one of its most sophisticated exponents (Hall and Modood 1982).

Hall and Modood argued that philosophy may legitimately offer practical solutions to political problems, hence paving the way for Modood's role as a public intellectual, and Hall's as an opinion poll analyst. In this respect Modood was following R. G. Collingwood, who was more representative of British Idealism in rejecting the divide between theory and practice than Michael Oakeshott. For Collingwood, all the forms of experience – art, religion, science, history and philosophy – had exhibited both theoretical and practical reason. Art found practical expression in play; religion in convention; science in utility; history in duty; and philosophy in absolute duty. Unlike Oakeshott, Collingwood conceptualised the different worlds of experience as a scale of overlapping forms, each harbouring a contradiction that was taken up and resolved in the immediate higher form (Collingwood 1924; cf. Boucher 1989, 1993). He argued his case for the overlap of theory and practice in his *An Autobiography* (2013), where he maintained that anyone who subscribes to a utilitarian philosophy will inevitably view the world instrumentally in terms of means and ends. Philosophy, he argued, begins in practice for the problems it confronts, and returns to practice for their resolution.

Oakeshott, on the other hand, posited no hierarchy among the modes and conceived them to be completely autonomous, related to each other only as arrests in experience as a whole. Following Bosanquet, he takes philosophy to be experience without reservation, presupposition or arrest (Bosanquet 1899: 2), a regulative ideal pursued but never attained. Furthermore, philosophy is 'the study of something as a whole and for its own sake' (Bosanquet 1899: 1), and because it is not a body of knowledge it is incapable of revealing or discovering new facts. Its purpose is to tell you the significance of what in some sense you already know (Bosanquet 1895: 166).

Because Oakeshott rejected the idea of an overlapping hierarchy of forms, he also rejected the idea that philosophy had anything by way of recommendations to offer the modes of experience. This is not to say that the philosopher may not offer practical advice, but in doing so philosophy is temporarily renounced for the delights of the world of practice, as, for example, when Oakeshott himself offers advice on how to pick the winner of the Derby (Griffiths and Oakeshott 2017).

Even though Modood rejects this aspect of Oakeshott's philosophy, he is explicit about his debt to him in other respects. However, he is equally indebted to Collingwood, who objected to the separation between theory and practice, not least because it denied the role of the committed intellectual, and absolved philosophy of social responsibility. It was the Oxford and Cambridge realists that Collingwood had firmly in his sights because of the consequences of their doctrines on the impressionable youths they taught.

Realists, such as Cook Wilson, Bertrand Russell, H. A. Prichard and G. E. Moore, contravened all of Collingwood's golden rules of philosophical interpretation: they did not satisfy themselves as to the relevance of their criticisms by reading the texts historically; they did not take pains to determine what question the author of a text was asking; and, in addition, assumed that the questions they were addressing were perennial. Their greatest crime was to ignore history as a form of knowledge, and formulate their own theories of knowledge on the methodology of the natural sciences (Collingwood 2013: 84–5). What was needed was more understanding of human affairs and more knowledge of how to deal with them. History was to provide not rules of conduct but insights in helping us diagnose our moral and political problems.

Hall and Modood in consequence embrace Collingwood's rapprochement between theory and practice, and attack Oakeshott's separation of the two. Oakeshott's error, they contend, rests on two unargued assumptions. First, that there is a definitive truth to which all philosophers would subscribe if they were sufficiently rational, and that 'plurality of practices and faiths is a necessary characteristic of practice' (1982: 164). They contend that the contrast entails a 'distorting asymmetry'. They maintain that Oakeshott contrasts practice, understood as men's diverse attempts to live as they ought, with the idea of a single, final philosophical account of reality. But the comparison, Hall and Modood maintain, should not be with the *idea* of a definitive account of philosophy, but with the actual variety of attempts by philosophers to express what they understood the truth to be; not the ideal of philosophy with the actuality of practice, but either the ideal or actual of both. Thus, 'we should compare not one eternal truth with manifold action, but thinking with acting; not a final philosophical account of ephemeral actions, but critical enquiry with practical action' (1982: 164).

To accuse Oakeshott of suggesting, or implying, that philosophers, if they were sufficiently rational, would arrive at a definitive truth, is to misunderstand Oakeshott's conception of philosophy. Philosophy, for him, is not a body of knowledge, and therefore cannot be applied to anything to resolve practical problems. It is instead a manner of enquiry; a disposition to remain dissatisfied with any claims to knowledge that are conditional, that is which make unquestioned assumptions. Furthermore, there can be no definitive account of reality, the modes change, new ones come into being, as for instance aesthetic experience did for Oakeshott, requiring a reassessment of their postulates, but not of their relation to each other, or of each to the whole. In other words, it is a very different conception of philosophy from the idea of Plato's Forms that all suitably educated and capable philosophers can come to know.

The Limits of Philosophy

The question to ask is: what in Oakeshott's view does philosophy enable us to do, and what is the status Oakeshott attributes to the different worlds or modes of ideas he identifies in terms of their postulates? It is imperative that we recognise that Oakeshott is not attributing a concrete existence to any of his constructs. When he characterises the modern European state, for example, he admits that no 'historic state' corresponds exactly to it because there are always contingent conditions which have to be considered (Oakeshott 1975a: 192, 247).

This is because what Oakeshott identifies are 'Ideal characters' (1975: 1–107). Ideal in this respect has no normative implication.[1] He says that ideal characters are aids to reflection, instruments of inquiry, and what he is doing is identifying the 'conditions of relevance in terms of which an enquiry may be recognized' as, for example, the scientific

(1983: 2, 23n8). Oakeshott's point is that we identify entities in terms of characteristics adequate to our purposes. Ideal characters composed of characteristics are required for achieving understanding. They are the instruments of identification which may be crude and unsophisticated or refined and complex. It is always open to us to modify what at first is an ideal character composed of relatively few characteristics into ideal characters far more complex. What is identified, Oakeshott argues, 'is always as intelligible as the terms in which it is being understood allow it to be' (1975a: 6).

Although Oakeshott did not reply to Hall's and Modood's criticisms, we may refer to Oakeshott's response to an earlier attack on his separation of philosophical explanation and practical action (Raphael 1964; Oakeshott 1965). Oakeshott contended that what he had ventured to do in *Rationalism in Politics* was to suggest that explaining conduct was very different from recommending that certain actions be performed, and from approving or disapproving of those actions. In response to D. D. Raphael's claim that most philosophers engaged in recommendation, Oakeshott acknowledged that many philosophers, such as Aquinas, offered some such recommendation, but rarely did they give specific advice on what to do in particular situations. Oakeshott maintained that this does not mean that there is something that may properly be called 'explanatory-cum-practical activity; it merely suggests that, like most of us, he [Aquinas] was both a philosopher (*sophos*) and a preacher (*phronimos*)' (1965: 90).

This is not to suggest, as Raphael does, that reasoning for Oakeshott is out of place in practical discourse. We find, Oakeshott suggests, diagnosis, prescription and justification, all directly connected to practical activity, but none of which is explanatory. In clarification, Oakeshott adds that the logic of arguments designed to recommend is different from that of justifying action. Reasoning, on Oakeshott's understanding, is an open-ended, ongoing activity and cannot be prevented from being extended into explanation. There will come a point, however, when explanatory reason becomes irrelevant to practical activity. Furthermore, without giving his reasons, Oakeshott contends, the process is irreversible: 'we cannot descend from explanation to practical argument in the same manner as we may ascend from practical argument to explanation' (1965: 89). Furthermore, the explanatory languages are not the languages of the participants. Speaking of historians, for example, he says that their language is distinct from the participants in events they depict: 'The historian is the maker of events; they have a meaning for those who participated in them, and he will not speak of them in the same way as they spoke of them' (Oakeshott 1950–1: 347).

It is a mistake to think that Oakeshott is legislating against the use of historical or aesthetic characters to teach lessons about political life. There are plenty of emblematic heroes in history, and paradigmatic villains in literature, and they may often be used to draw lessons about life. The point is that when such characters are appropriated for moral or practical purposes they cease to belong to the historical past, or aesthetic present, and we no longer understand them historically or delight in the aesthetic imagery. They have simply been (re)constituted to conform to the idiom of a different mode from history or aesthetics, namely practice (Oakeshott 1983: 18).

Oakeshott's arguments for the autonomy of philosophical explanation and practical injunctions needs to be distinguished from his distinction between technical knowledge and practical knowledge. They are, he says, 'distinguishable, but inseparable' (Oakeshott 1991: 12). Any activity, whether it is scientific experimentation, the writing of history, the cooper making a barrel or the cook following a recipe, Oakeshott contends, requires a combination of technical and practical knowledge.

Oakeshott, with his friend Guy Griffith, wrote such a manual for selecting the winner of the Epsom Derby. The set of rules and procedures they offer the reader are no substitute for, and have to be supplemented with, some practical knowledge of horses. The guide therefore assumes, as we can infer from something Oakeshott wrote in a footnote to *Rationalism in Politics* many years later, that the horse-racing fraternity generally knew something, first hand, about horses and were genuinely educated people. He remarked that the authors of *A Guide to the Classics* were aware of the distinction between technical knowledge and complete knowledge, and that beyond a certain point there could be no fail-safe rules for picking the winner because some intelligence not supplied by the rules themselves was required.

The point is, then, that the distinction between theory and practice, or philosophy and recommendation, is distinct from his discussion of technical and practical knowledge. They are inseparable in any human activity, and which philosophers, in their less philosophical moments, indulge themselves from time to time. By implication, if Tariq derives practical lessons from philosophical arguments, he has left philosophical explanation behind, and reconstituted its conclusions, divorced from the arguments, but which are nevertheless invoked. With reference to Wittgenstein, for example, Modood says, 'I thought – perhaps quite mistakenly – that I had learned from Wittgenstein that one does not start from theory, but that theory emerges in how one works through a series of puzzles and problems; theory flows in intellectual activity rather than precedes it' (2005: 2). A point, as we saw, that he also would have learnt from Collingwood.

Anti-Essentialism

Anti-essentialism has been a prominent feature of Modood's thinking throughout the various phases of his research. One of the pillars on which he anchors his criticism of Oakeshott's complete separation of philosophy and recommendation is that Oakeshott's conception of philosophy, he claims, is essentialist because of the expectation that all philosophical arguments conform to specific criteria, and that anything that fails to conform to them cannot be philosophy. Furthermore, that because criticism is common to philosophical enquiry, it can be found nowhere else, and conversely because recommendation is a necessary feature of the practical mode, it too can be found nowhere else.

The second point, I think, is misplaced. Just as there are for Oakeshott different pasts, an historical past and a practical past, constituted by the relatively coherent worlds of history and practice, there are different types of criticism; philosophical criticism is the commitment to interrogate all presuppositions which characterise the conditionality of the different modes, but this does not preclude historical criticism, practical and moral criticism, or scientific criticism. Each is appropriate to the type of activity to which it belongs, and each is categorially distinct. For example, if practical life entails the constant activity of changing what is into what ought to be, unless there are credible criticisms of what is, the process of wanting to change it into something better would be arbitrary and capricious (1933: 59).

However, the claim that Oakeshott is an essentialist has more credibility, but it needs qualification. The modes, or forms of experience, are for Oakeshott not aspects of reality, but the whole of reality taken from different standpoints. They are not separable and independent parts of reality. The business of philosophy is to determine the *differentiae* of each mode, and each begins with a system of postulates which distinguish each mode from the others and from the whole, which is, to remind ourselves, experience without reservation, presupposition or arrest (1933: 101). In identifying the postulates of the different modes, Oakeshott may justifiably be accused of being an essentialist. However, talking of taking respite within one of the modes, he is far from essentialist.

The question of finite individuality is central to Oakeshott's understanding of the modes, and is little noticed among commentators. In relation to characterising finite individuality, Oakeshott rejects an essentialist stance. The question which Oakeshott asks of each of the modes of experience is not what in a mode of experience is real, but what in each is an individual or a thing. The historical individual, for example, is an abstraction, a mere arbitrary characterisation, because not even birth and death exhaust the relations in which an individual stands to the world; the significant events that precede, as well as those that follow a person's life, add to the coherence of the characterisation. It is in practical life, Oakeshott contends, that we hang on most tenaciously to the idea of the autonomous self, or finite individual. In practical life, as in other modes, the thing, or the individual, is presupposed, not defined.

The criterion of the characterisation of the individual is not completeness, or self-completion, but what is separate and self-contained. The practical self is the creature of practical thought and presupposed in all action. This self is presupposed to be self-determining, and the freedom entailed requires no demonstration, because it belongs to the practical self, by definition. To deny it is to undermine the world of practice, and the principle upon which it is built, namely, the 'separateness and uniqueness' of the individual. The individual in practical life is just as much an abstraction, an arrest or modification of experience, as the individual, or thing, presupposed in all the other modes (1933: 268–74).

Modood cautions against too radical a rejection of essentialism, because, in his view, to be too dismissive is 'inherently destructive' (1998: 381). He takes Stuart Hall, who in some moods, casts doubt on both politically constituted multiculturalism, and the very idea of a unified self. Hall believes that because of the globalisation of economics, consumption and communications, as well as complex patterns of migration, it is not possible to consider societies constituted by relatively stable collective purposes, and identities that the nation-state organises territorially. As to a unified identity, it is a myth, a fantasy, perpetrated by those who feel the necessity to tell themselves comforting stories or narratives about themselves. Instead, there is a veritable proliferation of passing identities, any one, or number, of which we may entertain fleetingly (Modood 1998: 380; Modood 2007: 103–4; Hall 1992: 277).

Many radical anti-essentialists, nevertheless, acknowledge the necessity of accepting the fictions and of acting as if they were true. This Modood finds very worrisome because any intellectual position that reaches counter-intuitive conclusions, such as the claim that the self is a fiction, has to engage in all sorts of intellectual contortions in order to protect prized political projects from the logical consequences of the requirements of consistency, and is therefore inherently dishonest (1998: 381). Modood argues that there is no necessity to remain wedded to 'a rigid anti essentialism that requires us to think that historical continuities, cultural groups and coherent selves do or do not exist: Nothing is closed *a priori*; whether there is sameness/newness in the world, whether across time, across space or across populations are empirical questions' (2007: 182; Wittgenstein 1967, para. 108).

Again, this may be said to conflate the philosophical and the practical. Stuart Hall, and those who acknowledge but accept the imperfections of their characterisations, are making the philosophical point that idealists make, including Bradley and Oakeshott, that practical life requires dealing in necessary fictions which are in varying degrees imperfect (Bradley 1897: 434; Bradley 1914: 239). Outside of philosophy we are compelled to accept the unintelligible and use it in whatever ways work best. The person in possession of the ordinary knowledge required by practical life is fleetingly conscious of its imperfections, but to seek to complete that knowledge by eliminating inconsistencies is to leave the practical world and enter the realm of philosophy (Bradley 1914: 235).

The historical individual, for example, that is, an event, person or culture, Oakeshott argues, is a presupposition of history, not something given, but constructed and characterised by the historian. Oakeshott argues, 'what is required', of the historical individual, 'is that it should be stable and should be consistently adhered to, not that it should be absolutely clear and coherent' (1933: 120). This, too, is Modood's position, although he attributes the idea to Wittgenstein. Modood argues that the lesson is that we do not need to posit essences or resort to philosophical theories in order to go about our regular business: 'we can talk of there being ethnic groups, or a cultural plurality without having clear-cut ideas of what is an ethnic group or culture' (2007: 97p., cf. 152–3). The point is that on the issue of finite individuality, Modood, from within the mode of practice, accepts the reality of culture as a concrete identity, whereas Oakeshott, from the philosophical stance, emphasises its necessity as a postulate of practice, but nevertheless convicts it of abstraction.

Oakeshott uses the term 'character' to convey how we understand and portray the necessary fictions that practical life requires. The idea of character captures the sense in which an individual is a unity in diversity (1954). This is echoed by Greenleaf when he elaborates, by drawing upon Oakeshott, Wittgenstein's idea of family resemblance in order to characterise, rather than designate, the area of activity occupied by politics (Greenleaf 1968a: 7–8).

Oakeshott, in discussing identity, argues that in experience we are not confronted by bare, static and unchanging units, but with 'what changes and yet remains somehow the same' (1933: 65). Oakeshott further argues: 'Now, whatever else the notion of identity may imply, I take it, first, to signify a mode of behaviour, and secondly, to be a matter of degree. That is to say, all identity is qualitative because it consists in the maintenance of a certain character, and not in the mere retention of a fixed and original substance.'

The characterisation of the identity of a thing, Oakeshott contends, must be conceived in terms of, rather than in the denial of, its differences and changes. To understand an identity in terms of character implies and unifies differences: 'And if identity be this, it must be a matter of degree whether or not it is maintained' (Oakeshott 1933: 65). Identity is not maintained by pointing to one unaltered feature throughout a passage of differences. The past in history, for example, is composed entirely of differences from which a changeless identity is necessarily excluded (Oakeshott 1983: 99).

The character of an individual is established by the principles of continuity and discontinuity. Following F. H. Bradley (1932: 288; 1897: 347), Oakeshott argues that the historical individual persists over a period of time, changes but remains the same, and its identity is maintained on the principle of the identity of indiscernibles, which implies that both sameness and difference co-exist and what is the same remains the same however much in other ways it differs. The principle itself is not one that is established or examined. It is presupposed (Oakeshott 1933: 124).

Modood, of course, subscribes to these ideas of identity in difference, unity in diversity and continuity through change, which are hallmarks of Idealist thinking, but whereas they try to explain why they are necessary fictions, abstractions in the totality of experience, he gives the identities a concrete reality from within the world of practice. Modood argues that a person throughout his or her life undergoes changes in personality, and those changes constitute a single person, without having to subscribe to the idea that there is a primordial essential I to begin with, already formed, and which remains throughout. The same is the case with a culture or ethnic group. A culture is constituted through change; 'it is not defined by an essence which exists apart from change; a noumenon hidden behind the altering configurations of phenomena. In individuating cultures and peoples, our most basic and helpful guide is not the idea of an essence, but the possibility of making historical connections, of being able to see change and resemblance' (Modood 1998: 382).

The idealist conception of Identity in Difference seems to encapsulate what Modood perceives to be the elements, or features, of multiculturalism: 'Identities persist even when participation in distinctive cultural practices is in decline or these practices are undergoing considerable adaptation. This means that multiculturalism is characterised by the challenging, the dismantling and the remaking of public identities' (2007: 43). A culture, he argues, is not an ossified entity with essentialist characteristics, but a changing entity that implies continuity in change: 'at the end of one's life one might reflect on how one's personality changed over time and through experience, and see how all changes constitute a single person without believing that there was an original, already formed, essential "I" prior to the life experiences' (Modood 2007: 93).

Modood is anti-rationalist and pragmatic in his approach to multicultural citizenship. He suggests that National identity is not comprised of a list to which citizens are required to subscribe, but is instead formulated in debate and discussion. (2007: 152–3). He recoils from over-defined and over-determined values, arguing instead that in being too prescriptive in defining core values there is a danger of being too bland, or too divisive (Brown 2005).

Ideology and the Pursuit of Intimations

Whatever practitioners of politics think they are doing, whether they are conservative pragmatists or extreme ideological revolutionary rationalists, they are deluded if they think that they are formulating principles *tabula rasa* to recommend courses of action in resolution of particular problems. Even the Russian revolutionaries, Oakeshott contends, were merely continuing the tradition of the Tsars, despite believing that they had completely broken with it (Oakeshott 1950–1). More controversially, Oakeshott contends that the French Revolutionaries were not applying the new doctrines of natural rights to political arrangements in France, but instead formulating and applying the traditional rights of an Englishman. The Declaration of the Rights of Man on 4 August 1789 replaced the complex and bankrupt French system, not with new principles but with those derived from Englishmen and their common law rights. The result, not of independent premeditation, but of centuries of the everyday attention to the social and political arrangements of 'an historic society' (Oakeshott 1991: 53).

Modood sees ideology not as a necessary component of political action but instead as a threat to multicultural citizenship (Modood 2007: 128). Modood claims that multiculturalism is not an abstract ideology, it is expressive of and grounded in specific socio-cultural contexts, and develops out of a broadly consensual framework of norms, policies and politics: 'It works to reform the status quo by selecting, developing and organising ideas, tendencies and "intimations"' (Modood 2007: 8; Oakeshott 1962: 123). Modood's account is essentially a restatement of the dangers Oakeshott identified. An ideology, for Modood, is a perspective upon the social world that inadequately attends to the substance of a context to which it is directed. An ideology is an abstract set of ideas tangentially or partially connected to the social and political practices and institutions, of which it is critical, or seeks to defend. He is opposed to religious ideologies, for example, which can threaten the dialogical working through of multicultural citizenship (2007: 132). Muslims cannot be categorised in terms of political generalisations: 'it is no more plausible to ascribe a particular politics (religious or otherwise) to all Muslims as it is to all women or members of the working class' (2007: 135).

Modood adopts Oakeshott's characterisation of what is entailed in the pursuit of intimations. Rational activity within the practical world of politics entails identifying and resolving incongruities and injustices consistent with the lines of development the traditional political practices themselves indicate, not by applying principles independently premeditated, but by immersion in the tradition in question and in the lines of development intimated. Hall and Modood maintain that there is 'no expectation that we shall necessarily detect a single direction in which to move, for traditions contain intimations between which we have to choose' (1982: 158). Oakeshott had made this clear in 1965 when he was at pains to impress upon D. D. Raphael that we cannot expect straight answers from our miscellaneous approvals, disapprovals, beliefs and preferences. We cannot expect the presentation of a single unambiguous norm, but instead a number of intimations suggested by the tradition, with little indication of a single direction. There are many suggestive directions, but no unambiguous injunction. We are provided, not with a prescription, but with 'a number of aids to reflection to be used in deciding upon and in justifying our responses to practical situations' (Oakeshott 1965: 91).

Modood elaborates the concept while developing, with Simon Thompson, the idea of reiterative contextualism in which certain principles may have a cross-contextual existence. Such principles may be invoked in criticism of particular normative practices, while not dismissing them completely. The theorist values and acknowledges existing norms, which at the same time are criticised in the name of principles. It is a familiar tension addressed by Idealist thinkers. Henry Jones, for example, refers to self-criticism, that is, the criticism of one's own social practices, as the hardest and most necessary form of criticism, in the name of wanting the best for one's society (Jones 1910). Modood and Thompson once again invoke Oakeshott's idea of the pursuit of intimations (Oakeshott 1962: 123, 124, 128), to at least ease the tension between deference to, and criticism of, existing normative practices. They identify three important features of the concept. Firstly, the contention that political activity is always circumstantial because it takes place within recognised traditions of behaviour. Such traditions are equivalent to their understanding of contexts as 'complex networks of normative practices' (Modood and Thompson 2017: 353). Secondly, the traditions are neither fixed, nor finished, and have no changeless core immune from change. This aspect of Oakeshott's contention is a reflection of his subscription to the principles of identity in difference, and continuity through change (Oakeshott 1933: 64–5, 123–4; Oakeshott 1983). Thirdly, politics is the activity of identifying and pursuing what changes are intimated within the traditions, making oneself open to sympathies that are present but not put into practice, and acknowledging that now is the time for recognising them (Modood and Thompson 2017: 353).

There are a number of ways in which this formulation is a distortion of Oakeshott's idea that politics is the pursuit of intimations. Firstly, Oakeshott does not direct it at theorists and it is not a recommendation about how they might go about formulating, for example, principles of justice or equality. It is not something that the theorist or philosopher chooses to do, or apply. Secondly, it is a piece of descriptive theorising (Costelloe 1998: 336–9) about the practice of politics. It belongs to an ontology and not to an epistemology. Just as Gadamer's idea of a fusion of horizons is not a method in hermeneutics, but a description of what happens to us each and every time we engage in the act of interpretation, Oakeshott's claim that politics is the pursuit of intimations is a description of what happens to practitioners each and every time they formulate principles or policies, and implement them.

Conclusion

I have tried to show that Modood's early philosophical career laid the foundation for justifying the positions that he subsequently advocated in his role as a public intellectual. From Collingwood he learnt that theory and practice overlap, and that a philosophical theory may have a considerable bearing on how one acts. Philosophy provides a necessary self-awareness, and self-knowledge inseparable from the activities in which the self engages.

Despite disagreeing with Oakeshott's separation of theory and practice, and with the radical autonomy of the modes of experience, there is much for which Modood is indebted. He does not share Oakeshott's scepticism, for example, about the reality of the finite individual when understood philosophically, yet both Oakeshott and Modood characterise the finite individual in similar terms, as an identity in difference which exhibits a unity in diversity throughout change. He rejects Oakeshott's essentialism in relation to identifying the postulates upon which the modes rely, but accepts his anti-essentialism in relation to the finite individual within each mode. Furthermore, Modood is equally as distrustful of rationalism in politics as Oakeshott, especially as it manifests itself in ideological politics.

Modood's disposition of enquiry may be characterised as deeply imbued with the latter-day philosophical idealism of Collingwood and Oakeshott, two of the twentieth century's foremost exponents of the philosophy of the day before yesterday, or to paraphrase Oakeshott on the occasion of the publication of the Festschrift dedicated to him in 1968, a philosophy that was out of date before Tariq was born (Oakeshott 1968: King and Parekh 1968). While his achievements in the field of multiculturalism are rightly celebrated, it has to be acknowledged that he has also been one of the contributors to the revival of the philosophical tradition from which his principles of enquiry emanate.

Notes

1. They are not to be conflated with Weber's ideal types (Weber 2004), although there are affinities, in that their progenitors are the neo-Kantian rather than the positivist traditions in philosophy. As John G. Gunnell suggests: 'while Weber's primary concern was with the application of social science to public policy, Oakeshott was deeply suspicious of the idea of theory intervening in practice' (2009: 4).

References

Aristotle (2013), *Poetics*, translated by A. Kenny. Oxford: Oxford University Press.

Bosanquet, B. (1895), *The Essentials of Logic*. London: Macmillan.

Bosanquet, B. (1899), *The Philosophical Theory of the State*. London: Macmillan.

Boucher, D. (1989), 'Autonomy and Overlap: The Different Worlds of Collingwood and Oakeshott', *Storia, Antropologia e scienze del Linguaggio*, IV, 69–89.

Boucher, D. (1993), 'Human Conduct, History and Social Science in the Works of R. G. Collingwood and Michael Oakeshott', *New Literary History*, 24, 697–717.

Boucher, D. (2016), 'Invoking a World of Ideas: Theory and Interpretation in the Justification of Colonialism', *Theoria: A Journal of Social and Political Theory*, 63, 6–24.

Boucher, D. (2022), 'Apologia for Poetry and the Art of Conversation', *Cosmos and Taxis*, 10 (7), 50–61.

Bradley, F. H. (1897), *Appearance and Reality*, revised 2nd edn. Oxford: Clarendon Press.

Bradley, F. H. (1914), *Essays on Truth and Reality*. Oxford: Oxford University Press.

Bradley, F. H. (1928), *Ethical Studies*, 2nd edn. Oxford: Clarendon Press.

Bradley, F. H. (1932), *The Principles of Logic*, 2nd edn. Oxford: Clarendon Press.

Collingwood, R. G. (1924), *Speculum Mentis or the Mirror of Knowledge*. Oxford: Oxford University Press.

Collingwood, R. G. (1938), *The Principles of Art*. Oxford: Oxford University Press.

Collingwood, R. G. (1992), *The New Leviathan*, revised edn, by R. G. Collingwood. Oxford: Oxford University Press.

Collingwood, R. G. (1998), *An Essay on Metaphysics*, new revised edn, R. Martin (ed.). Oxford: Oxford University Press.

Collingwood, R. G. (2005), *The Philosophy of Enchantment*, D. Boucher, W. James, and P. Smallwood (eds). Oxford: Oxford University Press.

Collingwood, R. G. (2013), *An Autobiography and Other Writings*, D. Boucher and T. Smith (eds). Oxford: Clarendon Press.

Greenleaf, W. H. (1968a), 'The World of Politics'. An Inaugural Lecture at University College, Swansea.

Greenleaf, W. H. (1968b), 'Idealism, Modern Philosophy and Politics' and 'A Bibliography of Michael Oakeshott', in P. King and B. C. Parekh (eds), *Politics and Experience: Essays Presented to Professor Michael Oakeshott on the Occasion of His Retirement*. Cambridge: Cambridge University Press, 93–124 and 409–17 respectively.

Griffith, G. and M. Oakeshott (2017), *A Guide to the Classics or How to Pick the Derby Winner*. Exeter: Amphora Press.

Gunnell, J. G. (2009), 'Political Inquiry and the Metapractical Voice', *Political Research Quarterly*, 62 (1), 3–15.

Hall, D. and T. Modood (1979), 'Practical Politics and Philosophical Inquiry: A Note', *Philosophical Quarterly*, 29 (117), 340–4.

Hall, D. and T. Modood (1982), 'Oakeshott and the Impossibility of Philosophical Politics', *Political Studies*, 30 (2), 157–76.

Hall, D. and T. Modood (1982), 'A Reply to Liddington', *Political Studies*, 30 (2), 184–9.

Jones, H. (1909), *Idealism as a Practical Creed*. London: Macmillan.

Jones, H. (1910), *The Working Faith of the Social Reformer*, London: Macmillan.

McTaggart, J. M. E. (1934), 'Dare to be Wise', in S. V. Keeling (ed.), *Philosophical Studies*. London: Arnold, 37–45.

Martinez, D. O. (2013), 'Interview: Intellectual Biography, Empirical Sociology and Normative Political Theory: An Interview with Tariq Modood', *Journal of Intercultural Studies*, 34 (6), 729–41.

Modood, T. (1980), 'Oakeshott's Conceptions of Philosophy', *History of Political Thought*, 1 (2), 315–22.

Modood, T. (1984), *R. G. Collingwood, M. J. Oakeshott and the Idea of a Philosophical Culture*. Unpublished PhD thesis. University College, Swansea.

Modood, T. (1989), 'The Later Collingwood's Alleged Historicism and Relativism', *Journal of the History of Philosophy*, 27 (1), 101–25.

Modood, T. (1995), 'Collingwood and the Idea of Philosophy', in D. Boucher, J. Connelly and T. Modood (eds), *Philosophy, History and Civilisation: Essays on R. G. Collingwood*. Cardiff: University of Wales Press, 32–61.

Modood, T. (1998), 'Anti-Essentialism, Multiculturalism and the "Recognition" of Religious Groups', *The Journal of Political Philosophy*, 6 (4), 378–99.

Modood, T. (ed.) (2005), *Multicultural Politics: Racism, Ethnicity and Muslims in Britain*. Edinburgh: Edinburgh University Press.

Modood, T. (2007), *Multiculturalism*. Cambridge: Polity.

Modood, T. (2013), *Multiculturalism*, 2nd edn. Cambridge: Polity.

Modood, T. and S. Thompson (2017), 'Revising Contextualism in Political Theory: Outing Principles into Context', *Res Publica*, 24 (3), 339–57.

Oakeshott, M. (1933), *Experience and Its Modes*. Cambridge: Cambridge University Press.

Oakeshott, M. (1950–1), 'Mr. Carr's First Volume', *Cambridge Journal*, IV, 504–6.

Oakeshott, M. (1954), 'The Idea of "Character" in the Interpretation of Modern Politics', Presented to a meeting of the Political Studies Association, in M. Oakeshott (2004), *What is History and Other Essays*, L. O'Sullivan (ed.). Exeter: Imprint Academic, 255–78.

Oakeshott, M. (1962), *Rationalism in Politics and Other*. London: Methuen.

Oakeshott, M. (1965), 'Rationalism in Politics: A Reply to Professor Raphael', *Political Studies*, 13 (1), 89–92.

Oakeshott, M. (1968), Speech regarding *Politics and Experience*, in P. King and B. Parekh (eds), Oakeshott Papers. British Library of Political Science, Oakeshott 1/3 Various Speeches.

Oakeshott, M. (1983), *On History and Other Essays*. Oxford: Blackwell.

Raphael, D. D. (1964), 'Professor Oakeshott's *Rationalism in Politics*', *Political Studies*, 12 (2), 202–15.

Raphael, D. D. (1965), '*Rationalism in Politics:* A Note on Professor Oakeshott's Reply', *Political Studies*, 13 (3), 395–7.

Raphael, D. (1990), *Problems in Political Philosophy*, 2nd edn. London: Palgrave.

Toulmin, S. (1972), *Human Understanding*, Vol. 1. Oxford: Oxford University Press.

Uberoi, V. (2021), 'Oakeshott and Parekh: The Influence of British Idealism on British Multiculturalism', *History of Political Thought*, 42 (2), 730–54.

Weber, M. (2004), *The Essential Weber*, S. Wimster (ed.). London: Routledge.

TWO

Intimating or Iterating? Modood on Contextualism and the Danish Cartoons of Muhammad

Sune Lægaard

Introduction

Tariq Modood's work is distinctive in how it both discusses issues of general societal relevance and engages in the specific details of particular cases. Modood's work on multiculturalism originated from a debate that precisely combined the discussion of a general issue and the details of a particular case, namely the controversy surrounding Salman Rushdie's novel *The Satanic Verses*. The general issue in question concerned the nature of a multicultural society and the role of religious minorities, specifically Muslims, in it.

Modood has subsequently been engaged in discussions of many other similar cases. One of them concerned the controversy over the cartoons published by the Danish newspaper *Jyllands-Posten*. The cartoon controversy was sparked by the publication of twelve cartoons in *Jyllands-Posten* on 30 September 2005 under the heading 'The Face of Muhammad'. The cartoons were accompanied by a short text by the cultural editor of the newspaper, Flemming Rose, who explained that the cartoons had been solicited by the newspaper in response to a perception of widespread self-censorship among artists when it came to discussing or addressing issues related to Islam. Rose also wrote that some Muslims reject modern secular democracy and the freedom of expression that this involves. To begin with, the publication did not have much of an effect. There were a few local protests orchestrated by an action committee composed of representatives of several Danish mosques. During the fall of 2005, members of the same group travelled to the Middle East to raise support for protests. Simultaneously, a group of ambassadors from predominantly

Islamic countries wrote to the Danish prime minister asking for a meeting to discuss the cartoons and similar cases of what the ambassadors considered attacks on Muslims. The prime minister refused to meet with them (for discussion of this aspect of the controversy, see Brown and Lægaard 2021). The controversy did not really erupt before early 2006, when boycotts were initiated by many predominantly Islamic countries against Denmark, protests and demonstrations took place, as well as several attacks on Danish diplomatic representations in Iran, Syria and Lebanon. The protests ebbed out during the spring of 2006 but there have been several subsequent revivals of the cartoon controversy when the cartoons have been reprinted by European newspapers in response to threats against *Jyllands-Posten*, the cartoonists or freedom of the press more generally (for the most comprehensive scholarly treatment of the cartoon controversy, which also describes these and other aspects of the course of events, see Klausen 2009).

Modood has furthermore been engaged in methodological discussions about how scholars should approach and discuss such cases as part of building a more general political theory – in his case, a political theory of multiculturalism. Since Modood's general take on multiculturalism (as most systematically articulated in Modood 2013 [2007]) advocates the rethinking of several aspects of how society is constituted, such a political theory requires normative principles both to criticise existing practices and to prescribe how a multicultural society should be constituted.

This paper focuses on Modood's interventions concerning the cartoon controversy and discusses them in light of his general contextualist stance as well as his more specific methodological recommendations. The aim is to draw out how Modood works with specific cases like this and to note some examples of the challenges posed by how he does so. Furthermore, I will use Modood's engagement with the cartoon controversy as possible illustrations of the different methodological moves in his contextualist approach.

The structure of the paper is as follows. I first sketch the main contours of contextualist methodology as described by Modood. I focus on two central concepts, which designate methodological steps in political theory, namely 'iteration' and 'intimation'. I then summarise the main claims that Modood advanced in his various contributions to the debates about the Danish cartoons of Muhammad and the ensuing controversy. Then I examine the way in which Modood argued for these claims. My focus will be on whether and how his arguments fit with the kind of contextualist methodology he has advocated. I will mainly focus on some examples of how Modood's interventions regarding the cartoon controversy seem not to exhibit the kind of attention to context that follow from his own methodological recommendations. I end by reflecting on the significance of these examples of apparent tensions between Modood's methodological commitments and his normative arguments regarding the cartoon controversy.

Contextualism

One can distinguish between contextualism in a very broad sense and more specific forms of contextualism. In the broad sense, contextualism denotes all ways of doing political theory that involve attention to specific cases and to their particular circumstances. Much of Modood's work is clearly contextualist in this broad sense, for example, his discussions of *The Satanic Verses* and the Danish cartoons. Modood has recently remarked that his interest 'lies in developing concepts to understand specific cases, such as Britain, rather than using that as an opportunity for generalisation and greater abstraction . . . my concept formation is perhaps less Weberian and more a form of contextualised political theory' (Modood 2019: 19).

Contextualism in this broad and unspecific sense is compatible with different views of what it might mean for contextual facts to appropriately inform political theory and with invocation of context at different levels of political theory (see Lægaard 2015 and 2021a for two attempts to map different types of contextualism in political theory).

Regarding the level of political theory at which context is invoked, one might distinguish between the *description and characterisation* of specific cases and arguments about which *general principles* should be used to evaluate such cases. Modood's work is contextualist at both levels, but contextualism means different things at the different levels. Modood has articulated a sense of contextualism, which he calls 'iterative contextualism', that is a view about the latter question, that is, how political theorists can articulate and justify general principles in a contextualist way. In this section, I present Modood's iterative contextualism. However, it should be kept in mind that this is mainly a view about general principles and that contextualism also concerns the inclusion and description of particular cases, which will be central to the subsequent discussion of the cartoon controversy.

Together with Simon Thompson, Modood has argued that context has two important roles to play. One is that 'it is through the exploration and evaluation of multiple contexts that general principles are devised, revised and refined'. The other is that 'significant weight should be given to the norms to be found in specific contexts because the people affected by those norms strongly identify with them' (Modood and Thompson 2018: 340). According to Modood, general principles are on the one hand based on the local context. On the other hand, they are not limited to a specific context. This is where his concept of iteration comes in. The idea is roughly that a political theorist starts out from a particular context and the norms already established in it. The theorist formulates a general principle that captures the norms in question. But this general principle should then be applied to other similar contexts, for example, to similar types of laws or institutions in different states. There will then most likely be various differences between the original principle and the norms established in other contexts. This will sometimes give the theorist reason to adjust and revise the principle, and then repeat the procedure in relation to new contexts. This is the process of iteration (Modood and Thompson 2018: 346–8).

In this iterative process of formulation, application and revision of general principles, Modood and Thompson argue that political theorists should give special weight to the ideals and values that the people in a particular context presently endorse. This is because they see their iterative contextualism as a political theory that aims 'to understand what justice requires people to do in particular contexts, and therefore the character of the norms which characterise each context will play an important role in our thinking, not just as facts but as constituting the normative context' (Modood and Thompson 2018: 352). This so-called normative constraint 'implies a duty of care on the part of critics. While there will always be a limit to how far this can be practised, the point applies to majority and minority practices alike' (Modood 2019: 20).

The result of iteration will be that, even though the general principle is based on norms in specific contexts, it will also be to some extent independent from any particular context. The application of a general principle to a particular context may therefore result in recommendations which deviate to some degree from the prevailing norms in that context. This is how contextualism, according to Modood and Thompson, retains critical distance (for discussion, see Lægaard 2019).

When principles differ from local norms, Modood and Thompson argue that 'although justice requires something other than what local norms say, what is required is likely to be intimated by the relevant context' (2018: 341). They here draw on Michael Oakeshott's idea of political reasoning as 'the pursuit of intimations' (Modood and Thompson 2018: 353). They understand this as a sensitivity to the complexity and immanent possibilities of the specific context, which are matters of judgement, not of rational deduction (Modood 2019: 20). Since there will generally be more than one norm present in each context, and each of them may be interpreted in different ways, the theorist both must determine which norm is of most importance and decide how that particular norm should be interpreted. This enables the iterative contextualist 'to offer an account of what justice requires in a particular situation which narrows – even if it does not entirely close – the gap between the existing norms and her principle of justice. To put this in Oakeshott's terms, the contextualist can pursue those intimations which tend in the direction of the principle which she has developed through her consideration of contexts elsewhere' (Modood and Thompson 2018: 345).

Modood on the Cartoon Controversy

There are two phases in Modood's engagement with the cartoon controversy. The first phase takes place simultaneously with the events in 2006. Modood published an article in the online magazine *Open Democracy* on 8 February 2006, that is, precisely at the time when the controversy really took off globally. This article gave rise to a debate, organised by Randall Hansen from the University of Toronto, and published in the December issue of the journal *International Migration*, which also included a second article by Modood responding to the other contributions to this debate. Modood's first article (Modood 2006a) should accordingly be read as an occasional piece rather than a research paper, and not as Modood's considered view of the cartoon controversy. Nevertheless, the piece introduces most of the themes that continue through his more considered writings on the topic, and it also provides some examples that are useful for discussing contextualism in relation to the controversy.

The second phase consists of Modood's more considered treatments of the cartoon controversy, which is mainly found in his chapter written together with Geoff Levey (Levey and Modood 2009) as well as some parts of later articles (including Modood 2013, republished in revised form in Modood 2019).

In these contributions, Modood focuses on the publication of the cartoons rather than on the responses to them. He is concerned with the background for the publication and the motives for it, as well as with how to understand the publication. This focus is linked to the broader normative issue about how to assess and regulate acts of this kind, including whether the publication of the cartoons should be understood as a kind of hate-speech and, if so, whether it should be criminalised as such or regulated in some other way. This focus is similar to the questions Modood had already discussed in his work following the controversy over *The Satanic Verses* (Modood 1993, republished in Modood 2005).

In phase one, Modood characterises the cartoons as all unfriendly to Islam, as sending the message that the prophet was a terrorist, and as being racist in how they use stereotypical depictions of Muslims (2006a: 4). According to Modood, the publication of the cartoons was premised on the view that a collective effort involving twelve cartoonists was necessary to withstand Muslim opposition, and the republication of the cartoons across continental Europe was deliberately done to teach Muslims a lesson (2006a: 5).

Modood's main claim regarding the normative question of how to respond to this is his *distinction between censorship and censure*. His point is that, even if an utterance such as the cartoons is racist, this does not in itself mean that it should be banned. The primary response should be a social sanction in the form of criticism and, if necessary, protest, rather than legal criminalisation. However, if social censure is not enough, legal censorship might also be necessary, such as in the case of the British 2006 law against incitement to religious hatred.

Modood is not very specific as to where the line between informal censure and legal censorship should be drawn. Regarding the most discussed cartoon, Kurt Westergaard's drawing of a bearded man with a bomb in his turban and the *shahadah* (the Islamic creed) written on the bomb, Modood writes that 'the drawing is an incitement to hatred and therefore in the category of the kind of images that ought to be banned ... Nevertheless, I would not categorically say that even that cartoon should be censored rather than censured' (2006b: 54).

Modood adds another theme from his other work, namely that religious minorities like Muslims are not treated even-handedly, since most Western societies for instance accept various limits to freedom of expression but deny such limits and rather invoke absolute freedom of expression precisely in cases involving minority religions (2006a: 6). Modood's position is that accommodations and privileges already accepted in relation to majority religions, or to other types of minorities, should also be extended to religious minorities such as Muslims, as illustrated by the move from the British ban on blasphemy that only protected Christian beliefs to a general law against incitement to religious hatred (2006b: 60). This is a general theme in Modood's work (developed in Modood 2013 [2007]), which is here simply affirmed in relation to the cartoon controversy and the issue of legal regulation of utterances like the cartoons.

In phase two, Levey and Modood (2009) use the cartoon controversy, and specifically Westergaard's bomb-in-the-turban cartoon, to illustrate conflicting interpretations of what liberal democracy requires in multicultural societies. They assume that Westergaard's cartoon suggests that

Islam is violent and dangerous and that the cartoon thus targets either Islam or Muslims (Levey and Modood 2009: 220). Levey and Modood do mention that both the commissioning editor Flemming Rose and Westergaard presented their aim differently, namely to criticise how Islam has been hijacked by violent extremists, but they disregard this interpretation on the basis that the cartoons could be interpreted as targeting Islam and/or Muslims (2009: 221).

On this basis, Levey and Modood (2009: 220, 222) discuss three potential problems with the cartoons, namely, 1) as *representing* the prophet contrary to religious injunctions against this; 2) as identifying *Islam* with violence and terrorism; and 3) as identifying *Muslims* with violence and terrorism. Levey and Modood's general (some might say, liberal) point regarding the first issue concerning representation is that it would be a threat to liberty if people were obliged to observe religious injunctions and that this cannot be enforced in a free society (2009: 223–4).

Regarding the second issue of targeting Islam, Levey and Modood discuss whether blasphemy laws are applied equally to all faiths. They mention the existence of a Danish blasphemy law that covered Muslims. But they further write that all cases according to the Danish blasphemy law had concerned images of Jesus (2009: 225). The normative upshot of this part of Levey and Modood's discussion is that the decision of the Danish director of public prosecution not to raise charges against the cartoons for violation of the blasphemy law might be a form of discrimination against Muslims.

Levey and Modood also discuss the progression from blasphemy laws to religious hatred provisions (2009: 230–6). Whereas Levey and Modood hold that religion as such should not be protected by law, they think that it makes a difference if the cartoons are instead understood as targeting Muslims rather than Islam (2009: 236). They argue that the cartoons can be seen as an attack on Muslims as a group on the basis that some of the cartoons employ roughly antisemitic stereotypes, which 'marks a brush with racism' (2009: 237). Regarding this third issue, which would make the cartoons a type of hate-speech, Levey and Modood support their claim that the cartoons understood as such could be restricted under religious and/or racial hatred laws by a parallel to laws proscribing Holocaust denial (2009: 237–8), which they think should be understood as protection of a group from hatred and incitement.

Modood has subsequently (in Modood 2013, republished in revised form as chapter 3 of Modood 2019) reaffirmed and expanded on many of these claims. This includes the parallel to laws against Holocaust denial, which according to Modood (2019: 62) is criminalised in many countries, not because it is immediate incitement to hatred, but out of concern for the feelings of Jews given the historical context. Modood uses this to argue that limits to free speech out of concern for the feelings of specific groups can be justified even if they are broader than laws against immediate incitements to hatred. This applies to Muslims, who according to Modood (2019: 63) experience feelings comparable to those relevant to Holocaust denial laws when there are disrespectful attacks on their faith. Therefore, limits to attacks on Muslim beliefs are appropriate for the same reason as limits on Holocaust denial, not to protect a specific religion, but as a means to protect a vulnerable group (2019: 64; for discussion, see Lægaard 2021b).

Modood has also reiterated his distinction between censorship and censure (2019: 65–6): there should be laws against incitement to hatred, but it is better to censure than censor (2019: 68). Modood sees a learning process in the UK from *The Satanic Verses* to the cartoon controversy: contrary to most other European countries, British newspapers decided not to publish the cartoons, which according to Modood was an exercise of self-restraint out of a concern for civility (2019: 66, 120), even though some might also have refrained from republication out of fear of reprisals (2019: 67–8).

Modood now has a much more nuanced characterisation of the cartoons that qualifies several of the more sweeping characterisations made in phase one, but he still holds on to the central claim that at least the bomb-in-the-turban cartoon is about Muslims in general and as such is racist:

> Of the twelve cartoons that were published, some were only mildly offensive, some were innocuous and one was even poking fun at the very exercise. We assumed (perhaps because we did not see them) that they were all offensive when they were not. There was one that I would say was racist: the cartoon that became famous, of a bearded man wearing a large turban with an Islamic declaration and from which is protruding a lit fuse. Nothing in that cartoon showed that it was of Muhammad, but it was clearly of a Muslim. Its point was, I think, that Muslims are terrorists or that, at least, there is something about Muslims and terrorism that goes together. It was not, then, a remark about the prophet Muhammad as such but a remark about Muslims; and on this basis it was racist. (Modood 2019: 66–7)

Are Modood's Arguments Sensitive to the Context?

Do Modood's claims regarding the cartoon controversy fit with his contextualist methodology? Are these claims contextually grounded and do Modood's arguments for them take context into account in the ways one might expect in light of his methodological recommendations?

One might discuss these questions at several levels. Given that a claim or the argument for it should take context into account in some way, one might discuss whether it does this *at all*. If it does, one might then discuss whether the contextual facts invoked for the claim are *correct* or not, whether the context is characterised correctly, or whether it is the right context that is invoked. Finally, if a claim or the argument for it does take a relevant and reasonably characterised context into account, one might still discuss whether this actually provides a good *justification* for the normative claim advanced on this basis.

I will provide examples of all three kinds of discussions in relation to Modood's writings on the cartoon controversy. I will focus on examples where one might criticise Modood for not taking context into account, or for assuming a questionable characterisation of the context, or for making claims not supported by the context. The point of this focus is to discuss the challenges for a contextualist methodology like the one recommended by Modood. My aim is to illustrate methodological difficulties with a view to subsequent reflection on what we might learn from these. The types of criticisms change from phase one to phase two. Roughly, as one might expect, the more occasional writings in phase one provide more examples of the first kind of problems, that is, failure to take context into account or failures in getting the facts about the context right, whereas the more considered writings in phase two provide more examples where the disagreement rather concerns interpretation and what the normative upshot is of taking the context into account. Even though one might think that we should only discuss the more considered writings, I will nevertheless also discuss the writings in phase one, both because they provide pertinent examples and because there actually is a high degree of continuity in Modood's normative views across phases one and two.

The first thing to expect from a contextualist discussion of a concrete case like the cartoon controversy is an accurate description of the case. There are some examples from Modood's description of the cartoon controversy where one might find problems in this respect. This concerns the characterisation of the cartoons, the motives involved in the publication of them, and the legal framework invoked in relation to the subsequent discussion of how such publication should be regulated.

Regarding the description of the cartoons, Modood's initial claim that they are all unfriendly to Islam (2006a: 4) is simply wrong (as also pointed out in response to Modood by Erik Bleich (2006: 17–18), and as subsequently acknowledged by Modood (2006b: 54) and by Levey and Modood (2009: 218)). Some of the cartoons were critical of the newspaper's 'stunt' or of the author Kåre Bluitgen, whose claim not to have been able to find an illustrator for a children's book about Muhammad

was part of the impetus for the whole exercise. Others were satirical interventions in local Danish politics (cf. Klausen (2009: 14): 'Not all the
cartoons depicted the Prophet. Some mocked far-right politicians; others
portrayed Muslims as victims.' See further, Klausen (2009: 21–4)).

Modood's claim that the whole exercise was premised on the view
that a collective effort involving twelve cartoonists was necessary to withstand Muslim opposition (2006a: 5, reiterated by Levey and Modood
2009: 218) is also inaccurate. The commissioning editor, Flemming
Rose, explicitly motivated the invitation, which was sent to all members
of the Danish newspaper cartoonists association, as a *test* of whether
there was self-censorship among Danish artists relative to matters
pertaining to Islam. The stated main aim, which was described in the
text accompanying the cartoons, was to gauge the extent of such self-
censorship. Jytte Klausen describes it thus:

> the editors were conducting an experiment. They solicited drawings of
> the Prophet Muhammad from all the members of the union of news-
> paper illustrators (in Denmark everyone belongs to a union) in order
> to establish whether illustrators would refuse to participate. Prompting
> this experiment was a rumor, circulated earlier during the summer, that
> an author of children's books named Kåre Bluitgen had been unable to
> find an illustrator for a book about Muhammad. The editors wished to
> see whether such fear was widespread and if illustrators would therefore
> refuse the commission. (Klausen 2009: 14)

Modood's further claim that the republication of the cartoons across
continental Europe was deliberately done to teach Muslims a lesson
(2006a: 5) is also questionable. Some of the first republications of the
cartoons were by an Egyptian and a Bosnian newspaper (Klausen 2009:
48), which does not support the claim that republications were directed
against Muslims. Further, most of the republications took place *after*
the protests against the cartoons had taken off, that is, during February
2006, and the explicit justifications given by most of the newspapers
for reprinting the cartoons (or, usually, only Westergaard's cartoon) was
a response to the threats against *Jyllands-Posten*, to the trade boycotts
against Denmark, and to the perceived attempt by Islamic states to censor the press (cf. O'Leary 2006: 27, and as acknowledged by Levey and
Modood 2009: 219). Klausen writes that 'The newspapers also almost
invariably proclaimed that publication of the cartoon or cartoons was
a statement of solidarity with the Danes or a stand for freedom of the
press' (2009: 48) and 'The editors generally said the same thing: The
cartoons were offensive – so therefore we show just a little bit of them –
but the Muslim countries should not try to interfere with what we print'
(2009: 52).

The republications were interpreted differently by many Muslims (cf. Klausen 2009: 48–9). Modood is explicit about this and that he focuses on how the cartoons were seen by many Muslims:

> Everyone – Muslims and non-Muslims – 'views' them (whether literally or imaginatively) in a wider domestic and international context that is already deeply contested. From the Muslim side, the underlying causes of their current anger are a deep sense that they are not respected. (2006a: 5)

So Modood seeks to contextualise the cartoons, but only in relation to the contextual factors that many Muslims see as relevant and which plausibly explain some of the protests against the cartoons (although a main explanation arguably is how certain Islamic states and international organisations like the Organisation of the Islamic Conference (now the Organisation of Islamic Cooperation) instrumentalised the cartoons for other purposes, cf. Klausen 2009). But in restating the perception of some Muslims that the republications were intentional acts of disrespect and denigration of Muslims, Modood provides a one-sided view of the events. This is an example of how the same action can be interpreted differently. Modood presents how the cartoons were understood by some Muslims, which is central to understanding the subsequent events and a relevant consideration in relation to the discussion about how such acts should be assessed. But in ignoring the explicitly stated aims of the actors in question and jumping directly to how the acts in question were interpreted by some Muslims, Modood premises this discussion on only one perspective. Contextualist methodology should arguably take account of how different actors present and understand a given act or event. Modood has himself stressed this in his invocation of the normative constraint and the duty of care on behalf of political theorists that this according to him implies, which directs theorists to give special weight to the views and values of people in the context under discussion. If only some of these understandings are included and taken at face value whereas others are ignored or misrepresented, contextualism risks becoming a mere partisan intervention.

This illustrates one challenge facing all forms of contextualism, namely the need to decide what the relevant context is (cf. Lægaard 2021a: 18–19). On some forms of contextualism, selecting a particular context as the relevant one can be defended, for example, if context is viewed as a source of problems (Lægaard 2021a: 8–10). We might understand Modood as deliberately selecting only the context as understood by some Muslims in order to focus on the problems to which the events thus understood gave rise. But if contextualism is supposed to provide a fuller understanding of the object of inquiry as a basis for normative judgements that do not just cater to how a specific group understands an event, then selective inclusion of some contextual factors and exclusion of others seems problematic.

Moving from the interpretation of the general context in which the cartoons should be viewed to the more specific issue of how the cartoons, and especially Westergaard's bomb-in-the-turban cartoon on which most of the debate has focused, should be understood, Modood started out by stating very bluntly that the message of the cartoons was 'that the Prophet of Islam was a terrorist', that 'the cartoons are not just about one individual but about Muslims per se' and therefore racist (both 2006a: 4), since 'Muhammad is meant to represent Muslims as such' (2006b: 54). These are of course possible interpretations, and it might be true that many Muslims who saw the cartoons interpreted them in this way or, more likely, that many Muslims got the impression that this was the message of the cartoons even though they did not see them.

But why think that this is the right or the only relevant interpretation? The already noted fact that not all of the cartoons were even about the prophet and not all were negative towards Islam or Muslims should at least qualify these blunt claims. The commissioning editor Flemming Rose's accompanying text about the purpose of the whole exercise was mainly about supposed self-censorship due to fear among artists about retaliations and only said that *some* Muslims reject secular democracy and free speech. This does not support the claim that the cartoons should be interpreted as being about *all* Muslims. During the height of the controversy in February 2006, Rose further addressed the claim that Westergaard's cartoon is saying that the prophet is a terrorist or that every Muslim is a terrorist: 'I read it differently: Some individuals have taken the religion of Islam hostage by committing terrorist acts in the name of the prophet' (Rose 2006). As Klausen notes, Kurt Westergaard explicitly stated that his cartoon was about how fanatics misuse Islam and the prophet:

> Kurt Westergaard, who drew the cartoon, was angry that there were illustrators who were 'afraid' and wanted to prove there was no need to worry about such matters in Denmark. He intended his drawing to show that radical Muslims use the Prophet's name to justify violence. He did not for a minute consider that Muslims would interpret his drawings the other way around, as intended to show that the Prophet is the source of violence. (Klausen 2009: 22)

At least Rose's views were available already in 2006, so it seems selective that Modood did not even mention or engage with them in phase one.

In phase two, Levey and Modood did acknowledge Rose's and Westergaard's views, but set them aside on the grounds that 'the associations in
the image are so obviously open to being misinterpreted as an attack on
either Islam or Muslims, or both, that neither the cartoonist nor, especially, the editor is much let off the hook' (Levey and Modood 2009: 221).

If one acknowledges that there are different interpretations and that
a widespread interpretation might be a misinterpretation, why nevertheless focus only on precisely this possible misinterpretation, namely that
the cartoon identifies Islam and/or all Muslims with violence and terrorism, which is what Levey and Modood do? It is probably true that many
Muslims accepted this interpretation of the cartoons, and this might in
part explain some of the ensuing events. But even if we grant this, why
should the assessment of the cartoons only be based on this interpretation? A contextualist approach can clearly involve the social meanings
of given acts or events. But if a contextualist approach privileges one
among many interpretations as the basis for normative assessments, this
seems to give rise to a version of the problem of critical distance facing
some forms of contextualism (Lægaard 2019).

I now turn to the set of examples concerning the contextual elements
of Modood's discussion of legal regulations of utterances like the cartoons. Even though Modood's main point is his distinction between censure and censorship, which means that cases like the cartoon controversy
should not primarily be handled through legal regulations, Modood is
nevertheless clear that legal regulations are necessary in some cases, and
that at least Westergaard's bomb-in-the-turban cartoon, under Modood's
assumed interpretations of it, might be one such case. Modood's general
view here is that the type of incitement to hatred laws already in place
in relation to some groups should be extended to cover Muslims, that it
is a form of discrimination if they are not, and that such laws should be
understood as protections of the feelings of the groups in question.

The structure of this general argument is already contextualist in that
it takes its point of departure in already established laws in a given context and then argues for their extension or for applying them in a way
that does not discriminate against a specific group. Modood applies this
mode of argument to the specific Danish context in relation to how the
cartoons were handled. He notes (with reference to Bleich 2006) that:

> Danish law – like that of many other countries – already forbids dissem-
> ination of threatening, insulting, or degrading material on account of
> race, colour, national or ethnic origin, or sexual inclination, so extending
> it to cover religion is not making Muslims a special case but the reverse.
> (Modood 2006b: 60)

This is an instance of Modood's general argument about extending accommodations and protections already offered to other groups to religious minorities in general and Muslims in particular. But here it seems misplaced in a way that interestingly shows a lack of contextual accuracy. The Danish penal code §266b, to which Bleich referred, makes it a criminal offence to issue public utterances 'threatening, insulting or degrading to a group of persons due to their race, skin colour, national or ethnic origin, faith or sexual orientation' (Lægaard 2007: 485–6) and thus in fact already included religion as one of the protected traits. So precisely this case is a bad one for reiterating the general argument for extension of protection to religious minorities, including Muslims, because they are already covered. The fact that Modood nevertheless makes this argument in this case reveals that he had not, in phase one, done what his own contextualism would recommend, namely, to compare the principle he has arrived at on the basis of his investigation of other contexts (mainly of the British context) with what is the case in a new context (here, the Danish context). To use Modood's own terminology, it seems that he has not engaged in the process of iteration, which involves checking how an argument and recommendation based on discussion of one context (the British one) applies to another one (the Danish one).

Contrary to this phase one discussion of hate speech laws, Levey and Modood (2009) mention the existence of a Danish blasphemy law that did in fact cover Muslims. But they further write (with reference to private correspondence with the Danish scholar Jytte Klausen) that all cases according to the Danish blasphemy law had concerned images of Jesus (2009: 225). However, this is not true. When the Danish director of public prosecution in 2006 considered whether to raise charges against *Jyllands-Posten* for the publication of the cartoons, there had only been three cases where charges had been raised in relation to the Danish blasphemy clause since its introduction in 1930. None of these had concerned images of Jesus. The first case concerned denigration of the Judaic faith, and the subsequent cases concerned an act of dressing up as priests and performing a mock baptism of a doll, and performance of a song about sexuality with references to God, where the latter case in 1971 did not lead to conviction.

It is true that there had been other (at the time highly publicised) cases, where the director of public prosecution had *considered* whether to raise charges in relation to the blasphemy clause, which did involve offensive images of Jesus. This was the case for two prominent cases involving a Danish provocative artist in the seventies and eighties. In these cases, the director of public prosecution eventually decided not to

raise charges (cf. Klausen 2009: 144–5). The same was the case in relation to the cartoons, which the director of public prosecution considered in relation to the existing applicable laws and the legal precedent
(cf. Lægaard 2007: 486). The decision was not to raise charges – on similar grounds to those underlying the earlier decisions not to raise charges
against offensive depictions of Jesus. The normative upshot of this
part of Levey and Modood's discussion, namely their suggestion that
the decision of the director of public prosecution not to raise charges
against the cartoons might be a form of discrimination against Muslims,
is therefore questionable. From a contextualist point of view, the lesson
to be drawn regarding the (subsequently abolished) Danish blasphemy
clause and the cartoons might actually be the opposite, namely that the
cartoons and their offensiveness to Muslims was treated in the same way
as how the prosecutor had treated depictions of Jesus, which were offensive to some Christians (cf. Klausen 2009: 145–6).

These two examples illustrate how a normative claim might be
undermined if it is based on an argument with contextualist elements
but where the facts about the specific context do not support the contextual claims needed to justify the conclusion. These versions of Modood's
general argument are formulated regarding the Danish context, so the
claim is that specific already established Danish laws should either be
extended or applied differently. The problem is that the arguments
assume that a given law is restricted in a way that it is in fact not or that
it is applied in a way that it is in fact not. As such, these instances of
Modood's general argument are different from arguments about which
laws there ought to be in the first place where this is not justified on the
basis of features of the existing laws. Modood's iterative contextualism
seeks to provide a method for discussing this other question.

Before considering that, it is worth remarking on Modood's references to laws proscribing Holocaust denial. As part of the discussion
of extension of accepted limits to free speech to also cover attacks
against Muslims, Modood mentioned the imprisonment of Holocaust
deniers as an example of what Europeans regard as acceptable limits
to freedom of speech (Modood 2006a: 6). He presented the imprison-
ing of historian David Irving for Holocaust denial as an example of
how Western society protects certain vulnerabilities and sensibilities
but not those of Muslims (2006b: 54). Levey and Modood (2009: 237)
repeated this point but qualified it by saying that Holocaust denial
laws are not about protection of religion or sensibilities of Jews but an
act of solidarity and fraternity with a view to protecting Jews against
incitement to hatred (2009: 238). Modood further develops this interpretation of European Holocaust denial laws, which he argues can

only be understood as means to protect the emotions of victims of incitement (2019: 62).

Modood's invocation of Holocaust denial laws is relevant to two arguments. One argument is how existing laws provide unequal protection of Muslims compared to other groups, the other about how we already accept limits to free speech aimed at protecting the emotions of targeted groups. What is central from a contextualist point of view is that Holocaust denial laws are not in place in all European countries. Neither the UK nor Denmark have such laws (as Modood 2019: 73, acknowledges in a footnote), so how should we understand Modood's invocation of Holocaust denial laws from a contextualist perspective? One view might be that these laws are irrelevant in the British and Danish contexts, which do seem of particular relevance to the discussion of *The Satanic Verses* and the cartoons, respectively. At least one cannot mount the argument about unequal protection by existing laws or already accepted grounds for limiting free speech with reference to Holocaust denial laws in the British and Danish contexts. This is not to say that Holocaust denial laws might not be relevant in other ways, including in relation to Modood's iterative contextualism. But in relation to the specific case of the application of the two noted types of arguments to the cartoons, the relevance of these laws is less clear.

What is the Significance of Tensions between Contextualism and Normative Claims?

What do these examples from Modood's writings on the cartoon controversy where context might not have been taken adequately into account show? If specific claims are justified in a way that fits with a methodological prescription, then one can take this either as a reason in favour of the claims or as a support for the methodological prescriptions, or both. On the other hand, if there is tension, this might either show a problem in the specific claims, or it might show that the methodological prescriptions are inapplicable, either to the specific case or in general. These possibilities concern whether we should accept Modood's claims regarding the cartoon controversy or his methodological prescriptions, respectively. However, we might also use such a comparison as part of a constructive discussion of how to be aware of challenges and possibilities in contextual discussions like this. The comparison might finally illustrate the difference between the central moves in a contextual methodology, in Modood's case between iteration and intimation.

The discussion of the cartoon controversy provides a pertinent illustration of challenges facing contextually sensitive political theory. It is evidently not a simple matter even to describe the events in question. It is difficult to discuss the cartoon controversy without characterising the cartoons or the circumstances surrounding their publication. Such a characterisation can either be inadequate or inaccurate, if it is based on factually wrong claims or disregards facts of the case, or it can be one-sided if it is only based on how one party understood the case. The lesson to be learnt from this is that discussions of such cases should attend as much as possible to the facts of the case and either take seriously the different understandings of the case or declare clearly if the discussion approaches the case based on particular understandings of it. This can be inevitable, to the extent that characterisations of events like this cannot be completely objective and impartial, but then one should be as open about one's choice of perspective as possible. Explication of the choices made in the characterisation of the context are required.

I have noted some respects in which Modood's description of the case was inaccurate or inadequate, especially in the more occasional writings in phase one. This is not surprising, given the nature of these writings. Does this undermine any of Modood's normative claims? These claims consist of his argument about how the cartoons could be considered racist hate-speech, how protections and privileges already granted to other groups should be extended to Muslims, and the implication that it is a form of discrimination if this is not done, and how limits on free speech can be justified to protect minority groups. Modood's assertion of these arguments in relation to the cartoon controversy can be problematised on contextualist grounds. It is debatable whether even the bomb-in-the turban cartoon was racist hate-speech against Muslims – even if many Muslims understood it as such. The Danish laws against blasphemy and hate-speech did in fact extend to Muslims, and the decision not to raise charges against the cartoons based on these laws did not involve discriminatory treatment of Muslims relative to how other groups were protected under these laws.

Are Modood's normative claims therefore wrong? Not necessarily. One can distinguish between the general mode of argument and the application of it to a specific case. Even though Modood might be right that some utterances are racist and should be legally restricted hate-speech, the Danish cartoons perhaps did not provide an example of this. And one might endorse his general argument for extension of protections and privileges to Muslims but accept that this argument did not apply in the case of Danish blasphemy and hate-speech legislation. Such a response would save the general arguments by abandoning the claims made regarding the specific case.

The lack of fit can alternatively be used to problematise the general arguments. There is a high degree of continuity in Modood's normative claims from phase one, based on inadequate descriptions of the case, to phase two, where the description of the case is more accurate. This continuity might show that these claims are not contextually sensitive. It is understandable that occasional writings such as those in phase one draw on modes of argument already tried out in another context. But if it turns out that there are relevant differences between the contexts, then the considered response in phase two should have qualified the claims. If this does not happen, it puts in question the contextual sensitivity of the normative claims.

The proper contextualist response would be to engage in the kind of process of iteration that Modood later describes, where the general mode of argument is qualified and adjusted to take account of the facts of the new context – and in this process to exercise the duty of care towards the agents in this context by taking their perspectives into account. Such a process of iteration could provide a more informed version of the general arguments. The upshot might be that the laws in the Danish context should be changed, perhaps in a way similar to how the British laws were changed in 2006. This is a possible outcome of iterative contextualism but one where the contextualist argument has yet to be made. The lack of fit in the specific instances discussed here simply shows the need for further work for anyone committed to contextualism.

What about the other central element of Modood's contextualist methodology, namely his idea of intimation? There are several ways of understanding this idea. One is that intimation is something the political theorist engages in *after* the process of iteration, that is, when the theorist has applied a general principle to a new context, revised it in light of this context, and if the principle still yields criticism of the actually established local norms. Intimation in this narrow sense is what the political theorist does in considering possible ways of reforming the local context to comply with a general principle in a way that is most in tune with ideas and potentials already present in the context. But intimation might also be seen as *independent* of the idea of iteration. Intimation is then what the political theorist does in suggesting ways of reform based on consideration of the specific context which might (but need not) involve identification of principles in the context.

If intimation is a step following on iteration, and if Modood has not engaged in the process of iteration in relation to his arguments regarding the cartoon controversy, then there is not a place for intimation in these cases yet. However, if intimation can be independent of iteration, there might be room for intimation.

Modood's argument for the move from the British blasphemy clause to a general law against incitement to religious hatred (Modood 2005) is a possible example of intimation in the latter sense. This argument was based, among other things, on the fact that similar legislation was

already in place in Northern Ireland. This is one way in which a normative recommendation of change can be based on consideration of
features already present in part of the context in question. Modood
seems, however, to understand intimation as more than just attention
to such details. Pursuit of intimations is also a matter of interpreting the
deeper meaning of specific laws or practices, to understand how they
could be reformed or developed in light of this meaning, and to judge
which among several possible changes would be most valuable in light
of both these meanings and applicable general principles (Modood and
Thompson 2018: 353). Intimation is thus a matter of closer interpretative engagement with the systems of norms in a given context.

The best example of such an interpretative engagement in Modood's
writings about the cartoon controversy concerns the characterisation
of the cartoons and the exposition of how they might be problematic.
Especially Levey and Modood's extended discussion of three potential
problems with the cartoons is an example of such interpretative engagement (2009: 222–41). The problem here is not a lack of interpretative
engagement, but the already noted inaccurate assumptions about the
Danish context and the arguable somewhat one-sided perspective on
the cartoons. Levey and Modood do engage in pursuit of intimations,
but only relative to a context characterised in a way based on how some
Muslims understood the cartoons.

This shows a general problem facing contextualism, namely that contextualism must specify the relevant context. The delimitations following
from this are bound to exclude perspectives that might be relevant. However, one does not need to be critical of contextualism as such to find the
specific example problematic. The problem with the one-sided characterisation of the cartoons can also be explained with reference to the duty
of care towards ideals and values presently endorsed by people in a particular context that according to Modood and Thompson should be the
hallmark of contextualism (since this duty of care according to Modood
is a general constraint (Modood and Thompson 2018: 352; Modood
2019: 20) and therefore must be assumed to apply equally to minorities
and majorities, there is no need here to discuss who are the majority and
who the minority, which arguably changed when the cartoon controversy
expanded from being a domestic Danish to a global case).

Conclusion

I have discussed Tariq Modood's writings regarding the cartoon controversy in light of his views about contextualism. This comparison shows
the importance of attention to context and explicit attention to how

context is taken into account when one discusses cases like this. It also shows the difficulty of doing so in an adequate manner, since there are always several competing perspectives on such cases and since contextual sensitivity requires quite detailed knowledge. Modood's normative claims regarding the cartoon controversy reiterate some of the central arguments of his more general theory of multiculturalism. But the application of them in a contextually sensitive way turns out to be challenging, since some of the descriptions of the case on which Modood bases his arguments are either inaccurate or adopt characterisations drawn from one perspective while leaving other perspectives out. I have argued that this puts some of Modood's claims regarding the specific case in question, although it does not necessarily invalidate his more general arguments or his contextualist methodology. Rather, this shows how a contextualist defence and development of these arguments is a continuous work in progress.

References

Bleich, E. (2006), 'On Democratic Integration and Free Speech: Response to Tariq Modood and Randall Hansen', *International Migration*, 44 (5), 17–22.

Brown, A. and S. Lægaard (2021), 'Cosmopolitan Democratic and Communicative Rights: The Danish Cartoons Controversy and the Right to Be Heard, Even Across Borders', *Human Rights Review*, 22 (1), 23–43.

Klausen, J. (2009), *The Cartoons That Shook the World*. New Haven: Yale University Press.

Levey, G. B. and T. Modood (2009), 'Liberal Democracy, Multicultural Citizenship and the Danish Cartoon Affair', in G. B. Levey and T. Modood (eds), *Secularism, Religion and Multicultural Citizenship*. Cambridge: Cambridge University Press, 216–42.

Lægaard, S. (2007), 'The Cartoon Controversy: Offence, Identity, Oppression?', *Political Studies*, 55 (3), 481–98.

Lægaard, S. (2015), 'Multiculturalism and Contextualism: How is Context Relevant for Political Theory?', *European Journal of Political Theory*, 14 (3), 259–76.

Lægaard, S. (2019), 'Contextualism in Normative Political Theory and the Problem of Critical Distance', *Ethical Theory and Moral Practice*, 22 (4), 953–70.

Lægaard, S. (2021a), 'Contextualism in Normative Political Theory', in W. R. Thompson (ed.), *Oxford Research Encyclopedia of Politics*. Oxford: Oxford University Press.

Lægaard, S. (2021b), 'The Role of Alienation and Muslim Religious Beliefs in Debates About Establishment and Hate Speech', in T. Modood, R. Bauböck, J. H. Carens, S. Lægaard, G. Mahajan and B. Parekh, 'Ethnocentric Political Theory, Secularism and Multiculturalism', *Contemporary Political Theory*, 20 (2), 447–79.

Modood, T. (1993), 'Muslims, Incitement to Hatred and the Law', in J. Horton (ed.), *Liberalism, Multiculturalism, and Toleration*. London: Macmillan, 139–56.

Modood, T. (2005), *Multicultural Politics*. Edinburgh: Edinburgh University Press.

Modood, T. (2006a), 'The Liberal Dilemma: Integration or Vilification?', *International Migration*, 44 (5), 4–7.

Modood, T. (2006b), 'Obstacles to Multicultural Integration', *International Migration*, 44 (5), 51–62.

Modood, T. (2013 [2007]), *Multiculturalism*. Cambridge: Polity.

Modood, T. (2013), 'Censor or Censure: Maintaining Civility', in R. Griffith-Jones (ed.), *Islam and English Law*. Cambridge: Cambridge University Press, 216–24.

Modood, T. (2019), *Essays on Secularism and Multiculturalism*, London: Rowman & Littlefield.

Modood, T. and S. Thompson (2018), 'Revisiting Contextualism in Political Theory: Putting Principles into Context', *Res Publica*, 24 (3), 339–57.

O'Leary, B. (2006), 'Liberalism, Multiculturalism, Danish Cartoons, Islamist Fraud, and the Rights of the Ungodly', *International Migration*, 44 (5), 22–33.

Rose, F. (2006), 'Why I Published Those Cartoons', *Washington Post*, Sunday, 19 February 2006, Page B01. Accessed at: <http://www.washingtonpost.com/wp-dyn/content/article/2006/02/17/AR2006021702499.html>

THREE

Tariq Modood and the Politics of Recognition

Simon Thompson

Introductory Remarks

If Tariq Modood's large and ever-growing body of academic work could be said to revolve around one specific idea, that idea would be multiculturalism. He employs a range of other concepts to help him flesh out this idea, understand multicultural societies, and articulate a normative defence of them. My aim in this chapter is to explore the role that the concept of recognition in particular plays in Modood's thought. In a critique of Will Kymlicka's version of multiculturalism, he argues:

> Let us then put to one side Kymlicka's idea of the importance of cultural membership to individual autonomy. A better normative starting point is the politics of recognition of difference or respect for identities that are important to people, as identified in minority assertiveness, and should not be disregarded in the name of integration or citizenship. (Modood 2007: 37)

In this chapter, I take seriously Modood's claim that an idea of recognition – and more particularly a politics of recognition – is key both to understanding multicultural societies and to articulating a normative justification of them. Thus I ask what he understands by recognition, and I investigate what role it plays in his thought. I also want to bring a critical perspective to bear on his account. This will involve me questioning the clarity and coherence of his idea of recognition, and suggesting moves he might want to make in order to strengthen his concept so that it can play a greater role in his work.

To accomplish all of this, my discussion will revolve around four themes. For the sake of clarity, I shall sometimes refer to these by single words: equality, identity, struggle and inclusion. The first theme concerns the role of the idea of equality in Modood's normative framework. Here he suggests that 'equal citizenship' plays a foundational role in this framework. The second theme of identity encompasses both individual identity and group identity, as well as the complex relationship between them. The third theme introduces a dynamic element into the discussion. For Modood, we must accept that there is a constant struggle for recognition, in which some groups, hitherto unrecognised, make claims to be given appropriate acknowledgement, and other groups respond more or less constructively to these claims. I refer to the final theme I have chosen to discuss as inclusion. By this word, I intend to capture something of Modood's normative ideal, according to which a good multicultural society is one in which all citizens can feel included. Although these four themes are interrelated in complex ways, I think that, by distinguishing between them, and by presenting them in the order I have chosen, I shall be able to explicate Modood's account of recognition as clearly as possible, and to do so in a way which enables me to point to some deficiencies and limitations to this account.

The plan of the chapter goes like this. In section 2, I present Modood's account of recognition, focusing on the four themes just described. In section 3, I offer some critical remarks on each of these themes, and suggest there are certain lacunae in Modood's account that he might wish to address. Finally, in section 4, I conclude that Modood offers an interesting and valuable take on the idea of recognition, and uses this idea productively both as a means of understanding multicultural societies and as a normative standard for evaluating such societies. But I also suggest that his account of recognition needs further clarification and development if it is to play as fruitful a role as he intends for it.

Modood's Account of Recognition

In this section, as I have just said, my aim is to present what to my mind are the most important features of Modood's account of recognition.

Equality

My first theme is that of equality, where this also includes cognate ideas such as equal citizenship. This means that I begin with the most explicitly normative aspects of Modood's account, and I choose to begin here since Modood himself is at pains to insist that analysing struggles for recognition will always require the deployment of a normative frame-work. As he says:

> I make a multiculturalist plea for studying Islamophobia (and groups negatively perceived from the outside, generally) within a norma-tive framework which prioritises groups fighting outsider perceptions by boosting insider identifications and the struggle for recognition. (Modood 2019: 24; and see 85)

We shall focus on the idea of struggle later in this section. For now, the important point to take from this passage is that Modood distances him-self from any attempt to understand social conflict which uses the lens of recognition but which seeks to avoid normativity.

So far as his normative framework is concerned, I would suggest that the concept of equality is its most important component. In order to see this, let us reflect on the following brief and rather densely packed passage:

> the concepts of recognition and belonging . . . are interpretations of the idea of equality as applied to groups who are constituted by differentia that have identarian dimensions that elude socio-economic concepts. (Modood 2007: 153)

If we turn the various elements of this passage around, Modood begins from a commitment to equality, then applies this conception to identity groups, and as a result arrives at ideas of 'recognition and belonging'.

To understand more about how Modood understands equality, we need to appreciate that he makes a distinction between 'equal dignity' and 'equal respect' (2007: 51), a distinction which he believes can be found in Charles Taylor's well-known essay on 'The Politics of Recogni-tion' (1994). Modood understands these two forms of equality to cor-respond to Taylor's distinction between the 'politics of universalism' and the 'politics of difference'. Thus he understands equal dignity to be difference-blind, universalistic and uniform (2007: 51). In other words, when a number of individuals are treated with equal dignity, they are all treated in the same way, without reference to any of the characteristics which may distinguish them from one another. For instance, all citizens may enjoy the right to freedom of religion. As Modood understands it, equal respect, by contrast, is difference-sensitive, since it is a response to the belief that the failure to recognise relevant differences is oppressive (2007: 51–2). For instance, the Māori enjoy a number of reserved seats in the New Zealand Parliament in order to ensure that this important indigenous group can exercise an effective voice in their political com-munity (Pirsoul 2020).

Modood does not present these as alternative conceptions of equality. Rather, he insists that they always work in tandem, since individuals always stand in need of recognition both for what they have in common, and for what makes them distinct. Actually, one interesting feature of Modood's account is that he goes further than this, and argues that it is impossible to achieve either form of equality without simultaneously achieving the other. To put it slightly differently, we can say that equal dignity and equal respect are dependent on each other for their realisation (2007: 52). On the one hand, Modood argues that lack of equal respect undermines equal dignity because the stereotyping of groups undermines the possibility of each individual member regarding other citizens as equals (2007: 52). Even where two citizens enjoy the same basic rights, if one of them is identified with a group which is stigmatised, then they cannot regard each other as equals. On the other hand, a lack of equal dignity undermines equal respect. Here Modood's reasoning is a little more obscure. His claim is that equal dignity rests on equal respect's 'universalist foundations' (2007: 52). I think that the plausible idea at work here is that it is right to sometimes treat people differently, not because they are radically dissimilar, but rather because they have (or should have) the same moral status or standing.

Finally, let us bring these two conceptions of equality back together again. Here is how Modood puts it:

> genuine equality requires dropping the pretence of 'difference blindness' and allows marginalized minorities to also be visible and explicitly accommodated in the public sphere. This equality will sometimes require enforcing uniformity of treatment and eliminating discrimination . . . it may also require the recognition of distinctive disadvantages . . . or special needs . . . (Modood 2019: 201)

As we now know, 'enforcing uniformity of treatment' is a matter of giving individuals equal dignity, whereas recognising 'distinctive disadvantages . . . or special needs' is a matter of showing equal respect. We can also see other themes at work in this passage, including references to marginalised minorities and to public accommodation. I shall say more about both of these themes shortly.

Identity

My point of entry into Modood's account of recognition was the normative standard of equality. But of course this standard has to be applied to something – or rather someone. This brings us to the second theme of identity. To whom is the standard of equality applied? Who deserves to be treated with equal dignity and equal respect? It is not possible in this single short chapter to present a complete account of Modood's complex and subtle account of the nature of identity. Instead I shall highlight just a few aspects of this account which are particularly pertinent to the issues with which I am concerned here.

The first thing to say is that Modood focuses on particular kinds of person, rather than features of persons per se (even if assumptions about the latter are implicit in his work). This can be seen when Modood lists the various kinds of identities of interest to him, where this includes the usual sort of identity markers, such as 'gender, ethnicity, race, religion, sexuality' (2019: 185). I would suggest that he gives particular attention to what he calls 'ethno-religious identities' (2019: 185, 191), and that his most frequently discussed exemplar are 'British Asians and Muslims' (2019: 43). In saying this, I am in no way implying that Modood overlooks other identities; rather I think that he focuses his attention on this group for good reasons, including the fact that they have been relatively neglected in other academic analyses of race and ethnicity (2019: 43). Put positively, the focus on ethno-religious groups should be regarded as one of the distinctive strengths of Modood's work.

With these various kinds of groups in mind, the next question concerns how such groups are formed and how they persist over time. For Modood, identity groups are not natural kinds, of course.[1] In this case, we need to understand the processes that bring them into existence and sustain that existence over time. Here perhaps the best way to put it, although Modood himself never quite puts it this way, is that there is a dialectic going on between ascription and self-ascription, between the ascription of an identity to a group by others and the ascription of an identity of a group to itself. This declaration by Modood captures something of the dialectic I am talking about:

> I make a multiculturalist plea for studying Islamophobia (and groups negatively perceived from the outside, generally) within a normative framework which prioritises groups fighting outsider perceptions by boosting insider identifications and the struggle for recognition. (Modood 2019: 24)

To paraphrase, collective identities emerge from a complex and ongoing dynamic between what Modood neatly refers to here as 'outsider perceptions' and 'insider identifications'. Outsiders who are not identified – and do not identify – with a particular group have a certain perception of what that group is like (and they are likely to behave towards it accordingly). At the same time, insiders who do identify – and are identified – with the group in question have their own perception of their group. To say that there is a dialectical process going on here is to say that 'insider identifications' and 'outsider perceptions' are partly responses to one another. Outsiders believe that a certain group has a particular identity, with particular properties and characteristics. Insiders may agree to some extent with this account of what they are like. More often, however, they will disagree at least to some extent with the outsiders' perspective, and will struggle to change the way they understand their own identity as well as to change the way in which others perceive them.

Before closing my discussion of this second theme in Modood's account, I think it is worth emphasising the importance of his emphasis on specifically religious group identities. At the practical level, he has emphasised the growing importance of such identities in contemporary democratic societies. To take a case of central importance to him, in the British context, he comments that 'Asian Muslims, especially Pakistanis . . . in less than a decade transformed themselves from a relatively passive element of the "black" constituency into a highly energized, vociferous and mobilized group asserting a religious – not a colour-based or even an ethnic – identity' (2019: 43). At the theoretical level, he argues that what he calls 'the dominant multiculturalism in liberal theory' has failed to take the distinctive qualities of religious identities into account: for instance, 'Will Kymlicka argues that the strict separation of state and ethnicity, "the religion model", is incoherent but is content with the separation model as long as it is applied only to religion' (2019: 44–5). Finally it is worth noting that Modood is at pains to emphasise that recognising a religious group does not require or entail endorsing its beliefs and values: 'multiculturalist recognition of ethno-religious identities does not consist of' the endorsement of everything the state 'supports or funds'. Rather he advocates 'identity recognition as a form of equal citizenship and inclusion but without any strong evaluation or endorsement of any identities or ways of life' (2019: 11).

Struggles

In the previous subsection, it may have sounded as if the dialectic between identity groups is merely a matter of disagreement. As it stands, this is too abstract and anaemic an account of the relationship between groups and the individuals who are members of them. Insiders and outsiders do not just disagree about the former's identity; there is also a power struggle going on in which outsiders seek to impose an identity on the insiders while those insiders try to resist and counter that imposition as well as they can. Identity formation and maintenance, in other words, involves a struggle for recognition.

To be more specific, Modood's account of struggles for recognition factors in the different kinds and degrees of power which groups possess, where these differences play a crucial role in how struggles for recognition go. Again, a single passage will have to stand for his position here:

> Minorities . . . are never merely 'projections' of dominant groups but have their own subjectivity and agency through which they challenge how they are (mis)perceived and seek to not be defined by others but to supplant negative and exclusionary stereotypes with positive and prideful identities. Oppressive misrecognitions, thus, sociologically imply and politically demand recognition. Our analyses therefore should be framed in terms of a struggle for recognition. (Modood 2019: 78)

On one side of the dialectic, there are powerful or dominant groups, whose power gives them the ability to impose their version of the identities of other groups on those groups. On the other side, there are minority or marginalised groups, who have less power than the dominant groups to resist others' ascriptions and to formulate their own self-ascriptions.

In different places, Modood describes such struggles for recognition between unevenly matched groups in different ways. For my current purposes, I shall focus on how he sometimes explicates these struggles in terms of othering and resistance to this othering. In general, then, a dominant group 'others' a subordinate group, marginalising and excluding it from important processes and institutions. The latter group then tries to combat this othering, to get its identity positively revalued, and to be included fully as members of the collectivity in question.

Finally, it is worth emphasising that this theme of struggle in Modood's account tells us that his is a dynamic rather than static account of recognition. Since it is always possible for a group to make a novel claim about how it is being misrecognised or unrecognised, and since other groups will then have to respond to that claim either by accepting or rejecting its validity, it is clear that recognition is inevitably an ongoing process without the possibility of reaching an end-state in which all claims and counter-claims about recognition would cease. For Modood, in other words, it is never possible to specify a set of relationships between the individuals and groups in a particular political community which, if put in place, would mean that recognition had been achieved once and for all.

Inclusion

In order to introduce the fourth theme which I have identified in Modood's account of recognition, it may be useful to consider a question. Given the often painful reality of struggles between dominant and marginalised groups for recognition, how is it possible to approach a situation in which all members of these identity groups are treated with equal dignity and respect? To put it the other way around, what sort of political community would treat all of its members as equals, and provide space for the fair resolution of struggles for recognition? My suggestion is that, for Modood, an idea of inclusion, which he describes in various registers, provides the key to answering these questions. Once again, I shall use one passage from Modood's work to try to encapsulate his thinking on this issue:

> civic inclusion does not consist of an uncritical acceptance of an existing conception of citizenship, of 'the rules of the game' and a one-sided 'fitting-in' of new entrants (or 'new equals' – mostly ex-subordinates of the colonial experience). To be a citizen, no less than to have just become a citizen, is to have a double right: to be recognized and to debate the terms of recognition. (Modood 2019: 136–7)

Here Modood wants to distinguish his position clearly from those which suggest new citizens can and should achieve inclusion by complying with the norms set by and for existing citizens. For him, inclusion involves the ability to determine the terms of inclusion themselves. Thus a minority formed by immigration may play an active role in shaping every citizen's understanding of what it means to be a member of the political community in question.

I would suggest that in different contexts, Modood fleshes out this idea of inclusion in different ways. At some points, he associates it with deliberation between citizens:

> citizenship is a continuous dialogue. As the parties to these dialogues are many, not just two, the process may be described as 'multilogical'. The 'multilogues' allow for views to qualify each other, overlap, synthesize, modify one's own view in the light of having to coexist with others, hybridize, allow new adjustments to be made, new conversations to take place. Such modulations and contestations are part of the internal, evolutionary, work-in-progress dynamic of citizenship. (Modood 2019: 136)

This passage encapsulates Modood's complex views on the relationship between multiculturalism and multilogue very well. Let me pick out just the most important points from this passage. First, citizenship is not only a legal status; it is also a relationship which is multilogical in character. Second, such multilogues go on without end, since all of the parties can always make new points to – and make new demands on – their fellow citizens, their partners in the multilogue. Third, as I have just suggested, citizenship is not just a matter of being allowed to 'play the game', but also of being able to change the nature of the game itself.

I would suggest that Modood fleshes out his idea of inclusion in a rather different way when he talks about national identity and belonging. For instance, he describes the need for

> the creation of civic/public/national/state identities that incorporate minority ethnic and religious identities, guided by the ideal that all citizens should be able to see something of themselves in the overarching, yet internally plural, public identities. In short, they should be able to feel they belong to the country or countries of which they are citizens. (Modood 2019: 43)

Thus, while multilogues take place between citizens, and in their course it is possible to thematise the terms of citizenship themselves, for Modood such citizenship is always located in a national frame. In other words, to be included in the multilogue and to have the opportunity to change its terms can also be described as being included in the political community's sense of collective identity, where the incorporation of hitherto excluded groups requires 'a remaking of national citizenship so that all can have a sense of belonging to it' (2019: 1).

A Critique of Modood's Account

Having outlined what I regard as four key themes in Modood's account of recognition, I now want to present some critical comments on this account. These are intended in a constructive spirit, since, although I am persuaded that Modood's account is distinctive and valuable, I also think that it can be improved in a number of ways. I shall present my critical comments under the four themes I discussed in the previous section, focusing on equality, identity, struggle and inclusion in turn. While some of the points I want to make may not fit perfectly into this four-fold scheme, I think it is worth persisting with it for the sake of clarity of exposition.

Equality

If we begin, then, with the normative dimension of Modood's account, we may recall that he thinks individuals stand in need of two forms of equality, which he calls equal dignity and equal respect, and which he believes correspond to Taylor's distinction between the politics of universalism and the politics of difference.

The first and relatively minor semantic point I want to make here is that I don't think that Taylor himself uses these terms 'equal dignity' and 'equal respect' to refer systematically to the two types of politics of recognition which he distinguishes. In fact, he describes both the politics of universalism and the politics of difference at different points as forms of the politics of dignity and as forms of the politics of respect. Thus Taylor suggests that the 'original politics of dignity' (1994: 40) is difference-blind, but that the politics of difference 'grows organically out of' this original form (1994: 39). A page or so later, he suggests that both politics latch onto a *'universal human potential'* (1994: 41) in order to claim that every person 'deserves respect', although the potential they identify is different for each politics (1994: 41–2).

There is a difference in the way in which Taylor uses the words 'dignity' and 'respect', but it is not the difference that Modood identifies. Rather, Taylor uses the former word to refer to a quality or status that persons possess, and uses the latter word to refer to acts or attitudes which should be taken to people who possess this quality or status. For example, he says that, according to Kant, human dignity rests on 'our status as rational agents, capable of directing our lives through principles', and that it is in virtue of this status that 'each person deserves respect' (1994: 41). It is because human persons have dignity that they should be treated with respect. Ending this part of my discussion, I would emphasise that it is a relatively minor semantic issue. Whether or not they correspond to Taylor's two forms of politics, Modood does clearly distinguish between two forms of equality, and he does argue that a politics of recognition requires both to be applied in tandem.

The second and more substantive issue that I want to raise concerns the practical application of his two norms of equality. Modood insists that these are not alternatives since '*both* equal dignity and equal respect are essential to multiculturalism' (2007: 53; see also 2019: 118). Sometimes, he says, difference-blindness is appropriate, at other times difference-sensitivity is needed, and at yet other times some combination of the two is required. But how do we know when one is appropriate rather than the other? When should a political community treat its members in a way blind to their differences? When should it take those differences into account? And when should both be applied in some proportion or another?

I would suggest that Modood needs a metric capable of providing answers to these questions. I think such a metric can be found in his account, but that he does not connect it as explicitly as he could to his two-dimensional conception of equality. This passage is the closest I can find:

genuine equality requires dropping the pretence of 'difference blind-ness' and allows marginalized minorities to also be visible and explicitly accommodated in the public sphere. This equality will sometimes require enforcing uniformity of treatment and eliminating discrimination against (for example) religious affiliation, and it may also require the recognition of distinctive disadvantages (such as measures to increase the number of women in a legislature) or special needs (such as the provision of halal meat in state schools). (Modood 2019: 201; see also 117–18)

Here I want to pick up in particular on Modood's reference to the public accommodation of 'marginalized minorities'. A little later on, I shall connect this to the fourth theme of inclusion. For now, my suggestion is that a notion of accommodation, understood as inclusion or belong-ing, can provide the metric needed to determine if and when members of a political community should be treated with equal dignity and/or equal respect. If it would help some individuals to be included in, and feel they belong to, their political community by being treated exactly the same as their fellows, then difference-blind equal dignity is required. Consider, for example, Martin Luther King Jr's speech on the Montgom-ery Bus Boycott, in which he declares that 'we are American citizens and we are determined to apply our citizenship to the fullness of its mean-ing' (1955). If, by contrast, such a sense of inclusion and belonging can only be achieved if some individuals' distinctive qualities are acknowl-edged, then this suggests that difference-sensitive equal respect is called for. See, for example, Modood's argument for recognising 'Muslims *as* Muslims, rather than just as equal citizens' (2019: 11).

The third and final issue I want to raise about Modood's conception of equality concerns a significant absence rather than a matter of detail. While he is centrally concerned with what he often refers to as 'multicul-tural equality' (for example, 2007: 56, 71; 2019: 23, 52), I would suggest that this focus comes at the neglect of socio-economic inequality. Certainly Modood refers to this and cognate notions, including 'socio-economic disadvantage' (2007: 15), 'socio-economic inequalities' (2007: 17) and 'socio-economic location' (2007: 48), at various points. But he tends to use such notions as springboards for his theory of multiculturalism, sug-gesting that his theory captures sources of inequality that conventional socio-economic theories miss. Thus, as we have seen, some groups have 'identarian dimensions that elude socio-economic concepts' (2007: 153).

There is one point at which Modood acknowledges that both forms of inequality need to be held in mind at the same time:

The inequalities of 'difference' are of course connected with other forms of inequality, especially those to do with social status and economic

opportunities. For example, the groups in question are often disproportionately disadvantaged; the socio-economic disadvantage is one of the
sources of, as well as a consequence of, their stereotypical representation
as inferior, unintelligent, backward, alien and so forth. Moreover, socio-
economic disadvantage can be a basis for an ethnic group solidarity, for
enhancing groupness (though it can have the opposite effect too). So neither sociologically nor politically can these groups be seen as classless or
as distinct classes in their own right. (Modood 2007: 58; and see 60–2)

This is an isolated passage, however, since Modood does not make a
systematic and sustained attempt to keep these two forms of inequality
in focus at the same time. He admits as much himself: 'The issues of
"difference" . . . are as important as the socio-economic in relation to
equal citizenship and have to be understood on their own terms. The
bigger challenge, not attempted here, is to connect the socio-economic
with the issues discussed here' (2007: 198 n9).

My point is that, by moving away from a socio-economic theory to a
multicultural theory of equality, Modood is able to identify 'identarian'
sources of inequality which the former theory overlooks. But, by doing
so, he risks losing sight of forms of inequality generated by differences
of power and resources, wealth and income, on which the former sort
of theory focuses. What is needed, I would suggest, is a theory of justice
which seeks to keep multicultural and socio-economic equality in focus
at the same time.[2] Before closing this part of my discussion, I want to be
clear about the strength of my claim. I have not argued that Modood's
relative neglect of socio-economic inequality means that his theory is
fatally flawed. On the contrary, his application of two forms of equality
to identarian groups is important and valuable. My suggestion, rather,
is that he might consider incorporating a concern with socio-economic
inequality into his existing account.

Identity

Turning now to the theme of identity, while I am convinced that the
dialectical process of identity formation which Modood describes does
provide the foundation of a persuasive account of social identity, I do
want to raise a couple of questions about it.

My first question concerns the recognition of groups in general. To
introduce this question, it may be noted that Modood declares that multiculturalism requires the recognition of both individuals and groups. At
a fairly abstract level, he says, for instance, that 'the concept of equality
has to be applied to groups and not just individuals' (2007: 51). At a

more concrete level, he approves of the Report of the Commission for Multi-Ethnic Britain's contention that Britain should be regarded as a 'community of communities and individuals' (cited in Modood 2007: 17). I shall put aside individual recognition, assuming it to be a relatively uncomplicated part of this picture. When, for instance, the state grants its citizens the right to freedom of association, it is protecting the freedom of each individual to join with others in various kinds of collectivities.

In the case of the recognition of groups, however, I would suggest that this could mean different things. First, in the most unproblematic sense, what we may refer to shorthand as 'group recognition' may in fact be the recognition of a number of individuals identified by their association with a group. Thus it is Sikhs as individuals who are granted exemptions from wearing hard hats on building sites in virtue of their identification with Sikhs as a group. Second, and somewhat more trickily, but still quite common, rights may be granted to groups themselves rather than to the set of individuals composing that group. Some sorts of indigenous people's land rights probably fall into this category. Rather than granting each indigenous person a small tract of land, the whole group is granted ownership and control of a large area of land which the group must govern collectively. Third, and most problematically, it may be asserted that groups should be recognised as groups since they are themselves the locus of particular goods or values. Perhaps it could be argued that the Balinese people as a whole deserve recognition for the contribution that gamelan music has made to world culture.

My point, then, is that I am not sure which of these possibilities Modood is thinking of when he says that groups may deserve recognition. Consider, for example, the following passage in which he discusses the relationship between individual and group recognition. Taking Muslims as his example, he comments:

> The point I am stressing . . . is that they are not just being recognised as abstract individuals or as citizens in the abstract but as groups with identities. So, to recognise them as citizens is – contrary to standard liberal or civic individualism – to recognise their group identities. (Modood 2019: 11)

For me, this wavers between the first and second possibility I just described. The first sentence says Muslims are being recognised 'as groups with identities', which suggests recognition of the group per se. But the second sentence seems to emphasise individual recognition, implying that, in order to recognise Muslims 'as citizens', we need to take their group identities into account – rather than recognising those group identities directly. In short, I am suggesting that here and elsewhere Modood needs to be clearer about the nature of group recognition in particular. Should some groups be recognised for the sake of their individual members? Or are there circumstances in which some groups should be recognised in their own right?[3]

The second issue I want to raise about the theme of identity at work in Modood's account of recognition follows fairly closely on the heels of the first. As a way of introducing this point, consider how Modood discusses Kymlicka's work at a number of points, and does so in order to suggest the superiority of his own approach to multiculturalism. It is not my intention to enter this debate here. Rather, I want to suggest that these two theories may have opposing blind spots.

Let me explain. When laying out the fundamentals of Kymlicka's theory, Modood refers to his account of national minorities. He comments, for example, that, on Kymlicka's view, 'a liberal democratic society should be willing to give some degree of self-government and special rights to preserve national minorities' (2007: 31). Modood then suggests that Kymlicka's focus on such groups leads to his relative neglect and mis-conceptualisation of immigrant minorities. Thus Kymlicka's theory

> fails to capture the true situation of many immigrants and so the restrictive attitude to the rights of immigrants is based on a false conceptualization. It distorts the circumstances of some kinds of migrants in order to highlight the condition of national minorities and indigenous peoples. (Modood 2007: 33–4)

My second point about Modood's discussion of identity simply reverses the claim he makes here about Kymlicka's theory. I want to suggest, in other words, that Modood overlooks the situation of national minorities since his attention is focused on what he calls 'post-immigration socio-cultural formations' (2007: 18) or 'post-immigration multiculturalism' (2007: 32).

I would suggest, furthermore, that, if Modood did think about how groups like national minorities might fit into his approach, then he would have to address the issue I have just raised. When Scotland was granted a considerable degree of independence from Westminster, this right to partial self-determination was granted to the Scottish nation as a whole rather than to its individual members. In closing this discussion of the theme of identity, and echoing my comment about Modood's relative neglect of socio-economic inequality, I do not want to claim that Modood's focus on immigrant communities at a cost to national minorities is any kind of fatal flaw in his theoretical approach. Rather, my argument should be regarded as something more like an invitation to Modood to think about how groups like national minorities might fit into his theoretical scheme.

Struggles

The third theme which I identified in Modood's account of recognition concerns what might be called its agonistic dimension. Like a number of other theorists, he gives the idea of a struggle for recognition an important role in his account.

The question I want to raise about this aspect of Modood's account concerns practicality. Under what circumstances is it possible to resist and reverse othering? Under what circumstances, on the contrary, might such efforts fail? To answer these questions, we need to look a little more closely at the role of grievance, and related notions such as hurt and anger, in Modood's account. Here is a key passage:

> one of the principal ways of seeing the emergence and development of ethno-religious equality is in terms of a grievance of exclusion from the existing equality framework and its utilisation in order to extend it to address the felt exclusion and to develop and seek public recognition for a minority subjectivity ignored by liberal legislators. (Modood 2019: 48)

On this account, then, an ethno-religious minority is not treated equally, feels aggrieved by this state of affairs, demands public recognition, and achieves it by becoming included in an expanded version of 'the existing equality framework'.

To rephrase my earlier questions: does it always work as smoothly as this? Do aggrieved feelings always lead to demands for recognition? Do such demands always result in inclusion? I would suggest that there are various reasons why one or more of the stages of such a struggle for recognition might fail. First, there are cases when, although a group may be treated unjustly, and not receive the recognition it deserves, it may nevertheless not experience grievance. In the most extreme cases, it may come to believe that its treatment is justified, that it doesn't deserve any better than it gets. See, for example, Taylor's brief discussion of how women, people of colour and indigenous people may be 'unable to resist' internalising a 'demeaning image' of themselves (1994: 26). Second, there are cases in which the group in question may feel aggrieved, but this may still fail to motivate an effective struggle for recognition. In some such cases, this may be because such grievance is directed towards the wrong object.

For example, some citizens may blame immigrants, rather than the rapacious behaviour of a populist political elite, for their woes. In other such cases, a sense of grievance may be outweighed by a feeling of hopelessness that anything can be changed. Third, there are cases in which a group feels aggrieved, knows it deserves more, knows from whom that is due, but still fails to better its condition simply because it lacks the power, resources and opportunities to engage in effective struggle.

I realise that this is a very sketchy account of various possible reasons for failures of struggles for recognition, and unfortunately there is no space here to discuss these failures further or to describe how they might be overcome. Speaking for myself, I would try to do this in part by exploring the role of collective emotions in political struggles (Clarke, Hoggett and Thompson 2006; Hoggett and Thompson 2012). But I would not claim that this is the only option available if Modood did want to further develop his account of struggles for recognition. Finally, it should go without saying that, although struggles for recognition may fail, this is no reason to conclude that they should not play an important role in an account of recognition. My comment is intended once again as something like an invitation to Modood, this time to consider whether it would be useful to develop a more nuanced account of struggles for recognition, one capable of determining the likelihood of success of any particular struggle.

Inclusion

The fourth and final theme that I picked out of Modood's account of recognition focused on inclusion and belonging. I want to raise two issues about this aspect of his account. First, I would suggest that, at the moment, Modood's account is lacking in detail. What is meant by inclusion in dialogue? What is the content and style of such dialogue? What rights might it presuppose? What institutional forms might it take? One source of inspiration which comes readily to mind is the work of deliberative democrats, who place a notion of inclusive dialogue at the heart of their account of a democratic society. Consider, for example, Seyla Benhabib's definition of democracy as

> a model for organizing the collective and public exercise of power in the major institutions of a society on the basis of the principle that decisions affecting the well-being of a collectivity can be viewed as the outcome of a procedure of free and reasoned deliberation among individuals considered as moral and political equals.
> (Benhabib 2002: 105)

If Modood was happy to endorse this account of deliberative democracy as a key component of his theory of multiculturalism, then it might also enable him to flesh out his own idea of civic dialogue, providing, as it does, an account of the sorts of values, practices and institutions required to realise this type of democracy in practice.

The second issue that I want to raise takes us for one last time to what might be thought of as the outer limits of Modood's theory. As I mentioned earlier, at the centre of his account of multiculturalism are the groups he described at one point as 'post-immigration ethnic and religious minorities' (2007: 35). I would suggest that a focus on such groups makes sense if Modood's system rests on two postulates. The first is the assumption that immigration has already happened, so that Modood's job is to consider how to respond appropriately and justly to that fact. He does not, therefore, consider how would-be members of a political community, presently outside of that community, should be treated. In other words, he does not address issues of justice concerning immigration itself. Second, and perhaps underlying the first postulate, I think he assumes that there are – and will continue to be – more or less effectively bounded political communities in existence. In this case, bigger questions about the legitimacy of states, including, among other things, the justifiability of closed borders, fall outside Modood's purview.

In one sense, echoing what I have said earlier about other limits to Modood's system, there is nothing wrong with his focus on post-immigration minorities per se. Since no one can consider everything, it makes perfect sense for Modood to describe the aim of his *Multiculturalism* book thus:

> The multiculturalism I want to elaborate and defend in this book is rooted in recent and ongoing policies, politics and other real-world developments. It consists of ideas that influence policy-makers and public debates and are of great controversy. They have come to have the status that they have because of social and political struggles and negotiations surrounding racial, ethnic and religious differences largely led by immigrants and the second generation. (Modood 2007: 18–19)

In another sense, however, this post-immigration focus is less satisfactory. This is because it is not possible to make a clear and stable distinction between insiders and outsiders, between those who have achieved stable membership of the political community and those wanting to become members, now or in the future. The instability of this distinction is shown up most clearly in the UK by the treatment of the Windrush generation: immigrants from Caribbean countries in the postwar period assumed that they had achieved secure citizenship status, only to find much later that they were still regarded as possibly illegitimate immigrants (Joint Council for the Welfare of Immigrants).

Other theorists of recognition have sought to include these sorts of issues in their theoretical frameworks. Nancy Fraser, for example, offers a three-dimensional theory of justice, in which the third dimension, which she calls 'representation', encompasses those injustices generated by the way the borders of political communities are created and maintained (2008: chapter 2). Nothing would stop Modood adding such a dimension to his theory too.

At the end of previous subsections, I tried to be clear about the import of my remarks about Modood's system, and I shall do so for one last time now. My observation that this system rests on certain premises – premises which other theorists have thematised and critically analysed – does not imply that there is a fatal flaw in Modood's system. Certainly my remarks should not be taken to imply that I think that Modood is wrong not to consider the situation of would-be migrants rather than those who have already migrated. Rather, my remarks are more in the spirit of an invitation to Modood to look at this particular outer limit to his account of recognition and to consider whether at some point he might want to explicitly address the concerns that it generates.

Concluding remarks

I began this chapter with the suggestion that the concept of recognition plays an important role in Modood's approach to multiculturalism. Arguably it is one of just a small number of concepts which lie at the core of his thinking, and it is a concept he invokes at many points and in many contexts in order both to explain the nature of post-immigration multicultural societies and to determine what the appropriate normative attitude to such societies should be. On his account, in other words, we can better understand the nature of such societies by seeing that they are characterised by struggles for recognition, and we can better decide how such societies should be arranged by reference to the normative core of the concept of recognition.

In order to make good on these two interlinked analytical and normative claims, I presented a reading of Modood's account of recognition which focused on four particular themes, which I referred to at some points by four single words – equality, identity, struggle and inclusion. Following this exposition of Modood's account, I offered a number of critical remarks about it, organised again according to the same four themes. To sum up, one half of my critique involved calls for Modood to provide greater clarity about, or the further development of, particular parts of his thinking on recognition. The other half of my critique indicated some of the outer limits to his system, suggesting that he might want to move beyond those limits at some point. Whether he takes up that invitation or not, there is no doubt that Modood already offers a distinctive and valuable account of recognition, where this account is a key component in his theory of multiculturalism.

Notes

1. According to Alexander Bird and Emma Tobin, to 'say that a kind is *natural* is to say that it corresponds to a grouping that reflects the structure of the natural world rather than the interests and actions of human beings' (2023).
2. See, for instance, Nancy Fraser's theory of justice which integrates concerns with recognition and redistribution (2003; 2008).
3. The properties and behaviour of groups will also come up in the next subsection on struggles for recognition.

References

Benhabib, S. (2002), *The Claims of Culture: Equality and Diversity in the Global Era*. Princeton, NJ: Princeton University Press.

Bird, A. and E. Tobin (2023), 'Natural Kinds', in E. Zalta and U. Nodelman (eds), *The Stanford Encyclopedia of Philosophy* (Spring 2023 Edition). Accessed at: <https://plato.stanford.edu/archives/spr2023/entries/natural-kinds/>

Clarke, S., P. Hoggett and S. Thompson (eds) (2006), *Emotions, Politics and Society*. London: Palgrave.

Fraser, N. (2008), *Scales of Justice: Reimagining Political Space in a Globalizing World*. New York: Columbia.

Fraser, N. and A. Honneth (2003), *Redistribution or Recognition? A Political-Philosophical Exchange*. London: Verso.

Hoggett, P. and S. Thompson (eds) (2012), *Politics and the Emotions: The Affective Turn in Contemporary Political Studies*. Continuum.

Honneth, A. (1995), *The Struggle for Recognition: The Moral Grammar of Social Conflicts*. Polity.

The Joint Council for the Welfare of Immigrants (No date), 'Windrush Scandal Explained'. Accessed at: <https://www.jcwi.org.uk/windrush-scandal-explained>

King, M. L., Jr (1955), 'The Montgomery Bus Boycott', 5 December. Accessed at: <https://www.blackpast.org/african-american-history/1955-martin-luther-king-jr-montgomery-bus-boycott/>

Modood, T. (2005), *Multicultural Politics: Racism, Ethnicity and Muslims in Britain*. Edinburgh: Edinburgh University Press.

Modood, T. (2007), *Multiculturalism: A Civic Idea*. Cambridge: Polity Press.

Modood, T. (2019), *Essays on Secularism and Multiculturalism*. London: ECPR Press.

Pirsoul, N. (2020), 'Māori Recognition in New Zealand', in N. Pirsoul, *The Theory of Recognition and Multicultural Policies in Colombia and New Zealand*. London: Palgrave Macmillan.

Taylor, C. (1994), 'The Politics of Recognition', in A. Gutmann (ed.), *Multiculturalism: Examining the Politics of Recognition*, expanded edn. Princeton, NJ: Princeton University Press, 25–73.

Part Two

The Inclusion of Diversity

FOUR

What's to Be Done? Reuniting the People

Charles Taylor

i

How can we manage to overcome the multiple divisions which hamper, even cripple, our contemporary democracies? To bring about unity in a more stable and long-term fashion requires changes in identity, either in that of certain partial groups, or in their take on the political identity of the nation as a whole. This is the question I would like to examine in this chapter.

To understand what this requires we should look at the lines of possible fragmentation to which our contemporary democracies in the West are vulnerable.

First, there is a (well-founded) sense among non-élites that they are neglected by élites, both governing and economic (rich), and sometimes by professionals and managers in general. This neglect is visible in 'rust belts' today, with their loss of good, lifetime jobs – through global trade and robotics – so that workers, or their children, find jobs scarcer, more short-term, more precarious. We see this, for instance, both in the US and in France, and in a number of other countries. But we also see this sense of neglect in smaller centres: towns which have lost population, but also institutions, to larger cities, which in turn have been growing, and are largely where the new economic growth is occurring. Disadvantaged regions face downward social mobility, and the smaller centres also face the decline and potential disappearance of their traditional way of life. As workers, as members of viable communities, their identity seems to be at stake.

This élite–popular split is one source of 'populism', both good and bad. Resentment seeks redress. But in 'bad' populism this first split generates another one, between mainstream 'ordinary', 'real' or 'full' members of the society and some categories of 'outsider'. These are often immigrants, either recently arrived or on the point of (perhaps) arriving, like refugees. The connection between the two splits is that élites are blamed for favouring these 'outsiders' over the 'real' ordinary people that they ought to be helping. The priority is given to the needs of immigrants, or citizens which are somehow seen as second-class.

Of course, these two lines of division may not come together. We can have a 'populist' revolt against élites without the xenophobia (Bernie Sanders' campaign in the 2016 election); and we can have discomfort or worse at the arrival of people from outside without blaming élites (or the original reaction against guest workers in post-1960s Germany, or recent developments in Scandinavia). And indeed, when they do come together, 'outsider' is not always the appropriate term. Sometimes what is fuelling the resentment at the inappropriate 'favouring' of others is various (often largely unspoken, even unavowed) assumptions of hierarchy or preference. For instance, some people are the 'original' citizens; say, white, long-standing Americans, and others are the more recently arrived from other origins (say, Hispanics); or the crucial distinction singles out ancestral French people, as against recently arrived Muslims from the Maghreb; or native Germans as against Muslim *Gastarbeiter*. The arrival of these new populations may already have been creating a certain discomfort or cultural fear among natives. And so the supposed 'favouritism' they benefit from makes them targets of resentment along with the 'élites' which are helping 'them' before 'us'.

But the date of arrival may not be an issue. There are largely unspoken, often unavowed assumptions of hierarchy among ancestral populations; for instance, those white Americans who assume that their needs should be met before those of African-Americans; or those males who hold that women should remain in their traditional roles. Attempts to challenge these orders, like Black Lives Matter or MeToo, awaken anxiety and anger, and the same bi-directional resentment, against élites and the groups they 'favour'.

Of course, these hierarchical assumptions are incompatible with the ethic of equal citizenship which is officially espoused by many modern democracies. And so policymakers tend to reject and condemn such assumptions, in the name of the political identity of the nation. But these hierarchies are often an essential part of the identities of non-élite whites or non-élite males. Being above in race or gender may partly compensate for being disadvantaged in socio-economic terms. And people in declining industrial areas and small centres naturally (and rightly) feel disadvantaged.

And so a bitter dispute may break out between two readings of the nation's political identity: one which asserts unmodified the ethic of equal citizenship and another which subtly tempers it to accommodate long-standing notions of precedence.

ii

Either heading off or healing any of these splits requires a re-examination, often a redefinition of the political identity of the society, but the issues may be different for different types of division. Before examining these, it may be useful to review what this identity consists in, and how it relates to other kinds of identity.

Democratic societies need a strong sense of commitment on the part of their members. What unites them in a common allegiance is what I am calling their 'political identity'. This exists alongside, and sometimes in tension with, the (much more many-sided) identities of individuals, and the partial group identities that exist among the citizens – regional, racial, confessional, moral, gender and so on. The political identity of a modern democracy has two facets: on the one hand, it espouses certain general principles. Today these include human rights, equality, democratic rule itself. These are widely shared values.

But there is also a particular facet: each democracy is a unique historical project which aims to realise these principles after its own fashion. Allegiance to this project is what has been called 'patriotism'. Strong patriotism animates the pride peoples feel in their own democratic project (and when they fail to live up to it, the shame). Americans tend to think that they are the originators of modern democracy; we Canadians tend to think that we are the world champions in harmoniously uniting diversity. The French think that they invented the completed form of the Republic in one blaze of creativity. The British quietly know that the 'Mother of Parliaments' is really at the origin of the democratic age. And so on. Often innocent enough stuff – and believable, as long as we are not looking at the negatives in our history. But we can see already why political identities have to find expression in narrative, stories, potted versions of histories. It is in these that we define our particular project, our attempt to realise whatever universal values lie at the core of our society.

The stories I just gestured to make us (respectively, Americans, Canadians, French, British) feel warm and united, as far as they go. And at moments we may feel happy with this, but these halcyon periods cannot last. New people enter from outside (immigrants). Or a new generation of home-grown children raises new issues (the '60s). Or old inequalities and exclusions come under challenge (civil rights movement, feminism, gay rights). Or a new generation faces unprecedented difficulties (the new precarity of jobs). Or a whole new set of global challenges arise (global warming).

Instead of basking in the warm sun of self-congratulation, we have to work hard to recover the earlier unity. And the very brightness of that sun can blind us to the moment when we start to bend the identity to justify exclusion of certain groups of citizens or residents who would be citizens; or when we use our exceptional history as a reason to break ties with others (Brexiteers). This kind of exclusion is a disaster for a democratic society. It often leads to harsh, even cruel behaviour towards minorities. It divides the society and makes it more difficult to address common challenges. And it undercuts solidarity, or in terms of the famous 1789 trinity of values, Fraternity, which is crucial if we are to reverse the degenerations which are crippling democracies today. For this reason, there is an essential function which all democracies must assume today, that of consciously redefining an historically received identity, and/or its relation to important group identities in the population, so as to overcome the divisions which traditional readings have created and justified.

It is fatal to democracy to believe that the important, ultimately decisive formulations are all to be found in the past. All democracies live by their traditions, but this belief, alone and unmodified, freezes and stultifies the tradition. The revered principles always have to be applied anew and creatively as the world changes. For this reason political identities require a narrative, a story of its origins, what they were responding to (various forms of hierarchical rule), and an account of what has happened since, in terms of which one can define what an authentic continuation of the tradition entails. These narratives play a crucial role in politics. We could cite the campaign waged by Obama in 2008, around the phrase from the US constitution, 'in order to make a more perfect union', which calls for a progressive realisation in new conditions of the original principles; against this appeared another narrative, exalting the Boston Tea Party of 1774, and a return to neglected basic principle.

Or we could cite the narratives about the meaning of being British which confronted each other in the referendum over Brexit, one calling for a return of a past independence, the other for further engagement in a Europe yet to be built. Or the argument in France, with spillover effects in Quebec, about the meaning of the French legislation of 1904–5 defining 'laïcité', and its bearing on the rights of immigrants, as we go forward into the twenty-first century.

It is clear that democracies have a very powerful incentive to redefine their political identity, and/or, when this cannot be changed without betrayal, to redefine its relation to the group identities of citizens, so that a distinction between first- and second-class citizens can be avoided.

iii

I want now to look at different kinds of challenge to the unity-in-equality of the population. One such challenge often arises from immigration. A population which consists of a more or less homogeneous ethnic group, when faced with immigrants of different religions, customs, dress, etc., will almost inevitably feel some discomfort at first. This can lead to reactions which alienate the newcomers, who in turn can come to see themselves as in an adversarial relation to the original population.

We experienced this in Quebec and Canada, with the arrival of different waves of immigration. And sometimes, familiarity, mixing, the arrival of new generations can gradually make the sense of division less acute, and even make it disappear altogether. (To take a US case, the initial reaction to the arrival of the 'Papist' Irish in the first half of the nineteenth century has totally disappeared; the Know Nothing Party now seems bizarre.) But recently, the arrival of Muslims in Quebec has for some people provoked the same reaction. This can perhaps best be described as one of fear. What is feared is that these newcomers might change us, make our society unrecognisable. In the Commission we held in Quebec in 2007–8 on reasonable accommodation (Bouchard and Taylor 2008), the anxious question which recurred was: 'Est-ce que ils vont nous changer?' – 'Will they change us?'.

This is a very understandable reaction, and one shouldn't respond with liberal indignation to the *feeling* of anxiety. But in fact, it is unfounded, and when natives and immigrants get to know each other, it dissipates quite rapidly. In fact, our present-day immigrants are eager to join us and participate in our way of life. That's why they've tried so hard to be admitted. When we in the Commission asked immigrants why they wanted to come to Canada and Quebec, the first answer was 'freedom', and the second was: 'I wanted to give my children an education and a chance in life I could never have found in [the country of origin]'. All one has to do is avoid forms of exclusion (like denying women wearing the hijab jobs in important fields), which create a feeling of alienation. In fact, they are not going to change us native-born that much, considerably less than our children (and grandchildren) will as they grow up. So we should be upbeat. With time, with people from different backgrounds meeting and working alongside each other, everyone's fears should dissipate. Unless we create through our exclusions, a long-term, hard-to-reverse alienation.

But there's the rub. Important parties are still proposing to close certain public sector jobs, like education, to people wearing 'religious signs' (like hijabs, kippas, Sikh turbans). Montreal is much less of a problem. That's where most of the immigrants are, and mixing is very common. Indeed, in public schools where children from both backgrounds go to school together, the young people begin to wonder what their parents are so excited about. But outside Montreal, in the Province, there are very few immigrants and people rarely work alongside them.

Moreover, the very fact that this kind of exclusion is badly seen in modern liberal democracies can make the situation worse. Everybody has some consciousness of the fact that this runs against certain widespread conceptions of equal rights. So the parties proposing these restrictions can't just promise to exclude. In this era of rights and principles, you need a principled reason. So they say that such offending garments go against one of our basic principles, that of 'laïcité', or secularism. We're not proposing to restrict them just because we feel uncomfortable. Oh no. We're doing it because they're violating a basic principle of our way of life. Modern rights doctrine, far from protecting against this kind of discrimination, can make it more determined, moralistic and unwilling to compromise.

Of course, this slippage into false moralisation was aided and abetted by the geopolitical threat of militant jihadism. But this should have been, and in another situation would have been, an additional motivation to make the essential distinction between pious, practising Muslims and jihadis; the first can be allies of our society against the second. In fact, the rhetoric of laïcité has tended to elide the two. And now with Islamophobia on the rampage, it is harder than ever to make the crucial distinctions.

Here we have a classic case of democracy turning against itself. We might say its 'immune system', which should be detecting betrayals of its ethic, is turned against potentially 'friendly' cells. Democracy generates exclusion when its 'immune system' turns against itself. This is what we are witnessing today in France and Quebec, as well as other Western societies. To dismantle this pernicious muddle, we have to offer a saner definition of secularism. But this is not all. For there is also the fact that the traditional Quebec identity, formed in the struggle to survive as a French-speaking society against the pressures of a huge Anglophone North America, and often in the teeth of opposition from the Anglophone majority of Canada, is very much one of a beleaguered ethnic group.

So in order to defend the project of an open, diverse society, we also need to give a new definition of our identity. Some problem of this kind emerges for most societies which are admitting immigrants in significant numbers, not only in the Western hemisphere where large-scale immigration has long been an important fact, and essential to the building of the society, but also in certain European countries, which have just started to diversify through immigration in recent decades. In Germany, one often hears worries about where the society is headed on this score, and fears for the traditional culture, fears that are evident in the proposal to give precedence to a 'leading culture' (*Leitkultur*). Many European societies also need a new definition of identity which can allow for, say, someone to be fully 'German', even though their original language, or that of their parents, was Turkish or Arabic. As is generally the case, these definitions involve a story which will show the continuities in the change, how this new basis for German identity makes sense in relation to the traditional one.

In fact, Canada has produced two such narratively justified redefinitions, which have become widely known: multiculturalism and interculturalism. Canadian multculturalism is widely misunderstood, even caricatured in Europe, as a policy which is designed to slow down, even defeat integration; its basic thrust is supposed to be in encouraging immigrants to retreat into their communities of origin. In short, it fosters ghettoisation. This negative, ghetto-inducing idea of the point of multiculturalism is widely shared in Europe, as Canadians discover to their cost and horror when they discuss these questions with French, Germans or Dutch.

I remember reading a headline in a German newspaper, 'Multikulturalismus ist gescheitert', where the explanation was that the politics of laisser-aller which recognises difference with no concern for integration had brought Europe to a terrible pass, and that now was the time to get tough and make immigrants conform. In fact, in the last decade or so, heads of government of the three biggest EU countries – Merkel, Cameron and Sarkozy – have announced the end of this pernicious 'multiculturalism'. In France, 'Communautarisme' has been regularly stigmatized as the same kind of encouragement to retreat into closed cultural communities, while 'le multiculturalisme' is seen as an endorsement of a philosophy of closure. Canadians find it hard to recognise themselves in this travesty, because multiculturalism in this country has from the beginning been concerned with integration, putting a great emphasis, for instance, on teaching the national languages, English and French (Kymlicka 1995).

But the fact that the word has a different sense in Europe and in Canada is not just a harmless semantic shift. Anti-multicultural rhetoric in Europe reflects a profound misunderstanding of the dynamics of immigration into the rich, liberal democracies of the West. The underlying assumption seems to be that too much positive recognition of cultural differences will encourage a retreat into ghettos, and a refusal to accept the political ethic of liberal democracy itself. As though this rush to closure was the first choice of immigrants themselves, from which they have to be dissuaded through 'tough love'. Up to a point, we can understand why politicians with no great experience of the dynamics of immigrant societies fall into this error, because the tendency among immigrants is always at first to cluster with people of similar origins and background. How else can they find the networks they need to survive and move ahead in the new environment? We also see this clustering in globalised cities, like Bombay, where new arrivals seek out people from the same state or village.

But the major motivation of immigrants into rich democracies is to find new opportunities, of work, education or self-expression, for themselves and especially for their children. If they manage to secure these, they – and even more, their children – are happy to integrate into the society. It is only if this hope is frustrated, if the path to more rewarding work and education is blocked, that a sense of alienation and hostility to the receiving society can grow, and may even generate a rejection of the mainstream and its ethic. Consequently, the European attack on 'multiculturalism' often seems to us a classic case of false consciousness, blaming certain phenomena of ghettoisation and alienation of immigrants on a foreign ideology, instead of recognising the home-grown failures to promote integration and combat discrimination.

Given opportunities, and in the absence of discrimination, immigrants into our rich, northern, developed democracies will become integrated. But that is not to say that they will assimilate. Differences will remain, for example, in religion. And that prospect can awaken anxieties about how the newcomers might 'change' us.

Let me try to explain the distinction I'm invoking here.

Integration of immigrants is a question of the roles they take up in the host society. Of course, the primary one for most immigrant breadwinners is finding a job. But they are also invited, and often desire, to belong to certain associations and institutions. For instance, they send their children to school (this is more than an invitation, of course; it's required by law). Acting in these roles brings about contact with existing members of the host society. Even if the first association they found or join brings together members of their own culture/community/faith, this inevitably brings wider contact. Our association will, for instance, want to set up a meeting hall or a place of worship, and we may have to get permission from the mayor; or it will enter into some collaboration with other like associations: the people of our faith may find it necessary/prudent to associate with people of other faiths to achieve certain ends, for example, overcoming negative stereotypes.

The point is that through these contacts, members of our immigrant community make more and more contacts with the wider society. This inevitably leads to some degree of assimilation. Within the bounds of this discussion, this means cultural/religious/lifestyle convergence on the existing models in the host society. This assimilation is often not complete, but provided there is convergence on the political ethic underlying a democratic, egalitarian, diverse society, this is no problem. On the contrary, the differences which are not ironed out enrich the host society; that is the stance taken in Canada both by multiculturalism and interculturalism.

But the important thing is to realise that this process of convergence takes time. It begins to make serious progress often only with the next generation, those born here; who go to our schools, meet and form relations with children of other ancestral cultures and outlooks. And there are further effects later on.

It is important to have confidence in the process. Most of our immigrants come to Canada/Quebec, first, because they value positively our political ethic, even if there are some differences in detail; and second, because they can succeed in careers they couldn't in their home country; and third, and often crucially important, because they can give their children the education and the chance in life that they couldn't in the country of origin. If they succeed in this triple goal, there are no more patriotic Canadians.

But in countries that have little experience of integrating immigrants, there are often fears, provoked by the fact I mentioned above that immigrants tend to group together at first. But this is inevitable, as I argued above. In most cases, new arrivals don't know anyone in the host society – except people from the same background who have immigrated before. I seek out my brother-in-law; or the friend of my uncle at home, who has already come here. How else can I get a start, find a job, find a convenient place to live, etc.? Clumping is standard among immigrant populations. This applies not only to countries receiving immigrants, but to large cities in countries like India. Mumbai is full of quartiers where people from Gujarat, or from Karnataka, or wherever, concentrate in the same way and for the same reason.

But I have often heard in Europe people expressing anxiety about the eventual integration of immigrant communities. 'They're all living together!' said a Dutch friend to me, his face full of suspicion. But of course! How do they survive otherwise? But this says nothing about the eventual integration and partial assimilation of the children of this community – and that independently of what the parents might like.

There is only one thing which can stop this natural process from taking place, and that is discrimination, and/or frustration of the goals with which immigrants arrived. If the children don't get jobs, or the community is subjected to various expressions of hostility or fear; if as in France, young Maghrébins are stuck in certain banlieues, suffer discrimination so they don't get jobs (even if you send in a c.v. without a name, but you give your postal code, you don't get shortlisted), are frequently attacked as a danger to the society, even your old aunt's bourquini on a beach sends the Prime Minister (Vals) into paroxysms of panic; then integration, and even partial assimilation, will be seriously hampered.

The process should be allowed take its course, with a bit of nudging towards mixed neighbourhoods in the second and third generations.

But all this assumes that there isn't a dynamic of group segregation going on between the natives and recent arrivals; either because of racism (as in the US), or because of continuing mutual distrust or discomfort. If there is, we have to take action to dismantle this, or thaw it out. But the policies here have to be tailored to the nature and mainsprings of the particular dynamic at work in the society in question.

But this is not to say that Canadian multiculturalism is a formula for all modern diverse societies. Indeed, it is not accepted in Quebec, where the policy of 'interculturalism' prevails instead. The two policies are in fact very similar, and where they mainly differ is in the story they tell (but stories are crucial, as I argued above). One story fits a society which already has no majority ancestral culture (Canada as a whole); and the other makes sense in a society which still has such a majority identity (Quebec) (see Bouchard 2011; Taylor 2012).

Let me try to give a sense of what these two policies, and their respective stories, involve; and the debates they give rise to.

iv

In fact, it would be best to look here at the 'inter' story, and the hopes and fears that arise in connection with it. Of course, this story allows that the society will develop in ways which it wouldn't if only the native born were in charge. The hopes connected with that are that people coming from outside will contribute new ideas, new skills, new insights which will enrich our society. The obverse of this expectation is the fear that somehow what are considered essential features of our identity will be lost. In the Quebec case, these essential features include understandably the French language. After more than two hundred years' struggle to maintain the centrality of French, there can be no question of abandoning it. But there are other basic elements as well. Quebec has become a liberal society, sharing the same basic ethic as other similar ones. The central features of this are human rights, equality and non-discrimination, and democracy. But beyond the language and these basic principles, there is an indefinite zone of customs, common enthusiasms (hockey), common reference points, modes of humour and so on, each cherished to varying degrees, and more by some than by others, whose weakening, abandonment or demise may be feared.

The degree of acceptance of the intercultural story depends on the balance between these hopes and fears, and the public debate centres around them. But this debate is unavoidably imprecise and semi-articulate. As to the fear element, it seems focused disproportionately on the principles, in present-day Quebec. By that I mean that worries about the third element in our list, the customs and common reference points, etc. (let's call these for short 'folkways'), often get articulated as fears for the principles. So Quebeckers will often state their apprehension that immigrants don't want to adopt our way of life; then when asked for examples, they frequently come up with issues of male–female equality.

Now to some extent this arises from the fact that, as in other Western countries, the debate about integrating newcomers has focused disproportionately on Muslims; and fears around Muslims has focused on instances where women have been maltreated or given inferior status. But to some extent also, the choice of these examples reflects the fact that it is generally considered more acceptable to invoke universal principles in this context of argument, rather than more 'parochial' modes of cultural unease.

The frequent invocation of male–female equality also reflects the sense that our society has made serious strides in this direction only relatively recently, and that the gains may be fragile. Will these newcomers contribute to bringing about a retreat on this front? Lots of people expressed fear on this score during the hearings of our commission. These fears seem quite unfounded, since a) Muslim Quebeckers generally themselves support these principles (indeed, often came here because of them); and b) even if they were hostile, they are a relatively small minority. But if we see the invocation of this example as articulating a more unstructured fear about the possible loss or erosion of our way of life in its many facets, an articulation which has the advantage of being more generally acceptable, and more clearly defined, then the anxiety surrounding it becomes more understandable.

The Achilles heel of the inter story is thus the fears it can arouse that 'they' may change 'us'. The notion that 'they' can be equal collaborators in remaking our common culture rings alarm bells in all who share this anxiety. It seems safer and more sensible to insist that they conform first to what we consider the basics, before we let them become co-deciders. But this easily slides in practice towards imposing assimilation as a condition of integration; that is, towards insisting that they become like us before they can function beside us to shape our future. Logically, of course, the preconditions could be much more limited; we might just say: start learning our language and accept our basic ethic. But where even these demands are made in a spirit of fear and mistrust; and where they are motivated by a larger unstructured fear for our whole way of life; they begin to amount to something like: win back our trust (and we doubt very much that you can) before we can accept you as equals. That is, in any case, how the demands are perceived by their addressees. And we are on the road to creating and entrenching a deep rift in society, which can compromise democratic life.

Or the fear may take an alternative form. 'They' are hostile or recalcitrant to our way of life. But what they want to do is not so much transform 'us', as to set up their own self-contained communities in our midst; in short, build a ghetto. In fact, 'they' are carrying out the 'multicultural' programme (as this is widely misunderstood by those who see it as favouring cultural retreat into closed communities). And they are being assisted by naïve liberals who don't realise how disastrous this is. We have to demand that they conform. (And so we come to the same policy: assimilation as a condition of integration.)

Now the push towards assimilation undercuts the intercultural scenario, as indeed, it goes against any genuine recognition of the greater diversity of our present society. But how can one combat fears of the kind which drive this demand?

V

Here let me step beyond the parochial, and say what I've been building up to all along. The intercultural story is not simply made for Quebec. It also suits better the situation of many European countries. The features which make it applicable to Quebec also often apply in Europe. There (1) many countries have a long-standing historic identity which is still shared by the great majority of their citizens. (2) This identity frequently centres around a language which is not spoken elsewhere, and is under pressure from larger, 'globalised' languages. And (3) the same kind of not-fully-structured fears for the future of its culture and way of life may arise there as I noted in Quebec. Points (1) and (2) make the intercultural story a better fit than the multicultural one. Indeed, they may contribute to fears around the word 'multiculturalism' analogous to those encountered in Quebec, and to the misunderstanding that it amounts to encouraging ghettos. And at the same time, (3) may mean that a policy of openness to difference may trigger off some of the same reactions as we have found in Quebec.

These fears may be aggravated by several factors: a) European experience as immigrant receiving societies has been much shorter than that of societies in the Western hemisphere; b) much of that experience occurred under (what turned out to be) a disastrously wrong story, that summed up in the term *Gastarbeiter*, the idea that outsiders who came to fill the needed jobs would end up returning to their home countries, with the benefit of the funds earned during their time of employment in Europe. As a result, the necessary measures were not taken to integrate them and their children. For instance, programmes to ensure that immigrant children learn the language of the host country were not undertaken, and are only now being introduced. Thirdly (c) there is an important difference in the level of education and skills between immigrants to Quebec and those to many European societies. The former are selected on the basis of their skills and competences, which are usually much higher than those entering Europe. They are frequently professionals, or potential occupants of middle-class jobs. They often have a level of education, and hence outlook and way of life, which has been more influenced by 'globalised' trends, and thus find it easier to integrate into the host society.

The intercultural story thus faces additional obstacles and resistances to those encountered in Quebec (and God knows, these are great enough here). Because the necessary policies were late in coming, immigrant children may find themselves in an underclass where they lack the linguistic and other skills to succeed. And their skill set will probably already have been lower to begin with than their Quebec counterparts. In addition, they may be culturally more distant from the native born than we experience these days in Western hemisphere societies. The result can be a growing sense of alienation, especially among younger people in immigrant communities, a conviction that they are not welcomed, not treated as equals, discriminated against in employment, housing and in their treatment by police and other authorities.

This sense of alienation can lead to expressions of revolt and rejection of the host society, of the kind which were dramatically evident in the riots and car-burnings in the 'banlieues" of France in autumn 2005. And such movements obviously increase the fears of the majority, and their sense that the historic culture is under threat. Indeed, immigrant alienation and host society cultural fear are in a relation of mutual intensification. The fears stoke hostility to immigrants, and intensify demands for stern, even punitive measures of assimilation, or else more radically for an end to immigration, or even a repatriation of those already present. This hostility then entrenches further immigrant alienation, which leads to further expressions of anger; and so on into a dangerous spiral.

How to stop the spiral? The best antidote, perhaps the only one, is: successful enactments of the intercultural scenario. That is, leaders and members of the majority mainstream seek out leaders and members of the minority(ies), and together with them work out new ways of resolving the conflicts, then work together effectively to resolve them. (This is, for instance, what Jop Cohen did when he was mayor of Amsterdam.) The ensemble of such collaborative enterprises contributes in effect to the elaboration of a new, more inclusive culture of interaction.

So enactment of the scenario eases fears. But people also have to overcome their fears to enter into these enactments. So a catch-22 obstacle threatens to block our way forward. How to convince members of the mainstream to enter into this kind of collaboration?

Perhaps what they need is more familiarity with the immigrant situation. The vast majority of immigrants to the rich countries of the North are drawn to them because they hope for a better life for themselves and their children. Indeed, millions aspire to this, and sometimes risk their life on the ocean, or crammed into containers, on the outside chance of getting in. A better life, in what sense? For some this means a place of relative freedom, of security, of human rights. But for just about everyone, it means opening possibilities for themselves or their children, like particular jobs, with access to higher income, and education for their children leading to even better occupations and greater prosperity.

Success in these endeavours creates an enormous positive bonding with the host society, a sense of gratitude and belonging which one often hears expressed by immigrants to the USA, and sometimes Canada. And this is what tends to come about, provided . . . Provided the hope is not negated: the avenue to the hoped-for job systematically blocked, by discrimination or some other structural factors, avenues to other associations blocked by prejudices; or else one is stigmatised, and branded an outsider, a danger for the society. When this happens, the resultant bitterness is proportionate to the dimensions of the antecedent hope, and great alienation can result. But when things go as planned, newcomers can express a patriotism which makes natives blush. (This may be particularly the case in Canada where such fulsome expressions make people uneasy.)

In our Northern societies this kind of positive bonding should not be difficult to create. It takes some special factors to wreck it. These can be geopolitical, as one sees in ex-imperial countries, where relations with the ex-colonised are compromised by a heavy and problematic past. Or hatred and resentment may be mobilised today on the geopolitical level, as with various jihadist movements in the Muslim world, and these may find recruits among immigrants in Northern societies. But for the most part these movements have little success without a hefty assist from high levels of hostility and exclusion generated within these Northern societies themselves. Alienation within these societies is to a great extent created by the fear and mistrust they have generated against the new arrivals.

This is a sad fact, but it can be seen as a basis of hope: that more open policies may turn the situation around, and reverse the spiral. So that enactments of the intercultural scenario inspire further such enactments, and make the story itself come true.

vi

We need now to go beyond the issues arising specifically in societies which receive immigrants, and look at the divisions which exist between different segments of the population which have a long-standing presence and mutual relation in the society. These can indeed be much more difficult to overcome. I am thinking, for instance, of the discriminations against Blacks in the US, against aboriginals in Canada, or against non-whites (for instance, Chinese) in both countries; or against Hispanics in the US.

When we try to bridge these differences, and overcome these discriminations, we often run into the fact that the battle is interwoven with another conflict, that between rival interpretations of the national identity. Where this is not the case, one can hope that time, education, campaigns for recognition, mutual contact will gradually erode the stereotypes and heal the divisions. But where what I called above 'hierarchies of precedence' not only exist, but are felt by some people to be part of the national identity, the problem becomes much more intractable. Trying to heal one division runs afoul and envenoms further another struggle.

Something of the sort has bedevilled politics in the United States, where certain measures to extend equal rights have fallen afoul of a major battle between rival versions of what the American political identity consists in. And such battles are by their nature very difficult to resolve and even navigate.

It is time we look at this kind of threat to unity, and inquire what can be done about it. Of course, this kind of division is not specific to the United States. In fact, in many countries, riding on the back of con-troversies over what rights to accord immigrants are serious issues about how to define the national identity. Between the political mainstream and the Front National in France, there lies not only the issue of what rights are to be given to Muslims, but also the question of how we define the ethos of the Republic. Something of the same, of course, exists in Quebec, but the fight is on a much narrower front, that of defining secu-larism. It is not as total and wide-ranging as the one we see in France.

But there is something surprising, disturbing and intractable about the battle around the American identity. This is partly, but I don't think mainly, because of the seriousness with which this identity figures in American speech and thought. The disturbing and intractable nature of the conflict comes from the way in which a number of different issues, which could be handled, and perhaps even partly settled, on their own, have been inextricably bundled into the general identity struggle.

So issues of the public place of religion (Ten Commandments on the courthouse, school prayer, etc.) and issues of feminism, of gay rights, or the legal status of abortion, of state support for welfare versus self-reliance, of the right to own guns, have all been bundled together, and two opposed positions, 'Conservative' and 'Liberal', have been invented to describe the two sides in this mega-dispute; whereas, there are obvious crossover positions which are perfectly reasonable, and clearly adopted by some people, like economic conservatives who are for gay rights, or believers in the welfare state who think Christianity should receive higher recognition, or feminists who worry about welfare budgets, etc.

What holds these mega-positions together is the sense that each side co-defines a single definition of the American identity, and that a bitter battle is being fought between these two definitions. The idea seems to be that the 'conservatives' defend the original pristine identity which has since been eroded, and so there is dark talk of 'taking America back', as though it had been occupied by some alien force.

The negative consequences of this bundling are that it becomes impos-sible to negotiate, and perhaps find an accommodation, on any single issue, without seeming to cede to the adversary on the crucial question of what America really is and stands for. On some of these issues the contrast with Canada is striking. Many Canadians oppose gay rights, and they are unhappy with the decision which flowed from the supreme court, and was ratified in Parliament. But every citizen knows that you can't win every battle, and you live to fight another day about another matter. It would never occur to anyone to claim that there was something UnCana-dian about the decision. Besides, this labelling is what the Americans do, which immediately disqualifies it for many Canadians.

Folding into the one great identity battle does for these distinct issues what raising the moral stakes does to questions like whether Muslim women will be allowed to wear hijabs. Invoking laïcité makes the act heinous instead of unpleasant or inconvenient, and makes compromise seem like treason. Similarly, invoking the American identity in regard to a given issue renders it more intractable, and the battle around it more bitter and hostile.

What can be done to reunite societies which are going through such identity battles? Compromise may not be possible. And I myself would not accept it when it comes to fundamental rights like freedom of conscience, or the forbidding of discrimination between races, religions or identities. But a lot can be done to reduce the tension, and undercut the acerbity of the battle.

First of all, the bundles must be loosened, and the multiple cross-over positions given their just due. Here we're engaging on the round I described earlier, where we try to question not the principles behind an issue, but its relation to the national identity. There is no reason why either position on abortion, or on welfare, or on gay rights, important as these issues are, should place one on the other side of a divide where one is no longer a conversation partner.

Unbundling is necessary for what we might call 'normal' democratic politics, where at any given time, we will be 'winning' on issue A and 'losing' on issue B. In this regard, there are analogies between the American situation and what we observe in societies in which a totalising ideology squares off against its polar opposite: the situation, for instance, of Muslim societies where 'islamism' is in mortal combat with some 'secular' opponent. As long as the totalising ideology holds, democracy cannot take hold, as we see tragically in Egypt in the aftermath to the Arab Spring in Tahrir Square. Whereas in Tunisia, first steps have been taken towards a fully democratic regime (fingers crossed!), largely because Ennahda was willing to abandon the totalising programme and engage in the 'normal' democratic process, where you win some contests and lose others.

Second, conversations should be started on all these previously bundled questions between people on opposite sides, where they frankly exchange views, go into issues in detail, and search for common ground.

We have had a lot of proof of this on the small scale. The problem is how to upscale it. The various experiments with small groups have been interesting and encouraging. For example, in the United States, there have been encounters between advocates who are pro-life and pro-choice, say, bringing people together for a weekend from both sides. And then they talk to each other, and they find out that they are not a million miles apart from each other. There's some kind of common ground, and they find that the other is not a monster. Things begin to thaw. We did the same thing when we had big constitutional problems in Canada. Again, small scale: people brought together for a weekend – a Quebecois, an Ontarian, someone from BC, etc. – and they sat around and talked. The same thing happened: the great fears and suspicions melted.

Moreover, if you're not just talking but working together on something, a common project, that greatly strengthens the effect. And in addition, you find here that you're not only breaking down the barriers, but you're also increasing what might be called democratic intelligence. The dumbing-down effect is countered by the fact that you're trying to work out common projects, actually confronting the difficulties, and where things have to be changed, and where the levers for change are to be found.

But this is just the beginning. The obstacles to this kind of meeting of minds will include partial group identities, which are partly built on a rejection of other groups (hardcore Front National voters in France, in relation to Muslims), or at least relegate others to an inferior role. Unfortunately some identities of this latter sort are powerful in the US. The legacy of slavery has been that for many whites, and not just in the South, Blacks should in some ill-defined way come second. And for others, this category of those who deserve second priority extends to include other ethnic groups (for example, Hispanics), or more generally to recent immigrants as such. As a result, the normal procedure of welfare state provision, which is to redistribute resources to those most in need, comes to seem like a reversal of the proper priority, disrespecting the status of the 'first' Americans.

The image that Arlie Hochschild (2016) developed in her study of Southern whites in Louisiana, of a long line climbing a hill towards the American dream, which her interlocutors enthusiastically accepted, says it all. In this imagined line, as in all lines, some people are ahead of others. And in the imagination of these Southerners, the first Americans were up there at the front. And these people were not well off. In the light of all this, redistributive welfare programmes benefiting Black and more recent arrivals amounted to a kind of illegitimate elbowing into line by people whose normal position was farther back.

In the US, as in many other Western democracies, this kind of – largely tacit – assumption of precedence is very widespread and often powerful, in spite of the 'official' doctrine stipulating that all citizens are equal. But, as with the prejudices against Muslims in Quebec, squaring the two requires some false moralisation, to the effect that the less-favoured populations are lazy, or prone to violence, or in other ways don't 'fit'.

A direct attack on these assumptions of precedence, as violations of the ethic of equality, in an attempt to shame those who are in their grip, may have little effect. Indeed, ridicule, and dismissing the people concerned as 'rednecks' or 'deplorables', will just backfire. On the contrary, we need a more indirect approach. Without in any way abandoning the basic principles of democratic equality, we need to gain a sympathetic understanding of what drives people to entrench themselves in them, and also of the connections between different facets of their motivation, which are more complex and many-sided than the hierarchical identity itself. Here the attempt is not to reject the identity itself (say, of Southern whites), but to change its felt relation to the common American identity.

To take the US case: We should look first at what leads people to vote on the basis of their hierarchical identity; for instance, the votes for Trump in the 'rust belt'. We can point to a sense of diminished citizen efficacy and the need for its recovery. A man's (this gendered term still applies in many milieux) efficacy is measured not only by his political clout, but also by his ability to feed his family by his work. This is essential to his dignity. Michael Sandel makes the point that the obscenely astronomical 'bonuses' on Wall Street, alongside the fact that people on Main Street were losing their jobs, were seen as a statement by élites in government and finance that work has no value for them, no dignity in their eyes. The obvious contrast in rewards arouses strong indignation – which paradoxically and maddeningly has helped produce the solid Republican majority. But this assault to male dignity (felt as such by lots of men, even though women also lost jobs) connects to one facet of identity, which many men, and the women who shared this view, saw as slighted.

This raises difficult questions of rhetorical appeal for the Left. Many of the aspects of Republican (and Trumpian) electoral appeal are pretty ugly: the real Man who wants to be able to provide for his family through his work may also bridle at the idea that he can't own a gun; or that women should have equal pay. And then he may not be too unruffled by discrimination against gays. And he may think that the old-time religion and morality is essential to a good society. And he may buy into the idea that the line marching towards the American dream puts some people ahead of others, etc.

There are connections here, which the Left has to tease apart. We have to appeal to the ex-worker who feels degraded because he can't operate as (sole or principal) breadwinner, without buying into all aspects of this identity. But above all, we have to communicate that we understand, and can sympathise with his loss and his pain. And there is real pain here. It is possible in fact to feel how devastating this kind of assault on someone's identity can be, without sharing or endorsing all aspects of the (necessarily complex) identity. A new solidarity, across the chasm of existing anger and resentment, can be built on this basis.

This is not just a matter of choosing a rhetoric, but of being the kind of person who can carry this message across. The impact of Bernie Sanders shows this. Impeccably liberal though he be, he was not identified as part of the 'Liberal élite'.

But secondly, we have to go farther and understand the life position of many of those who excoriate the 'élites', and how this relates to the stances they take and the votes they cast. I quote from Joan C. Williams (2017: 20) in a recent book:

> To working class members of all races, valuing hard work means having the rigid self-discipline to do a menial job you hate for 20 years and reining yourself in so you don't 'have an attitude' (i.e., so that you can submit to authority). Hard work for élites is associated with self-actualization; 'disruption' means founding a successful start-up. Disruption, in working class jobs, just gets you fired. Free spirits born working class can't count on the second chances available to élites. That's why blue collar families are so big on stability and self-discipline, and they embrace institutions which support these traits. Chief among these is religion. The devout have greater impulse control and 'tend to do better in school, live longer, have more satisfying marriages and be generally happier' (quote from Tierney, 2008).
>
> Regular church attendees commit fewer crimes, are in better health, live longer, and finish college more frequently than those who don't attend church at all (Vance, 2016; Gorman, 2005). Churchgoing can also provide a financial safety net.

The message that this passage contains, along with its quotes from other works, is this: we need a sympathetic understanding of the life condition of people with a different group identity; here that of the white working-class, Protestant (Scots-Irish), the earliest Europeans to arrive in the Appalachian rust belt. Of course, the above focus on the need for discipline applies to many others, including Blacks and Hispanics, but the focus here is on the WASP identity, because this was so easily recruited by Trump's campaign.

The essential point is to see how these people, in their struggle to give a liveable order to their lives through discipline, turn to this identity, to its religious traditions, and also its folkways more generally. To ridicule this turn is to ridicule them. On the other hand, this group's identity, as all such identities, is multifaceted and can change. Our goal should be to help this community to downplay and eventually detach itself from the assumptions of precedence which it has traditionally enshrined.

Of course, the detachment will not be complete, nor will it happen among all those who share this identity, but even a partial delinking among a significant number will allow the healing process to begin.

How will this process take place? First of all, in the political realm. Because on the back of this greater mutual understanding, we can try to build coalitions on particular issues between people on both sides. The worker who voted for Trump because he felt cheated and slighted might easily vote for a believable programme which would really get him a good job.

How can this best be done? In the electoral process itself, across the boundaries that presently divide people. If I may once again invoke the Quebec experience, here is another example of how complexity and multiple facets of identity can open the way to a shift in political alignment. During the debate in Quebec on the Parti Québécois' Charter of Values, which would have denied women wearing hijabs the right to work in the public sector, polls steadily gave majorities in the upper 50s in favour of the Charter. But when you asked another question: should anyone be fired as a result of the charter?, similar majorities said 'no'. This was flagrantly inconsistent on the part of those in the intersection between 'yes' to the first, and 'no' to the second. But it shows that lots of people are cross-pressured, and you can get to them by another route than just condemning them as anti-liberal beasts. There are in fact may reasons in traditional Quebec culture and experience to find the kind of victimisation proposed very distasteful, as well as traditions of local solidarity which pull in another direction.

The consideration which would give power to all these efforts is that our unnecessary divisions are doing us a lot of harm; they are disempowering us to face real problems and challenges, like global warming, declining jobs, greater inequality. Coming to appreciate this would give extra strength to these attempts to cut through the paralysis induced by the rigid identity struggle between inflexible bundles of the supposed super-positions, Conservative and Liberal.

References

Bouchard, G. (2011), 'What is Interculturalism', *McGill Law Journal / Revue de droit de McGill*, 56 (2), 435–46.

Bouchard, G. and C. Taylor (2008), *Building the Future: A Time for Reconciliation*. Toronto: Canadian Scholars.

Gorman, L. (2005), 'Is Religion Good for You?', National Bureau of Economic Research. Accessed at: <https://www.nber.org/digest/oct05/religion-good-you>

Hochschild, A. (2016), *Strangers in their Own Land: Anger and Mourning on the American Right*. New York: The New Press.

Kymlicka, W. (1995), *Multicultural Citizenship*. Oxford: Oxford University Press.

Taylor, C. (2012), 'Interculturalism or Multiculturalism?', *Philosophy & Social Criticism*, 38 (4–5), 413–23.

Tierney, J. (2008), 'For Good Self-Control, Try Getting Religious about it', *New York Times*, 29 December. Accessed at: <https://www.nytimes.com/2008/12/30/science/30tier.html>

Vance, J. D. (2016), *Hillbilly Elegy: A Memoir of a Family and Culture in Crisis*. William Collins.

Williams, Joan C. (2017), *White Working Class: Overcoming Class Cluelessness in America*. Boston, MA: Harvard Business Review Press.

FIVE

The Unfinished Tasks of Multiculturalism: Thinking *of* Multiculturalism, Thinking *with* Tariq Modood

Gurpreet Mahajan

Tariq Modood is perhaps the most engaged, vocal and persuasive face of multiculturalism today – of not just British multiculturalism, or the 'Bristol school of multiculturalism' (Brahm Levey 2019), but of multicultural political theory in general. In the post-9/11 world, when multiculturalism has faced the heat from many European leaders, and the 'war on terror' has made security and integration the primary concerns, Tariq has been, and continues to be, a staunch advocate of the multicultural path – someone who unhesitatingly challenges the dominant nationalist and liberal narratives relating to the Muslim immigrant populations in the West. What is unique to Tariq Modood is that he acknowledges his subject position, as an immigrant and a second-generation South Asian Muslim, owns that subjective experience to make a reasoned normative argument for the need to be more inclusive, and explores ways by which this goal can be pursued in Western democracies. Confronting the rising tide of majoritarian nationalism, he makes a strong case for a positive recognition of diverse religious/cultural/ethnic identities, arguing that extending respect and nurturing trust are better ways of pursuing the goal of integration.

For many normative theorists, offering rational arguments requires placing oneself behind the 'veil of ignorance', distancing oneself from personal and subjective experiences, being neutral and distant from different subject positions. Tariq's political theory, in my view, draws its strength from the contrary position. It shows that reasonable arguments, which inform our public thinking and policies, require an understanding of embedded subjective positions. Without the latter, reason will remain a slave to the prevailing constitutive prejudices.

Tariq will probably disagree with this representation of his work. He is likely to say that his focus on Islamophobia and the Muslim community is on account of the prevailing context (Modood 2021). While there are a number of minorities who face various forms of disadvantage, it is the Muslims who are treated, at this moment, as the quintessential 'other'; they, more than others, are vilified, presented in negative terms and treated as the 'problem'. Hence, it is the current state practices in Europe and elsewhere that compel him to focus on this religious, racialised community. Ever since the Rushdie Affair and the controversy that erupted around *The Satanic Verses*, it has been necessary to intervene and explain the Muslim perspective. All this is undeniable, although one could say that his concern for the position of the Muslim, more specifically South Asian Muslim, community predates those events. These minor details aside, what is more important, and what comes through sharply as I read Tariq's writings, is that reflection begins with some concrete experiences. The latter presents us with questions and that is, as it were, the start of the journey. While the direction we follow and the arguments we make are not determined by subjective experience, the latter reveals an aspect of reality that is not readily available to others. Reflecting on his early years, Tariq notes the difference between the disadvantages faced by the South Asians and the Blacks. Music, for instance, gave the latter a social advantage and made them more popular than the South Asian minority. In this instance, experience drew his attention to the differences between the minorities and the different ways in which each is disadvantaged. It also posed a question – were the South Asian Muslims worst off? Experience not only draws our attention to specific issues, it also compels us to ask if certain representations of them are adequate. It triggers, to borrow Ricoeur's phrase, a 'hermeneutics of suspicion', compelling one to look for meanings that are not immediately given; to question the dominant narrative and explore alternative ways of reading a text and making sense of an event.

In the 1990s, when Will Kymlicka and Charles Taylor (1994) made a compelling case for valuing cultural membership and diversity[1] and giving 'national' (Kymlicka 1995) minorities the right to govern themselves, multicultural theory focused on the claims of the indigenous populations and the Francophones, each of whom had a distinct linguistic cultural identity. The indigenous people had been colonised and displaced from their homeland. Not only were they victims of 'historical wrongs', their world view embodied a form of non-instrumental rationality – something that was valued in the post-Heidegger world. The social norms that governed the Francophones in Quebec were not significantly different from those of the Anglophones in the rest of Canada. Hence, making a case for accepting their difference, rather than coercing them to assimilate, stood alongside other critiques of high modernity, which opposed the urge to homogenise and hegemonise the political and the natural world.

In England, where the primary concern was the immigrant populations and their cultural differences, multiculturalism faced a new and different challenge. It was confronted with social norms and practices that were starkly different from that of the majority population. Whether it is gender-specific roles or priority given to the family and community vis-à-vis the individual and her autonomy, these differences brought into play another set of values that liberal secularists were prone to decry rather swiftly. In this context, multiculturalism had to be reinvented, and we see this happening in the writings of Tariq Modood. He foregrounded equality; instead of extrapolating why diversity is valuable for us and the society as a whole, Tariq showed how its absence may be a source of unfairness and inequality. It is through this lens that he took up issues relating to diverse populations and cultures, especially those relating to the Muslim immigrant population.

Bhikhu Parekh had already rearticulated some key ideas of multiculturalism. While Charles Taylor spoke of the intrinsic and equal worth of all cultures (1994a),[2] Parekh viewed cultural diversity to be a necessary condition of critical self-reflection. Tariq shifted the ground still further; in the 1980s and '90s he raised the question of equality, more specifically, of inter-group equality. Did different communities enjoy the same opportunities? Were they treated alike in the public domain? If, as the data showed, Muslims were lagging behind on several social and economic parameters, should they not receive some form of special consideration?[3] If there was fairly wide support for women's movements that demanded special measures to ensure equality, why were similar claims from the Muslim population not entertained? Why was there reluctance to extend similar provisions for these cultural and religious communities?

Tariq has continued to pose these hard questions, and each one of them calls for some self-reflection on the part of the liberals. Over the years the questions he has asked have only become more difficult: if protections under the Race Relations Act are extended to other religious communities – the Jews, for instance – then why not for the Muslims? Why should we not consider Muslim bashing, and the accompanying Islamophobia, as a form of racial discrimination? Even when Muslims are often targeted for their 'Muslimness', why are Muslims not treated as a racial minority? In these and several other ways, Tariq continues to pose the multicultural question in England as an issue related to equality – something that is unquestionably an important democratic value. This

rendering of multiculturalism is strikingly different from its earlier formulations, particularly those that emerged within the Canadian context.

Will Kymlicka had argued that culture is a context of choice and its
loss is a source of harm to the members (1989: 162–81); hence, one
needs to make cultures secure. Giving vulnerable communities the right
to govern themselves was a way of ensuring that their cultures (the context which informs their choices and conditions of good) can survive
and flourish. In England, the primary multicultural concern was not the
security and protection of diverse/minority cultures, but *understanding*:
that is, it called for a hermeneutic exercise to make sense of the meaning
that certain actions and ways of thinking have for the members. Above
all, to interrogate liberal perceptions and prejudgements about other
cultures and communities (Parekh 1994b). Bolstering tolerance, avoid-
ing misjudgement of the other, and nurturing some communication
and dialogue across communities and cultures required transcending
one's prejudices, even those through which we are socially and historically constituted.

Multicultural political theorists had already shown that forced assimilation was a form of discrimination (Kymlicka 1989: 175–6), and it
is preferable to foster solidarity among fellow citizens instead of asking them to assimilate into the majority culture. Integration involved,
among other things, pursuing policies that engender a sense of psycho-
logical (and not just legal and political) belonging and membership
(Carens 1995: 12–13); a sense of attachment – something that would
be better achieved through accommodating, and one might add, understanding their difference. Tariq Modood pursued this line of reasoning
as he intervened in the debates that followed the controversies around
The Satanic Verses and the publication of the Danish cartoons. Europe, to
quote him, 'has to choose which is more important, the right to ridicule
Muslims or the integration of Muslims' (2006: 6).

Although multiculturalism is often accused of fragmenting and ghet-
toising society, integration has always been a primary concern within this
framework. Integration is not, however, possible if some communities
remain vulnerable, or if their voices remain unheard and uncounted.
Integration therefore required both a positive recognition of difference
and an accommodation of that difference. Tariq Modood, at least while
intervening in the debates around *The Satanic Verses* and the Danish cartoons, added that it also entailed 'restraint in the use of freedom directed
against religious people' (ibid.: 7). One had to understand that a different
rationality was at work in diverse cultural and religious perspectives, and
one must acknowledge this in a plural and diverse society. One could in
fact say that a different rationality is at work when we are dealing with

religious world views and the actions of religious believers. Tariq's later work (if one may use that term) has in fact moved in that direction. If his earlier work, written in the shadow of the Rushdie Affair, alluded to 'working class anger' and 'hurt pride' of the marginalised Muslims, his work over the last decade or so grapples with the nature of religious identity and the place of religion in the liberal democratic state.

There is, as it were, a natural progression in his work, from understanding the position and rationality of the Muslim immigrant (a particular) to examining the governance of religion in the public domain. Or, to put this another way, from understanding the predicament of a particular group, to understanding the nature of religious identity and membership, the nature of other significant identities, such as, national identity or citizenship, as well as the relationship between these identities. These questions have brought him back to the concept and the practice of secularism, and in recent years his work on this subject has shaped the debate in four significant ways. First, it has pluralised the discourse on secularism; second, his intervention has changed the terms of discourse by considering religion as a form of 'public good'; third, he has aligned multiculturalism with secularism and nationalism, or made these pursuits compatible with each other; and lastly, he has presented what I would call a nationalist multiculturalism.

For a long time, the debates on secularism took the French conception of laïcité or the American model of 'separation' as the definitional norm. Even those who rejected the adequacy of this framework, or its applicability to non-Western societies, associated secularism with the ideal of keeping religion and state apart (Madan 1987; Nandy 1995). Alternatives to this so-called 'Western' model were sought in the Indian experience and its conception of the state–religion relationship. Bhargava wrote extensively of the 'Indian' conception of secularism and pitted it against the 'Western' conception of the same (2010). When Charles Taylor and Gerrard Bouchard differentiated between 'rigid' and 'open' secularism (2008: 135–8), they too invoked the French and the American framework as the basis of the former and the Indian variant as an embodiment of the latter. The debate on secularism was thus constructed around the issue of the adequacy of the 'Western' model: that is, whether Western democracies and their idea of secularism can successfully accommodate religiously diverse communities. It also hinted at the superiority of the Indian model in this regard. Over the last decade, Tariq Modood has systematically challenged the assumed homogenisation of the Western experience to argue that a strict separation of religion and state is not the dominant norm in many parts of Western Europe (Modood 2021; 2022). Patterns of state–religion relationship, and with it the idea of secularism, vary across the Western world. Although this fact figured in many historical accounts and political analyses, debates on secularism tended to bracket out this plurality. As an interlocutor and active participant in those debates it is Tariq, more than others, who brought in the diversity of European experience and institutional arrangements. More recently he has offered a more complex schema to comprehend the varieties of state–religion relationships that prevail in contemporary democracies.

Pluralising the conception of secularism and pointing to the differences within Europe (the West) was a way of asking Europe to take a closer look at itself, and learn also from its own experiments. Instead of focusing only on the non-West and how it has negotiated the challenge of living with deep diversity, the West could learn from each other.[4] Although it may not have been his intention, this offered a way of moving beyond self-doubt. Against the backdrop of several accounts of the failure of Western liberal democracies to deal with diversity (particularly one that came with the immigrant people), this presented a way of restoring Europe's confidence in itself and arguing that things can easily be different. This narrative of Europe, and refocusing the gaze on its different journeys and ways of making society more equal and fair in its treatment of different religious and ethnic communities, should have made multiculturalism more acceptable. At least it should have mellowed the critics. This has not, or so it seems, happened, but this is a point that I will return to later.

When one turns to the European experiences, it is evident that in many societies – Britain, Belgium, Denmark and Finland (taking a cue from the examples given by Tariq) – religion is actively present in the public domain. It is, to use his phrase, considered to be a 'public good' (2010). In many different ways it continues to shape public policies, especially relating to education, social welfare and health. For Tariq then, not only is complete separation not the norm, one can justifiably make a case for including religious inputs and involve communities. A possibility exists within these societies of finding ways, and expanding spaces, by which diverse communities can be involved in shaping the public domain, policies and laws.

That is not all. If religion has a public presence and some communities are involved in framing policies, then one can make space for new entrants to be included. Minorities can be given a voice in the system, and their perspective can also be included to inform the outcomes. This kind of secularism can be, and for Tariq it is, aligned with multiculturalism. It has the potential of being inclusive and sensitive to the concerns of the minorities. Tariq Modood writes about 'multiculturalising secularism'

(Modood 2017; Modood and Sealey 2021); but in making this argument he is not suggesting a new form of secularism (more so, as secularism does not have one standard form), but deepening aspects that are already present in the way state–religion relationships are shaped in some parts of Western Europe. This addresses liberal apprehensions about multiculturalism; it shows that in practice many secular democracies already have mechanisms for including religious groups and one can now include significant minorities to be a part of that consultative process. What is being advocated by multiculturalists is not therefore very far from what already exists.

Contemporary Britain is, for Tariq, an example of multicultural secularism at work. It sees religion as a public good; accords recognition to minority schools/educational institutions; and as a society finds ways of recognising minority festivals, their cultural events and, to some extent, their cultural practices. It has gradually built a multicultural sensibility: after all, no newspaper in Britain published/reprinted the Danish cartoons; it is fairly accommodative of diverse religious dietary norms and dress codes; the head of state makes significant symbolic gestures of inclusiveness. So, it has a form of secularism that is moderate and multicultural. The two do not necessarily push in different directions; if anything, secularism and multiculturalism sit together comfortably, if not all the time, then most of the time. To a considerable extent, this coming together of secularism and multiculturalism is made possible by thinking of religion as a public good. At least implicitly, Tariq suggests that societies that regard religion positively, as a public good, are more inclined to be sensitive to the sensibilities of other religious communities. It can buttress a form of secularism that is inclusive and accords positive recognition to diverse religious identities.

One could extend this argument to say that one can, indeed, one should envisage a more inclusive form of nationalism. It is not clear if Tariq Modood thinks that England has also evolved a form of nationalism that includes minorities. Perhaps a multicultural nationalism has yet to emerge, but such an ideal appears achievable in this context. Tariq's writings communicate a subtle sense of pride in the way Britain, as a secular democracy, has evolved and become more receptive to the concerns of the minorities. Much more needs to be done; he does not deny that. But, for him, Britain presents a positive story of what is possible and doable within the framework of contemporary democracies and state–religion relationship, and this needs to be acknowledged by both the secularists and the multiculturalists. I refer to this orientation as nationalist multiculturalism, in part to underline that his writings express a sense of belonging and pride in the society he lives in, and this coexists with his ability to take a critical look at that society and see how the spirit of multiculturalism can be infused in it more fully. In Europe, where multiculturalism and its policies are frequently associated with nurturing group loyalties and neglecting the nation (and its many achievements), his narrative puts the spotlight on what Britain has been able to do by way of recognising and accommodating its diversity, and this marks a shift in the narrative on secularism and multiculturalism.

In multiple ways, Tariq Modood's ideas extend the multicultural thinking and offer good reasons to the majority community to take this framework seriously. Even the most provocative idea – that religion is/should be seen as a public good – requires serious engagement. In a context where few people identify themselves as believers and, on the other side, we see orthodox voices surfacing within religious communities, it may not be easy to agree with him. His suggestion poses many questions: if religion is a public good, should we welcome close partnership between state/political rulers and religion? What implications would such an alliance have for the non-believers and atheists? Since we can only speak of diverse religions and communities (and not religion per se), are we envisaging a public sphere saturated by religious symbols and narratives? When scientific studies question the truth of some religious beliefs/conceptions, such as stories of creation, what will prevail?

These questions need to be addressed. That being said, Tariq's view on religion as a public good hints at something significant. It suggests that religious beliefs and observances configure the lives of many people in subtle, and often unacknowledged, ways. Taking note of them, being aware of them and accommodating them is a public good. Vice versa, ignoring these constitutive elements does more public harm than good. Take, for example, the case of hijab, or turban, or some other dress code. Many of these are linked to notions of dignity and personal identity (Mahajan 2017). It is not necessary that everyone in the community accepts these dress codes and makes them a part of their daily life. It is also possible that at times individuals feel socially compelled to accept these norms, and left to themselves they would not wear those external markers of identity. Yet, if they are prohibited, then even the less compliant members are likely to endorse the right to wear these markers.[5] They may not see religion as a public good, but infringement and denial of specific religious values and observances would be seen as 'harm'. It would therefore be better to recognise religion as a source of value and good, and see if the perspectives they offer can positively inform our decisions.

One might also think of religion in non-theological terms; as a collective, community way of life or a world view which prioritises certain values and patterns of social life. It is possible then to say and accept, without the apprehensions that institutionalised forms of religion (with their history of conflicts and wars) generate, that there may be something valuable in each religion. Or, at least accept that these diverse ways of life and thinking may provide different perspectives and we will be better off, or public policies would be enriched by listening to, considering and incorporating the insights that come from them. In other words, Tariq Modood's claim that religion is a 'public good' could be read more creatively. Instead of viewing it as a pronouncement about the value of religion (opposed to the non-religious outlooks that are often less sympathetic to notions of 'sacred' and collective good), one could read in it a plea to be inclusive; to be willing to bring in voices from different cultural frameworks, many of which stand outside of the liberal tradition.

Tariq Modood offers, as I have noted even earlier, a form of multiculturalism – an inclusive and accommodative politics – that sits comfortably with a certain kind of moderate secularism and national identity. It also offers a reasonable way of recognising diverse communities in positive ways, bringing them into the public domain, and, in the process, strengthening the nation-state. One would have thought that this representation of multiculturalism would have quelled the opposition. By making a case for group equality rather than protection of difference, he would also have assuaged the critics, and assured them that multiculturalism is not seeking to protect and defend all minority cultural practices; nor is it ignoring the steps that Britain has taken to accommodate the minorities. Yet, despite Tariq's efforts to engage in public debate on almost all major political events and pronouncements, specifically in relation to the Muslim immigrant population, the critics of multiculturalism remain unpersuaded. The shrill voices against multicultural secularism continue to prevail. When the term multicultural is appended to any other concept, it becomes suspect, and is dismissed rather quickly.[6] One could of course attribute this to prejudice and an unwillingness to have a reasoned discussion. These factors cannot be discounted, but one has still to ask: what else could multiculturalists do (beyond what Tariq has done and is doing)? Or could they do something differently to alter the negative perception? In other words, what explains the continued resistance to multiculturalism? Are there certain ideas that need further enunciation and clarification? Are there silences within the contemporary multicultural discourse that need to be addressed? These are questions that I want to turn to in the rest of this paper.

There are, it appears to me, four unfinished tasks of multiculturalism. They call for further engagement and clarification. Although these are issues on which some theorists have written, yet, in the present context they require further consideration from multiculturalists. First, in popular perception multiculturalism has come to be associated closely with the resurgence of religion in the public domain. Even though multiculturalists do not endorse or espouse any religious values in their writings, their plea to involve religious communities/organisations in some spheres of state policy, or at least to see religion as a relevant factor in a person's life and actions, has created the impression that multiculturalism is blind to the dark side of religion and religious conflict. Many societies are witnessing more orthodox and rigid expressions of religious views; religious symbols are visible everywhere; demands to withdraw or ban artistic and literary expressions are on the increase. In such a situation, one can appreciate these concerns, and multiculturalists need to address them. They need to clarify the envisaged role of religion. Do they welcome the growing presence of religion in the public sphere? Do they support the display of religious symbols everywhere? Will we see prayers being offered before any or all major events?

Not so long ago, left-liberals frequently stood alongside multiculturalists in the fight against racism and minority discrimination. Today, they have reservations. They are apprehensive about the space that multiculturalism is willing to give to religion in the public domain. For them the issue is not about the sovereignty of the state or its autonomy. Neither may be threatened by the resurgence of religion, but they see the increased space given to religious claims vis-à-vis other kinds of claims as a worrying trend: one that is likely to engender more conflict, intolerance and prejudice, not to mention diminished room for expressing dissent against prevailing religious beliefs, all of which are likely to be counterproductive for realising the main goals of multiculturalism. Four decades back one could have said that these worries emanate from a narrow understanding of secularism, which is only comfortable with a privatised religion. However, this is no longer the case. Even those who accept that religion has a public and collective dimension and that complete separation of state and religion is not possible, are voicing these concerns. Perhaps they are pointing to gaps in multicultural theory that need to be filled in.

In the 1980s and '90s, when multiculturalists pointed to the absence of visible mosques in Berlin, or pleaded for diverse dress codes and dietary requirements to be permitted in institutions and public spaces, they were pointing to sites of minority disadvantage and discrimination that still existed in many liberal democracies. They were not making a case for

prioritising religion or religious practices over all else. Nor were they saying that practices backed by religious commitment must necessarily be
accommodated. When objections were raised against *The Satanic Verses*,
again the plea was to understand the views of the community. Instead
of dismissing the perspective of the devout Muslim, or any other religious believer, to show that a different rationality was at work here. The
willingness to consider a contrary point of view was a precondition for
dialogue and arriving at a negotiated settlement of differences.

Again, on the issue of religious symbols, the multicultural argument
was that we need to be 'evenhanded' (Carens 2000). Since the public
institutions and spaces were dotted with symbols that had a religious
root, or bore an affinity to a specific religious community, one could
now make space for the symbols of other communities. This was a way
of signalling their equality and not a claim for granting a special status
to religion; nor was it asking for the inclusion of religious symbols in the
cultural imagination of the nation. Somewhere this element has been
lost as multiculturalism has been mis-presented as a theory seeking special rights for minorities, including religious minorities.

There is a distinction between accommodating claims to pursue
equal treatment of religions and justifying/affirming religious claims.
Multiculturalism can, and often does, slide from one to the other, and
this has led to considerable confusion. I am among those who maintain that religious beliefs are different insofar as they are linked not
only to a person's sense of identity but also to their conception of what
is right, appropriate or good for them. Hence, certain actions – such as
forcing someone to remove their hijab, turban or yarmulke or some
other mark of their identity – are taken as an assault on one's dignity; a
source of their humiliation by others/outsiders. In recognising this, one
accords a special, or a different, status to religious beliefs. But does this
mean that all religious claims must be placed in a separate basket and
treated differently from other claims made by groups and individuals?
This is an issue which certainly needs more discussion and clarification.
I have argued for sometime now that we need to approach the other
(those with strong religious beliefs) with sensitivity and awareness of
how their selfhood is closely linked with these beliefs; we should therefore ask just what is lost or compromised when a person wishes to
abide by their beliefs.

Living with deep diversity requires inculcating such forms of mutual
understanding and accommodation. As a society we need that ethic,
but accepting the need to understand is not the same as affirming those
beliefs/observances or justifying them. It is not a plea to accept all claims
that come in the name of religion and recognised religious or community

authority. Perhaps, as multiculturalists, we have not stated this categorically. Perhaps there are ambivalences that need still to be addressed.

Over the years the terms of discussion have changed. In Western
Europe it is the minorities who are more observant of their religious practices, and multicultural discourses do make a case for accommodating
these religious-cultural practices. They also reject a rigid form of secularism that opposes the presence of religion in the public domain. Some
even turn to countries like India, where the public domain is marked by
the presence of multiple religions, their symbols and observances. As they
look at other experiences of living with deep diversity and argue that it
is necessary and desirable to accommodate some aspects of religion and
community practices, the question that invariably arises is: how much
space and in which form? This remains an open question – one that
theorists of multiculturalism/multicultural secularism have not attended
to sufficiently.

In most contemporary democracies, even in India (a case that figures
so frequently in these discussions), the presence of religion in the public
domain is accepted but it is subject to state regulation. While religious
initiatives receive state support, the state can, and it does, intervene to
ensure that basic constitutional values and individual rights are upheld.
Perhaps in the debates that occurred in the West, where the challenge
was to move away from a narrow view of secularism, which privatised
religion, to a more inclusive and accommodative form of secularism,
this dimension received relatively less attention. The emphasis placed
on accommodating visible aspects of religion, and making different
communities a partner in policy discussions, has fostered the impression that multiculturalism makes religion and communities active play-
ers in the public domain without subjecting them to other constraints.
In other words, after arguing that religion cannot be, or should not be,
restricted to the private domain, one still needs to address the space
religion can occupy in the public domain, and reflect on the conditions
that should circumscribe that role.

Second, multiculturalism requires a deeper and more intense engagement with the minorities. This may appear puzzling, as multiculturalism
speaks for the minorities. It takes up their perspective and interrogates
the norms that structure the public domain and place minorities at a
disadvantage. When multiculturalism points to the rationality embedded in the choices that minorities make, it tries to translate a minority's
way of life to the majority. It does not engage with the multiplicity of
claims that come from that minority on specific issues.

To take an example: when Tariq Modood discusses the demand for
Muslim minority schools/educational institutions, he examines the

arguments that come from those who oppose this demand (2019). He points to the unfairness involved in allowing and supporting educational institutions of some minorities – Catholics and Jews, for instance – but not those of the Muslim minority. He also addresses liberal objections to minority educational institutions and argues that when they follow the same national curriculum, they should be permitted and given support from the state. That is, there is no good reason to deny the Muslim community, or others, from having separate schools. Here and elsewhere, he points to the reasonableness of the Muslim minority demand, and the unreasonableness of those who oppose it. Needless to say, we do need such interventions but minorities speak in multiple voices. Not all who ask for minority educational institutions accept that these schools should endorse and follow the national curriculum. At least some want the freedom to set their own curriculum, in part if not entirely. Multiculturalism needs to debate these diverse minority positions while exploring what can be reasonably accommodated. At present, it responds (and we see this also in Tariq's work) more systematically to the perspective that comes from the dominant majority, and not the different positions taken by a minority on this subject. One could of course say that Tariq is already positioning himself with a specific minority claim – namely, that minority schools would abide by the accepted national curriculum – but it appears as if this is the only claim that is being made by the minorities. Since there are a range of different positions taken by the minorities, there is a need to argue with other minority perspectives on this and other issues.

A critical engagement with minority perspectives is a necessary condition for a meaningful dialogue between diverse communities – the majority and the minorities – one where both parties are willing to take a critical look at their respective positions, listen to each other and be willing to alter their understanding. In the late 1990s, Bhikhu Parekh posed the question of the 'limits of permissible diversity'. His contention was that no society can be expected to endorse all forms of diversity. One has to build a consensus across various groups – particularly the majority and the minorities – on specific issues. Minorities have to understand the historically constituted identity of the country, and the majority needs to take note of the disadvantages faced by the minorities. Both need to reflect on their perspectives in order to arrive at a consensus. He went on to suggest that 'operative public values' (1994a) enshrined in the constitution could be the basis of drawing the boundaries of what is permissible in a society. One may or may not agree completely with his answer. In fact, I have argued elsewhere that the constitution is a historical document and open to interpretation; it does not always speak in a single, clear voice;

there may also be contradictions between different clauses and values affirmed in the constitution. Nevertheless, the question that he raised is an important one, and it needs our attention more urgently today.

By posing the question of permissible diversity, Bhikhu Parekh recognised that every dialogue involves a two-way process. The majority must reflect on its position, and see if their conclusions are warranted: for instance, if accommodating certain preferences – a dress code, for instance – violated a liberal principle; and, on the other side, the minorities have also to acknowledge that some values are identified with the British way of life, and they cannot be completely ignored. Issuing death threats to back a demand or using coercion to enforce community norms were therefore off the table. The latter were beyond the limits of permissible diversity. Interventions of this kind are needed from multiculturalists. Bhikhu Parekh mediated in the controversies that surrounded the publication of *The Satanic Verses* from this perspective. The negotiations required him to not only translate the concerns of the minority to the majority, but also to question the position taken by sections of the community. The latter is equally essential, and multiculturalists need to continuously ask if a given position of the majority and the minority is reasonable and acceptable.

Third, while attending to the question of inter-group equality, there is an equally pressing need to attend to the concerns of intra-group equality. In the post-9/11 world, the latter has slipped to the back, and been nearly forgotten by the multiculturalists. The discourse on securitisation has set the agenda not only for the state but also for multiculturalism. Today there is a pressing need to ensure that the space for accommodating minority cultures and communities is protected and defended. With the result that attention has shifted away from the needs of vulnerable groups within the community. While struggles on these fronts continue to be fought by individuals and groups, multiculturalism has not surfaced as an immediate ally. Group equality and minority protection appear to have parted company with the battles being fought for intra-group equality.

In the 1980s and '90s, theorists of multiculturalism addressed questions of intra-group equality alongside the preponderant concern for inter-group equality (Eisenberg and Spinner 2005). They explored ways of dealing with and accommodating dissenting voices within the community. Some argued for democratising community institutions and creating space for deliberation by involving different groups within the community; others suggested a structure of multiple jurisdictions (Shachar 2001). But in recent times, this dimension of multiculturalism has been eclipsed by the concern for due recognition and inter-group equality.

Although the question of group equality has gained singular importance as a counter to extreme right-wing rhetoric that drapes the nation-
state in the colours of the majority community, delinking the concerns of
inter-group/community equality from intra-group equality has strength-
ened the appeal of the Right. As they (the right wing) take up the issue of
changing or disallowing what are seen as 'oppressive practices', they gar-
ner the support of vulnerable groups within the community, and simultaneously stigmatise the community as a whole. Taking up some issues
related to intra-group equality, they push for stronger forms of external
intervention, such as laws that prohibit and penalise some community
practices. Multiculturalism would gain lost ground if it spoke for minority communities as well as vulnerable groups within the community.

Lastly, identity-based discourses speak of a group, a collective.
Whether it is feminists or multiculturalists, each refers to a shared identity. Most theorists who write on identity issues clarify that the members
of a group differ in many significant ways. As Tariq explains, members
of the Muslim community are not all the same. They make different life
choices; they differ on matters of belief and practices; they have different
opinions on particular subjects. Yet, as multiculturalists speak almost
always of a community, it is their sameness that is foregrounded. How
should we deal with this homogenising impulse that is built into identity-based discourse? Tariq suggests that we see the community and its
members through the lens of 'family resemblances' (2021) rather than
complete identity. This is a significant intervention but de-essentialising
the discourse on community/minority needs something more. At present it is merely a footnote in the larger narrative of the fate of minorities,
and that is not sufficient.

We have seen that minorities get stigmatised as a collective. When a
crime, particularly a violent crime, is committed by an individual member of the minority community, it is the community as a whole that is
blamed. The individual differences get submerged. How can multiculturalism challenge this major site of misrepresentation and discrimination?
Since it too speaks of the community, the tendency to view the minorities as a collective gets reinforced. How can one check this tendency to
homogenise the community? How can we, as multiculturalists, speak of
sameness and difference simultaneously? How can we weave the idea
of a de-essentialised community within multicultural theory? This is the
methodological challenge that confronts multiculturalists today.

One could add to the list of these unfinished tasks. How should multiculturalism address inter-minority conflicts? While many minorities are
disadvantaged by current laws and policies, they rarely join hands to support the changes sought by a particular minority. All these elements limit

the pursuit of the multicultural agenda, and its capacity to effect significant changes in the public domain. So, there are many more challenges
facing multiculturalism today. But in drawing attention to a few issues
that need further attention of the multiculturalists, my primary purpose
is to stress that a political theory that seeks to intervene in some of the
most contentious and troubling issues of our time has to continuously
rethink and represent its own conceptual framework. It has to confront
difficult questions – perhaps none more difficult than seeing if we need
to make a distinction between minimising sites of discrimination which
may require accommodating diversity, and promoting diversity as an
intrinsic value that we must seek to protect and promote in itself.

Notes

1. While emphasising the value of cultural membership, Will Kymlicka makes a
   case for valuing cultural diversity. If culture provides the condition for a good
   life, then different groups must have an opportunity to secure their own way
   of life. For Kymlicka, liberals – Rawls, Dworkin, Raz – recognise the value
   of cultural membership, except that they treat the political community as a
   homogeneous cultural community. If we begin with the idea that a political
   community is culturally heterogeneous, then we would have to make space for
   cultural diversity. What is perhaps even more important is that the commitment to justice and to 'revisability' of received practices requires the presence
   of others, who are different, who do things differently. If we do not 'decide our
   life-plans *de novo*, but by . . . examining the models and ways of life of those
   who have preceded us' (1991: 164), then it follows that the presence of others
   in our society (those who are different) would similarly enhance the capacity
   to choose by offering concrete alternatives to our way of life. A 'secure cultural
   pluralism' (81) would be an essential condition for developing our capacity
   to choose what we consider to be good and desirable. Charles Taylor rests his
   argument on the presumption of 'equal worth': '. . . the claim is that all human
   cultures that have animated whole societies over some considerable stretch of
   time have something important to say to all human beings' (1994: 66).
2. For Taylor, we could have a religious ground for respecting diverse cultures.
   'Herder, for instance, had a view of divine providence, according to which all
   this variety of culture was not a mere accident but was meant to bring about a
   greater harmony. I can't rule out such a view.' But equally, at the human level,
   '. . . it is reasonable to suppose that cultures that have provided the horizon of
   meaning for large numbers of human beings . . ., over a long period of time . . .
   are almost certain to have something that deserves our admiration and respect'
   (Taylor 1994: 72).
3. The 1980s Labour Force Survey showed that the non-white groups, Pakistanis
   and Bangladeshis, had the highest rates of unemployment, along with low educational qualifications and highest profiles in manual work (Modood 1990).

4. Comparative study remains a central part of Tariq's work. The experiences of other societies, including the non-West, continues to be an important mode of enriching one's understanding. But the diverse ways in which Western Europe has dealt with questions of religion and religious diversity over the decades are also significant for him, and he presents this in his more recent work (Modood and Sealey 2022).

5. They may, and this is something that we have seen happen, themselves don those markers of identity to underscore the solidarity with community members and their predicament.

6. Much of this is, as Uberoi and Modood argue, on account of misrepresentation of what is multiculturalism. The latter has come to be associated with ghettoisation and separatism – something that multiculturalists do not themselves endorse (Uberoi and Modood 2013).

References

Bhargava, R. (2010), 'The Distinctiveness of Indian Secularism', in A. Singh and S. Mohapatra (eds), *Indian Political Thought: A Reader*. New Delhi: Routledge.

Bouchard, G. and C. Taylor (2008), *Reasonable Accommodation of Minorities in Quebec*. Quebec: Government of Quebec.

Brahm Levey, G. (2019), 'The Bristol School of Multiculturalism', *Ethnicities*, 19 (1), 200–26.

Carens, J. H. (1995), 'Citizenship and Aboriginal Self-Government'. Paper prepared as part of the Research Program of the Royal Commission on Aboriginal Peoples, January. Accessed at: <https://publications.gc.ca/collections/collection_2016/bcp-pco/Z1-1991-1-41-106-eng.pdf>

Eisenberg, A. and J. Spinner-Halev (eds) (2005), *Minorities within Minorities: Equality, Rights and Diversity*. Cambridge: Cambridge University Press.

Kymlicka, W. (1989), *Liberalism, Community and Culture*. Oxford: Clarendon Press.

Kymlicka, W. (1995), *Multicultural Citizenship: A Liberal Theory of Minority Rights*. Oxford: Clarendon Press.

Mahajan, G. (2017), 'Living with Religious Diversity: The Limits of the Secular Paradigm', in A. Triandafyllidou and T. Modood (eds), *The Problem of Religious Diversity: European Challenges, Asian Approaches*. Edinburgh: Edinburgh University Press.

Modood, T. (1990), 'Muslims, Race and Equality in Britain: Some Post-Rushdie Affair Reflections', *Third Text*, 4 (11), 127–34.

Modood, T. (2006), 'The Liberal Dilemma: Integration or Vilification?', *International Migration*, 44 (5), 4–7.

Modood, T. (2010), 'From Anti-Racism/Decolonisation to Religion and Secularism'. Accessed at: <https://www.uregina.ca/education/assets/docs/pdf/events/20170310-11-Decolonizing-Teacher-Education-Presentation-Tariq-Modood.pdf>

Modood, T. (2017), 'Multiculturalizing Secularism', in P. Zuckerman and J. R. Shook (eds), *The Oxford Handbook of Secularism*. Oxford: Oxford University Press, 354–68.

Modood, T. (2019), *Essays on Secularism and Multiculturalism*. London: ECPR Press, Rowan & Littlefield International.

Modood, T. (2021), 'Islamophobia and the Struggle for Recognition', *Oxford Law Faculty's Annual Equality and Diversity Lecture*, University of Oxford. Accessed at: <https://www.youtube.com/watch?v=9Mz0mqtQLhw>

Modood, T., R. Berthoud et al. (1997), *Ethnic Minorities in Britain: Diversity and Disadvantage*. London: Policy Studies Institute.

Modood, T. and T. Sealy (2021), 'Freedom of Religion and the Accommodation of Religious Diversity: Multiculturalising Secularism', *Religions*, 12 (10), 868.

Modood, T. and T. Sealy (2022), 'Developing a Framework for a Global Comparative Analysis of the Governance of Religious Diversity', *Religion, State and Society*, 50 (4), 362–77.

Parekh, B. (1994a), 'Cultural Diversity and Liberal Democracy', in D. Beetham (ed.), *Defining and Measuring Democracy*. Thousand Oaks, CA: Sage Publications.

Parekh, B. (1994b), 'Equality, Fairness and Limits of Diversity', *Innovation: The European Journal of Social Science Research*, 7 (3), 289–308.

Shachar, A. (2001), *Multicultural Jurisdictions: Cultural Differences and Women's Rights*. Cambridge: Cambridge University Press.

Taylor, C. (1994), 'The Politics of Recognition', in A. Gutmann (ed.), *Multiculturalism: Examining the Politics of Recognition*. Princeton, NJ: Princeton University Press, 25–74.

Uberoi, V. and T. Modood (2013), 'Has Multiculturalism in Britain Retreated?', *Soundings*, 53, 129–42.

SIX

From the Race Relations Act 1968 to the Great Repeal Act 2018: Back to Square One in 50 Years?

Maleiha Malik

Fifty years separate the Race Relations Act 1968 and the European Union Withdrawal Act 2018 (known as the Great Repeal Act 2018). During this time, race discrimination law developed from a fragmented body of legislation and case law into a sophisticated structure of legislation, case law and policy. The UK Equality Act 2010 was the epitome of 'state of the art' harmonised anti-discrimination law that was the envy of European liberal democracies. Fifty years also captures the time frame within which Tariq Modood's research on racism, migration and multiculturalism made a crucial intellectual contribution to our understanding of how Britain could adapt to complex demographic change and increasing racial, cultural and religious diversity.

These are remarkable achievements in research, law and policy that put the UK in a prime position to adjust to the challenges of twenty-first-century migration and multiculturalism. This chapter explores this fifty-year time frame to understand why, despite fifty years of race relations law and policy, anti-migrant sentiment and racism 'pushed the Brexit vote over the line' to deliver a victory for Vote Leave. If, as I argue, a key driver for Brexit was anxiety about race, migration and a 'pure' vision of what it means to be 'British', then why did the seemingly progressive trajectory of race relation law, equality policy and vision of multiculturalism fail to address the racism that secured Brexit. Why Brexit, despite five decades of sophisticated race discrimination law and policy and multicultural politics?

In this chapter I want to explore the question of what has gone wrong in the last fifty years. I will focus on the early British race relations legislation, which later acted as the precedent for European race discrimination law, and has been heralded by some as the epitome of British tolerance and fair play towards minorities. Last year, 2023, marked wide-ranging national public celebrations of the *Windrush* arrival that took place seventy-five years ago. In this chapter I want to push the analysis back further to the period before the *Windrush* arrival in order to engage with the legacies of the British Empire. I argue that this wider geographical and temporal analysis allows for a deeper understanding of race discrimination law and race relations policy. I treat the arrival of post-1948 Commonwealth migrants in Britain as the starting point for analysis, while at the same time acknowledging the significance of earlier historical periods. By setting 1948 or *Windrush* as the start date for analysis, there is a danger of minimising the significance of the legacy of the British Empire and its impact on the contemporary legal regulation of racism. This, in turn, prevents us from observing the clear patterns of colonial prejudice and racism that cross arbitrary geographical and temporal divides. Understanding the reverberations of the racial hierarchies from Britain's colonial past into the present is crucial not only for minorities, but also for the whole British population, who are enduring the negative political, social and economic consequences of Brexit.

Fifty years after the passing of RRA 1968, the debates that preceded the Great Repeal Bill of 2018 illustrate the tensions that Adrian Favell has mapped out in what he has described as 'Crossing the Race Line' in the Brexit debate. Yet, despite the introduction and enforcement of complex race discrimination legislation and policy in the fifty years that passed between RRA 1968 and the Great Repeal Bill 2018, a racialised discourse still pushed the Leave vote over the majority that it needed to secure Brexit, and thus destabilised decades of British achievements in racial equality and multicultural politics. How do we understand this startling – for some, shocking – success of UKIP and the Leave campaign that was able to benefit from the political mobilisation of racism? One key aspect of a better understanding of this period is to recognise that although the disciplines of law and politics are rooted in the present, the 'past is prologue'.

'What's Past is Prologue': From British Empire to Brexit Britain

Within the popular narrative of race discrimination law, the originating moment is often taken to be the arrival of *Windrush* in 1948, so prominently marked on the 75th anniversary on 22 June 2023 as National Windrush Day, with celebrations in schools, museums and public institutions. The '*Windrush* tale' has been promoted vividly through the dramatic visual image of a ship arriving on British shores full of Black migrants, and subsequently those from less prosperous countries, who were all seeking economic advancement and a better way of life in Britain.

Yet any celebrations should heed the warnings of scholars such as Stuart Hall and Barnor Hesse that this comforting instrumentalising of *Windrush* distracts us from the challenge of a deeper understanding of the historical, social, political and economic role of empire that led to these citizens arriving on the shores of Britain. This deeper analysis of the *'Windrush* moment' is crucial to understanding the creation of racial hierarchies that were carried over from empire into Britain in the 1950s: the creation of racialised hierarchies whereby white Britons came to perceive themselves as more civilised and 'born to rule' (Colley 1992: 324); imperial roots of the racism that leads to the exclusion of some British citizens from social, political and economic goods; and the exclusion of non-white Britons from full citizenship.

At its zenith in 1922, the British Empire ruled over a vast geographical area and racial, religious and culturally diverse populations of nearly 458 million people, which had enormous consequences for the British people in its metropole. Professor Katherine Wilson, cited by Linda Colley in her analysis of 'Britishness and Otherness', suggests that Britons responded to this vast empire not only at the level of politics and trade, but also in popular awareness:

> Possession of such a vast and obviously alien empire encouraged the British to see themselves as a distinct, special and often superior people. They could contrast their law, their standard of living, their treatment of women, their political stability, and above all, their collective power against societies that they only imperfectly understood but usually perceived as far less developed. Whatever their own individual ethnic backgrounds, Britons could join together vis-à-vis the empire and act out the flattering parts of historic conqueror, humane judge, and civilizing agent.

These assumptions that the British Empire was a 'civilising mission for the good of its subjects', with its 'imperial nationalism' and racial hierarchies that powered the distinct form of British colonial governance, all had dramatic implications for politics, economics and society in contemporary Britain. One of the saddest ironies of Brexit is that the pressing need to link the British present to its colonial past was distorted in precisely the opposite direction from what was needed to allow contemporary Britain to adjust to reality. Instead of a sober, realistic reckoning with the past as the basis for making sense of Britain's present challenges, Brexiteers glorified the British Empire as a precedent for how post-Brexit Britain could stand alone as a global superpower and reclaim its former glory at the head of a contemporary Anglosphere empire (Campanella 2019).

We must keep in mind a wider geography as part of our analysis of UK race relations law and policy, to make clear the connections between the governance of migrants within UK borders and jurisdiction and previous British colonial governance. After all, at the height of the British Empire just after the First World War, it controlled roughly a quarter of the world's population and land mass. The Commonwealth migrants who entered the UK in the 1950s and 1960s had been colonial subjects of this empire only a few decades before they arrived as migrant workers. An important part of understanding race discrimination law and policy, therefore, is to connect the presence of racial and cultural migrants as 'minorities over here in the metropole' to crucial continuities with the period when the British Empire treated them as subjects 'over there', where they were majorities subject to British colonial governance (Gilroy 1990).

After the Second World War, the transition from British Empire to New Commonwealth provides a crucial backdrop for understanding many of the key foundational concepts and contexts for the subsequent decades of UK race relations law and policy, including the fifty-year journey from RRA 1968 to Brexit. The geography of the British Empire may have shrunk, but this did not mean that the foundational premise of British colonial rule could be so easily or quickly 'de-colonised'. British colonial subjects had never been represented within British political and administrative systems in London: no matter how civilised, educated or 'liberal' these subjects may have become under British colonial rule, it was unthinkable that they would have any direct representation in London. The belief that white Britons were more superior and civilised than their 'coloured' colonial subjects and that Britain was 'a white country' continued beyond the transition of the British Empire into the New Commonwealth.

Britain's imperial legacy and the fictions that had underpinned it meant that the British Empire was a single legal entity exercising colonial governance over vast populations, and therefore large numbers of those very colonial subjects had the right to move to the UK. But when Black and Asian British subjects exercised their right to live in the UK, those beliefs that Britain was a 'white country' resulted in their being excluded through a pattern of violence, abuse and discrimination.

This was not the first time that concern about 'foreigners' and a distinct racial and religious minority entering UK borders had led to immigration controls. At the beginning of the century, the UK Aliens Act 1905 was introduced in response to Russian and Polish Jews who arrived in the East End of London fleeing persecution. Linking racism faced by these groups in its wider historical context and relating it to the wider geography of the British Empire is important because all these historical racialised groups – Jews, Roma, Irish as well as non-white British subjects of the British Empire who arrived as Commonwealth immigrants – were included within one category of 'race' as a protected group in UK anti-discrimination law. It is crucial to note this early response to Jewish immigration, because the cultural racism that focused on their religious difference prefigured later instances of cultural racism and discrimination against Muslims, who were often excluded from the protection of anti-discrimination law. Tariq Modood's significant scholarship demonstrated the specific form of racism against British Muslims at a time when it was argued that they should remain outside the protection of race relations legislation and policy. Tariq Modood's scholarship on Muslims and cultural racism established a fundamental conceptual framework that anti-Muslim racism (or Islamophobia) was rooted in attributing to Muslims cultural or religious characteristics to vilify, marginalise, discriminate or demand their assimilation, thereby treating them unfairly and as second-class citizens (Modood 2018: 2). This crucial scholarship has transformed our thinking about racism and the accommodation of Muslims as a minority in liberal democracies: in the field of sociology (Modood 2020), and a range of other academic disciplines such as politics (Modood 1998) and theory (Modood 2013), as well as having an impact on concrete social policy through initiatives such as his contribution to the Commission on the Future of Multi-ethnic Britain (2000).

Both state and popular responses to postwar migration are complex. Polling data from this period confirms that there was consistent public opposition to non-white migration (Hansen 2000: 4–5). At the same time, the state response to non-white migration was more complex than a simple rejection and racialisation. As Randall Hansen has argued, the state's free entry policy for nearly a decade before restrictions were introduced cannot be understood as a simple process of racialisation. It was a complex set of factors: most notably a desire to maintain historic relationships with the old Dominions of Australia, New Zealand and Canada, which ensured a definition of British citizenship that included former imperial subjects and a resistance to immigration controls (Hansen 2000: 16–18). By the 1960s, when the first race relations legislation was introduced, this laissez-faire approach had shifted to restriction through immigration law and policies. Hansen concludes that British immigration policies have succeeded in reducing the numbers of immigrants arriving in the UK and keeping migration to lower levels than other European countries, despite claims by successive politicians and most recently Brexiteers that Britain has 'lost control of its borders' (Hansen 2000: 21–2).

Regulating Racism

After the Second World War, as the British Empire shrank and transitioned into the British Commonwealth, immigration controls were passed to limit the numbers of Black and Asian migrants entering the UK who were exercising their right to citizenship by moving from the peripheries of the British Empire to live in the 'metropole'. There was public debate about the status and treatment of the new Britons and race relations law. This was a national moment at which there could have been a deeper conversation enabling Britain to come to terms with its colonial past. Yet instead of treating this transition as a moment of open debate, there was instead a 'foreclosure' within theory, politics and society, representing a tragic missed opportunity.

At the level of liberal theory, as Barnor Hesse notes in his critique of traditional liberal political theory, there was a 'colonial racial foreclosure' as exemplified by Mill's defence of the colonies and most recently Isaiah Berlin's *Two Concepts of Liberty* published in 1958; this was a statement of the liberty/freedom issue which failed to address the complicity of liberal political thought in Western colonialism and racial governance (Hesse 2014: 288), although Berlin did address the challenge of representation and freedom for formerly colonised peoples in his brief lecture on Tagore and nationalism (Baum and Nichols 2012).

Outside Britain, ideas of racial and civilisational superiority provided the justification for projects that exported liberalism and democracy to the former colonies, based on the belief that 'the only right ordering of all humanity globally is the gradual establishment of European style, ideal republican or constitutional states that legally recognize individuals as negatively free, formally equal and substantively unequal, and dependent on a single system of laws and representative government' (Tully 2008: 144). This foreclosure had a profound hold on political theory and practice, despite the dramatic social change that was taking place as a result of Commonwealth immigration. Decades later, multiculturalism as a theory and policy broke through this denial, developing a sophisticated analysis of how liberal societies could respond to the social fact of diversity.

In the 1950s, as British influence in the world waned, there was another missed opportunity for an honest confrontation of the British nation and state's continuing deep connection to empire, which needed to be discussed and reconfigured in the new situation of imperial decline. This could have been a moment to challenge and define what it meant to be 'British' without a British Empire, particularly if, as David Marquand has argued, Whig imperialism was central to British national identity (Marquand 1995). Yet instead of defining a different image of modern Britain, the period that preceded the introduction of the first Race Relations statutes (1958 and 1965) continued to be dominated by public assumptions of British exceptionalism and ethnically charged nationalism, which emerged as the basis for national identity just as non-white immigration from the former colonies was increasing.

Writing about this period of British history, Chris Waters has argued that the period between 1947 and 1963 saw a fragmentation of the previous British national unity that had been sustained during the national struggle against a common enemy (fascist Germany). Waters argues that the end of the Second World War led to an erosion of stable national identity and a crisis of national self-representation that was compounded by the rapid emergence of the United States (rather than the United Kingdom) as the military, political and economic hegemonic global power. Instead of an open debate that addressed the imperial decline of the UK, there were attempts to recreate this role through the Commonwealth. At this time of imperial decline, Waters argues, questions of race became central to questions of national belonging. He concludes:

> Especially in the 1950s, discussions about the rapid increase of 'new Commonwealth' migration to Britain could not wholly be separated from discussions of what it now meant to be British. In that decade, the characteristics of Black migrants in Britain were mapped against those of white natives, serving to shore up definitions of essential Britishness. (Waters 1997: 208)

As Harry Goulbourne has argued (Goulbourne 1991), the 'most powerful and influential attempts to redefine the post-imperial British national community have depended on a conception of the nation which excludes non-white minorities who have settled on these shores since the Second World War'. This definition of the post-imperial British nation provided a context for the racism faced by newly arrived non-white migrants in the UK; and, moreover, for the Race Relations Act 1965 (RRA 1965), which was a direct response to the Notting Hill riots and increased migration. All these developments need to be understood in a longer historical, geographical and temporal context.

So, concerns about non-white migration into the UK provided the key backdrop for the introduction of the RRA 1965; this was the first specific UK legislation to prohibit racial discrimination, on the grounds that it was becoming a social problem that justified legal regulation. The Act determined the use of criminal law against those who discriminated against racial minorities. The key social problem that RRA 1965 identified was public disorder; its focus, therefore, was to regulate racism in public places by making 'incitement to hatred on the grounds of colour, race, or ethnic or national origins' an official offence. The immediate context for RRA 1965 was the UK Nationality Act 1948, which allowed entry into Britain by Commonwealth citizens. In 1958 there were race riots in Notting Hill, when white gangs, encouraged by fascist troublemakers and far-right organised political parties, went on the rampage in areas where Commonwealth citizens had settled.

The central misdemeanour that RRA 1965 addressed was the outward manifestations rather than the root causes of the Notting Hill riots. In relation to RRA 1965, the Labour Home Secretary Sir Frank Soskice, who led the legislation, stated, 'Basically, this Bill is concerned with public order' (House of Commons 1965). Yet the term 'public order' is not a sufficient explanation of the Notting Hill riots or the complex dynamic of racism that was a response to non-white migration in the 1950s. In 1958, the Notting Hill riots were frequently framed as either hooliganism and individualised acts of violence or a response of white working-class communities who were competing with newly arrived non-white migrants for scarce jobs and public services such as housing. Yet blaming the riots on young white men, violent Black communities and dysfunctional working-class communities fails to address the structural causes for these public acts of violence or the possibility that the centuries-old racial hierarchies of the past that had underpinned the British Empire continued to have material impact in the present.

Recent research on the Notting Hill riots challenges this explication. Christopher Hillyard's research is an analysis of arrest data that maps where the violence took place; comparing those facts with where the rioters lived confirms that few of the white people involved in the riots lived alongside Black people or competed with them for housing (Hillyard 2022). As Hillyard concludes, this way of charting the Notting Hill riots suggests that the race riots were more complex than individualised disorder:

> In any case, historians have long been warned against assuming that popular protest can be read off material conditions without culture getting in the way. Rather than a 'spasmodic' response to economic conditions, collective violence is often an attempt to reassert a conception of the proper order of things. (Hillyard 2022: 11)

In the case of the Notting Hill riots, the 'proper order of things' had been disrupted by the presence of Black and Asian migrants and social change. Although officials and the police had tried to play down the role of racism as a trigger for the violence, internal police files that have recently been released confirm that the Notting Hill riots were predominantly led by 300–400-strong 'Keep Britain White' mobs who deliberately went 'nigger-hunting' among West Indian residents of Notting Hill (Travis 2022).

The strategy of denying racism and treating resistance to organised political racism as natives running 'amok', 'riots', public disorder and common affray was a common strategy in response to political resistance to colonial governance and racism (Jenkinson 2009; Van Rossum 2013). RRA 1965 treated racism as a problem of public order rather than addressing the deeper root causes of the racial hierarchies that defined the order of things as 'white' Britons being inherently superior free citizens who were justified in exercising power over less civilised non-white subjects. The presence of Black and Asian individuals in the metropole who claimed rights as equal citizens was a shock to this world view of what it meant to be British.

This could have been a moment for a national debate: to look back at the decades since the arrival of former colonial subjects, to understand why they had left their homes to come to Britain. There was an opportunity for understanding why migrants self-identified with the category 'British', their understanding of themselves as subjects of the British Empire, and their enthusiasm for migration to Britain as a basis for a modern conception of what it means to be British. This conception of being British could have integrated the perspective of citizens' own emotions, identification and grassroots practices of daily living side by side with white Britons. Instead, a focus on immigration control and legislation made Britishness ever more narrowly defined as a juridical category through the prism of immigration law and concerns about public order and race relations (Perry 2018).

The focus on connecting race to public disorder was within the comfort zone of the public officials who drafted RRA 1965; they were actually drawing on the anti-sedition laws used to suppress resistance to colonial rule in British India. The conceptual legal structure of early race relations legislation transplanted definitions of racial incitement that were themselves borrowed from colonial legal regulation in British India; these had prohibited incitement to racial and religious hatred and criminalised the political speech of Indians who challenged colonial rule (Malik 2011).

What developed now was a tense and increasingly contradictory lock-step in legislation: on the one hand attempts at public order to quell the riots, and the passing of race relations legislation in 1962 and 1968 to protect those racial minorities who were already in Britain; on the other, attempts to limit immigration in the face of public discourse that the increasing presence of non-white Britons was changing the 'face of Britain' or 'British culture'. These two strands of legislation – race discrimination law and immigration law – were and remain intimately and paradoxically connected.

As Colin Yeo has noted (Yeo 2020a), UK immigration law evolved from the British Nationality Act of 1948 that created early subdivisions of UK citizenship, through to the Commonwealth and Immigrants Act of 1962 that abolished the right of British subjects whose British passports had formerly been issued by colonial authorities to arrive at UK borders and live in the UK. A parallel skilled-workers scheme at the time was, as Yeo notes, designed to allow 'white' Commonwealth subjects from Australia, Canada and New Zealand to enter, live and work in the UK.

Throughout the 1950s, the Labour Party position had been to oppose immigration controls: their reasoning was, inter alia, the need for migrant labour because of economic demand; and a commitment to the Commonwealth as a sphere for international influence and community (Miles and Phizacklea 1984: 35–45). Although in the general election of 1964 Wilson's Labour government won a slim overall majority, the Smethwick West Midlands constituency, which should have been a safe Labour seat and where there was a significant Sikh immigrant minority, was won by Peter Griffiths, who had run an anti-immigrant campaign that had gained national media coverage.

There had been Private Members' Bills to prohibit race discrimination throughout the late 1950s and 1960s, and they were gaining increasing support among some MPs, especially Labour MPs, and civil society. Harold Wilson was committed to introducing race relations legislation to defend what he stated was the country's international image as a tolerant, multiracial society that respected equality in the rule of law. But at the same time, the political lesson from the Smethwick by-election was that Commonwealth immigration could be a liability among voters who viewed Britain as an island nation that needed to be defended against a siege of newly arrived non-white migrants. The lesson that the Labour leadership learnt from the Smethwick seat – that was to be later echoed by New Labour and then by many in the Labour Party before and after Brexit – was summed up in a statement by Labour Minister Richard Crossman (Crossman 1975: 160–75): 'since the Smethwick election it has been quite clear that immigration can be the greatest potential voteloser for the Labour Party'.

Wilson's Labour government pursued a dual strategy: on the one hand, his immigration policy specifically targeted non-white migration through immigration controls; at the same time, there was a focus on addressing the social 'problem' of non-white immigrants through race relations legislation (Perry 2018: 190–202). This dual strategy ensured that immigration control to exclude non-white migrants was a constant shadow in public debates about race relations.

The Race Relations Act 1968 was introduced by a Labour government alongside the Commonwealth Immigrants Act 1968 that prohibited Kenyans holding British passports from coming to the UK. Commenting on these early immigration controls, Colin Yeo concludes:

> And this is why British immigration law and debate about immigration was and continues to be tainted by racism. Immigration laws did not divide the world into *citizens* who had a right to live in the country and *non-citizens* who did not. Instead, citizenship was massively and widely defined and then immigration laws were introduced to limit which citizens were to be allowed into the United Kingdom. These laws were devised specifically in order to prevent Black and Asian citizens from doing so. (Yeo 2020b)

RRA 1965 did contain legal innovations, with the potential to address racial discrimination and the disadvantages facing Black and Asian Britons. There was potential within RRA 1965 to address racism as a structural problem: a group of Labour lawyers lobbied for a US model to address private discrimination in housing and employment and the introduction of an innovative administrative body (the Race Relations Board) with some investigative and enforcement powers (Lester and Bindman 1972). That potential depended on a number of key factors, including, inter alia: securing the confidence of minorities to take complaints to the body and abide by its decisions; support by trade unions and business interests to integrate minorities into the labour market on fair and equal conditions; and, crucially, political and financial support by successive governments (Hepple 1969: 256–7).

In the years that followed, these factors for success were never put in place to allow this remedial mechanism to succeed. Trade unions excluded and discriminated against Black workers, as exemplified most dramatically by the refusal of the TGWU to support Asian women workers during the Imperial Typewriters strike in Leicester (Virdee 2000). Governments failed to provide the support that the Race Boards and their successor, the Commission for Racial Equality, needed to fulfil their function, as testified by Peter Newsam, Chairman of the Commission for Racial Equality, in 1982 (Newsam 1987; Solomos 2022). During the three years between the RRAs of 1965 and 1968, immigration control, race riots and public violence remained the crucial backdrop to the early

UK race discrimination legislation and the prism through which Black and Asian migrants were made visible in the public sphere.

RRA 1965 did nothing to prevent or provide a remedy for the racism in the public and private sphere that generated the 'colour bar' against Black and Asian migrants in fields such as housing, employment and education. As Sheila Patterson recorded in 1969 (Patterson 1969: 96–7), of the 309 complaints received between the implementing of RRA 1965 and 31 March 1967, the overwhelming majority related to employment, housing or financial services (only 85 out of the 309 complaints fell within the scope of RRA 1965).

This lacuna in RRA 1965 in turn entrenched systemic discrimination and disadvantage for newly arrived Commonwealth immigrants in key spheres such as employment, housing and public services (PEP 1967; Daniel 1968). Subsequent race relations legislation in 1968 did remedy the lacuna by extending the scope of unlawful race discrimination to housing, employment and some key public services, which became the basis for modern UK discrimination law in RRA 1976 and the Equality Act 2010. Yet this legislative framework treated discrimination as a problem of individual acts, rather than a systemic problem that was related to the historical and economic legacy of British colonialism.

While the underlying aims of immigration law were to limit non-white immigration, RRA 1968 and subsequent race relations legislation were premised on the principle that those New Commonwealth citizens who had the right to enter the UK were British citizens with the right to equal treatment. Once again, public debates that preceded RRA 1968 missed the opportunity of honestly addressing and untangling definitions of Britishness from their imperial legacy. This longer history and framing of racism as a problem of public order and immigration policy, that was predicated on a definition of British citizenship as white, exacerbated rather than addressed the structural problem of racial hierarchies that had their origins in the British Empire and impacted on all aspects of British institutions and British identity.

Political and public debates continued to treat racism as a problem of individual acts that went against the grain of the superior civilised British values of tolerance and fair play. The Smethwick election, Powellism and violent racism led to the development of a paradigm that treated racism as a social, political and electoral challenge coming from within white working-class communities. The central image of RRA 1965 was of white working-class communities confronting angry Black men; and this focus on legislation to deal with incitement to racial hatred sent the signal that racism was a problem of speech that was leading otherwise good British people astray. This suggested an assumption that racism was a problem that could be rooted out and overcome, 'stamped out' through the assertion of a general political will that would regulate individual conduct. By focusing on racism as a problem of individuals rather than a historical and structural legacy linked to the British Empire, RRA 1968 and subsequent race discrimination law were never able to address the structural causes of discrimination and disadvantage faced by minorities who had been workers in the periphery colonies of the British Empire, and had subsequently become racialised migrant workers in the metropole.

Diamond Ashiagbor's work sets out a research agenda for this analysis (Ashiagbor 2021: 521) by pointing out the process through which migrant workers continue to be exploited when they move from the periphery of what was the British Empire to the core metropolis: through coercive immigration law that structures the terms of entry of migrants into the labour market; the segmentation of host labour markets between migrant and non-migrant sectors; and exclusion from collective bargaining processes that leaves migrants vulnerable to exploitation in precarious forms of employment.

The individual employment contract that was the focus for RRA 1968 and subsequent race discrimination law assumed an atomised bilateral relationship and bargaining power between the employer and employee. Direct race discrimination, and later indirect race discrimination, was prohibited in access to employment, housing, education and some private services. Yet in the key area of access to labour markets, which is a precondition for migrants' life chances, the narrow strictures of the law ignored the wider structural context that framed this relationship, which was in turn rooted in legacies of colonialism that structured patterns of global migration as well as labour markets.

Moreover, as Ashiagbor argues, this standard form of employment contract does not fit well with the labour market experiences of migrant workers, who are often clustered in precarious and informal forms of work that fall outside the scope of employment protection law. Race relations legislation seeks to remedy these exclusions, but it does nothing to address the structural causes of labour market disadvantage faced by non-white minorities. Moreover, political and economic developments subsequent to RRA 1968, that is, the Race Relations Act 1976, made the situation worse. The White Paper that preceded RRA 1976 had always envisaged that the legal regulation of race discrimination would be accompanied by supply-side measures to ensure equal treatment in employment, education and housing. However, immediately after the introduction of the new race discrimination law, an economic recession and a turn to neoliberal economic policies cut the budget for these measures, as well as for the Race Relations Board and later the Commission for Racial Equality.

The Thatcher years led to the marketisation of the public sector, and a greater use of non-standard forms of contract had a disproportionate effect on racialised minorities: with a greater concentration in zero-hours contracts; agency work; and into insecure forms of employment (Ashiagbor 2021: 529, n. 34; Modood et al. 1997). Research by Yaojun Li and Anthony Heath confirms that ethnic minority groups (particularly Black African, Black Caribbean, Pakistani and Bangladeshi) continue to face an ethnic penalty and are more likely to face unemployment and greater barriers to re-employment (Li and Heath 2020).

While the focus on labour markets and employment is understandable, race relations legislation also seriously overestimated the extent to which labour market disadvantage was the only source of discrimination and disadvantage, or the main source of concern for minorities themselves. As Tariq Modood's work demonstrated, culture and religion were also significant, and increasingly prominent, factors in discrimination and disadvantage. This was especially true for British Muslims, who self-identified as Muslims, and who were subject to increasing securitisation after the 9/11 and 7/7 suicide bombings in the US and UK respectively. Definitions of racism and anti-discrimination law from the 1950s and 1960s that focused on colour and ethnicity were insufficient to capture the claims of British Muslims, particularly after the Salman Rushdie affair and the increasing securitisation of British Muslim communities between 2001 and 2015 (Modood 2004).

Moreover, in relation to British Muslims, the Salman Rushdie affair and the protests over the Danish cartoons, as well as the condemnation of Muslim veils as a barbaric misogynist practice, had set up a stark dichotomy between being Muslim and being British. Liberals, who should have been allies for a minority group such as British Muslims and especially British Muslim women, invoked freedom of speech or gender equality as necessary conditions for 'being British'. A closer examination of these 'British' values (Mamdani 2008; Ridley 2021) would have revealed a more complex reality. Certainly, the racialisation of Islam and British Muslims played an important role in the political mobilisation of racism to 'get Brexit done', as Favell argues in his analysis of how subliminal representations of Muslims assisted the UKIP case for taking back control of British borders (Favell 2020). The racialisation of Muslims during this time followed a similar process to other Western European states and has deep historical roots (Daniels 2009; Malik 2010), even as there were differences in the form of racism in the specific social, political and economic context of different European member states. For example, while veiling was criminalised in some European countries such as France and Germany, it was mainly permitted in the private and public spheres in the UK (Brems 2014). In the UK, however, the specific anxiety was with ideas of migration and Britishness that were the political context of the rise of UKIP as a political force in mainstream UK politics. Anti-European politics in the governing Conservative Party coincided with popular sentiments of hostility to refugees and migrants stemming from nativism, racism and anti-Muslim prejudice to produce a narrow majority for the Brexit vote.

Brexit and Back to Square One?

Despite the evident disadvantages suffered by Black workers, debates from the 1950s all the way to Brexit usually prioritised the 'white working class', who were said to have been marginalised by increasing migration and diversity. As with the lesson of the Smethwick by-election, racism is consistently understood within the paradigm of placating the white working class, rather than a structural challenge for the whole population on how to adjust their national identity after the end of the British Empire. Nevertheless, as noted by Satnam Virdee, what distinguished the key period of the 1950s and 1960s with the emergence of the welfare state settlement, 'was the extent to which the state, employer and worker came to adhere to a common belief in British nationalism underpinned by a shared allegiance to whiteness' (Virdee 2014, in Ashiagbor 2021: 523). While these earlier forms of racism focused on ideas that British- ness was synonymous with an allegiance to 'whiteness', later forms of racism took specific forms that focused on civilisation, culture and reli- gion in relation to British Muslims (Modood 2014) as well as refugees, migrants and Eastern European workers (Rzepnikowska 2019).

There were also, before Brexit in 2018, positive moments of solidar- ity and inclusiveness that co-existed with social processes that excluded non-white Britons: for example, multiethnic and multicultural national celebrations such as the opening celebration of the Olympics in 2012 are significant national moments that complicate any attempt to draw a straight line between the 1950s and Brexit (Uberoi and Modood 2013). More recently, the multiculturalist approach to the Coronation of King Charles III continues this vein of optimism of an inclusive, diverse pol- ity that can find a place for diverse minorities (Uberoi 2023).

This argument of prioritising the white working class reverberated decades later during Brexit, when not only UKIP but also respectable political commentators justified racism as the understandable response of white working-class communities to migration. Commentators such as David Goodhart criticised liberal elites defending open borders and multiculturalism (Goodhart 2013), arguing that they would erode the solidarity necessary for a welfare state, without scrutinising the racial origins of these constructed solidarities. While seeking to identify and 'represent' white working-class communities, these commentators sought to be well-intentioned 'friends' in the fight against racism. This representation relies heavily on essentialist methods, through which the white working class are represented as a homogeneous block who oppose migrants without any critical deconstruction or understanding of the structural root causes for the disadvantage of white working-class communities (Portes 2013). Nor is there an engagement to examine and unearth the complex relationship of working-class communities with the category British, based on a tradition of cooperation and solidarity across racial and ethnic boundaries (for example, in relation to diverse categories such as Irish, Scottish, Catholic) (Virdee 2014). John Holmwood has accurately summarised the error of this essentialist method in analysing race and working-class solidarity in his observation, 'The point is not that immigration has now begun to undermine solidarities, but that solidarities were formed on a racialized politics of colonial encounters' (Holmwood 2016, in Ashiagbor 2021: 525).

The popular narrative linking immigration, race and the welfare state, especially around Brexit, also ignored the fact that racial minorities were disproportionately poor, and concentrated in low-paid, precarious work. In fact, as Robert Shilliam has demonstrated, Brexit was never about defending the interests of the poor. Rather, underlying Brexit was a key ideological construction (Shilliam 2018) that distinguished between the 'deserving poor' (associated with hard-working white Britons) who were pitted in competition against the 'undeserving poor' (non-white migrants who had recently arrived to take advantage of Britain's generous welfare state).

Looking forward, it is instructive to note the response of the Brexiteers to the rise in lawful migration in May 2023. The Brexiteers and their intellectual enablers remain dissatisfied that lawful migration to the UK remains high, even after they had supposedly gained control of migration from the EU and introduced domestic policies that delivered high-skilled immigration. Could it be that the issue was never about unlawful or low-skilled migration, but rather an objection to any and all migration and – crucially – a visceral aversion to migrants? Aditiya Chakrabortty summarised this reality in punchy terms (Chakrabortty 2023): 'First, it was no to Polish plumbers, then Afghan refugees. Now the right doesn't want any migrants at all: [. . .] the furore over entirely legal migration proves it was never the kind of foreigner you were, simply your foreignness.'

Brexiteers who called for a points-based system to deliver high-skilled migration remain dissatisfied – or as Chakrabortty puts it, 'men who got everything they wanted now have a case of buyers' remorse'. This response to lawful high-skilled immigration should not be understood as an unfortunate 'paradox' or a contradiction. Instead, this Brexiteers' 'buyers' remorse' when they got what they wanted demonstrates the fundamental fallacies of Brexit. It was always, and still remains, false to assume that the job of 'getting Brexit done' can provide closure on the central global dilemma of how a complex services economy such as the UK's can manage its demand for labour migration, which in turn ensures that racial, religious and cultural diversity are, and indeed always have been, permanent facts about British society. In fact, as Adrian Favell argues:

One of the ironies of the virulent anti-'immigration' politics that, as I will argue, drove the Leave vote to victory, is that its triumph will very likely land Britain with far higher levels of unregulated 'neo-liberal' immigration than was ever likely under the hated obligations of EU freedom of movement. (Favell 2020)

These contradictory responses and the incoherence of the arguments used to justify Brexit should encourage us to ask a more fundamental question: was Brexit fundamentally about migration, or were there other forces driving the politics of Brexit? It is important to scrutinise the Brexiteers' own arguments about whether their concern was over illegal migration or indeed any type of migration. But to accept that Brexit was largely about migration is to miss important continuities between the Brexiteers' vision of Britishness, their visceral response to non-white migration – whether illegal or legal – and the fact that the same politicians who led the Brexit debate had also never really accepted that established racial or religious minorities (BAME) communities were 'really British'. Once this crucial connection is documented and scrutinised, it becomes easier to understand that the Brexit debate inevitably crossed what Adrian Favell has called the 'race bar'. As Favell and the recent 'Brexit regret' over lawful migration that was introduced by Brexiteers themselves suggest, the anxieties that powered the Brexit vote were not only about EU Eastern European migration or Syrian refugees who might get to France and then cross the Channel to the UK; Brexit was also about a racialised vision of what it means to be British in terms of racial hierarchies. As Favell notes, one of the most pernicious aspects of the politics of Brexit is that it has unsettled what many BAME communities assumed were settled issues of belonging; for post-Brexit they too have been rendered foreigners and migrants in the country in which they were born and where they have lived for generations.

Brexit illustrated that EU nationals who had entered the UK as part of their right to free movement within the EU were racialised as non-British 'foreigners', just as previously after the Second World War, British subjects of the British Empire had become 'foreigners' when they had exercised their right to enter Britain. The mobility of refugees and migrants from the Global South to Europe and then to the UK were represented not only in the far right or UKIP fringes but in the Leave campaign and in almost all sections of the media and mainstream political debates as an invasion of the British body politic. These images and language drew on and reinforced 'the racialized mix of knowledge and historical amnesia that reproduce age old hierarchies of the colonial systems' (Polowska-Kimunguyi 2022). Within this UKIP and Leave political discourse, an ideal vision of Britain being a 'white' and 'bordered' nation echoed the debates about immigration after the Second World War: about who constituted the 'true' British population.

More than this, as Favell notes, Brexit had consequences beyond newly arrived EU citizens and for all non-white Britons who had previously been included within the categories BAME, Black British and Asian British. The political discourse on refugees and migration that played a crucial role in the Brexit vote also reopened what were assumed to be settled public debates about the role of race relations and anti-discrimination law: this vision had been assumed to be that BAME communities should be integrated and accommodated through law and policies. As Favell notes:

> The return of Powellite 'immigration' discourse, in the era of UKIP, Farage and Leave, to classify and distinguish 'foreigners' indexed by colour or nationality, that means they can never really be indigenous or 'true' or original British (code for 'white English'), is thus one of the most egregious and disturbing (aspects) of the Brexit era. (Favell 2020)

Five decades have passed between the early Race Relations Acts and this Powellite immigration and race discourse, but we are not back to where we started in the 1960s, when the first race relations legislation was introduced. Unlike then, Tariq Modood and other theorists have provided theoretical and practical frameworks for multiculturalism that resist the earlier foreclosure of concepts of liberty and equality that excluded minorities, and therefore continue to have relevance to key questions for our societies. The UK also has the Equality Act 2010, which remains untouched despite the Brexiteers' rhetoric and resistance about 'woke' liberals. Attempts to roll back progress, such as the widely criticised Sewell Report, were sidelined by a government committed to Brexit, rather than enthusiastically implemented (Syal 2022).

The Great Repeal Bill 2018 formally ends the supremacy of EU law: and from the date of its enactment, UK courts are not required to consider the jurisprudence of the Court of Justice of the European Union (CJEU) – a binding precedent, although the two bodies of jurisprudence can continue to be in dialogue with that body of case law by having regard to CJEU judgements. Yet this does not necessarily mean a regression for the protection offered by UK discrimination law. At an ESCRC-funded Chatham House rules seminar on 28 September 2017 at the British Academy, an expert group considered the impact of Brexit on equality law. Noting the resistance to the label 'European', the conclusion of the round table was to frame the discussion around values such as equality, rather than European origins. The expert round-table report concludes:

> The feeling around that table was that the future flexible relationship between the CJEU and the UK courts could have benefits for the development of equality law in the UK. One view was that Brexit is a chance to leave behind CJEU jurisprudence that curtails the growth of equality, particularly in the area of affirmative action, and that there may be future areas of equality law where the UK can surpass the CJEU. (Oxford Human Rights Hub 2017)

At the same time, one lesson from fifty years of regulating racism in the UK and USA is that law in the form of judicial action is a necessary but not sufficient means for addressing structural racism. One lesson looking back at the impact of the 1968 and 1976 RR Acts is that judicial action needs to be accompanied by a legislative will to achieve viable social change (Malik 2007; Rosenberg 2008).

Moreover, to be effective and sustainable, it is essential that progressive legal forms are rooted in social practices and attitudes, rather than grafted on to the daily lives of individuals and communities (Malik 2000). To that end, while theoretical concepts, public ideas and political leadership are essential to support the goals of race discrimination law, it is also crucial that law is supported by local action and social movements with deep roots in communities.

There is no doubt that Brexit was a victory for those who find comfort in a national vision that Britain's Empire was a 'civilising mission', justified by the superior British values of the rule of law, tolerance and freedom of speech. As Caroline Elkins has demonstrated, this vision underlies the image that powered the Brexiteers' vision of the 'Great' in Britain. Elkins notes that memories of the British Empire played a significant role in the Brexit campaign, citing for example (Elkins 2022) Boris Johnson's evocation of Churchill and empire when he stated: 'Churchill was right when he said that the empires of the future will be empires of the mind and in expressing our values I believe that Global Britain is a soft power superpower and that we can be immensely proud of what we are achieving.'

At the same time, despite the narrow victory for Brexiteers, there remains substantial resistance to this false narrative and an alternative vision. Churchill may be cited by Brexiteers to justify their imperial fantasies, but there are many others who challenge this view. In 2020, after the murder of George Floyd in the US and the emergence of the Black Lives Matter movement, protesters marched to Parliament Square chanting 'Churchill was a racist'; they stopped at Churchill's statue and spray-painted the words 'was a racist' after his name. Following the Rhodes Must Fall movement, the statue of Edward Colston, a former Royal African Company director, was toppled in Bristol in 2020. Despite a backlash against these movements, the mainly young demographic of the protesters and their willingness to protest confirm that there is significant support for these ideas and political movements. Despite concerted government attempts to hinder the dissemination of these ideas (Trilling 2022), the ideas that animate these movements are 'out' and cannot be 'put back in the box'.

At the level of social practice, too, there are some reasons for optimism. Despite the unrelenting commentary that white working-class communities resent non-white migration, new research from the UK ESCRC-funded project 'Northern Exposure: Race, Nation and Disaffection in "Ordinary" Towns and Cities after Brexit' confirms that there is potential for solidarity and alliances. It concludes:

> Amid these dislocations and risks, we find delicate, differentiated, and predominantly informal infrastructures of community governance and intervention attempting to build alliances and resolve tensions: a grounded local-view that belies the kind of image of the North established in mainstream national understandings of the dramatic politics of Brexit and after. (Wallace and Favell 2022)

These green shoots of solidarity require well-designed public politics and funding to respond to the needs on the ground; social and political movements that allow us to confront and debate the truth about Britain's imperial past, such as the Black Lives Matter and Rhodes Must Fall movements, which are crucial to constructing a post-imperial British identity. As the costs of a Brexit victory secured through the political mobilisation of racism mount up for all British citizens, it is becoming clear that an honest national debate about the issues raised by Black Lives Matter and Rhodes Must Fall are not just 'woke' peripheral issues for non-white minorities; they are crucial to the prosperity of all Britons.

References

Ashiagbor, D. (2021), 'Race and Colonialism in the Construction of Labour Markets', *Industrial Law Journal*, 50 (4), 506–31.

Brems, E. (2014), *The Experiences of Face Veil Wearers in Europe and the Law*. Cambridge: Cambridge University Press.

Campanella, E. (2019), 'A Diminished Nation in Search of an Empire', *Foreign Policy*, 24 October.

Chaterjee, P. (2012), 'Berlin, Tagore and the Dubious Legitimacy of Nationalism', in B. Baum and R. Nicholls (eds), *Isaiah Berlin and the Politics of Freedom: Two Concepts of Liberty*. New York: Routledge.

Chakrabortty, A. (2023), 'First, It Was No to Polish Plumbers, then Afghan Refugees. Now the Right Doesn't Want Any Migrants At All', *Guardian*, 25 May.

Colley, L. (1992), 'Britishness and Otherness: An Argument', *Journal of British Studies*, 31 (4), 309–29.

Crossman, R. (1975), *The Diaries of a Cabinet Minister, Vol. 1: Minister of Housing 1964–66*. London: Hamish Hamilton.

Daniel, W. W. (1968), *Racial Discrimination in England*. London: Penguin.

Daniels, N. (2009), *Islam and the West: The Making of an Image*, 3rd edn. Oxford: Oneworld Publications.

Elkins, C. (2022), 'Britain Can No Longer Hide Behind the Myth that its Empire was Benign', *Time*, 2 April.

Favell, A. (2020), 'Crossing the Race Line: "No Polish, No Blacks, No Dogs" in Brexit Britain? Or, The Great British Brexit Swindle', in F. Duina and F. Merand (eds), *Europe's Malaise: The Long View*, 103–30.

Gilroy, P. (1990), 'Nationalism, History and Ethnic Absolutism', *History Workshop*, 30, 114–20.

Goodhart, D. (2013), *The British Dream: Successes and Failures of Post-War Immigration*. London: Atlantic Books.

Goulbourne, H. (1991), *Ethnicity and Nationalism in Post-Imperial Britain*. Cambridge: Cambridge University Press.

Hansen, R. (2000), *Citizenship and Immigration in Post-War Britain*. Oxford: Oxford University Press.

Hepple, B. A. (1969), 'The British Race Relations Acts, 1965 and 1968', *University of Toronto Law Journal*, 19, 248–57.

Hesse, B. (2014), 'Escaping Liberty: Western Hegemony, Black Fugitivity', *Political Theory*, 42.

Hillyard, C. (2022), 'Mapping the Notting Hill Riots: Racism and the Streets of Post-war Britain', *History Workshop Journal*, 93 (1), 46–68.

Holmwood, J. (2016), 'Moral Economy Versus Political Economy: Provincializing Poloyani', in C. Karner, and B. Weicht (eds), *The Commonalities of Global Crisis: Markets, Communities and Nostalgia*. London: Palgrave Macmillan.

House of Commons Debates, Vol. 711, Columns 926–7, 3 May 1965.

Jenkinson, J. (2009), *Black 1919: Riots, Racism and Resistance in Imperial Britain*. Liverpool: Liverpool University Press.

Lester, A. and G. Bindman (1972), *Race and Law in Great Britain*. Cambridge, MA: Harvard University Press.

Li, Y. and A. Heath (2020), 'Persisting Disadvantage: A Study of Labour Market Dynamics of Ethnic Unemployment and Earnings in the UK (2009–2015)', *Journal of Ethnic and Migration Studies*, 46 (5), 857–78.

Malik, M. (2000), 'Governing After the Human Rights Act', *Modern Law Review*, 63 (2), 281–93.

Malik, M. (2007), 'Modernising Discrimination Law: Proposals for a Single Equality Act', *International Journal of Discrimination and the Law*, 93 (2), 73–94.

Malik, M. (ed.) (2010), *Anti-Muslim Prejudice in the West: Past and Present*. London: Routledge.

Malik, M. (2011), 'Angare, the Burning Embers of Muslim Political Resistance', in M. Maussen, V. Bader and A. Moors (eds), *Colonial and Post-Colonial Governance of Islam*, IMISCOE Research Series. Amsterdam: Amsterdam University Press.

Mamdani, M. (2008), 'On Blasphemy, Bigotry and the Politics of Culture', in B. Ertru and M. Gursoy Sokmen (eds), *Waiting for the Barbarians: A Tribute to Edward W. Said*. Turkey: Verso, 176–84.

Marquand, D. (1995), 'After Whig Imperialism: Can There Be a New British Identity?', *Journal of Ethnic and Migration Studies*, 21 (2), 183–93.

Miles, R. and A. Phizacklea (1984), *White Man's Country: Racism in British Politics*. London: Pluto Press.

Modood, T. et al. (1997), *Ethnic Minorities in Britain: Diversity and Disadvantage*. London: Policy Studies Institute.

Modood, T. (1998), 'Ethnic Diversity and Racial Disadvantage in Employment', in T. Blackstone, B. Parekh. and P. Sanders (eds), *Race Relations in Britain*. London: Routledge.

Modood, T. (2004), 'Muslims and the Politics of Difference', *Political Quarterly*, 74 (1), 100–15.

Modood, T. (2005), *Multicultural Politics: Racism, Ethnicity and Muslims in Britain*. Edinburgh: Edinburgh University Press.

Modood, T. (2013), *Multiculturalism*, 2nd edn. Cambridge: Polity.

Modood, T. (2018), 'Islamophobia: A Form of Cultural Racism. A Submission to the APPG on British Muslims in response to the Call for Evidence on "Working Definition of Islamophobia"', Centre for the Study of Ethnicity and Citizenship, University of Bristol.

Modood, T. (2020), 'Islamophobia and Normative Sociology', *Journal of the British Academy*, 8, 29–49.

Newsam, P. (1987), 'The Commission for Racial Equality 1982–1987', *Journal of Ethnic and Migration Studies*, 14 (1), 17–20.

Oxford Human Rights Hub (2017), 'The Impact of Brexit on Equality Rights'. Accessed at: <https://ohrh.law.ox.ac.uk/the-impact-of-brexit-on-equality-rights/>

Patterson, S. (1969), *Immigration and Race Relations in Britain 1960–1967*. London: Institute for Race Relations.

Perry, K. H. (2018), *London is the Place for Me: Black Britons, Citizenship and the Politics of Race*. Oxford: Oxford University Press.

Political and Economic Planning Report on Racial Discrimination (1967). London: National Committee for Commonwealth Immigrants.

Polowska-Kimunguyi, E. (2022), 'Echoes of Empire: Racism and Historical Amnesia in the British Media Coverage of Migration', *Humanities and Social Science Communications*, 9 (3).

Portes, J. (2013), 'An Exercise in Scapegoating', *London Review of Books*, 35 (12).

Ridley, C. L. (2021), 'When the British Empire Waged War on Free Speech', *Tribune*, 20 April. Accessed at: <https://tribunemag.co.uk/2021/04/pernicious-messaging>

Rosenberg, G. N. (2008), *The Hollow Hope: Can Courts Bring About Social Change?*, 2nd edn. Chicago: Chicago University Press.

Rzepnikowska, A. (2019), 'Racism and Xenophobia Experienced by Polish Migrants in the UK before and after Brexit Vote', *Journal of Ethnic and Migration Studies*, 45 (1), 61–77.

Shilliam, R. (2018), *Race and the Undeserving Poor: From Abolition to Brexit*. NY: Columbia University Press.

Solomos, J. (2022), *Race and Racism in Britain*, 4th edn. London: Macmillan.

Syal, R. (2022), 'Government Strategy Sidesteps Sewell's Race Report's Most Criticized Conclusions', *Guardian*, 16 March.

Travis, A. (2022), 'After 44 Years Secret Papers Reveal Truth about Five Nights of Violence in Notting Hill', *Guardian*, 24 August.

Trilling, D. (2022), 'Why is the UK Government Suddenly Targeting Critical Race Theory?', *Guardian*, 23 October.

Tully, J. (2008), *Public Philosophy in a New Key – Imperialism and Civic Freedom*, Vol. 2. Cambridge: Cambridge University Press.

Uberoi, V. and T. Modood (2013), 'Inclusive Britishness: A Multicultural Advance', *Political Studies*, 61 (1), 23–41.

Uberoi, V. (2023), 'Is King Charles a Traditionalist, a Multiculturalist or Both?'. Accessed at: <https://blogs.lse.ac.uk/politicsandpolicy/is-king-charles-a-traditionalist-a-multiculturalist-or-both/>

Van Rossum, M. (2013), '"Amok!": Mutinies and Slaves on Dutch East Indiamen in the 1780s', *International Review of Social History*, 58, 109–30.

Virdee, S. (2000), 'Racism and Resistance in British Trade Unions, 1948–1979', in P. Alexander and R. Halpern (eds), *Racializing Class, Classifying Race*. London: Macmillan, 122–49.

Virdee, S. (2014), *Race, Class and the Racialized Outsider*. London: Palgrave.

Waters, C. (1997), 'Dark Strangers in Our Midst: Discourses of Race and Nation in Britain 1947–63', *Journal of British Studies*, 36 (2), 207–38.

Wallace, A. and A. Favell (2023), 'In the Wake of Brexit: Negotiating Diversity and Majority–Minority Relations in the North of England', *Journal of Ethnic and Migration Studies*, 49 (9), 2070–89.

Yeo, C. (2020a), *Welcome to Britain: Fixing Our Broken Immigration System*. London: Biteback.

Yeo, C. (2020b), 'Race, Racism and Immigration'. Accessed at: <https://freemovement.org.uk/black-lives-matter/>

Part Three

Multiculturalism, Nationalism and Transnationalism

SEVEN

Multicultural Nationalism as an Ethics of Social Membership[1]

Will Kymlicka

In public debates, multiculturalism and nationalism are often seen as expressing incompatible values or commitments. Nationalists view multiculturalism as corrosive of national identity and solidarity; multiculturalists view nationalism as entailing an assimilationist or exclusionary approach to difference. In practice, however, multiculturalism and nationalism often seem to co-exist. Indeed, insofar as contemporary states have adopted multiculturalism as a public policy and a public value, it has often taken the form of a multicultural nationalism. Multiculturalism has been understood as a way of belonging to the nation, opening up new ways of being Canadian, say, or being British. Multiculturalism, we might say, seeks to pluralise the nation. The nation is still taken as the locus of belonging and membership, and multiculturalism creates new ways of belonging to and participating in the nation. Many commentators have therefore described actually existing multiculturalism in Canada (Kernerman 2005), Australia (Levey 2019; Moran 2011), Scotland (Hussain and Miller 2016; Bond 2017) and Britain (Modood 2020; Uberoi 2018) as forms of 'multicultural nationalism'.

This linkage between multiculturalism and nationalism is a source of debate and dispute among supporters of multiculturalism. For some multiculturalists, the emancipatory potential of multiculturalism is lost if it is bound by the nation. A multicultural nationalism might create new ways of belonging to the nation, but why should the nation be privileged as the site of membership and belonging? Minorities may have identities and aspirations that transcend or compete with the nation. Why should they need to fit themselves into the nation to qualify for multicultural recognition? Indeed, for some commentators, the progressive potential of multiculturalism is precisely its potential to decentre the nation as the locus of identity, loyalty or belonging (for example, Fleras 2015; Walton-Roberts 2011; Sharma 2011). On this view, the rise of multicultural nationalism reflects the capture and domestication of multiculturalism by the nation-state.

Other theorists, however, including Tariq Modood, whose work we are here to celebrate, have argued that the linking of nationalism and multi-culturalism is not artificial, but rather reflects a kind of elective affinity or mutual interdependence, and that each offers a potential resource for the other (for example, Modood 2018; see also Uberoi 2018). In this chapter, I will not attempt to resolve this debate, but I will suggest that we can bet-ter understand the links between multiculturalism and nationalism, and the strengths and limits of actually existing multicultural nationalism, by situating them in relation to what I will call an 'ethics of membership'. I will begin by explaining what I mean by ethics of social membership, and why it is a central issue for political theory. I will then explore how the need for an ethics of social membership pushes in the direction of both nationalism and multiculturalism, and how this illuminates both the potential to reconcile the two and the limits of doing so.

An Ethics of Social Membership

There are many different forms of justice, and many different ways of thinking about what we owe each other. But in the modern world, two frames of justice are particularly powerful. The first frame grounds claims simply on our shared humanity. Wherever humans interact with each other, we should treat each other in a way that acknowledges and respects our common humanity, and hence that avoids treating others in a degrading or dehumanising way. This generates claims to universal human rights, which many people have argued provide the moral foun-dation for the postwar world.

But all modern societies also have a second framework of justice, which grounds claims in the fact of shared social membership. The idea here is that where people are members of a shared society with a shared scheme of social cooperation, they have distinctive rights and obligations to participate in the governing of that society, and distinc-tive claims to a fair distribution of the benefits and burdens entailed by the cooperative scheme. The right to vote, for example, is usually restricted to members – to those who are permanently resident in the country – rather than to tourists, guests, international students or short-term business visitors. Voting is therefore often seen as a 'citizenship right' or 'membership right' rather than a universal human right, such as the right not to be tortured, or subjected to medical experimentation, or imprisoned without due process, which do not depend upon someone's membership status.

This distinction between universal human rights and citizenship rights is a familiar one, even if there is debate over which rights fall into which category.[2] In my view, however, the normative logic of membership rights has not always been made explicit, and I think it is worth distinguishing two different roles that the idea of membership plays.

First, and perhaps most obviously, the fact of social membership operates as a *criterion of eligibility* for citizenship rights. As I noted before, membership rights are typically limited to those who have settled in a society, as distinct from transient tourists, foreign students and business visitors. This raises complex questions about where this threshold of membership is set, and what are the procedures for people to transition from transient to settled, from visitor to member. There is a rich and sophisticated literature in political theory on this topic.[3]

However, social membership plays a second fundamental role which has been less discussed in the literature – namely, as a *goal* or telos of membership rights. One of the central purposes of membership rights, I would argue, is to promote social membership as an identity and a practice: to enable and encourage people to think of themselves as members of a shared society, and to enact and enjoy their social membership.

While recent debates have largely focused on the first role of membership as a criterion of eligibility for rights, an older literature on citizenship emphasised the second role of membership as the goal of rights. One particularly striking example is the work of T. H. Marshall, the postwar British sociologist who studied evolving ideas of citizenship, and in particular the rise of social democratic ideas of citizenship tied to the welfare state. He famously said that the theory and practice of citizenship rights depends on 'a direct sense of community membership based on loyalty to a civilisation that is a common possession' (Marshall 1950: 40). This dense passage is much-quoted in the citizenship studies literature, but in my view, its full meaning and implications have rarely been unpacked. So let me try to unpack this Marshallian view of membership rights into a set of six premises or presuppositions:

- First, citizenship implies that there is such a thing as a 'shared society'. It implies a vision of the world as organised into 'societies';
- Second, citizenship is understood as membership of this shared society;
- Third – and this is arguably the crucial normative step – this shared society is seen as a 'common possession' of its members;

- Fourth – and here we shift to more empirical claims or predictions – when citizens view society as their common possession, they will feel a sense of loyalty and commitment to the shared society and to their co-citizens;
- Fifth, this sense of loyalty to society as a common possession generates the solidarity that underpins the democratic welfare state;
- Sixth, none of these ideas are innate or natural. People are not born with the idea that there are such things as 'shared societies', or that people are 'members' of societies, or that such societies are the 'common possession' of their members. On the contrary, throughout much of British history, the upper and lower classes have seen themselves as forming two separate societies, captured in Disraeli's famous description of England as 'Two Nations'. For Marshall, a central task of citizenship rights and the welfare state was precisely to *create* a shared society that would belong as much to the working class as to the upper class, and that could then be seen as the common possession of all classes. In that sense, a sense of forming a shared society is both a cause and an effect of citizenship. This was not just a matter of giving workers the material resources needed to access and enjoy the wider society, but also creating the 'public things' that define a shared society, such as the BBC, museums, libraries, public transportation, parks and so on.[4]

In short, Marshallian politics is *society-making* and *membership-making*. Membership rights, on this view, are not only or primarily about acknowledging some pre-existing fact of social membership. Rather, membership rights are intended to create and make visible a 'shared society', to enable and encourage individuals to think of themselves as 'members' of such a society, and to feel that the society is their 'common possession' – or as he elsewhere puts it, membership rights are the 'right to share to the full in the social heritage' of a society (Marshall 1964: 74).

Marshall's focus was on how citizenship rights can enable the working class to enact and enjoy social membership, but this basic template has arguably underpinned many other 'citizenship struggles' of the past sixty years, including struggles for gender equality, racial desegregation, and LGBT+ and disability rights. These are not just struggles for universal human rights, but also struggles to claim and enact social membership. They too are society-making and membership-making: they demand the kinds of membership rights that would help create a 'shared society' that is truly a 'common possession' of its members, and that would enable previously excluded groups to enjoy social membership.

I would argue that this image of citizenship-as-membership-making has implicitly or explicitly shaped social-democratic politics for the past hundred years in the West (and so we might equally call it the 'social-democratic' model of membership rights). And this helps to explain why social democracy in the twentieth century has been closely aligned with the nation-state (Berman 2006). While social democrats rarely self-identify as 'nationalists' – and Marshall himself would have rejected that label – they are committed to an idea of society-making, and for most social democrats, the obvious unit of society-making is the nation. As a result, society-making has de facto involved nation-building, and membership-making has de facto been tied to national citizenship.[5]

The Turn Away from Marshall

While the Marshallian view has dominated the social democratic imagination for several decades, it is now under severe strain, and there has been a marked turn away from Marshall on the left. To give just one example, during the 2021 federal elections in Germany, the Green Party held a party convention to debate their election manifesto which was entitled 'Germany. Everything is possible'. While the substance of the manifesto received general approval among party members, there was a rebellion against the inclusion of the word 'Germany' in the title, with critics arguing, 'At the heart of our politics are people in their dignity and freedom, not Germany' (Huggler 2021).

It would be difficult to find a more explicit repudiation of the Marshallian project. For Marshall, it is a central task of progressive politics to orient people to a shared society – to encourage people to put on their social membership hat, as it were, and to claim Germany as their common possession. For the rebel Green Party members, by contrast, any effort to render the nation salient is a betrayal of progressive values, which should only be about 'people in their dignity and freedom', not any idea about building the nation as a common possession.

Of course, Germany is a special case, but the retreat from Marshall can be found across the West. An increasing number of legal and political theorists are warning us that 'membership is an ideal that is not only overrated but dangerous' (Kukathas 2021: 5), and encouraging us to 'give up on citizenship as an aspirational project altogether' (Bosniak 1998: 33). There are many factors underlying this retreat, but to oversimplify, we might divide them into global and domestic factors.

Let's start with the global concern. One natural worry about Marshallian politics is that orienting people to a shared society will erode any sense of obligation to the rest of the world, whether in relation to refugees, global poverty or climate change. Of course, as I noted earlier, the commitment to membership rights is not intended to substitute for universal human rights: membership rights are supposed to be layered on top of universal human rights. But we might worry that focusing too much on society-making and membership-making may distract people from their obligations to the rest of humanity.

Does Marshallian politics at the national level diminish feelings of global obligation? It's not clear how we would test that assumption, but it is interesting to ask which countries have in fact been most support-ive of global human rights and development initiatives. Alison Brysk's study of these 'global good Samaritans' suggests that those countries which have been most successful in building robust national schemes of social-democratic citizenship are also those most inclined to sup-port global justice initiatives (Brysk 2009). She also suggests that their sense of global obligation derives in part from their national solidarity: global citizenship is seen as an expression of their national identity, it is part of 'who we are' as Swedes or Canadians, and understood as a form of national responsibility. This has sometimes been theorised as a kind of 'rooted cosmopolitanism' (Kymlicka and Walker 2012), in which sentiments of global citizenship are rooted in Marshallian national citizenship.

Of course, some individuals have a sense of global citizenship that does not pass through the nation, and who may indeed disavow any sense of national identity. But the survey evidence suggests that such unrooted cosmopolitans – those who say their only or primary iden-tity is citizen of the world rather than citizen of the nation – have a rather thin sense of global obligation (Reeskens 2023). While opposed to racial discrimination and religious intolerance, they tend to endorse meritocracy and market inequalities, and reject redistributive policies. They are, in effect, neoliberal cosmopolitans, levelling down rather than levelling up. There is growing evidence that the turn away from Marshall is producing this sort of desolidaristic cosmopolitanism, at least among the university educated (Gelepithis and Giani 2022).

So it is not clear that national solidarity and global solidarity are necessarily zero-sum or hydraulic, as if the only way to increase feel-ings of global solidarity is to abandon or weaken Marshallian projects of national solidarity. More work is needed to sort out which forms of Marshallian politics promote or inhibit which forms of global justice.

In any event, I don't think global justice is the main reason for the left's turn away from Marshall. The more significant concern is how Marshallian politics creates hierarchies and exclusions *within* the state. Historically, Marshallian society-building and membership-building has often been on the backs of minorities. In the name of creating a 'loyalty' to 'shared society' that is a 'common possession', social democrats have at times endorsed a host of oppressive and violent policies against minorities who are not seen as 'fitting' into the nation, including policies of eugenics and sterilisation, forced assimilation, ethnic cleansing, and racially exclusionary immigration and citizenship laws.[6] And one reason why minorities are not seen as fitting into the nation is that the prevailing national narratives - the 'stories of peoplehood' (Smith 2003) – have often been defined precisely in opposition to Indigenous peoples, racialised groups and religious minorities. Marshallian politics seeks 'loyalty to a civilization that is a common possession', but all too often this civilisation has in fact been seen as the achievement of the (white, Christian) dominant group that needs to be defended against, and imposed upon, uncivilised minorities. Marshallian politics seems to privilege those who 'fit' into the nation, while penalising those who do not fit.

Against this history, it is perhaps not surprising that many on the German left argue that 'At the heart of our politics are people in their dignity and freedom, not Germany.' Even if Marshallian politics does not undermine global solidarity, it seems to organise domestic politics around ideas of nationhood and peoplehood that are prone to hierarchy and exclusion. And so, across Europe, we see the retreat from Marshall, and the spread of an 'anti-nationalist European' left that rejects any privileged status for the nation as the object of loyalty or attachment (Caiani and Weisskircher 2022).

Rescuing an Ethics of Membership through Multicultural Nationalism

Not everyone on the left, however, is willing to give up on the Marshallian vision, which runs so deep. And so alongside the retreat from Marshall, we also see efforts to rescue Marshall's vision, and to show it can avoid the dangers of exclusionary nationalism. In particular, latter-day Marshallians defend the overarching commitment to society-making and membership-making, but argue that the underlying conception of the 'shared society' can be pluralised, and the prevailing 'stories of peoplehood' can be changed, so as to define minorities not as outsiders or threats, but as constituent members of the 'we'. In the Canadian context, for example, the shared society could be redefined as a bilingual society, a federal society, a treaty-based society and a multicultural society. Indeed, this is arguably what the 1982 Constitution Act does: bilingualism, treaties, federalism and multiculturalism are all now recognised as defining features of Canadian society (Uberoi 2009). We can see similar trends in other countries.

In my view, this is one important source of the rise of actually existing 'multicultural nationalism'. Multicultural nationalism can be seen as an attempt to maintain the Marshallian vision of politics as society-making and membership-making, but in a pluralised form, acknowledging and remedying the exclusions and hierarchies that too often accompanied the original social democratic vision.[7] Not surprisingly, social democratic parties are the main champions of multicultural nationalism in many countries, precisely because it can combine a newer pro-minority politics of recognition and anti-racism with an older politics of society-making.[8]

Yet social democrats are not uniformly enthusiastic defenders of this approach. Social democrats are deeply divided on this issue, and even those who support it tend to downplay or even deny the extent to which it retains a distinctly national orientation. We see, in effect, a form of multicultural nationalism that dares not speak its name: a longing for a multicultural national solidarity yet a reluctance to highlight the nation as a potential object of membership commitment, and a scepticism that it is legitimate to ask or expect minorities to orient themselves towards the nation.[9]

This ambivalence and scepticism is understandable and healthy, but it raises the question: is multicultural nationalism a viable basis for an ethics of membership? Can the Marshallian vision be pluralised in a way that truly makes room for minorities? Or is the Marshallian vision inherently biased against minorities, imposing a set of nationally oriented identities and expectations that does violence to their identities and aspirations?

This is a complicated question, whose answer is going to vary from group to group, and country to country. But for our purposes, I think it's useful to distinguish two different ways in which multicultural nationalism might succeed or fail as an ethics of membership.

First, we can explore multicultural nationalism from the perspective of minorities themselves. Does multiculturalism enable a sense of membership and belonging among minorities? If a country redefines itself as multicultural, do minorities in fact feel a sense of membership in it, and a sense of attachment and loyalty to it? Do they come to see it as their common possession? And does this allow them to express their authentic political aspiration? Marshallian politics understands membership claims as vehicles for claiming and enacting social membership – as enabling different ways to be Canadian – but are minorities able to formulate their aspirations in this way, as ways of being Canadian?

In many ways, this is the most obvious test of multicultural nationalism, and so not surprisingly, there is a great deal of empirical research on it, including Modood's influential work showing the importance of religious accommodations to a sense of belonging among Muslims in Britain (Modood 1994). I have tried elsewhere to review this body of research, but let me just say here that while the results are predictably mixed and uneven, the results are more encouraging than many critics suppose. Where minorities are recognised and represented as constitutive elements of the larger society, we see positive effects on minorities' feelings of belonging and political participation (Kymlicka 2012, 2021), including for Indigenous peoples (Schmid 2023). More research is needed to figure out the limits and conditions of these positive effects, but my provisional conclusion is cautious optimism about the prospects for nurturing a sense of belonging among various minority groups.

In any event, for the purposes of this paper, I will assume that multicultural nationalism can generate a sense of belonging at least some of the time, for some minority groups in some countries. However, we then confront the second test of multicultural nationalism, which concerns *majority perceptions* of minorities' membership. Do majority groups recognise and accept that minorities have a sense of attachment and commitment to the larger society?

I think this is a crucial but under-studied question. It is crucial for Marshallian politics, because his vision of solidarity is triadic. On Marshall's view, my willingness to make sacrifices for your citizenship rights depends not just on whether I am committed to the larger society, but whether I think you share that commitment. My solidaristic commitment to you goes through the belief that we are both committed to the larger society as our common possession. And so it's vital to Marshallian politics to know whether, or under what conditions, majorities perceive minorities as attached and committed to the larger society.

So what do we know about majority perceptions of minority commitment to the larger society? Surprisingly little. We know a great deal about the sense of national identity and pride of members of the majority group, and we also know a great deal about the sense of identity and attachment of minority groups, but we know virtually nothing about whether members of the majority view members of the minority as committed or attached.

To remedy this gap, a group of us have attempted to measure what we are calling 'perceptions of membership commitment' (Banting, Kymlicka, Wallace and Harell 2020; Harell, Banting, Kymlicka and Wallace 2022). We developed a battery of survey questions that are intended to tap perceptions of whether others are committed to the larger society. For example, respondents were asked whether they believe that members of a particular minority *care* about the larger society, or whether they believe that members of a minority group are willing to *make sacrifices* for the larger society. The survey has been run in seven countries, focusing on different groups that are particularly relevant in each country. In the Canadian version of the survey, for example, respondents were asked about three different minorities: immigrants, Indigenous peoples and francophone Quebeckers. In other countries, respondents were asked about Blacks, or about Muslims.[10]

The results were consistent: across all seven countries, members of minority groups are seen as less committed to the larger society – for example, they are seen as caring less about other members of the society, and as less willing to make sacrifices for the larger society. Perhaps this is not surprising in and of itself. As I noted earlier, one might expect minorities to have ambivalent feelings towards a society and 'civilisation' that has dispossessed, enslaved, excluded and oppressed them.

However, if the Marshallian story is correct, these perceptions of membership commitment are consequential for solidarity. So the next step in our survey was to see whether these perceptions of membership commitment affect support for the citizenship rights of minorities, including their social rights (for example, access to the welfare state), democratic rights (for example, to engage in political protest) and civil rights (for example, to wear religious garb).

And here the results are sobering. I will start with the Canadian case, and then widen the focus. We first examined the impact of membership perceptions on support for social rights in Canada, illustrated in Fig. 7.1. What this figure shows, on the left, is that majority Canadians are less supportive of redistribution to minority groups: majority members see minorities as less 'deserving' of social rights. That's the bad news. However, the figure also shows that support for redistribution substantially increases when majority respondents see the minority as committed to Canada, as we move to the right of the graph.

Let's shift now to democratic rights, such as the right to engage in political protest. This is arguably the crux of an ethics of membership: the real test of whether society is understood as a common possession is who is entitled to make decisions about the future of that shared society. The results are shown in Fig. 7.2. What this figure shows, on the left, is that majority Canadians have depressingly low levels of support for the right of minorities to engage in disruptive political protest, such as blockades: the support is only half the level of support for mainstream groups such as seniors or farmers. However, here again, moving to the right, the more that respondents see members of minorities as committed to Canada, support for their democratic rights substantially increases. Indeed, in the case of Indigenous peoples, it actually exceeds support for mainstream groups.

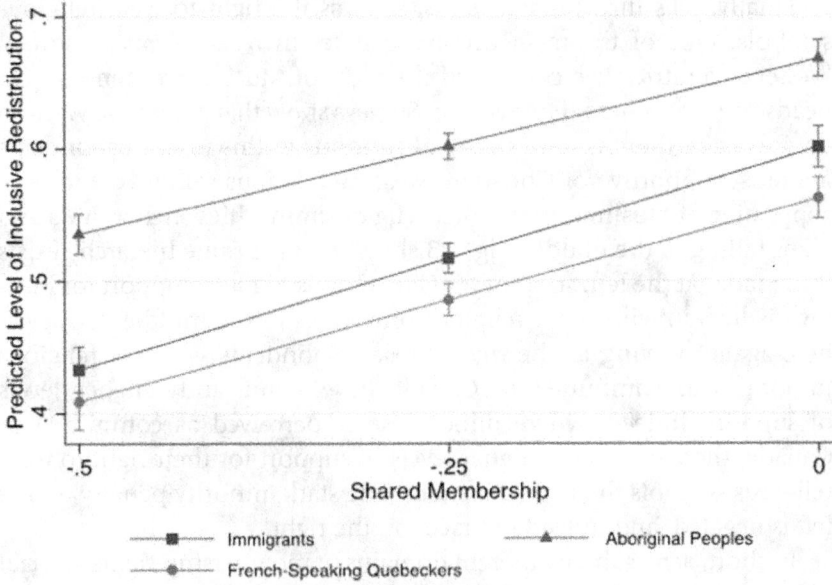

Fig. 7.1: Impact of Membership Perceptions on Support for Redistribution (Canada)
Source: Banting, Kymlicka, Harell and Wallace 2020.

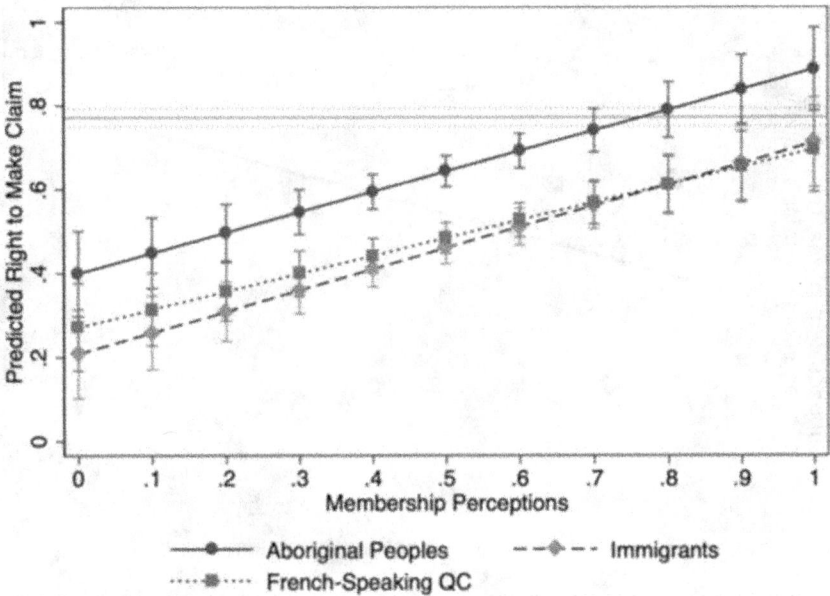

Fig. 7.2: Impact of Membership Perceptions on Support for Democratic Rights (Canada)
Source: Banting, Harell and Kymlicka 2022.

Finally, let's turn to civil rights, such as the right to wear religious symbols. One of the most divisive debates in recent years in several Western countries has concerned the right of Muslim women to wear headscarves or other religious garb. Surveys show that across the Western democracies, there is a hierarchy of support on this issue: respondents are most supportive of Christians wearing religious symbols, and least supportive of Muslims, with other religious minorities such as Jews and Sikhs falling in the middle. Fig. 7.3 shows that the same hierarchy exists in Canada. At the left, support for Christians is highest, support for Muslims is lowest, with other religious minorities in the middle. However, here again, moving to the right, those respondents who see religious minorities as committed to Canada have significantly higher levels of support. Indeed, where minorities are perceived as committed to Canada, there is actually higher levels of support for their right to wear religious symbols than for Christians. The stark minority penalty on the left is negated, and indeed reversed, on the right.

In short, across three different domains of membership rights – social rights, political rights and civil rights – we see the same dramatic effect: support for the membership rights of minorities is strongly tied to perceptions that they are committed to the larger society.

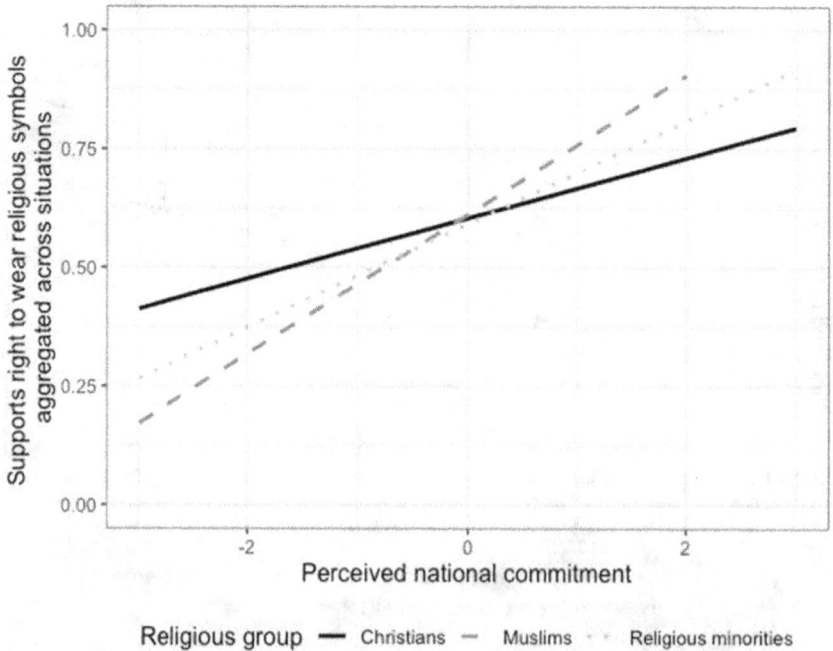

Fig. 7.3: Impact of Membership Perceptions on Support for Religious Symbols (Canada)
Source: Scott 2023.

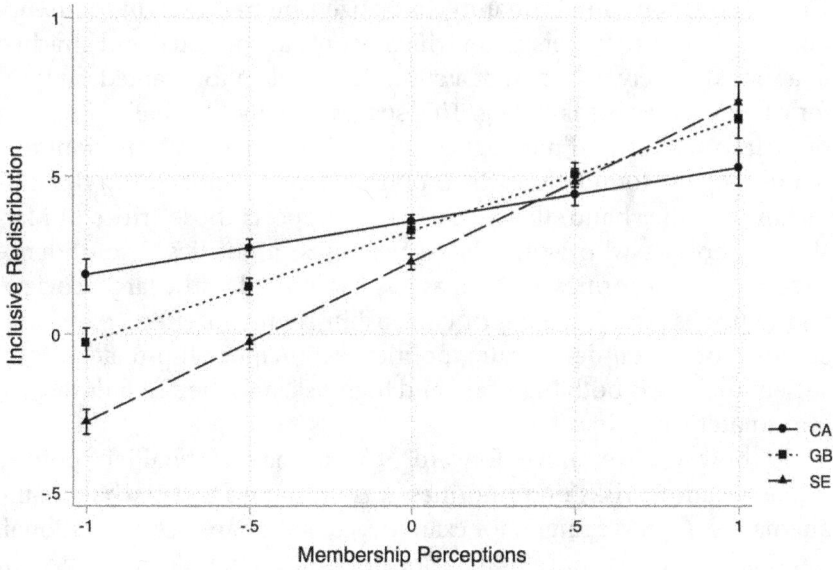

Fig. 7.4: Impact of Membership Perceptions on Solidarity (Cross-National)
Source: Harell, Banting and Kymlicka 2023.

One might wonder whether this is somehow a uniquely Canadian phenomenon. Our cross-national survey shows that it is not: the same basic pattern is found in all seven countries. In fact, the slope of the line is flatter in Canada than in most other countries (see Fig. 7.4, which compares Canada (CA) and Great Britain (GB) with Sweden (SE)). In other words, membership perceptions actually have a more powerful effect in other countries than in Canada.

Marshallian Politics Revisited

What does all of this tell us about the prospects for multicultural nationalism as a pluralised form of Marshallian politics? As I said earlier, this question of majority perceptions of minority commitment is understudied, and so we need more research to confirm these findings, and to identify potential limits and counter-examples, before drawing any firm conclusions. But assuming that future research confirms these patterns, I would highlight two potential lessons from this research.

On the one hand, I think this research supports a basic empirical premise of Marshallian politics – namely, that the practice of citizenship rights rests on the idea of loyalty to a shared society as a common possession. We owe certain basic human rights to all people simply in virtue of our common humanity, but citizenship rights seem to presuppose an ethic of membership in which people are oriented and attached to a shared society. Where that assumption is taken for granted, support for citizenship rights is strong. This suggests that a Marshallian politics of society-making and membership-making can play an important role in building the foundations for a robust practise of citizenship rights.

On the other hand, the research also supports those critics of Marshallian politics who worry that it penalises minorities. The evidence suggests that minorities are seen as less committed to the larger society, and hence as less deserving of citizenship rights. In effect, Marshall's account of social-democratic politics as membership-making and society-making is both high gain and high risk, and the risk falls disproportionately on minorities.

So how do we move forward? Given that Marshallian politics imposes chronic risks on minorities, it is important to ask what are the alternatives to it. We might, for example, consider various post-national, transnational or cosmopolitan visions of politics that do not expect or require people to orient themselves to a common shared society. One of the tasks of political theorists is to expand our political imagination, to envisage other ways of doing politics. So I welcome proposals and models for a post-Marshallian progressive politics.

However, I will just note here that while Marshallian politics carries risks, so too do these alternatives. I would highlight two risks. First, it is not clear how a stable democratic order can be constructed without some degree of society-making and membership-making. Democracy arguably requires a stable and bounded 'we' that is widely accepted as the unit for democratic governance (Kymlicka 2022). Second, there is the risk that giving up on membership-making will not lead to greater solidarity with minorities, but simply an across-the-board decline in solidarity. As I noted, there is some evidence that those who identify primarily or exclusively as citizens of the world are less supportive of redistribution, and more supportive of market inequalities. And I don't think this should be surprising. After all, it's worth recalling why social democracy emerged in the first place. According to Karl Polanyi – that other great mid-century theorist of social democracy – the fundamental task of social democracy is to subordinate markets to society, to ensure that markets serve a social purpose (Polanyi 1944). He argued that markets have a tendency to become 'dis-embedded' from society, such that society serves the market, rather than vice versa. We might view neoliberalism as the most current version of this historic tendency for markets to become dis-embedded from society. And the task of social democracy, he argued, is to reassert the primacy of society, to re-embed markets in a social project. But that of course presupposes that citizens have some vision of the society into which markets are being embedded, and that arguably requires a politics of society-making.

So, I think it is worth asking how we can update Marshall to address the realities of modern pluralistic societies, and in particular, whether we can revise Marshallian politics in a way that minimises the risks and burdens to minorities. Clearly, this is an uphill battle, and requires overcoming what are deep-seated tendencies towards membership penalties. However, I do think the evidence discussed earlier suggests glimpses of a truly inclusive Marshallian politics. If we look again at the figures on support for social, political and civil rights (Figs 7.1–7.3), in each case we can see that there is in fact a zone of inclusive solidarity. In the top right of each figure, we have a body of public opinion in which citizens view minorities as fully deserving of citizenship rights – including rights to protest and to express their religious and cultural differences – and in which the exercise of these rights is seen as a legitimate way of enacting their membership in and commitment to the larger society. That, in my view, is one way to understand the goal of a truly multicultural nationalism, and the evidence suggests that it is not a purely theoretical possibility, but in fact has a toehold in public opinion. The question – and the next step in our research – is how can we shift society towards the top right of these figures?[11]

Notes

1. Thanks to the organisers for the invitation to present at a conference in honour of Tariq Modood, at the University of Bristol, 28–30 September 2022, and to all the participants for their helpful feedback, and in particular to Tariq, not only for his generous comments on this paper, but also for thirty years of intellectual debates. In the past, we have sparred on issues of liberalism and secularism, but in this paper I focus on one of our core agreements, on multiculturalism as a conception of membership. Thanks also to Allison Harell and Keith Banting, with whom I have been collaborating closely on the research discussed in the final section of this paper.
2. For example, in recent Canadian debates, there is widespread agreement that asylum seekers are owed basic health care as a human right, but disagreement over whether full access to publicly funded health care should be conditional on having their asylum claim accepted and so granted permanent residence.
3. The literature here discusses how many years of residence should be sufficient to claim membership status, and whether countries can require additional tests of commitment to the society, such as loyalty oaths, language tests, renunciation of prior citizenships and so on. For a sample of the range of views, see Bauböck and Joppke 2010.

4. For the importance of 'public things' to a viable conception of social member-ship, see Honig 2017.

5. A fuller account of membership-making in the West would need to situate the national welfare state within imperial histories. As Bhambra has argued, the building of relations of redistribution among citizens within Britain was tied to relations of extraction among subjects in the Empire (Bhambra and Holmwood 2018; Bhambra 2022).

6. For one representative example of this toxic combination of social democracy and racial eugenics in the Canadian context, see J. S. Woodworth's *Strangers within our Gates* (1909). This is not just a pathology of social democracy in settler colonial societies: on social-democratic support for eugenic and assimi-lationist policies towards the Sami and Roma in Sweden, see Roll-Hansen and Broberg 2005; Barker 2017.

7. The Marshallian influence may help to explain how multiculturalism involves both 'bottom-up' and 'top-down' dynamics. Defenders of multiculturalism often suggest it is the result of 'bottom-up' mobilisation and contestation by minorities, who see it as 'a tool of civic voice for historically excluded and oppressed people' (James 2010: 60; Hinz 2010). Critics respond that multicul-turalism is instead the result of 'top-down' governance strategies by the state, which sees it as a 'tool of domestication' (Mitchell 2004: 92) aimed at con-stituting 'nationally oriented multicultural selves' (Mitchell 2003: 399). But if we see multicultural nationalism as a pluralised form of Marshallian politics of society-making and membership-making, then it is not surprising that it is advanced by both minority and state actors. Insofar as Marshallian politics seeks to orient people to a shared society as the common possession of its members, then we might say that the state is primarily interested in the 'orienting people' part, and minorities are primarily interested in the 'common possession' part. But the two are difficult to disentangle in practice, and often feed each other. For further discussion of this dialectic of minority mobilisation and state regu-lation, see Kymlicka 2013.

8. In fact, the partisan polarisation around multiculturalism appears to be increasing. Centre-right parties were not uniformly opposed to multiculturalism, but they have stiffened their opposition to avoid losing votes to virulently anti-multicultural far-right populist parties. On this dynamic, see Westlake 2020.

9. See Ruiz Jimenez et al. 2015 for a fascinating discussion of the inarticulacy of the Spanish left in relation to nationhood, simultaneously 'longing' for a Marshallian national solidarity yet unable and unwilling to express a positive attachment to the nation as an object of orientation and attachment. As Laxer 2001 notes, this is not a new phenomenon, nor uniquely Spanish.

10. For details about the survey, including the wording of the membership percep-tions battery, and the list of groups mentioned in the different countries, see Harell, Banting and Kymlicka 2023.

11. The research is ongoing, but we are particularly interested in studying what counts as 'signals' of membership commitment, and how public policies can shape how these signals are interpreted. For a first step, see Harell, Soroka, Polacko and Kymlicka 2023.

References

Baines, D. and N. Sharma (2002), 'Migrant Workers as Non-Citizens: The Case against Citizenship as a Social Policy Concept', *Studies in Political Economy*, 69 (1), 75–107.

Banting, K., A. Harell and W. Kymlicka (2022), 'Nationalism, Membership and the Politics of Minority Claims-Making', *Canadian Journal of Political Science*, 55 (3), 537–60.

Banting, K., W. Kymlicka, A. Harell and R. Wallace (2020), 'Beyond National Identity: Liberal Nationalism, Shared Membership and Solidarity', in G. Gustavsson and D. Miller (eds), *Liberal Nationalism and Its Critics: Normative and Empirical Questions*. Oxford: Oxford University Press, 205–25.

Barker, V. (2017), 'Nordic Vagabonds: The Roma and the Logic of Benevolent Violence in the Swedish Welfare State', *European Journal of Criminology*, 14 (1), 120–39.

Bauböck, R. and C. Joppke (2010), *How Liberal are Citizenship Tests?* EUI RSCAS, Working Paper 2010/41, EUDO Citizenship Observatory.

Berman, S. (2006), *The Primacy of Politics: Social Democracy and the Making of Europe's Twentieth Century*. Cambridge: Cambridge University Press.

Bhambra, G. (2022), 'Relations of Extraction, Relations of Redistribution: Empire, Nation, and the Construction of the British Welfare State', *British Journal of Sociology*, 73 (1), 4–15.

Bhambra, G. and J. Holmwood (2018), 'Colonialism, Postcolonialism and the Liberal Welfare State', *New Political Economy*, 23 (5), 574–87.

Bosniak, L. (1998), 'The Citizenship of Aliens', *Social Text*, 56, 29–35.

Bond, R. (2017), 'Multicultural Nationalism? National Identities among Minority Groups in Scotland's Census', *Journal of Ethnic and Migration Studies*, 43 (7), 1121–40.

Brysk, A. (2009), *Global Good Samaritans: Human Rights as Foreign Policy*. Oxford: Oxford University Press.

Caiani, M. and M. Weisskircher (2022), 'Anti-nationalist Europeans and Pro-European Nativists on the Streets: Visions of Europe from the Left to the Far Right', *Social Movement Studies*, 21 (1), 216–33.

Fleras, A. (2015), 'Beyond Multiculturalism', in S. Guo and L. Wong (eds), *Revisiting Multiculturalism in Canada*. Rotterdam: Sense, 311–34.

Gelepithis, M. and M. Giani (2022), 'Inclusion without Solidarity: Education, Economic Security, and Attitudes toward Redistribution', *Political Studies*, 70 (1), 45–61.

Harell, A., W. Kymlicka and K. Banting (2022), 'Boundaries of Generosity: Membership, Inclusion and Redistribution', in M. Crepaz (ed.), *The Edward Elgar Handbook on Migration and Welfare*. Cheltenham: Edward Elgar, 102–17.

Harell, A., K. Banting, W. Kymlicka and R. Wallace (2022), 'Shared Membership beyond National Identity: Deservingness and Solidarity in Diverse Societies', *Political Studies*, 70 (4), 983–1005.

Harell, A., K. Banting and W. Kymlicka (2023), 'Inclusive Redistribution and Perceptions of Membership: A Cross-National Comparison', Paper presented to 2023 annual meeting of the Council for European Studies.

Harell, A., S. Soroka, M. Polacko and W. Kymlicka (2023), 'Communicating Commitment to the Nation? A Simulated Social Media Experiment', Paper presented to 2023 annual meeting of the Canadian Political Science Association.

Hinz, B. A. (2010), 'The Untold Story of Australian Multiculturalism: How It Was Shaped from Below by Ethnic Communities', Paper presented to Midwest Political Science Association 68th Annual Conference, Chicago.

Honig, B. (2017), *Public Things: Democracy in Disrepair*. Oxford: Oxford University Press.

Huggler, J. (2021), 'German Greens Election Lead at Risk amid Mutiny over Use of Word "Germany" in Manifesto', *The Telegraph*, 7 May. Accessed at: <https://www.telegraph.co.uk/news/2021/05/07/german-greens-face-mutiny-use-word-germany-manifesto/>

Hussain, A. and W. Miller (2006), *Multicultural Nationalism: Islamophobia, Anglophobia, and Devolution*. Oxford: Oxford University Press.

James, M. (2013), 'Neoliberal Heritage Redress', in J. Henderson and P. Wakeham (eds), *Reconciling Canada: Critical Perspectives on the Culture of Redress*. Toronto: University of Toronto Press.

Kernerman, G. (2005), *Multicultural Nationalism: Civilizing Difference, Constituting Community*. Vancouver: University of British Columbia Press.

Kukathas, C. (2021), *Immigration and Freedom*. Princeton, NJ: Princeton University Press.

Kymlicka, W. (2012), *Multiculturalism: Success, Failure, and the Future*. Washington, DC: Migration Policy Institute.

Kymlicka, W. (2013), 'Neoliberal Multiculturalism', in P. Hall and M. Lamont (eds), *Social Resilience in the Neoliberal Era*. Cambridge: Cambridge University Press, 99–125.

Kymlicka, W. (2021), 'The Precarious Resilience of Multiculturalism in Canada', *American Review of Canadian Studies*, 51 (1), 122–42.

Kymlicka, W. (2022), 'Nationhood, Multiculturalism and the Ethics of Membership', in L. Organ and R. Koopmans (eds), *Majorities, Minorities, and the Future of Nationhood*. Cambridge: Cambridge University Press, 87–128.

Kymlicka, W. and K. Walker (eds) (2012), *Rooted Cosmopolitanism: Canada and the World*. Vancouver: University of British Columbia Press.

Laxer, G. B. (2001), 'The Movement that Dare not Speak its Name: The Return of Left Nationalism/Internationalism', *Alternative*, 26 (1), 1–32.

Levey, G. B. (2019), 'Australia's "Liberal Nationalist" Multiculturalism', in R. Ashcroft and M. Bevir (eds), *Multiculturalism in the British Commonwealth Since 1945: Comparative Perspectives on Theory and Practice*. Berkeley: University of California Press, 83–103.

Marshall, T. H. (1950), *Sociology at the Crossroads*. London: Heinemann.

Mitchell, K. (2003), 'Educating the National Citizen in Neoliberal Times: From the Multicultural Self to the Strategic Cosmopolitan', *Transactions of the Institute of British Geographers*, New Series 28 (4), 387–403.

Mitchell, K. (2004), *Crossing the Neoliberal Line: Pacific Rim Migration and the Metropolis*. Philadelphia, PA: Temple University Press.

Modood, T. (1994), 'Establishment, Multiculturalism and British Citizenship', *Political Quarterly*, 65 (1), 53–73.

Modood, T. (2018), 'A Multicultural Nationalism', *Brown Journal of World Affairs*, 25, 233–46.

Modood, T. (2020), 'Multiculturalism as a New Form of Nationalism?', *Nations and Nationalism*, 26 (2), 308–13.

Moran, A. (2011), 'Multiculturalism as Nation-Building in Australia: Inclusive National Identity and the Embrace of Diversity', *Ethnic and Racial Studies*, 34 (12), 2153–72.

Polanyi, K. (1944), *The Great Transformation*. New York: Farrar & Rinehart.

Reeskens, T. (2023), 'A Bridge over Troubled Water? Territorial Identification and Solidarity across Europe', Presented at Boundaries, Membership and Belonging workshop, Edinburgh, May.

Roll-Hansen, N. and G. Broberg (2005), *Eugenics and the Welfare State: Norway, Sweden, Denmark, and Finland*. East Lansing: Michigan State University Press.

Ruiz Jimenez, A. M., M. T. González-Fernández and M. J. Sanchez (2015), 'Identifying with the Nation: Spain's Left-Wing Citizens in an Age of Crisis', *South European Society and Politics*, 20 (4), 487–508.

Saldin, R. (2011), 'Strange Bedfellows: War and Minority Rights', *World Affairs*, 173, 57–66.

Schmid, S.-P. (2023), 'Individual or Collective Rights? Consequences for the Satisfaction with Democracy among Indigenous Peoples in Latin America', *Democratization*, 30 (6), 1113–34.

Scott, C. (2023), 'Supporting the Right to Wear Religious Symbols: The Importance of Perceived Commitment to the Nation', *Politics and Religion*, 16 (1), 90–109.

Sharma, N. (2011), 'Canadian Multiculturalism and its Nationalisms', in M. Chazan et al. (eds), *Home and Native Land*. Toronto: Between the Lines.

Smith, R. (2003), *Stories of Peoplehood: The Politics and Morals of Political Membership*. Cambridge: Cambridge University Press.

Uberoi, V. (2009), 'Multiculturalism and the Canadian Charter of Rights and Freedoms', *Political Studies*, 57 (4), 805–27.

Uberoi, V. (2018), 'National Identity – A Multiculturalist's Approach, *Critical Review of International Social and Political Philosophy*, 21 (1), 46–64.

Uberoi, V. (2020), 'Multiculturalism: A Tradition of Political Thought that Liberal Nationalists Can Use', *Nations and Nationalism*, 26 (3), 531–3.

Walton-Roberts, M. (2011), 'Multiculturalism already Unbound', in M. Chazan et al. (eds), *Home and Native Land*. Toronto: Between the Lines.

Westlake, D. (2020), 'Following the Right: Left and Right Parties' Influence over Multiculturalism', *Canadian Journal of Political Science*, 53 (1), 171–88.

EIGHT

Integrating Modood and Kymlicka on National Inclusion

Geoffrey Brahm Levey

Introduction

Much multicultural political theory attaches little or no importance to nationalism and national identity (for example, Castles et al. 1988; Young 1990; Phillips 2007; Vertovec 2007; Eisenberg 2009; Patten 2014). For some, this is a matter of indifference; for others, it is a matter of conviction in pursuing post-nationalist visions. Two theoretical approaches to multiculturalism which recognise the continued place of nationalism and national identity go by the monikers of liberal nationalism and multicultural nationalism. An unusual aspect of these theoretical approaches is that their respective leading exponents, Will Kymlicka and Tariq Modood, cannot agree on whether their positions disagree. Kymlicka has consistently maintained that Modood's multicultural nationalism, and the Bristol school of multiculturalism (BSM) with which it is more generally associated, are little different from his own liberal nationalism (Kymlicka 2001a, 2019). As if to underscore the point, Kymlicka (2023: 117; Chapter 7, this volume) has occasionally described his position as a form of multicultural nationalism. Modood, on the other hand, has long criticised Kymlicka's liberal defence of multiculturalism in propagating his own political-sociological argument (Modood 2007, 2013, 2019). Recently, Modood (2022, 2023) has sharpened his differences with Kymlicka specifically around the issue of national identity and inclusion.

In this chapter, I want to consider Modood's recent objections to Kymlicka's liberal nationalist treatment of national inclusion in the light of Kymlicka's own recent emphasis on national solidarity. I do not accept Kymlicka's assessment that he and Modood are essentially arguing the same position on national identity: 'But here again, many – if not most

– liberal multiculturalists are multicultural nationalists, on par with the Australian and Bristol schools' (Kymlicka 2019: 977). Nor do I fully accept Modood's assessment that his multicultural nationalism is more fundamental theoretically and more suited to post-immigration ethnic minorities than liberal nationalism: 'from what we might call the political theory of liberal multiculturalism ... there is no logic that gets us from special rights [for post-immigrant minorities] to national, multicultural inclusivity' (Modood 2022: 6). In my view, there are both crucial differences and points of intersection between the two approaches on national inclusion (as with their broader accounts). I have some issues with parts of Modood's recent critique of Kymlicka's liberal nationalism and with Kymlicka's recent revision of his earlier cultural rights approach. However, these concerns are no reason to discount these two perspectives. On the contrary, I will argue that an efficacious multiculturalism needs to incorporate features of both liberal and multicultural nationalisms, and then some. There are good reasons why such an integration is both possible and desirable. We need *all* effective resources in building more inclusive democracies.

I begin by rehearsing Kymlicka's revised cultural rights argument, after which I consider Modood's recent criticisms of this revision from the perspective of his own multicultural nationalism. I attempt to clarify what Modood variously means by broadening a national identity. I then offer an assessment of the respective strengths and limitations of each approach, and of how they might effectively work in tandem.

Kymlicka's Revised Cultural Rights Argument

To grasp Kymlicka's recent recalibration of his original liberal theory of minority rights, a brief recap of the original theory is in order.

Like many liberals, Kymlicka begins with the valorisation of individual autonomy, although, in his case, not as an end in itself but rather because autonomy enables individuals to pursue what they value (Kymlicka 1995; 2002: 222). For Kymlicka, membership in a societal culture is a primary good to which every individual is entitled. Such cultures set the horizon of options that provide the platform for individuals to exercise their autonomy. However, cultural minorities are typically disadvantaged in realising or accessing the good of societal cultural membership, a situation that entitles them to various kinds of remedial cultural rights. As national minorities and Indigenous peoples are said to constitute their own societal cultures, they are entitled to self-government, land, language, and political representational rights. In contrast, post-immigrant ethnic minorities join the established liberal-national societal culture and are entitled to more modest measures, such as exemptions from standing laws and regulations, public subsidies for their ethnic practices, some symbolic recognition of their practices and traditions, and some modest representation to government. A state that recognises these entitlements practices differentiated or multicultural citizenship.

Another aspect of Kymlicka's argument is that while he recognises the inevitability and even legitimacy of the liberal state reflecting the historic or established culture, he limits these state endorsements to the lingua franca and its associated traditions, drawing internal boundaries, education and core curriculum (including transmitting the shared history), and symbolic recognition such as public holidays, flags, anthems and state insignia (Kymlicka 1995: 108, 111, 115; 2001b: 18–20; 2002: 265). A 'thin' national culture of this sort is deemed necessary to make room for and not overbear fellow citizens from cultural minorities. The idea is that by limiting the state's endorsement of the dominant culture and providing an infrastructure of compensatory minority rights, not only will justice be served, but a more inclusive national community (Kymlicka 1995: 190–2) and 'redistributive solidarity' (Kymlicka 2023: 104) will develop over time. This is the kind of 'nation-building' that Kymlicka says liberal nationalists like himself defend (Kymlicka 2001b: 19–21; 2002: 263, 352–4).

In recent work, Kymlicka admits that the expected solidarity has not occurred, though he maintains that multiculturalism policies have moved the needle in the right direction (Kymlicka 2021, 2023, this volume). Survey research across Western democracies consistently finds that cultural minorities are viewed as the least deserving of welfare support among various nominated groups. In Canadian survey research by Kymlicka and his associates, perceived undeservingness was found to limit support also for other redistributive measures for minorities, and even though the latter were considered law-abiding and hard-working (Banting et al. 2020; Harrell et al. 2020). Probing further, the researchers found that this perception of undeservingness is mainly due to the majority doubting minorities' loyalty and moral commitment to the national community. This finding applied across Indigenous, Quebecois and immigrant minorities. Kymlicka interprets these findings to suggest that the 'stories of peoplehood differentially locate majorities and minorities' (Kymlicka 2023: 114). Majorities' mobilisation and claims-making is taken to demonstrate their concern for and commitment to the country, whereas minorities' mobilisation and claims-making is viewed as selfish behaviour. Kymlicka thus suggests a modest revision to his original cultural rights approach. While remedial cultural rights remain primary, they should be understood, claimed and promoted differently: not as limits on majority dominance or as protections against societal values, which may accentuate differential peoplehood, but rather as affording minorities the opportunity to participate in and contribute to the society at large.

I have some reservations about this interpretation and policy reform, which I will come to below. Here, let us consider Modood's criticisms of Kymlicka's recent take, of which there are four.

Modood's Recent Critique

Modood's first criticism is really a preliminary point that he has long made about Kymlicka's theory, namely, that it is suited to national and Indigenous minorities and ill-suited to post-immigration ethnic minorities (Modood 2007, 2013, 2022). This is because national and Indigenous minorities are credited with constituting their own societal cultures, entitling them to substantial group accommodation, whereas immigrant minorities join the established majority societal culture. Not only does the theory grant immigrant minorities more modest 'polyethnic rights', but, says Modood, it is unclear how even these modest measures follow from the theory's philosophical individualism (Modood 2022: 6).

There is, I think, something to this criticism, but it is important to identify what that is exactly. In fact, Kymlicka does theorise the situation of immigrant minorities in terms of individual autonomy and societal cultures as contexts of choice. His argument is that immigrant minorities endure a different kind of disadvantage from that faced by national and Indigenous minorities, namely, in gaining *access* to the wider, liberal society (Kymlicka 1995: 101, 114). This argument lends itself to being interpreted in two quite different ways. One is to understand it in the vein of direct and indirect discrimination, the former being deliberate and invidious, the latter unintentional but adversely impacting particular groups. The protection against such discrimination is commonly defended as ensuring 'access and equity'. This reading of Kymlicka's 'access to one's societal culture' argument treats immigrants' ethnic identity as a given background condition. So understood, the argument would seem to support various cultural exemption claims, public subsidies for minority community festivals and the like, and perhaps even some symbolic recognition, where this involves adjusting the uniforms of national services and the form of oath- taking for public office. If anti-discrimination legal precedent is any indication, the argument would not sustain redesigning public holidays, state symbols (flags, anthems and insignia) or the national story.

The other interpretation of Kymlicka's access argument is more literal and sensitive to the surrounding theoretical propositions that Kymlicka advances in defence of polyethnic rights. In particular, it is informed by Kymlicka's key theoretical points that most immigrants chose to leave their own societal culture to join another, and that the kind of culture to which they are entitled as a primary good is the broader liberal societal culture that took them in. From this perspective, the access idea might work for some limited exemption cases, such as a Sikh needing relief from hard hat or motorcycle helmet regulations to be gainfully employed as a construction worker or mail deliverer. However, its force wanes in many other exemption claims, such as the ritual slaughtering of animals (kosher and halal meat can be imported, as it now is in some Scandinavian countries) or being buried in a shroud rather than a coffin. It is unclear how the argument sustains public subsidies for minority ethnic festivals and the like, which measures are about enabling minorities to continue to access their own traditions rather than the societal culture (Levey 1997: 220–1). And like the first interpretation, only more so, this interpretation of the access argument scarcely supports symbolic recognition. Indeed, one might reasonably conclude that Kymlicka's theory provides a basis for insisting that post-immigration minorities either put up with some inconvenience or else conform with the societal cultural patterns they chose to join.

Modood's criticism could conceivably be aimed at either of these two interpretations of Kymlicka's polyethnic rights. His scepticism that these rights follow from philosophical individualism suggests perhaps a reading of Kymlicka's argument in line with the second account. However, Modood's particular interest in national identity would also find a focus on individual rights of non-discrimination to be inadequate (Modood 2012). The broader point I would make is that liberal nationalists do not need Kymlicka's theory, on any reading, to grant immigrant minorities cultural rights. They can appeal directly to the values of liberty, equality and democracy. Liberty must include some cultural liberty, equality must include people of diverse backgrounds and with different interests, and democracy must include all citizens and allow different voices to be heard. Thus, even non-multiculturalist democracies grant some minority cultural accommodation (Joppke 2017). As Modood (2022: 5) himself acknowledges, '[j]ustice warrants that they [immigrant minorities] should be allowed to maintain some distinctive cultural practices, which may indeed require some recognition and accommodation from the state'. To be sure, these measures are typically construed as elaborations of individual rights and not the kind of group rights that Modood and the BSM say they also want to endorse. Nevertheless, these are the bases upon which real-world multiculturalist democracies such as Canada and Australia accommodate the cultural identities and practices of immigrant minorities. To use BSM terms, they are the operative public values of these liberal national communities. Even if Kymlicka's liberal nationalist theory may not work well for immigrant minorities, liberal nationalists can otherwise support many of the same sorts of cultural rights claims. Again, there are limits at the symbolic level, to which I will return.

Modood's second criticism is that Kymlicka's recent concern with national membership and inclusion exposes the problem with his liberal argument that national identity should be kept 'thin'. Modood appears to read the recent Kymlicka as making a significant shift in the direction of national identity. I read him as reiterating his 1995 caution against enlisting national identity in the service of multiculturalism. Kymlicka writes, for example, that '[t]he fundamental priority in terms of justice cannot be to ramp up nation-building, but on the contrary to constrain nation-building by minority rights'. He notes how national states create exclusionary peoplehood based on the cultural majority, and the pattern of differential deservingness found in the Canadian data is, for him, further evidence that the solution is *not* to be found in focusing on national identity or stories of peoplehood, at least in the case of immigrant minorities, as it plays to the majority's hand (Kymlicka 2023: 97–9). One iteration of his recent position is even titled 'Beyond national identity: liberal nationalism, shared membership and solidarity' (Banting et al. 2020).

Yet there is a tension running through Kymlicka's analysis. For he also argues that 'imparting stories of peoplehood' that explain how the polity and the national 'we' came to take form is one of the few areas in which it is *appropriate* for a liberal state to propagate cultural commitments (Kymlicka 2023: 93). As noted, Kymlicka makes much the same argument in his earlier work: it is legitimate for the state to teach a core curriculum and the shared history of its people under his thin conception of national identity. The tension is explained and potentially eased in the case of Indigenous and national minorities, whose alternative accounts of peoplehood Kymlicka accepts as legitimate contestations which the parties should strive to reconcile as 'something "we" (majority and minorities) do together' (Kymlicka 2023: 117). However, the tension is left hanging in the case of immigrant minorities who, it

seems, simply must wear that '[s]tories of peoplehood ... put immigrants under a cloud of suspicion' (Kymlicka 2023: 98). Kymlicka's best
offer on this score is to keep a lid on national identity while seeking to
fortify 'we-ness' through recasting cultural rights.

In contrast, Modood's multicultural nationalism takes this bull by
the horns regarding immigrant minorities. He agrees that the prevailing story of peoplehood – in his terms, national identity – will reflect
the cultural predilections of the established majority culture. And it is
precisely for that reason, on his account, that the prevailing story needs
to broaden and be made more inclusive. Where Kymlicka seeks to arrest
majority cultural dominance and extend solidarity by means of minority cultural rights, Modood seeks to arrest majority cultural dominance
and extend belongingness through an inclusive national identity.

Which brings us to Modood's third criticism, namely, there is no
basis in Kymlicka's liberal nationalist theory for remaking national identity. That may seem to follow from the contrast just drawn and yet it is
not exactly the case. Though Kymlicka's theory does not *aim* to remake
national identity but rather to extend equality of membership and foster
solidarity and national inclusion, there is nevertheless some implicit provision to this effect. National and Indigenous minority rights include self-
government, land and language rights, all of which potentially impinge
on the character of the established national identity. And we have noted
how Kymlicka (2023) allows that national and Indigenous minorities
might agitate to have their own experiences of peoplehood incorporated
into the national story. There is more to Modood's criticism in the case of
immigrant groups and national identity for the reasons canvassed above:
Kymlicka's normative argument for polyethnic rights is suspect on one
reading, and, in any case, the degree to which polyethnic rights include
symbolic recognition (flags, anthems, insignia, public holidays, government declarations) or rewriting the national story is very limited.

However, at this juncture we need to probe what Modood means by
remaking a national identity. There are many ways by which a national
identity might be made more inclusive. Table 8.1 presents a list of some
such ways, with illustrative examples. Some cases are the province of
state authority or the government of the day, others of civil society.

One kind of state intervention involves the government directly and
deliberately making policy or issuing directives in this area (#1). This kind
includes the historical narrative or story of peoplehood (of such concern in
Kymlicka's recent work), as taught, for example, in the school curriculum.
However, direct intervention might also involve informal statements or
activities by government members in support of certain characterisations
of 'who we are'. Another kind of state intervention involves extending the
'mosaic' or 'quilt' of national identity. That is, new distinctive elements

Table 8.1: Remaking National Identity: Some Processes and Examples

Process	State Intervention	Society Driven
Government directive	1. government policy, directive, or other <u>endorsement</u> (for example, teaching the national story inclusively)	
Extending the mosaic or quilt	2. state institution itself <u>incorporates</u> some minority cultural difference (for example, a dual-language national anthem)	5. widespread <u>adoption</u> of, or <u>participation</u> in, a minority practice (for example, use of Yiddish: chutzpah, Chinese New Year)
New creation from old and new: melting pot	3. state institution <u>merges</u> constituent traditions or experiences in new form (for example, entrance to Canadian Museum of History)	6. cultural <u>fusion</u> (for example, cuisine, dress, music)
Reinterpretation	4. an established tradition is <u>redefined</u> (for example, monarch becomes ceremonial and unifying figure)	7. an established tradition <u>acquires new meaning</u> (for example, St George's Cross in state emblems no longer viewed as a religious symbol)

are added to the established patterns and embraced as part of the national 'we'. For example, a state institution might incorporate a minority cultural difference, such as a national anthem including stanzas in a minority language or otherwise referencing the minority or minorities (#2).

A national identity might also be modified through merging traditions to create something new (#3). This is the classic melting-pot model (Zangwill 1909). There are many spheres in which a new amalgam might take form, public architecture being a notable one. For example, the building of the Canadian Museum of History was designed by an Indigenous architect and features an entrance that abstractly represents a turtle's head, a symbol of great significance in the local Indigenous culture. Similarly, the National Museum of Australia features a zigzag wall on the Indigenous wing (seemingly modelled on Daniel Libeskind's Jewish Museum in Berlin), capturing the jagged, fraught historical relationship between settler and Indigenous Australians. Last, governments might invest established traditions with new meaning, an historically significant but still resonant one being the redefinition of the British monarchy as a ceremonial and unifying institution (#4). In the same vein, Italy's Supreme Administrative Court determined, in the famous *Lautsi* case, that the crucifixes hanging in the country's school classrooms symbolised 'liberty, equality, human dignity and religious toleration, and thus the *secular* nature of the State' (as cited in *Lautsi*, 2011 Eur. Ct. H.R. §§ 15–16; italics added).

On the societal side, the mosaic or quilt of national identity might be extended through the popular adoption of a minority practice, such as the routine borrowing and thus incorporation of certain words from a minority language (#5). Or it might be extended through the widespread participation in a minority festival, such as Chinese New Year. The melting-pot process is increasingly evident also in everyday social practices, from fashion to music, but perhaps none more so than in culinary fusion (#6). Finally, official reinterpretations of established practices are matched by the changing perceptions of mass publics over time (#7). Once a powerful and unmistakable religious symbol, St George's Cross, for example, now adorns many a state and university emblem as simply part of the institutional furniture, seemingly devoid of any contemporary religious significance (Levey 2018).

Modood would, I believe, welcome all these various ways of remaking a national identity. However, he returns time and again to the same five processes, as highlighted in Table 8.2. He endorses, of course, the government broadening the national story (#1), applauding, for example, the inclusive portrayal of the British people at the opening ceremony of the London Olympics (Modood 2013: 200–1; 2014a: 33). He often cites the example of broadening the religious education curriculum and the 'provision of religious instruction and worship in schools if and when requested by minority communities' (#2) (for example, Modood 2014b; 2022: 7), which are examples of state institutions incorporating diversity into their fare. He notes how then Prince Charles has made a point of redefining his role as 'Defender of Faiths' instead of the traditional and official 'Defender of the Faith', that is, the Church of England alone (#4), which involves the redefinition of an established tradition (for example, Modood 2010: 6; Thompson and Modood 2022: 7). One societal initiative – fusion cuisine in the form of chicken tikka masala (#6) – is accorded national identity significance only in conjunction with then Foreign Secretary Robin Cook publicly describing it as 'now a true British national dish' (#1) (Cook 2001). The only exclusively societal action that Modood regularly cites as helping to reshape British national identity is how religious minorities fancy maintaining the Established Church of England to protect the role of religion in public life more generally (#7) (for example, Modood 1994, 2010, 2022). The 'reshaping' here is again by way of retaining a tradition but investing it with new meaning.

Table 8.2: Remaking National Identity: Modood's Favoured Examples

Process	State Intervention	Society Driven
Government directive	1. government directive or endorsement (for example, a) inclusive storytelling at the Opening Ceremony of the London Olympics; b) Foreign Secretary Robin Cook declaring chicken tikka masala a true British dish)	
Extending the mosaic or quilt	2. state institution itself incorporates some minority cultural difference (for example, religious instruction in schools)	5. widespread adoption of, or participation in, a minority practice (for example, use of Yiddish: chutzpah, Chinese New Year)
New creation from old and new: melting pot	3. state institution merges constituent traditions or experiences in new form (for example, entrance to Canadian Museum of History)	6. cultural fusion (for example, chicken tikka masala: see also #1)
Reinterpretation	4. an established tradition is redefined (for example, British monarch as Defender of the Faiths instead of Defender of the Faith	7. an established tradition acquires new meaning (for example, Established Church of England supported by non-Anglican religious minorities for symbolising the public place of religion)

Two points are notable about Modood's recurrent examples, along with a third, more general point about his approach to multicultural- ism. First, the emphasis is very much on the state or government being involved in the remaking of national identity. In this sense, it is a decid- edly top-down approach to national identity, which point I take up below. Second, one of Modood's favoured examples for broadening and 'thickening' the national identity – religious education and instruction in schools (#2) – involves the kind of state institutional inclusion of minorities that Kymlicka could endorse as a polyethnic cultural right. I say *could endorse* because, as Modood notes, Kymlicka did not initially favour this kind of 'pluralistic religious thickening' (Modood 2022: 7), viewing the relationship between the state and religion as rightly one of separation in contrast to the deep entanglement between the state and ethnicity (Kymlicka 2002: 344–5). In *Multicultural Citizenship*, Kymlicka allows legal exemptions to Muslims, Sikhs and Jews and otherwise discusses the Amish, Hutterites and Hasidic Jews as segregationist groups, whereas he mostly chooses (non-religious) ethnic minorities to illustrate rights to group representation in the democratic process, public subsidisation and the institutional inclusion of cultural minorities (Modood 2007: 26–7). More recently, Kymlicka (2015) has clarified that he now agrees that ethnic and religious identity should be treated alike under multiculturalism. Modood (2022: 8) finds this extension problematic because Kymlicka has not shown how religion fits into theory. However, I can see no reason why Kymlicka's access to societal culture argument could not also apply to religious minorities (insofar as one is willing to credit the argument at all). Thus, it is fair to conclude that the state's incorporation of greater diversity in religious education and instruction or, for that matter, of greater ethnic representation in the curriculum could qualify as a cultural right claim as covered in Kymlicka's theory of polyethnic entitlements.

This intersection between Kymlicka's liberal nationalism and Modood's multicultural nationalism at the accommodation level prefigures, thirdly, a more general point about Modood's treatment of national identity. And that is he is inclined to view almost every instance of public recognition and accommodation of cultural minorities as helping, or potentially helping, to remake and broaden the national identity. This follows from his sociological-cum-political approach to multiculturalism, which proceeds from both groups' positive self-understanding of their identity and from their response to 'negative difference' or how the state and society negatively characterise and treat their group (Modood 2007). Affirmative state or public recognition and accommodation of minorities is at once the ethic, the ethos and the practical building blocks of remaking a national identity. But this means that all Kymlicka's polyethnic rights – legal exemptions, public subsidies and grants, symbolic recognition, representation – are likely to qualify as such building blocks; the two theorists simply understand the work of the same measures differently. As Modood puts it: 'once we have an idea of a multicultural national inclusivity, that our co-citizens stand in need of recognition and their identities should be respected and should be seen as part of our national, multi-faceted, plural 'we', we can argue for appropriate forms of accommodation – "rights", if you will' (Modood 2022: 6).

Table 8.3 represents this coincidence of measures. Kymlicka's allowance of some symbolic recognition for immigrant minorities would cover government directed national ceremonies (#1), state institutions themselves incorporating minority cultural differences (#2), and various ways the state may otherwise accommodate and provide for minorities' cultural differences (#3), which, in Modood's theoretical terms, also amount to broadening the national identity.

Table 8.3: Remaking National Identity and Membership: Coincidence of Modood's and Kymlicka's State Measures

Process	State Intervention
Government directive	1. government directive or <u>endorsement</u> *(for example, inclusive storytelling at the Opening Ceremony of the London Olympics)*
Extending the mosaic or quilt 1	2. state institution itself <u>incorporates</u> some minority cultural difference *(for example, religious Instruction in schools)*
Extending the mosaic or quilt 2	3. <u>accommodating</u> some (minority) cultural difference *(for example, legal exemptions, public subsidies, representation)*

Returning, then, to Modood's claim that there is no basis in Kymlicka's liberal nationalist theory for remaking national identity as far as immigrant minorities are concerned, the assessment must be a 'yes' and 'no'. The claim is correct at the philosophical level: Kymlicka's theory does not aim to remake national identity, as such. However, the claim is incorrect at the practical level: Kymlicka's theory posits various cultural rights that potentially contribute to the remaking of a national identity, as Modood himself understands what it practically takes to engage in building that new identity.

This raises the question of whether, if the practical measures are the same or similar, it even matters how we think about and present them. Both Kymlicka and Modood think it does and so do I. Which leads us to Modood's fourth and concluding criticism, namely, that liberal nationalism cannot match multicultural nationalism's reach in securing national inclusion, thus showing multicultural nationalism to be the more fundamental and effective approach. It is to this issue that I now turn.

Cultural Rights or Remaking National Identity?

Modood contends that his multicultural nationalism is the more fundamental and effective approach because it can both broaden the national identity *and* generate wide-ranging rights-like provisions for post-immigration minorities, whereas Kymlicka's liberal national-ism can at best bequeath a limited set of cultural rights. I think each approach is fundamental to its own purposes, so the real question is one of efficacy. In my view, both liberal nationalism and multicul-tural nationalism have something valuable to contribute to an effica-cious multiculturalism, as well as having limitations. Let me then try to explain why and what.

Liberal nationalism and multicultural nationalism approach mul-ticulturalism and national inclusion very differently, even putting aside that Kymlicka seeks to present a liberal theory, a framing which Modood rejects. For Modood, the animating concepts and concerns are identity, difference, equality, recognition and belonging (see Thompson, this volume), whereas for Kymlicka they are political membership, culture, equality, accommodation, and solidarity and a broader social justice (that is, beyond cultural disadvantage). Both theorists invoke multicultural citi-zenship as a framing concept for their respective positions. One of several ironies in this debate is that Modood's focus on particular minorities and their felt marginalisation leads him to advocate for a remade whole – a broader, 'thicker' and more inclusive national identity – which is then expected to reshape and equalise relations between the majority and minorities on the ground. Meanwhile, Kymlicka's focus on social justice in general leads him to defend minority cultural rights, which are then expected to extend solidarity at the national and societal levels. What, then, can be said of their efficacy?

Taking Kymlicka's liberal nationalism first, his own assessment, as we have seen, is that it has not been entirely successful in producing the hoped for solidaristic democratic society, with the majority still suspect-ing the commitment of minorities to the broader society (at least in Canada). His solution to this blockage is to rebrand cultural rights as opportunities to contribute to the society from their conventional defence as protections against majority dominance. I have no issue with *adding* this understanding of cultural rights. Presenting cultural rights as oppor-tunities to contribute does capture an important dimension of them and should be part of the arsenal of their defence. However, there is a prob-lem if this account is meant to supersede rather than complement the original understanding of cultural rights, as appears to be the case. For then it would have an illiberal aspect to it. Like some members of the majority, some minority members will be self-absorbed and have little interest in or appetite for contributing to the society. Some, like the Amish, will remove themselves from the society and live alone. Some, like Hasidic Jews, will segregate themselves and do their own thing in cities. If they are law-abiding, a liberal society ought to be able to accommodate people who wish only to be let alone. Such groups may not serve the sought-after solidarity but their entitlement to be themselves must be part of a liberal society.

Emphasising contribution to society is not without moral hazard either. While such a contribution can come in many forms and degrees, it can also morph into unrealistic expectations. I am reminded of my own experience growing up in a minority community. Every Rosh Hashana, the Jewish new year, state and federal political leaders would extend goodwill greetings to their Jewish communities by rehearsing Jews' contribution to business, science, the arts, the legal profession and so on, and concluding how they were a welcome and valued presence in Australia. It was well intentioned, but it made me wonder where that left struggling communities with less conspicuous achievement. Why shouldn't law-abidingness, raising families and holding a regular job be enough to be welcomed and valued?

My main concern about Kymlicka's rebranding of cultural rights, however, goes to the reasoning behind it. Others have challenged this reasoning for assuming there is nothing to the national majority's claims (Da Silva and Weinstock 2023: 134–5). I think it can be faulted for doing almost the opposite: further privileging the majority's perspective. First, Kymlicka and his associates treat the majority's perceptions of minorities as the dependent variable and the character of minorities' pursuit of their cultural commitments and attachments as the independent variable. The entire onus is thus put on minorities and the way in which their cultural pursuits are presented. Kymlicka acknowledges the 'perverse injustice' of minorities continually having to prove their moral commitment to the nation, and simply concludes, with resignation, 'that is the world we live in' (Kymlicka 2023: 118). Reinforcing this unfairness is an odd position for multiculturalists to take. It will always characterise the world we live in if it goes unchallenged.

But secondly, the rebranding exercise is also unlikely to achieve its objective of alleviating majority suspicions of minorities. Clara Sandelind (2023) has questioned these postulated links between minority rights and majority attitudes by citing contemporary evidence and data. In *The Origins of Totalitarianism*, Hannah Arendt (1973) provides some historical grounds for scepticism. She observes that Jews in Western Europe made two fatal errors of judgement during their emancipation in the eighteenth and nineteenth centuries. The first was to assume that the Jewish question – whether, and on what terms, Jews could be integrated into modernising Western societies – would be solved through their legal emancipation and acquisition of equal rights of citizenship. They soon discovered that legal emancipation did not bring 'social emancipation' or their acceptance by the broader society. Their second error, says Arendt, was to suppose that they could win social acceptance by reforming their religious and cultural traditions, dress and behaviour to accord with the dominant societal patterns. Instead, where previously they were accused of being clannish, too foreign in their ways, unable to intermarry and so on, now assimilated Jews were accused of being too socially and economically successful, too powerful, taking the jobs of ordinary Germans, etc. (Arendt 1973: chapters 3 and 4). This story ends tragically in the ashes of the Holocaust.

While the Jewish experience of antisemitism cannot simply be applied to that of other ethnic and religious minorities in the West today, Arendt's analysis stands as a cautionary tale about the propensity of majorities to reinvent their suspicions about minorities as circumstances change. They have a habit of doing this everywhere. That is why the Canadian researchers could find that majority suspicions persist despite viewing minorities as law-abiding and hard-working. Yesterday's prejudices are replaced with today's. Multiculturalists who are hoping that a recasting of cultural rights will assuage majority suspicions of minorities should not hold their breath.

I fully agree with Kymlicka that multiculturalism will be most effective when it 'is designed with transformative as well as protective functions in mind' (Kymlicka 2023: 118). However, rebranding liberal cultural rights as opportunities to contribute to society is too slim a reed to do that transformative work. Realising inclusive membership needs to be tackled both more directly and wholistically, in my view.

First, at the ground and more immediate level, the established cultural majority should be made to assume some of the responsibility of adjustment. It needs to be invested in this project. It needs to be constantly reminded that the institutions of state and the society's bounty and opportunities are not its exclusive preserve. It needs to be made to understand that the situation of minorities is as much, if not more, its problem as it is minorities' problem. This is a long, grinding, perhaps never-ending campaign of education, messaging and policy interventions, just as it has been to get to the point that sexual assault and harassment are better understood today as men's problem and no longer only as women's problem. The nuts and bolts of multiculturalism policy are a key part of this effort, including cultural rights variously understood as cultural liberties, the right to participate as an equal member, and, yes, the opportunity to contribute to society. Protective cultural rights, in other words, need not be construed and defended only defensively;

they can and should be defended on the offensive. None of this is to deny that the national cultural majority may have legitimate interests of its own. It is only to reiterate why multiculturalism was called forth in the first place.

For all the reasons canvassed above, however, we should not expect cultural rights on *any* account to be sufficient to dislodge majority suspicions of minorities. Thus, the challenge simultaneously needs to be tackled at a more wholistic level. This is where Modood's multicultural nationalist approach comes into its own. It seeks to sew together the social fabric by reconstituting the national imaginary, thus obviating many of the tensions and disparities between the majority and minorities. While several of Modood's favoured examples of extending the national identity involve the accommodation of minorities' culturally different traditions and practices, some, like Prince Charles saying he will be 'Defender of the Faiths' and Foreign Secretary Robin Cook declaring chicken tikka masala a true British dish, are more about the symbolic signalling that minorities rightly belong. This kind of affirmation of the generalised presence of minorities, not necessarily connected to accommodating a particular cultural practice, is an oft-overlooked area of multicultural politics (Chin and Levey 2022a, 2022b). Modood's sociological-cum-political approach to multiculturalism, highlighting minorities' positive self-understanding in conjunction with their often negatively ascribed differences, has the theoretical advantage of speaking to this more symbolic and affective side of multicultural politics. Kymlicka's cultural rights approach cannot really compete in this domain regarding post-immigration minorities. More is involved than citizens having a right to see themselves in the institutions that govern them (Kymlicka 2023: 99), the measure of which also tends to be the accommodation of different practices. It concerns, as well, how specific minorities and minorities in general are addressed, spoken of, thought about, acknowledged and signified. In short, how public space in its broadest sense is constituted and represented. Liberal nationalism thus needs something like multicultural nationalism to help complete its own multicultural ambitions. Varun Uberoi (2020) makes a similar point in assessing Yael Tamir's (2019) account of liberal nationalism, that it can benefit from the Bristol schoolers' valorisation of national identity as a way of unifying diverse societies.

Yet, the Bristol school's multicultural nationalism has its own limitations. One is that shifting the dial on national identity and culture, and sentiment about those things, takes more time than is usually acknowledged. The theory is that once it is understood and accepted that citizens not of the majority also need to have their identities respected and included in the national story, this will arrest 'us' and 'them' thinking, reform institutions and issue accommodating policies. It may well *begin* to do all those things, but attitudinal and structural changes do not happen overnight, especially where the expressed goal is to change the national identity, as this provokes resistance. Witness the public controversy that erupted in response to the Parekh Report at the mere suggestion that British identity needed adjustment (CMEB 2000; Parekh 2001). Modood and his BSM colleagues rightly note how attitudes, even among some conservative politicians, subsequently began to shift towards more inclusive visions of Britain and Britishness (Meer and Modood 2009; Modood 2014a; Uberoi and Modood 2013). However, I think even they would agree that there is still a long way to go before multicultural nationalism is institutionalised as the reigning British public philosophy. The involvement of religious minorities at King Charles' Coronation and his delicate affirmation of the primacy of the Church of England while acknowledging Britain as a 'community of communities' are, for example, applauded by one Bristol schooler as 'a good start' with more to be done (Uberoi 2023).

It follows that until the multicultural nationalist ethic has seeped into public consciousness and transformed public institutions and national self-understanding, cultural minorities are going to need the (continued) protection and entitlement offered by cultural rights as conventionally understood and defended on liberal democratic principles of freedom, equality and toleration. Multicultural nationalism thus needs the assistance of liberal nationalist multiculturalism to help establish its own alternative vision of these measures.

Conclusion

Kymlicka's liberal nationalism and Modood's multicultural nationalism strive to do different things, albeit each as a defence of multiculturalism. Kymlicka's multiculturalism is primarily a component of and vehicle for securing a broader social justice, beyond cultural matters, and which appeals to a solidarity among citizens. Modood's multiculturalism is primarily a component of and vehicle for securing the belonging of cultural minorities to the political community and their sense of belonging. From these overarching interests and concerns, the two approaches deploy different strategies for achieving the kind of inclusion they respectively deem to be vital. Each approach has its strengths and limitations. I have argued that the particular alignment of these strengths and limitations should make liberal nationalism and multicultural nationalism partners rather than rivals in advancing the multicultural project. In a very real and practical sense, each needs the other in this project.

Liberal nationalist cultural rights need to be supplemented with the kinds of generic affirmation, acknowledgement and symbolic recognition that multicultural nationalism theorises as important. And multicultural nationalism needs the concrete protections of minority cultural practices that liberal nationalism affords until its own vision of an enlarged national identity is embraced to the point that it has reshaped institutions and rendered cultural rights unnecessary (if indeed such a point is ever reached).

Both approaches would benefit from measures that directly engage and serve national inclusion, that is, without making this depend either on minorities' contribution to society (Kymlicka) or on wrapping it in the language of national identity. Modood's multicultural nationalism is singularly focused on national identity as the medium of national inclusion. Kymlicka's concern with this, as we saw, is that priming national identity runs the risk of further empowering the cultural majority (Kymlicka 2023: 97–9). My own concern is that it entrusts politicians with a matter that is essentially developed by the people, on the ground, through their myriad everyday interactions and enterprises (Levey 2008, 2019), what Michael Billig (1995) calls 'banal nationalism', but which in fact is vital, rich, complex, dynamic and creative. Politicians may do good in effectively broadening the national identity, which is why I do not reject outright any of the government processes or examples Modood recurrently cites. Political leaders certainly have an obligation to rebut xenophobic, racist and discriminatory accounts of the national identity. However, in trying to say what the national identity *is* rather than what it is *not*, they also tend to get it woefully wrong. They aren't alone in that, as trying to distil and bring to speech, let alone engineer, something as organic, nebulous and complexly interconnected as a national identity and culture is a difficult and fraught exercise. The attempt usually results in cliché, caricature or jingoism, if not worse.

The goal of multicultural nationalism is to secure the inclusion and belongingness of and for cultural minorities. So it is important to consider how these goals might be served more directly, without constantly summoning national identity and inviting the controversies and caricature that can evoke. It is worth recalling that, as a revolutionary creed, liberalism began with a realisation that inclusion was no less important a *political* value than either liberty or equality. However, the third of the tricolour values, *fraternité*, never really acquired the same standing as *liberté* and *égalité* in Western democracies beyond France. This is especially notable in the Anglosphere. While latter-twentieth-century multiculturalism policy may be understood as something of a corrective in this regard, the detail of Anglospheric multiculturalism has tended to follow cultural form and view inclusion simply as the corollary of respecting cultural liberty and of protecting access and equity (Levey 2013). That misses, as Arendt forensically detailed, how formal rights do not necessarily bring social acceptance. So there is an opportunity and a need here for culturally diverse liberal democracies to retrieve a part of their historical vision and reinscribe inclusion and belongingness as political values independently worthy of respect. Much good might be done in their name. Table 8.4 presents this additional approach to national inclusion, with accompanying examples, in relation to the approaches and measures previously canvassed.

Table 8.4: Remaking National Identity and Membership: A More Inclusive Account

Process	State Intervention	Society Driven
Government directive (minimal liberal cultural rights)	1. government directive or endorsement (*for example, teaching the national story inclusively*)	
Extending the mosaic or quilt 1 (liberal cultural rights)	2. state institution itself incorporates some minority cultural difference (*for example, religious instruction in schools*)	7. widespread adoption of, or participation in, a minority practice (*for example, use of Yiddish: chutzpah, Chinese New Year*)
Extending the mosaic or quilt 2 (liberal cultural rights)	3. accommodating some (minority) cultural difference (*for example, legal exemptions, public subsidies, representation*)	8. commercial and civil society accommodation and sponsorship of multicultural initiatives (*for example, cultural diversity training; ritually prepared food available at work canteens*)
New creation from old and new: melting pot	4. state institution merges constituent traditions or experiences in new form (*for example, Canadian Museum of History*)	9. cultural fusion (*for example, cuisine, dress, music*)
Reinterpretation	5. an established tradition is redefined (*for example, British monarch as Defender of the Faiths instead of Defender of the Faith*)	10. an established tradition acquires new meaning (*for example, St George's Cross in state emblems no longer viewed as a religious symbol*)

| Inclusion of people (instead of difference) | 6. Inclusive political signification and practices
• *ceremonial representation*
• *inclusive public rhetoric*
• *official/public acknowledgement*
• *made to feel valued*
• *public space access and representation* | 11. Inclusive social practices
• *social acceptance*
• *intermarriage*
• *inclusive public rhetoric*
• *mutual respect*
• *respectful treatment by the media* |

Political values are implicitly understood by all to be the legitimate province of public administration. That is not always the case with national identity and culture. Core political values are also educative as well as regulatory. Over time, they are likely to be understood as part of the national identity and culture as well, creating a virtuous circle. Inclusion and belonging should thus be restored to the status of core political values. In this way, political inclusion and multicultural nationalism will work in concert to make nuts and bolts multiculturalism truly transformative. The 'multi' in multiculturalism should encompass not only the diversity of peoples but also our best ideas and strategies for building inclusive multicultural democracies.

References

Arendt, H. (1973), *The Origins of Totalitarianism*. New York: Andre Deutsch.

Banting K., W. Kymlicka, A. Harrell and R. Wallace (2020), 'Beyond National Identity: Liberal Nationalism, Shared Membership and Solidarity', in G. Gustavson and D. Miller (eds), *Liberal Nationalism and its Critics*. Oxford: Oxford University Press, 205–25.

Billig, M. (1995), *Banal Nationalism*. London and Thousand Oaks, CA: Sage.

Castles, S., M. Kalantzis, B. Cope and M. Morrisey (1988), *Mistaken Identity: Multiculturalism and the Demise of Nationalism in Australia*. Sydney: Pluto Press.

Chin, C. and G. B. Levey (2022a), 'Recognition as Acknowledgement: Symbolic Politics in Multicultural Democracies', *Ethnic & Racial Studies*, 46 (3), 451–74.

Chin, C. and G. B. Levey (2022b), 'Theorizing Acknowledgement: Sourcing, Grounding and Politicizing Recognition', *Ethnic & Racial Studies*, 46 (3), 512–20.

Commission on the Future of Multi-Ethnic Britain (CMEB) (2000), *The Future of Multi-Ethnic Britain: The Parekh Report*. London: Profile Books.

Cook, R. (2001), 'Robin Cook's chicken tikka masala speech: extracts from a speech by the foreign secretary to the Social Market Foundation in London', *The Guardian*, 20 April.

Da Silva, M. and D. Weinstock (2023), 'Reconciling the Cultural Claims of Majorities and Minorities', in L. Orgad and R. Koopmans (eds), *Majorities, Minorities, and the Future of Nationhood*. Cambridge: Cambridge University Press, 129–50.

ECtHR 11 March 2011, Case No. 30814/06, *Lautsi and Others v. Italy*.

Eisenberg, A. (2009), *Reasons of Identity: A Normative Guide to the Political and Legal Assessment of Identity Claims*. Oxford: Oxford University Press.

Harell, A., K. Banting and W. Kymlicka (2020), 'Nationalism, Membership and the Politics of Minority Claims Making', Paper presented at the National Identity in an Angry Age workshop, Uppsala, 3–5 Feb.

Joppke, C. (2017), *Is Multiculturalism Dead?*. Cambridge: Polity.

Kymlicka, W. (1995), *Multicultural Citizenship: A Liberal Theory of Minority Rights*. Oxford: Oxford University Press.

Kymlicka, W. (2001a), 'Liberalism, Dialogue and Multiculturalism', *Ethnicities*, 1 (1), 128–37.

Kymlicka, W. (2001b), 'Western Political Theory and Ethnic Relations in Eastern Europe', in W. Kymlicka and M. Opalski (eds), *Can Liberal Pluralism Be Exported?*. Oxford: Oxford University Press, 13–105.

Kymlicka, W. (2002), *Contemporary Political Philosophy: An Introduction*, 2nd edn. Oxford: Oxford University Press.

Kymlicka, W. (2015), 'The Three Lives of Multiculturalism', in S. Guo and L. Wong (eds), *Revisiting Multiculturalism in Canada: Theories, Policies, Debates*. Rotterdam: Sense Publishers, 15–35.

Kymlicka, W. (2019), 'Deschooling Multiculturalism', *Ethnicities*, 19 (6), 971–82.

Kymlicka, W. (2021), 'Multiculturalism and the Ethics of Membership', Paper presented at the Multicultural Citizenship, 25 Years Later conference, Université Paris 1 Panthéon Sorbonne, 18 November.

Kymlicka, W. (2023), 'Nationhood, Multiculturalism, and the Ethics of Membership', in L. Orgad and R. Koopmans (eds), *Majorities, Minorities, and the Future of Nationhood*. Cambridge: Cambridge University Press, 87–128.

Levey, G. B. (1997), 'Equality, Autonomy, and Cultural Rights', *Political Theory*, 25 (2), 215–48.

Levey, G. B. (2008), 'Multiculturalism and Australian National Identity', in G. B. Levey (ed.), *Political Theory and Australian Multiculturalism*. New York: Berghahn Books, 254–76.

Levey, G. B. (2013), 'Inclusion: A Missing Principle in Australian Multiculturalism', in P. Balint and S. Guérard de Latour (eds), *Liberal Multiculturalism and the Fair Terms of Integration*. London: Palgrave Macmillan, 109–24.

Levey, G. B. (2018), 'Religion, Culture and Liberal Democracy: The Issue of Majority Cultural Precedence', in K. Alidadi and M.-C. Foblets (eds), *Public Commissions on Cultural and Religious Diversity: National Narratives, Multiple Identities and Minorities*. Abingdon: Routledge, 251–65.

Levey, G. B. (2019), 'The Bristol School of Multiculturalism', *Ethnicities*, 19 (1), 220–6.

Meer, N. and T. Modood (2009), 'The Multicultural State We're In: Muslims, "Multi-culture" and the "Civic Re-balancing" of British Multiculturalism', *Political Studies*, 57, 473–97.

Modood, T. (1994), 'Establishment, Multiculturalism and British Citizenship', *Political Quarterly*, 65, 53–73.

Modood, T. (2007), *Multiculturalism: A Civic Idea*. Cambridge: Polity Press.

Modood, T. (2010), 'Moderate Secularism, Religion as Identity and Respect for Religion', *Political Quarterly*, 81 (1), 4–14.

Modood, T. (2012), 'Post-Immigration "Difference" and Integration: The Case of Muslims in Western Europe', Report prepared for the British Academy. London: The British Academy.

Modood, T. (2013), *Multiculturalism: A Civic Idea*, 2nd edn. Cambridge: Polity Press.

Modood, T. (2014a), 'Multiculturalism and Britishness: Provocations, Hostilities and Advances', in R. Garbaye and P. Schnapper (eds), *The Politics of Ethnic Diversity in the British Isles*. London: Palgrave Macmillan, 21–37.

Modood, T. (2014b), 'Multiculturalism, Interculturalisms and the Majority', Kohlberg Memorial Lecture, *Journal of Moral Education*, 43 (3), 302–15.

Modood, T. (2022), 'Is Multicultural Nationalism Possible? If it is, What Benefits Follow?', Paper presented at Toronto Metropolitan University, 26 May.

Modood, T. (2023), 'Multiculturalism without Privileging Liberalism', in L. Orgad and R. Koopmans (eds), *Majorities, Minorities, and the Future of Nationhood*. Cambridge: Cambridge University Press, 201–24.

Parekh, B. (2001), 'The Future of Multi-Ethnic Britain: Reporting on a Report', *The Round Table: The Commonwealth Journal of International Affairs*, 90 (362), 691–700.

Patten, A. (2014), *Equal Recognition: The Moral Foundations of Minority Rights*. Princeton, NJ: Princeton University Press.

Phillips, A. (2007), *Multiculturalism without Culture*. Princeton, NJ: Princeton University Press.

Sandelind, C. (2023), 'Linking Minority Rights and Majority Attitudes: Multicultural Patriotism', in L. Orgad and R. Koopmans (eds), *Majorities, Minorities, and the Future of Nationhood*. Cambridge: Cambridge University Press, 151–75.

Tamir, Y. (2019), *Why Nationalism*. Princeton, NJ: Princeton University Press.

Thompson, S. and T. Modood (2022), 'The Multidimensional Recognition of Religion', *Critical Review of International Social and Political Philosophy*. Accessed at: <https://doi.org/10.1080/13698230.2022.2115228>

Uberoi, V. (2020), 'Multiculturalism: A Tradition of Political Thought that Liberal Nationalists Can Use', *Nations and Nationalism*, 26 (3), 531–3.

Uberoi, V. (2023), 'Is King Charles a Traditionalist, a Multiculturalist or Both?', *LSE British Politics and Policy blog*, 10 May. Accessed at: <https://blogs.lse.ac.uk/politicsandpolicy/is-king-charles-a-traditionalist-a-multiculturalist-or-both/>

Vertovec, S. (2007), 'Super-Diversity and Its Implications', *Ethnic and Racial Studies*, 29 (6), 1024–54.

Young, I. M. (1990), *Justice and the Politics of Difference*. Princeton, NJ: Princeton University Press.

Zangwill, I. (1909), *The Melting-Pot: Drama in Four Acts*. New York: Macmillan.

NINE

Transnational Experiences: Redefining Solidarity and Nationalisms

Riva Kastoryano

In 1916, essayist Randolph Bourne argued in favour of a 'transnational America' (Bourne 1916). He developed a conception of American identity that would take into consideration the population's diversity and a vision of the United States as the 'first international nation' (Vaughan 1991) – a nation that would take differences into account and a nationalism that would include the history of migrations and allow migrants to maintain their attachment to their country of origin without calling into question the common feeling of belonging to a single political community. He thus combines loyalty to national or ethnic origins and allegiance to the national community. His conception of the American identity laid down the premises of 'cultural pluralism' that would later be developed by Horace Kallen (Kallen 1924). The concept, developed at the time of massive European migration, has been considered later as the premise of multiculturalism, in, however, a different historical and political context. Multicultural critic to cultural pluralism focused on Europe-centrist America, and the absence of Black population, Asian immigrants as well as native Americans, form a democratic egalitarian diverse American society (Hollinger 1995; Walzer 1990).

Since the 1980s multiculturalism, settled in the social science vocabulary in relation to cultural pluralism, has been studied as a theory, a narrative and political paradigm in response to the management of cultural diversity within the nation-state in order to redefine citizenship, equality and solidarity, a solidarity for Tariq Modood 'where group identities would be included into composite national identities' (2022). The normative vision of multiculturalism combined with public policy to achieve integration thus led Modood to develop the concept of 'multicultural nationalism'. For Tariq Modood (2017), multiculturalism is the extension of the concept of national citizenship and of nationalism, and he suggests a 'multicultural nationalism' as a way 'to accommodate British Asian Muslims' political assertiveness'.

He focuses on remaking of British national identity and implies the extension of the concept of national citizenship so that it is neither understood in terms of liberal neutrality nor monocultural majoritari-anism, but a multicultural nationalism (Modood 2017). He argues that multiculturalism is a mode of integration that does not just emphasise the centrality of minority group identities, that integration is incom-plete without remaking national identity so that all can have a sense of belonging to it (Modood 2020). The central normative claim is that citizenship and national identity must be remade to include group iden-tities that are important to minorities as well as majorities. He argues that 'this is double-aspected: the right to recognition of difference, to distinct cultural needs and provision but also the right to be included, to full membership, which includes the sharing of the national-public space or culture and in the sharing to remake it'. He suggests a 'multi-cultural nationalism' that is only civic in nature because it is based on the recognition of groups rejecting membership as ascriptive, as well as the concept of 'Otherness that refers to Ethnicity'. The concept chal-lenges therefore narrow and exclusivist conceptions of nationalism and national identity while still giving a multicultural citizenship and inclusive nationalism a high significance and goal as a political project (Modood 2019; Fossum et al. 2023).

History matters. While migrants made the nation of the United States of America, migration to Europe is a postwar, postcolonial and economic phenomenon. In France, the historian Gérard Noiriel, in his book *The French Melting Pot* published in 1987, translated into English in 1999, drew attention to the absence of migration in the French historiogra-phy, because assimilation was considered as a 'natural' process. Today, according to Tariq Modood, 'Britain is where the normative value of the concept of multiculturalism is most elaborated' (2018). But hyphenated identity to which Bourne refers is a part of 'transnational America', and does not seem the case for 'multicultural nationalism'. Tariq Modood asserts that hyphenated identity means that the reference to the country of origin is 'an aspect of their Britishness, namely as a way of belonging to Britain'. He relates this process to his understanding of multiculturalism as a part of civic integration, and of the result of multicultural policies that lead to forming a shared common national political space. With regard to Joppke's analysis on 'civic integration' as a way of inclusion in citizenry, through education, language and political participation (2004:

60), Modood emphasises the 'civic idea' (2007, 2013) in relation to multiculturalism as a way to share common values, the basis of a national cohesion or Britishness (Meer and Modood 2009). Therefore citizenship is not only confined to the state, but has also an important social dimension, in order to ensure a 'multicultural citizenship'.

Multiculturalism as politics of integration has been analysed in relation to receiving states and societies based on recognition of groups' identities, claims-making, rules of participation, laws on citizenship, principles of equality. But the increasing importance of solidarity *beyond* national borders on the grounds of one or several identities – national, religious, ethnic, regional – and interests, take away claims, mobilisations and participation from a national to a *trans*national level, questioning the understanding of a shared political space as being only national.

Transnationalism thus raises the question of the limits of national borders and extends the concept of integration beyond borders, challenging the normative theories of multiculturalism. According to Nancy Fraser, transnationalism is about a distinct constellation of cultural pluralism and identity politics, focused on groups but beyond the traditional national public space (Fraser 2007). As a new approach to the analysis of participation, related to globalisation, transnationalism affects how public space is structured, which raises the question of boundaries: territorial, cultural and political (Basch and Glick Schiller 1994). The process redefines solidarity beyond borders, and involves a multilevel interaction between home and host countries and the transnational community spread throughout several countries, which, together, create a transnational space of action for states and communities.

Such a space becomes a site for confrontation of two kinds of transnationalism: transnationalism of groups and/or communities on the one hand, and transnationalism of states on the other. Both situate territory at the core of the analysis. For groups and communities, transnationalism leads to a new imagined community that is not territorial. For states, transnationalism leads to what is called 'diaspora politics'. This reflects the extra-territoriality of citizenship as a means of maintaining the loyalty of the citizens on both their territory of origin and 'abroad'. Such transnationalism of states leads them to extend their power *beyond* their territories.

The two understandings of transnationalism raise questions with regard to membership and belonging; what becomes of the relationship between citizenship and identity; between territory and the nation-state; between rights and identities, culture and politics, states and nations? This chapter will explore the emergence of transnationalism as practice and experience, and will analyse its effects on producing a sense of identification and belonging of groups and communities to a non-territorial unity, and on states' transnationalism as a strategy to extend their power and sovereignty beyond borders in order to react to globalisation and transnationalised identities.

The Emergence of Transnationalism

Transnationalism portrays the bonds of solidarity based on an identity – national, religious, linguistic or regional – and interest, often both, across national borders. The concept is in large part the result of the development of means of communication, the appearance of large regional groups and the increased importance of supranational institutions which either originate or facilitate their administration. Intensified by the magnitude of international migration, transnational networks favour not only cultural, social, political or ideological transfers but also both guide the activities that link the countries of origin to countries of current residence and give migrants 'the illusion of non-permanence'[1] of their departure.

Transnationalism is not a new phenomenon (Foner 1997). Clearly, migrants have always lived in more than one setting, at least for one or two generations. Economic migrants, who usually perceived immigration as temporary, have spontaneously maintained ties with their country of origin. What is new about transnationalism is its organisational aspect: constructed networks and structured communities. Its institutionalisation requires a coordination of activities based most of the time on common references – objective or subjective – and common interests among members (Held et al. 1999).

The emergence of transnational communities appears as a logical next step to cultural pluralism and to identity politics (Kastoryano 2000). The liberalism which favours ethnic pluralism has privileged the cultural activities that are guided by the association of immigrants, at the heart of which lie reappropriated identities, organised and redefined, to place them before the state. They thus acquire a political legitimacy in the countries of immigration that redefine these solidarities and attempt to institutionalise their links with the country of origin and beyond.

It would be nearly impossible to cite all the literature on the phenomenon of transnationalism since the 1990s. It is important to note that they all agree on the fact that the transnational community is constructed out of solidarity networks across national borders from populations displaying a communal identity, whether it be religious, national, regional or ethnic.[2] The economic networks which govern the transfer of funds and goods and the associative networks across which cultural activities, ideologies and ideas circulate between the country of origin

and country of immigration claiming the universality of rights, constitute – either together or separately – the underpinnings of solidarity and
transnational communities. The immigration experience binds together
two national spaces where both networks intersect and where new forms
of interaction occur, creating new symbols and engendering identities
which seek to assert themselves in the two countries (Faist 1998, 2000;
Pries 1999). According to this perspective, transnationalism corresponds
to a new identity space relying on cultural references of both the country
of departure and country of arrival, creating a new space of identification. In their study of Haitians in New York and the multiple links they
develop with their fellow citizens back in Haiti, Nina Glick Schiller and
her co-authors show how, for the immigrants, these two spaces in effect
constitute one single space (1994).

Transnationalism, developed as an experience of migrants and/or
minorities, settled in different national societies interacting with each
other beyond borders, making explicit multiple memberships, questions the very concept of citizenship in a single political community territorially bounded as well as a trans-border solidarity and identification.
Thus, a transnational form of participation allows the immigrant populations to bypass national policies and generates a new space of sociali-
sation for those involved in building networks beyond national borders,
interacting with each other in a new global space where cultural and
political specifics of national societies (both host and home) are combined with emerging multilevel and multinational activities. But at the
same time they reinforce solidarity to a 'communal' identity, creating
a sense of 'peoplehood' unbound and non-territorial, sustained by the
desire to belong to a 'people' through a process of nominal appropria-
tion of its actions and discourses, a sense of participation in its 'destiny'.
The process is opposed to multicultural nationalism suggested by Tariq
Modood, in the sense that group identities are not part of a bounded
national identity by expressing themselves beyond borders as a separate
'us', a 'communal us' that is non-territorial. Their demands fit however
into a dual, nevertheless paradoxical, logic: minorities fight for equality
and recognition before the state of settlement and its institutions; on the
other hand, they assert a collective identity based on a shared experience
of dispersion and mobilisation on a religious or linguistic basis without
a territorial reference.

Transnational Nationalism – Unbound and Non-territorial

Transnational communities based on common identity and/or interest
are characterised by their internal linguistic, ethnic, national diversity.

The internal diversity of transnational communities is 'unified' around norms and values diffused by supranational institutions and through the process by which the same institutions give the diversity a legitimacy on the international stage. Transnational activists draw the boundaries of the transnational community based on inclusive normative discourses on human rights, the fight against racism and discrimination or any other form of social, political and cultural exclusion. The same internal diversity to transnational communities also finds itself 'unified' around a common identity element constructed around events and controversies, around a common experience of segregation and discrimination and/or exclusion as a cause to find refuge either in the home country or in a transnational network as a new basis for identification. Globalisation generates identification, with globalised identities rejecting belonging to both the country of origin and country of settlement, so challenging the local and national cohesion.

With regard to Muslims as minorities in Europe, the anthropologist Pnina Werbner, taking the case of Pakistanis in Britain, points out that they have for a half-century settled in Britain, and as citizens of their new state have worked to build a diaspora linking the two countries through transfers of money, goods and ideas. At the same time, redefining their original identity as Muslim has led them to 'invent a Muslim diaspora' – concerned with the situation of minority Muslims living outside the lands of Islam, and in places such as Palestine, Chechnya, Bosnia, Iraq and Kashmir – and to develop 'a sense of co-responsibility' with regard to the plight of their coreligionists (2002). According to a Pew survey taken in July 2006, one year after the 7/7 attacks in London, 81 per cent of British Muslims considered themselves first as Muslims (the percentage is 66 per cent in Germany and 46 per cent in France). When the same question is asked in Pakistan, 87 per cent of respondents say also that they consider themselves first as Muslims.[3] This identification is expressed in transnational solidarity within the 'Muslim diaspora', extra-territorial to the United Kingdom: loyalty to the Islamic community, or ummah, and to Pakistan, a postcolonial nation.

More generally with debates on Muslims in Europe, with controversies on mosques, headscarves, halal meats (Göle 2015) or even broadly, with the Israel–Palestine conflicts, Islam becomes a 'refuge' or source of identification with the causes that 'trouble the world' at the local as well as transnational or global level. Mobilisation around the Israel–Palestine conflict reunites not only Muslim identity but associates other political groups consequently that align themselves with their cause. This opening towards 'the universal' and justice gives a greater legitimacy to the 'identitary recentralisation' of Islam.

This process of 'identity recentralisation', in addition to any longer-term political arrangements, also expresses itself in everyday life; it develops in different domains and territories – real or symbolic – which endeavour to re-establish social relationships and a communal identity. Anthropologists are huddled over the question of territory as an important variable of the transnational phenomenon. For A. Appadurai, deterritorialisation has become a central force of political modernity. 'Delocalised' populations, he writes, invent themselves as new spaces he calls 'ethnoscapes', which he defines as a non-localised territory and perceives as the sheer product of imaginary resources (Appadurai 1996).

The same argument can be applied to Asian Americans or the Asian diaspora in general with regard to Covid-19, and the populist and exclusionist public opinions towards the Chinese diaspora to bear the responsibility. Thus forces external to the country of birth and/or residence combine to create collective identification, particularly by developing a unifying narrative around international current issues that affect the sense of belonging. Another example is a study of young people with an immigration background in the Netherlands that shows how the younger generation of Hindustanis, detached from their homeland, invent new forms of transnationalism and a sense of belonging (Gowricharn 2009).

This new understanding of a 'communal identity' beyond borders creates new expressions of belonging. This new community is imagined upon the basis of a religion or ethnicity that encompasses linguistic and national differences and asserts itself as a non-territorial unity constructed around an identity or an experience constructed out of immigration, dispersion and a minority situation. The territorial boundaries of these communities are not disputed; on the contrary, their non-territorial boundaries follow formal and/or informal network connections that transcend the territorial limits of states and nations, thus creating a new form of territorialisation – invisible and unbounded – and, consequently, a form of political community within which individual actions become the basis for a form of non-territorial transnational nationalism that seeks to strengthen itself through speeches, symbols, images and objects.

Transnational nationalism breaks away from the territorialised nationalist project and attests itself beyond national borders, without geographical limits, as a deterritorialised nation in search of an inclusive (and exclusive) centre, around an identity to achieve legitimacy and recognition not only from states, but also from supranational or international institutions. This engenders a political engagement that reflects the nationalisation of communitarian sentiments along with new subjectivities, guided by an 'imagined geography', leading to a transnational nationalism, that is non-territorial (Kastoryano 2015). It translates the transnationalisation of community sentiment (whatever its content may be) or the communalisation of networks of transnational solidarity. Transnationalism leads to a new 'imagined community' (Anderson 1983) that goes against the unified community brought together around the same territorialised political project.

Self-determination for the transnational nation does not imply cultural autonomy on a territorial basis, but recognition within the framework of state structures, serving as the basis of equality for the differences that arise in the public space of Western democracies. From that standpoint, demands for recognition take on a racial or ethnic, even a religious, character, depending on the interactions with the community's states of residence, and are based on forces outside the state territory. The terms of this recognition vary from one state to another according to the definition that each gives to minorities and how the latter express their demands for equal rights. In the United States, for example, Black nationalism, born in 1850, is perceived as the foundation of a sense of multifaceted solidarity: territorial, religious, cultural or even class-based, with an aim to combat racial discrimination. The primary objective expressed by the proponents of Black nationalism is to be 'in charge of their fate' by controlling and preserving their own political and cultural organisation, and to find a political alternative to the racial policy in the United States, a way of 'de-racializing' themselves (Robinson 2002). Of course, it would be misleading to limit the Black question in the United States to a nationalist differentiation inside the nation. But the 'Black nation' in this context refers to a 'homogenised' culture based on colour and the quest for political recognition.

Studies in the United States have also developed other concepts, such as that of 'pan-ethnicity'. According to its author, Y. L Espirirtu, this concept underlines 'the generalization of solidarity among ethnic subgroups' (1992). He is referring, in particular, to the Asian population established in the United States, a population that is internally diverse in terms of nationality, language and even religion. Pan-ethnic identity would thus, by definition, be a multiple identity, in which groups of various origins blend into a single group, with the aim of building a political unity that draws its legitimacy from its institutions and asserts its self-determination upon the basis of 'race'. Other times, other 'races', but the issue remains the same. Like Black nationalism, analysed as an innovative policy developing new paradigms to understand the history of racial and ethnic relations in the United States, pan-ethnicity is hailed, by its author, to be the future of ethnicity, in which the group's internal diversity will be bound together by identity-based and institutional links, thus giving rise to new dynamics (Jones-Correa 1998).

Transnationalism expands then beyond the connection between home and host countries. For younger generations, the country of origin does not have the same meaning as for the generation who emigrated. Opposed to the first generation and their affective ties with the country of origin, the attachment to the land becomes abstract and imaginary for the generation born abroad; it does not therefore nourish the same emotions, does not produce the same affective ties and does not create the same identification. Territory does not have the same meaning and is not a basis for a collective identification, and neither for self-determination. A new 'imagined transnational global identity' becomes a third dimension of belonging, where individuals, groups and transnational communities are connected in global networks, and the traditional understanding of diaspora loses its territorial bases, in which home is an imagined place to express precisely 'co-responsibility' without a territorial reference as 'home', more so for the younger generation who have an abstract image of the home country of their parents. The objective of such an invented non-territorial belonging is ultimately to achieve legitimacy and recognition not only from states, but also from supranational or international institutions.

Such transnational belonging, a transnational nationalism as a non-territorial nationalism, differs from 'long-distance nationalism' as elaborated by Benedict Anderson, and from *diaspora* nationalism that Ernest Gellner qualifies as 'historical fact' and considers as a subspecies of nationalism. Long-distance nationalism is analysed as a new type of nationalism generated by the development of capitalism. Gellner sees *diaspora* nationalism as the result of a social transformation, a cultural renaissance and a desire of this minority to acquire a territory (Gellner 1983: 88–110). For Anderson, the development of emigration, the evolution of means of communication, the new industrial civilisation and the ensuing social and geographical mobility, have all raised consciousnesses and led to an identity-based withdrawal which has fuelled nationalist claims, to the effect that repressed ethnic identities should take the form of ethnicity-based nation-states (Anderson 1998). In their own definition of a similar concept, N. Glick-Schiller and G. Eugene Fouron suggest that long-distance nationalism is reconfiguring the way in which many people understand the relationship between populations and the states that claim to represent them. According to these authors, the political agenda associated with this type of nationalism relates to 'the vision of the nation as extending beyond the territorial boundaries of the state [that] frequently springs from the life experiences of migrants of different classes, whose lives stretch across borders to connect

homeland and new land' (Glick Schiller and Fouron 2001). This is remi-
niscent of the projects of reconstruction of nation-states elaborated in
exile that Benedict Anderson also mentions. Both are projects that are
territory-based, with self-determination or the redefinition of the nationalist foundation for the building of the state. Transnational nationalism, or
nationalism without territory, I argue, appears to be the result of a historical evolution a priori linked to what has become a global market, to the
emergence of a so-called global space and the rising influence of supranational institutions, in short, to changes related to what is known as the
process of globalisation.

States' Transnationalism – Extra-territorial Nationalism

Even if such a non-territorial identity characterises the new élan for a
transnational or a non-territorial nationalism, an important number of
transnational actors bring states and territories back in, by collaborating
with both states, of origin and of settlement. In some cases, they have
become 'private ambassadors', in charge of rebuilding a link between
statehood, nationhood and peoplehood, with regard to both countries.
Some leaders of voluntary associations become 'ethnic entrepreneurs' or
elected representatives in the parliaments in the country of settlement
and of citizenship. By acting in two political spaces, they also contribute
to the development of a new diplomacy, and to the reconfiguration of
a new diplomatic space (Kastoryano 2016). Their involvement in both
countries shows their important role in building transnational networks
and identification to a transnational space. It also contradicts the assumption that transnationalism sets against incorporation of migrant populations in the country of settlement. Kivisto argues that incorporation and
transnationalism are two theoretical models in interaction. He bases his
argument on empirical evidence showing that a perfect integration in the
country of settlement does not prevent the second generation from keeping ties with the country of origin of their parents (Kivisto 2003). As for
a transnational mobilisation of actors, leaders of voluntary associations
active in transnational mobilisation are often socially and institution-
ally assimilated, and in the majority of cases, legal citizens of two states,
developing links with other countries, becoming countries of reference
through their action.

Transnational organisations and multiple identifications compel
home states to position themselves and develop what is called 'diaspora
politics', with the objective to promote a resource for identity and for
mobilisation for individuals and/or groups of immigrant descent. This
means maintaining a link with citizens 'abroad'; it involves, at the same

time, the extension of its power beyond its territories. The state of origin thus takes part in defining or creating a diaspora, even in identifying its citizens with a diasporic identity. This is reflected in changes in citizenship laws or the granting of a special status with dual citizenship which becomes a way to institutionalise both immigrants' involvement in the home country, and home countries to ensure the extraterritorial belonging of their citizens abroad. The logic comes to dissociate citizenship and nationhood; it transforms the latter into an identity rooted in the country of origin and it makes citizenship an entitlement within the country of residence. On such a view, citizenship becomes a legal status, and nationhood merely defined along religious, ethnic or cultural lines promoted by home states. The process leads to the *de*-territorialisation of nationhood from the home state perspective. It therefore designs a 'diasporic identity' that keeps the legality of the citizenship of the country of origin, as an extraterritorial belonging.

Many cases show such processes established by different countries like China, India, Brazil and Mexico (Dufoix et al. 2010). They all intervene in the countries of settlement, through economic, cultural and political means, and contribute to ensure a permanent loyalty on the one hand and control their integration in the country of settlement, on the other, as paradoxical as it seems. Such a diaspora politics is now applied by many countries, which want their citizens to maintain an ethno-religiously defined national identity. They mobilise consular networks and other institutions, and organisations propagate the nation's official nationalism (Levitt and de La Dehesa 2003). Waldinger enumerates states' action to maintain transnational communities through voting abroad, legalising lobbying, promoting hometown associations, and for some like Mexico printing ID documents abroad (Waldinger 2015). Recently, states of origin have appointed official interlocutors – civil servants, attachés at consulates, or representatives of national voluntary associations – and attributed them the role of intermediary between emerging political actors from immigrant backgrounds and the state of origin. These actors provide the link between public and private spaces, as well as economic, social, cultural and political spaces, through the various family, commercial and organisational networks in both countries of settlement and in the country of origin. In general, such an extraterritorial nationalism has become an important element of their foreign policy. Such is the case of the relations between the Maghreb and France or between Mexico and the United States.

At the same time, states of origin – in their process of developing an extraterritorial nationalism – aim to re-territorialise 'globalised' identities, expressed through a transnational nationalist perspective. In Europe, among the countries of origin of migrants, Morocco and Turkey, where national and religious identities are combined, are those active in diaspora politics, as a means to re-territorialise Islam. They both created specific ministries in charge of their 'citizens abroad'. Their objective is to bring their citizens abroad 'back' to a national identity, that is, to 'a national Islam' as opposed to the 'global Islam' promoted by international organisations in Europe (Tozy 2009). Therefore, all initiatives coming from the home state had the objective of ensuring the integration of their migrants in their countries of settlement, in order to avoid the attraction of the young generation to radicalised identities spread through the Internet. It has become then important for the Moroccan authorities to stress the difference between the understanding of Islam that migrants are developing abroad – because of the influence of international organisations and their influence in the promotion of a global Islam – and the nationalist/traditional Islam promoted by home states and nations (Mohsen-Finan 2005). Their action is therefore extraterritorial – external to national territory –and therefore the objective of Morocco is to re-territorialise national/traditional Islam in the country of settlement as an extension of the home country (Kastoryano 2016). Turkey's motivations, on the other hand, are to combine a national identity abroad with 'global Islam', of which Turkey declared itself to be its protector; a motivation expressed in terms of a fight against exclusion and 'islamophobia' linking a non-territorial global Islam that co-exists in the fight against discrimination. The Tunisian case, on the other hand, focuses on the economic integration of its citizens abroad in their country of settlement as a way of institutionalising their attachment to the home country.

Receiving countries are driven to collaborate with the home countries in order to ensure the integration to 're-territorialise' citizenship and identities. They maintain the power of incorporation and citizenship, they establish rules of political participation and control the institutional structures for mobilisation. Minorities and/or communities express their claim before states of settlement in order to gain recognition, equal citizenship and representation. Facing increasing transnational participation of migrants and the increasing influence of countries of origin in migrants' cultural and political attitudes, the states of settlement also expand their influence beyond their territories in order to maintain the 'power' of incorporation and citizenship and compete with transnational communities in their engagement of the process of globalisation. What is at stake is the integration of the states (both states, host and home) and that of transnational communities into a global space. In reality, both states play an important role in the promotion of transnationalism by extending their sovereignty beyond borders. Transnational politics reflect therefore the changes in the 'paradigms of integration': have 'their' citizens to belong 'here and there' (Kastoryano 2016)? In this configuration, politics of integration are not a single-state policy. States (home and host) cooperate for integration to ensure re-territorialisation of globalised identities with transnational action.

Transnationality thus introduces a new relationship to states that is characterised by 'mutual dependence', to use J. Armstrong's expression; mutual dependence between a liberal, pluralistic state and the 'mobilised diaspora'. Whereas diasporas occupied a significant place, especially in international trade, in pre-modern states, 'mobilised diasporas' today find themselves, according to Armstrong, in a position of 'international negotiation' of political decisions (Armstrong 1976). The increased interdependence between scattered populations and both the states of origin and of settlement, and even beyond, is part of a global and complex system of interactions and is subjected to internal and external negotiation processes.

Transnational nationalism, a product of liberal states, leads to negotiations between transnational actors and states. From the actors' standpoint, such a nationalism becomes a means to wield pressure, even political clout; from the states' standpoint, governments must negotiate the means to include in their political strategy identity-based expressions born of their relations with minority populations and 'reterritorialise' their action, or else develop their own 'deterritorialised' power strategies to maintain the link and loyalty of individual citizens of states despite nationalist expressions that surpass them. For states, this boils down to their acting as transnational actors in constant interaction in a deterritorialized global space where cultural and political specificities of national societies intersect with multinational activities. This becomes the state's process of integrating the globalisation process. In both cases, the objective is to maintain the 'power' of incorporation and citizenship while expanding state influences beyond territories and to compete with transnational communities in their engagement in the process of globalisation. What is at stake is the integration of the states (both states, host and home) and that of transnational communities into a global space. As for communities, transnationalism becomes a way to negotiate their identities and means of citizenship from outside.

To Conclude

Thus, transnational politics of both communities and states create new configurations of nation and nationalism, of territory and power in globalisation. Communities, based on cultural, ethnic and religious identifications and recognised by states that increasingly rely on transnational solidarities, have sparked new upsurges of nationalism. States, on the other hand, expand their nationalism to maintain the 'power' of incorporation and citizenship, in order to reterritorialise identities here and/or there.

The development is inscribed in a global space that *does not translate* but rather *produces* an identity and generates a mode of participation across borders, as shown by the engagement of actors in the consolidation of transnational solidarities through action and mobilisation. By reflecting on the state 'deficiencies' regarding human rights or citizenship, the actors seek to channel the loyalty of individuals from a territorialised political community towards a non-territorialised political community to redefine the terms of belonging and allegiance to a 'global nation'.

Such an evolution challenges the multicultural nationalism of Tariq Modood. Transnational nationalism focuses on an 'invented', abstract identification with an 'imagined global community' fuelled by external events such as wars, conflicts in other countries, and colonial relations yielding to an expression of local and transnational autonomy. Diaspora politics of home states, in their objective to reterritorialise globalised identities, come to 're-ethnicise' them, which in return affects their attitudes in the country of settlement. It would be interesting to empirically determine how transnational actors perceive multiculturalism and how diaspora politics affects their involvement in multiculturalism as a policy and as a discourse. In any case, opposition to normative multicultural nationalism and the emergence of an 'imagined' transnational nationalism, old-fashioned, ethno-cultural nationalism, renamed populism, started to proliferate all over Europe. Their rhetoric, political programme and capacity to mobilise public opinion nourished exciting discourses on the failure of multiculturalism and revitalised state nationalism based on the protection of territorial boundaries and national identity. The 'return' of nationalism, with new populist discourses targeting migrants in certain European countries, has used the migrants' crises, attributing migrants and/or asylum seekers a transnational solidarity perceived as a threat to national sovereignty, even though the phenomenon has nothing to do with transnational networks and group membership.

Notes

1. An expression utilised by Myron Wiener in 'Labor Migration as Incipient Diasporas', in Gabriel Scheffer (ed.), *Modern Diasporas in International Politics*. London, Croom Helm, 1986, 47–74, cited by Nicholas Van Hear, *New Diasporas. The Mass Exodus, Dispersal and Regrouping of Migrant Communities*. London, UCL Press, 1998, 5.

2. It is important to mention that the magnitude of the phenomenon of the transnational subject has given rise to the creation of a special five-year program at
Oxford University directed by Steven Vertovec called *Transnational Studies*. The
program has supported dozens of research projects on the formation of transnational communities in multiple and varied populations in a comparative and
interdisciplinary perspective.

3. 'Muslims in Europe: Economic Worries Top Concerns about Religious and Cultural
Identity', Pew Research Center, 6 July 2006. Accessed 9 July 2016 at: <http://www.
pewglo bal.org/2006/07/06/muslims-in-Europe-economic-worries-top-concerns-
about- religious-and-cultural-identity/>

References

Anderson, B. (1983), *Imagined Communities. Reflections on the Organization and Spread
of Nationalism*. London: Verso.

Anderson, B. (1998), *The Spectre of Comparisons: Nationalism, South East Asia and the
World*. London: Verso.

Appadurai, A. (1996), *Modernity at Large. Cultural Dimensions of Globalization*.
Minneapolis: University of Minnesota Press.

Armstrong, J. A. (1976), 'Mobilized and Proletarian Diaspora', *American Political
Science Review*, LXX (2), 393–408.

Basch, L. and N. Glick-Schiller (1994), *Nations Unbound: Transnational Projects, Postcolonial Predicaments and Deterritorialized Nation-states*. New York: Gordon and
Breach Publishers.

Bourne, R. S. (1916), 'Trans-National America', *Atlantic Monthly*, 118, July, 86–97.

Dufoix, S., C. Guerassimoff and A. de Tinguy (eds) (2010), *Loin des yeux, près du cœur.
Les États et leurs expatriés*. Paris: Presses de Sciences Po.

Espiritu, Y. L. (1992), *Asian-American Pan-Ethnicity. Bridging Institutions and Identities*. Philadelphia, PA: Temple University Press.

Faist, T. (1998), 'Transnational Social Spaces out of International Migration. Evolution, Significance and Future Prospects', *European Archives of Sociology*, XXXIX
(2), 213–47.

Faist, T. (2000), *The Volume and Dynamic of International Migration and Transnational
Social Spaces*. New York: Oxford University Press.

Faist, T., M. Fauser and E. Reisenauer (2013), *Transnational Migration*. Cambridge:
Cambridge University Press.

Foner, N. (1997), 'What's New about Transnationalism? New York Immigrants
Today and the Turn of the Century', *Diaspora: A Journal of Transnational Studies*,
6 (3), 355–75.

Fossum, J. E., R. Kastoryano, T. Modood and R. Zapata-Barrero (2023), 'Governing
Diversity in the Multilevel European Public Space', *Ethnicities*, Online First. DOI:
10.1177/14687968231153838.

Fraser, N. (2007), 'Transnationalizing the Public Sphere. On the Legitimacy and
Efficacy of Public Opinion in a Post-Westphalian World', *Theory, Culture and
Society*, 24 (4), 7–31.

Gellner, E. (1983), *Nations and Nationalisms*. Oxford: Blackwell Publishing.

Göle, N. (2015), *Musulmans au quotidiens*. Paris: La Découverte.

Glick-Schiller, N. and G. E. Fouron (2001), *Georges Woke Up Laughing. Long-Distance Nationalism and the Search for Home*. Durham, NC: Duke University Press.

Held, D. (ed.) (1999), *Global Transformations*. Cambridge: Polity Press.

Hollinger, D. A. (1995), *Postethnic America. Beyond Multiculturalism*. New York: Basic Books.

Jones-Correa, M. (1998), *Between Two Nations. The Political Predicament of Latinos in New York City*, Ithaca, NY: Cornell University Press.

Joppke, C. (2017), *Is Multiculturalism Dead?*. Cambridge: Polity Press.

Kallen, H. M. (1924), *Culture and Democracy in the United States*. New York: Transaction Publishers.

Kastoryano, R. (2000), 'Immigration, Transnational Community and Citizenship', *International Journal of Social Sciences*, 165, 353–61.

Kastoryano, R. (2007), 'Transnational Nationalism. Redefining Nation and Territory', in S. Benhabib and I. Shapiro (eds), *Identities, Affiliations and Allegiances*. Cambridge: Cambridge University Press, 159–81.

Kastoryano, R. (2016), 'States and Communities competing for Global Power', *Philosophy and Social Criticism*, 42 (4–5), 386–96.

Kastoryano, R. (2022), 'Transnationalism. Theory and Experience', in R. Zapata-Barrero, D. Jacobs and R. Kastoryano (eds), *Contested Conceptions in Migration Studies*. London: Routledge, 243–58.

Kivisto, P. (2003), 'Social Spaces, Transnational Immigrant Communities, and the Politics of Assimilation', *Ethnicity*, 3 (1), 5–28.

Levitt, P., R. de La Dehesa (2003), 'Transnational Migration and the Redefinition of the State: Variations and Explanations', *Ethnic and Racial Studies*, 26 (4), 587–611.

Meer, N. and T. Modood (2009), 'The Multicultural State We're In: Muslims, "Multiculture" and the "Civic Re-balancing" of British Multiculturalism', *Political Studies*, 57 (2), 473–97.

Modood, T. (2013 [2007]), *Multiculturalism: A Civic Idea*. Cambridge: Polity Press.

Modood, T. (2019), 'A Multicultural Nationalism?', *Brown Journal of World Affairs*, 25, 233–46.

Mohsen-Finan, K. (2005), 'Maroc: l'émergence de l'islamisme sur la scène politique', *Politique étrangère*, 1, 73–84.

Noiriel, G. (1999), *The French Melting Pot. Immigration, Citizenship and the French National Identity*. Minneapolis: Minnesota University Press.

Pries, L. (ed.) (1999), *Migration and Transnational Social Spaces*. London and Aldershot: Ashgate.

Robinson, D. E. (2002), *Black Nationalism in American Politics and Thought*. New York: Cambridge University Press.

Safran, W. (1991), 'Diasporas in Modern Societies: Myths of Homeland and Return', *Diaspora*, 1 (1), 83–99.

Tozy, M. (2009), 'L'évolution du champ religieux marocain au défi de la mondialisation', *Revue internationale de la politique comparée*, 16 (1), 63–81.

Vaughan, L. J. (1991), 'Cosmopolitanism, Ethnicity and American Identity: Rudolph Bourne's "Trans-National America"', *Journal of American Studies*, 25 (3), 443–59.

Waldinger, R. (2017), *The Cross-border Connection. Immigrants, Emigrants and their Homeland*. Cambridge, MA: Harvard University Press.

Walzer, M. (1990), 'What Does it Mean to Be an "American"?', *Social Research*, 57 (3), 591–614.

Werbner, P. (2002), 'The Place Which Is Diaspora: Citizenship, Religion and Gender in the Making of Chaordic Transnationalism', *Journal of Ethnic and Migration Studies*, 28 (1), 119–33.

TEN

What Can Migration and National Identity Look Like in the Mid-twenty-first Century? Transnational Diasporas and Digital Nomads

Anna Triandafyllidou

Introduction

While it has been over twenty years that scientists have been speaking about the internet of things and the fourth technological revolution, we witness today, nearly every day, an acceleration of technological innovation that affects all areas of public, social and personal life. This technological transformation is intertwined with important socio-economic and political changes as it facilitates connectedness and simultaneity, intensifies economic globalisation, and through these two elements further reshapes geopolitical relationships. A common element that permeates this 'great transformation' (Polanyi 2001) of the twenty-first century is the role of human migration and mobility (Castles 2010; Vertovec 2021) in its different forms and facets. Such migration or mobility (I will provide definitions of the two concepts below) is not always nor necessarily spatial or physical, it can also be virtual/digital. The Covid-19 pandemic has shown how people can be trapped by closed borders but may also work remotely or connect and mobilise in very different locations as if they were physically present.*

Beyond the economic implications of remote work and the overall (important) discussion on the future of work or on trade nationalism, it is pertinent to reflect on how such complex forms of migration and mobility – physical and virtual – influence our sense of identity and belonging. Virtual mobility and transnational remote work can create

---

* The reflections included in the first two sections of this chapter originate from Triandafyllidou et al. (2024).

important gaps in the social and political participation of a person. At the same time, it can also contribute to mobilising transnationally for workers' rights or conversely against minorities or migrants. How can we analyse and codify these developments from our theoretical perspectives on national identities and nationalism? What kind of atomised or collective identities will emerge among transnational diasporas at destination or virtual nomads at origin? Do we need to invent new concepts and forms of membership?

These are the main questions that this chapter asks, and in ways that take heed of at least two key elements in Tariq Modood's thinking that, in my view, signalled a breakthrough in the discussion on multiculturalism from sociological perspectives: first, that individuals belonging to minorities live and negotiate their complex identities actively and in complex ways – internal differentiation is not a feature of majority groups only, minorities are internally differentiated too; and second, minority and majority communities also may choose which markers of difference are most important for them and may choose to mobilise in one direction or another in line with the importance they attribute to a particular feature. Modood (2007) argued that some post-migration minorities may mobilise around religious issues while others mobilise with reference to language or culture. Indeed, during the last twenty years sociologists and political theorists have spent considerable energy discussing how to integrate cultural and religious diversity in liberal democracies and how to forge strong feelings of belonging and trust among culturally diverse political communities. Despite anti-multiculturalism rhetoric proliferating for a good part of the 2000s, Tariq Modood stood his ground and affirmed his role as a publicly engaged intellectual and one of the foremost theorists of multicultural citizenship. He has brought to the fore important insights as regards the interplay of individual and collective identities and modes of belonging, and how these should inform political theory as well as multicultural policy and practice (Modood 2007).

The chapter starts by commenting on the transformations that have been happening in the last ten years and their impact on physical and virtual migration and the conundrums or contradictions that these create. It will then discuss how theories of everyday nationhood (Fox and Miller Idriss 2008; Skey 2009; Skey and Antonsich 2017), plural vs neo tribal nationalism (Triandafyllidou 2020), multicultural nationalism (Modood 2019) or transnational nationalism (Kastoryano 2018) can inform our thinking about identity in a world of mixed physical and digital migration. The question I want to ask and seek to answer is to what extent these observations hold in a world of mixed digital and physical mobility.

The chapter starts with setting the background. I will discuss what are the new forms of migration and mobility emerging today and what are their implications for the people involved. In section three I discuss the contributions of the different theoretical approaches outlined above and the ways in which these can help us understand better these new social phenomena. Section four presents my tentative conclusions on whether we should start considering digital identity as another layer of identity that intersects with our other social identities.

New Forms of Migration and Mobility

The future of being human is inextricably related to mobility or the lack thereof. The recent humanitarian emergencies in Afghanistan and Ukraine; the ongoing crises in Venezuela and Syria; the breakdown of mobility during the pandemic and the current frantic return of travelling for both business and leisure; the connection through smartphones of families torn apart by war or because of employment; and the transnational mobilisation whether against vaccines (in Canada and across North America or Europe) or in favour of democracy (for example, Canadian activism in favour of democracy in Hong Kong or to support farmers in India), are but different sides of the same process: human mobility.

While global movements existed for thousands of years, advanced technologies and socio-political-economic dynamics within and across nations have contributed to intensified cross-border mobility of people – with different reasons and objectives (McAuliffe and Triandafyllidou 2022). In a recent study, Recchi et al. (2019a) estimate global transnational mobility at 3 billion trips annually worldwide (in the period 2011–16) compared to an estimated 10 million migration episodes annually in the early 2010s (Abel and Sanders 2014). The rise of global mobility is both a global challenge and an opportunity; it fosters social and technological innovation but may also exacerbate social inequalities and socio-political tensions; there are also questions regarding its environmental consequences, the potential for pandemics' spread, and the emergence of global systemic risks (Centeno et al. 2015).

In conceptualising human migration and broader types of mobility, we need to consider it as an intrinsic part of broader processes of socio-economic, technological, political and demographic transformation (De Haas 2021; Castles 2010). We need to see it as a complex social process rather than as a response to development imbalances, or as a solution to problems like unemployment, poverty or population ageing. As such, migration and mobility are shaped by broader processes of globalisation,

208 / Anna Triandafyllidou

development, technological transformation and urbanisation, and in turn contribute to shaping these.

Human mobility today is acknowledged as a right (the right to emigrate, to leave one's country), as a positive element in people's lives (the capacity and freedom to move) and as a crisis (when people are forced to move because of a natural disaster, a war or simply the search for a better future). People move for leisure, to visit family and friends, to search for better living and working conditions, but also to seek protection. Communities may also be displaced internally or across national borders (Sassen 2014) both spatially and culturally (Tomiak 2017; Dorries et al. 2019).

Mobility today, and increasingly in the future, is not always nor necessarily spatial or physical, it can also be virtual/digital. Advanced digital technologies do not only facilitate connections and collaborations but are also promising a new level of virtual 'presence' soon (see the recent announcement of the Metaverse by Facebook). One may borrow the term 'saturated mobility' from the natural sciences and consider the case of young people who may be extremely virtually mobile but physically stay put. Their mobility experience is not spatial but social and inter-subjective: through virtual mobility and connectivity, they may be experiencing the breaking down and reorganisation of social and kinship networks, as well as a level of political alienation or of anti-social radicalisation, as they may feel they have lost connection with national governments but have not found any other political actors or institutions to fill the vacuum except for online communities. On the other hand, we cannot ignore that there are many people who aspire to move physically but are not able to because they lack the resources or the right documents, and additionally there are entire communities that may be forced to leave their traditional lands whether because of natural disasters, environmental deterioration or conflict.

Taking stock of these observations, I am distinguishing among four types of mobility today: travel (people moving for business or leisure); migration (notably people moving in search of better living and working conditions or to reunite with family); asylum (people moving to seek international protection); and displacement (people or communities being forcibly moved). We consider these as separate but interconnected mobility spheres because of their different motivations, modalities and legal/policy frameworks.

It was more than twenty years ago when, commenting on globalisation, the Polish sociologist Zygmunt Bauman (1998) wrote about the emergence of two types of 'sans papiers' people travelling in the world today: the cosmopolitan 'nomads', moving across borders whether for work or leisure, seamlessly, without visas because they are in possession of the 'right' passports; and the 'vagabonds', those willing but unable to move or moving illegally because they are in possession of the 'wrong' passports or of no passports at all. In recent decades, mobility of the first group (for business or leisure) has grown exponentially, as evidenced by the $4.7 trillion (2020, pre-pandemic) value of the current broader travel and tourism industry (including accommodation, transport, attractions and more) (Lock 2021).

Migration has also grown significantly: international migrants account today for 3.6 per cent of the global population or 381 million people (World Migration Report 2022: 3), up from 173 million or 2.8 per cent of the global population in 2000. Mobility for leisure and business has been facilitated by developments in global travel and the digitalisation of many services. Migration has benefited from increased connectivity and cheaper transport too, but has also faced increased restrictions as major destination countries have adopted sophisticated digital tools to regulate mobility (Triandafyllidou and Ambrosini 2011; Kenwick and Simmons 2020; McLeman 2019). While Bauman's stratification remains timely, there has been little effort to analyse these two divergent types of mobility and how they will evolve given the important technological advances of today as well as the increased restrictions for the 'vagabonds' and evolving concerns about climate change and pandemics.

During the last decade there has been increasing recognition that migration is mixed, in the sense that flows cannot be clearly classified as economic vs humanitarian, and rather we need to account for combined drivers and mixed motivations which may even change during the migration project of an individual or household (Triandafyllidou 2017; Kent 2020; Mixed Migration Centre 2019). The term of forced migration has been put forward by many also in criticising how global governance tends to compartmentalise between refugees and migrants without accounting for the complex situations on the ground (Jubilut and Casagrande 2019). It is more than ten years ago that Betts (2013) discussed 'survival migration', pointing to people moving because their governments cannot guarantee their basic conditions of existence. A comprehensive view of the future of human mobility requires us to take a closer look into community displacement – particularly the loss of habitat through forced evictions for market purposes (because of acquisition of lands by foreign governments and investors or because of gentrification within large cities), because of climate change (desertification, rising waters) or because of changes in environmental conditions brought about through plantation agriculture, mining or manufacturing (Sassen 2014). Community displacement has so far been analysed separately from studies on economic or family migration. They have also not been sufficiently connected to the mobility of the cosmopolitan 'nomads' of Bauman or of the 'creative class', as Richard Florida labelled them (2019 [2003]), who may follow opportunities arising in an interconnected global economy – opportunities that may be intimately connected with the displacement or migration processes that the 'vagabond' groups experience.

Speaking of 'nomads', it is worth delving into the ways in which nomadic pastoralists transform mobility into resilience. In a recent study, Scoones, Triandafyllidou and co-authors (Scoones et al. 2022) critique global migration governance by bringing together the analysis of international migration with that of nomadic pastoralist communities. Pastoralists must engage dynamically with uncertainty and variability, and as a result they challenge linear, uniform and predictable notions of mobility. Rarely do they move predictably from point A to B; a move from dry to wet areas or from home to host territories. Moving and stopping is part of a continuous and contingent flow, where ideas of mobility and immobility are not opposites, but part of the same experience (Maru 2020). The lived experiences of mobility rupture the binaries of start and stop, source and destination, fixed and flexible, mobility and immobility, as pastoralists seek to respond opportunistically to contextual dynamics. This is not so different from the ebb and flow of international migration but what is different is the way policymakers categorise economic or family migration and the way these communities manage their own patterns of annual migration, seasonal cycles, micro-mobility within and around their camps and, for instance, the ways they fulfil both livelihood-based and religious obligations while en route (Maru 2020; Scoones et al. 2022).

Concepts of National Identity in a Complex Mobility World

Taking stock of these complex and multidimensional forms of mobility discussed in the previous section, I would like to recall my recent argument (Triandafyllidou 2022a) that not only nationalism and the ways in which we define and negotiate our minority and majority identities needs to be seen in their specific socio-political context, but that also our conceptual toolkit requires the same critical contextual reading. Reviewing some of the main theories of nationalism, I have tried to make sense of why nationalism theorists have focused on specific theoretical and empirical questions or have adopted methodologies of broader political sociology or more of cultural anthropology and qualitative sociology in understanding the evolution of nations and nationalism. I have defined three periods in the last forty years within which I identify the main research questions that dominate national-ism studies (Triandafyllidou 2022a). In the first period that extends from the early 1980s till the mid-1990s, nationalism studies are domi-nated by a focus on grand theoretical questions and the methods of political sociology. The most important nationalism theorists seek to explain whether nations are perennial or modern and whether nation-states and nationalism as a political movement is mainly ethnic or civic in its orientation. Political theorists during the same period also seek to define the contours of 'good' liberal nationalism, investigating the tensions between liberalism and nationalism. The main nationalism theorists of this period disagree on their explanations but agree on the focus of their research questions. This focus persists until shortly after 1989 and the landslide changes that happened in Europe and the world after that date.

Looking at the contrasting developments of the 1990s – the focus on national minority and religious identities and their revival in Central Eastern Europe on the one hand, and the process of European integra-tion and reconnection of Europe under a common Union on the other – it comes as no surprise that nationalism theorists focus on what people 'do' with their identities and how they re-elaborate political and media discourses in their everyday encounters. Even though perspectives in this period may differ between those that see in the new socio-economic and political realities the emergence of a cosmopolitan and post-national world and those that emphasise the persistence of the nation, the focus in both perspectives is on everyday nationhood. The methodology is constructivist and discursive rather than focusing on institutions.

A new turn is registered though in the mid-2000s, with the emergence of international terrorism and increased tensions between national majorities and ethnic minorities, particularly Muslims. The discursive and constructivist turn persists as a methodology, but the focus now is on the interaction between the nation and the Other, and the ways in which diversity and even transnational influences may shape nations and nationalism. This preoccupation with the interaction between the nation and the Other reflects also the relevant politics in Europe where several far-Right and generally conservative political parties seek to capi-talise on anti-immigrant and anti-Muslim sentiment.

Taking note of how our research questions are interactively and per-haps at times inadvertently shaped by the socio-political developments in the context in which we work suggests the need for more self-reflexive work in nationalism studies. It is important to acknowledge that our perspective, research questions and even methodologies are indirectly guided by the important socio-political developments of the society in which we live, rather than simply by our intellectual curiosity. This invites a more self-reflexive approach to our own work which resonates particularly with the current pandemic context and the renewed anti-racism mobilisations in 2020 and 2021. Looking at the challenges that emerge today for the coming decades, three issues arise: the pandemic and the upheaval as well as the innovation it has brought; the persistent rise of populist tendencies that are closely intertwined with nationalism; and the powerful emergence of anti-racism and de-colonisation as a potential new political narrative. Scholars in nationalism studies need to consider what the pandemic re-bordering and 'vaccine nationalism' tell us about hierarchies of membership and transnational interdependence. During the pandemic lockdowns we witnessed innovative approaches to membership that valued 'effective residence' over legal status of a migrant (as temporary or permanent) (Triandafyllidou 2022b). We saw a reconsideration of temporary migrants or asylum seekers as 'essential workers' that should be given a preferential path to permanent residency or citizenship on the basis of their contribution to the community (by ensuring the food supply chain or that care services continue to function).

So, the question arises of how our current theories of identity and nationalism can help us make sense of the new forms of mobility and migration and the ensuing identity/diversity dichotomies that arise.

I have argued elsewhere (Triandafyllidou 1998, 2001) that we need to pay less attention to the ethnic or civic content of national identity and rather focus more on the ways in which a given understanding of the nation and nationalist ideology interacts with 'others', whether real or imagined. I have argued that globalisation requires us to pay more attention to that interaction with Others and have proposed the notion of plural vs neo-tribal nationalism (Triandafyllidou 2020).

While the conceptual and empirical inquiry into the onset of nations and their ethnic or civic configuration and historical circumstances of formation offers rich insights into how nations were formed into national states, with a particular focus on Europe in the last two centuries, it falls short of providing a useful analytical tool in the twenty-first-century context. The socio-economic developments of the last thirty-five years, particularly since 1989, including the collapse of Communism, the intensification of socio-economic and cultural globalisation, the advent of the internet of things, and the increasing relevance of migration and diversity, compel us to rethink what are the main driving forces behind nationalism and nation (trans)formation. While the ethnic or civic 'materials' that make a national identity and the historical process of nation formation ought not to be neglected completely, they need to be considered under a more interactive lens that puts mobility and diversity centre stage in the discourses and practices of nationalism and nation consolidation or change in the twenty-first century. I have thus proposed (Triandafyllidou 2020) the notions of neo-tribal vs plural nationalism as the main analytical categories through which to make sense of contemporary nationalism discourses and ideologies.

My analytical framework on plural vs neo-tribal nationalism is premised on two observations. First, our world is more interconnected and more mobile compared to the post-Second World War period, and even compared to the 1980s and 1990s, when Benedict Anderson, Ernest Gellner, Anthony D. Smith and other renowned theorists of nationalism developed their conceptual work. Our everyday lives today are imbued by services and products generated in other countries and continents.

Cultural and ethnic diversity has acquired an ever more important everyday consumption feature that is no longer confined to cosmopolitan habits of small elites. Not only has the distinction between high (elite) culture and low (popular) culture receded but ethnic cultural consumption has also become popularised. Tasting food from other continents, listening to ethnic music, reading cartoons from distant cultures, and watching TV series produced in other continents is increasingly common among wider population strata. We live in a world of frequent mediated or real interaction with people from other cultures, countries, ethnic backgrounds. This interaction with diverse cultural products and services makes Others, both real and imagined ones, more salient and more relevant in our understanding of who we are and who 'others' are. Such cultural consumption and indirect contact, however, do not necessarily imply openness or acceptance of other cultures and peoples. On the contrary, such multi-cultural tasting may trigger the urge to clarify one's own identity and sense of belonging in a world of increased complexity and inter-cultural contact (Lemaine et al. 1978).

Second, today groups of reference for individuals, and boundaries among different groups have become more blurred, potentially permeable, 'liquid' (to borrow Zygmunt Bauman's term). As Bauman (2000) argues, while free individuals in modernity were to use their freedom to find the appropriate niche where to settle and adopt the rules and modes of conduct identified as appropriate for that location, free individuals today have lost their stable orientation points. Their point of reference is universal comparison, argues Bauman (ibid.), generating too many patterns and configurations available to the individual – indeed, an 'unbearable lightness of being' – to use Milan Kundera's words (Kundera 2005).

In this twenty-first-century context of liquid identity and multi-cultural connectedness and consumption, nationalism – and particularly that of the populist and nativist variety – re-emerges with new force, filling the cracks of a 'liquid' and uncertain later modernity condition. However, it does so in different ways. It can propose neo-tribal identities that seem to restore the certainty and 'solidity' of the past, or it can acknowledge uncertainty (Scoones 2018) and 'liquidity' and create a nuanced and complex sense of belonging that acknowledges mixity and interdependence. The pattern that different countries follow and the ways in which different nationalism discourses (and related policies and practices of inclusion and exclusion) develop is not, I am arguing, a function of their ethnic or civic content but rather depends on how different nationalisms have reacted to increased exposure to mobility and diversity (Triandafyllidou 2013, 2020).

Thus we need to analyse new waves and discourses of chauvinist, populist nationalism or of transnational, universalist solidarity, and of mixed belonging along a continuum that ranges from *plural nationalism* (an open form of nationalism that acknowledges diversity, interacts with it and eventually embraces and synthesises a new national configuration) to *neo-tribal nationalism* (a reactive form of nationalism that is exclusionary, based on the construction of an authenticity and homogeneity that is organic and does not change). Neo-tribal and plural nationalism are of course ideal types, not black-and-white distinctions. They make more sense as the two extreme points of a continuum along which we can position the re-emerging nationalisms of today.

Plural nationalism acknowledges that the nation is based in some commonality. Such commonality may invariably be based on cultural, ethnic, religious or territorial and civic elements. What is important is that the ingroup perceives such commonality and identifies with it, organises around it. Within this plural nationalism there is certainly a majority group that to a large extent has made its imprint on the national identity, through the historical process of nation formation which may have been smooth and gradual or traumatic and conflictual. However, this majority national cultural, ethnic or civic imprint does not monopolise the national identity definition and the relevant dominant discourse. By contrast, plural nationalism acknowledges openly a degree of diversity in the nation that may stem from the period of nation formation and the existence of minorities within the nation or may have evolved later through the experience of immigration. Plural nationalism acknowledges the changing demographic or political circumstances of the nation and the nation-state, and through a process of tension, even conflict, and change it creates a new synthesis.

A concept similar to plural nationalism has recently been advanced by Tariq Modood (2019), who has argued for a multicultural under-standing of nationalism. Modood's notion builds on his earlier writings arguing that British national identity should accommodate post-migra-tion ethnic minorities who ask for recognition and inclusion within the national self-concept (Modood 2003). My notion of plural nationalism is not in reality particularly distant from the multicultural nationalism of Modood, albeit with a caveat: I am concerned not only with minori-ties within the state but also with real or imagined Others outside the boundaries of the nation-state which may include – to take into account the new forms of mobility and displacement – globetrotters and trans-national 'frequent flyer' business or scientific elites, as well as indigenous peoples and other communities displaced by extraction processes and environmental degradation.

In contrast to plural nationalism's interactive and dialogical relation-ship with diversity and Others, neo-tribal nationalism is predicated on a rejection of diversity. I use the term tribal to emphasise that this type of nationalism, regardless of whether the ingroup is defined in territorial-civic or blood-and-belonging terms, is predicated on an organic, homo-geneous conception of the nation (see also Chua 2018). The nation is represented as a compact unit that does not allow for variation or change. The only way to deal with challenges of mobility and diversity is to close ranks and resist and reject them. Neo-tribal nationalism is not static. It is dynamic and interactive too. Albeit its reaction to new challenges and to diversity from within or from outside is one of closure and rejection. I call this nationalism tribal, not in the sense of an ethnic, genealogical commonality but to emphasise that such a nationalism advocates for an organic type of national identity that is somehow amorphous, non-self-reflexive and develops also beyond or in contrast to political institu-tions. Neo-tribal nationalism may be seen as pre-modern in this respect.

However, it is not pre-modern and hence the prefix neo- before the adjective tribal: this type of nationalism develops and thrives not only in a world that is ever more interconnected and mobile but also in a reality that is also dominated by electronic and in particular by social media. While social media may be seen as the epitome of the modern, technological evolution, they bring within them the seed of a return to a tribal, closed understanding of the world. Social media and internet algorithms allow for people who are transnationally connected to the world (through videogames, YouTube channels, social media influenc-ers, on-demand television shows) to be confined within their own little echo-chamber, within their digital bubble of like-minded people. They create a transnational digital community that is neo-tribal. Chauvinist nationalists of the world can unite today. They may share the same zero-sum, competitive, nationalistic view of the world and through their sharing of Instagram and Facebook groups may feel that their views are very mainstream, not extremist at all. It is in this sense that neo-tribal nationalism is not simply tribal.

Discussing neo-tribal nationalism, I was considering the effects of simultaneity and connectedness that the internet of things and social media create, but I had not considered the possibility that a person lives in one country but works (and pays taxes?) in another country in a semi-permanent (or at least not too short-term) manner. However, the pandemic has accelerated those processes of digital nomadism which may include both highly educated globetrotters that chose to be based in Mexico while working for a firm in New York; *pater* or *mater familias* that pursue better career opportunities in Brussels while staying with their family in Cairo or Rome; or South Asian computer experts that work through digital platforms for companies in Dubai or Doha while continuing to live in their home towns. Some have argued for creating zoom towns and internet countries, and Estonia's digital citizenship is certainly a step in that direction, hailed as innovative and efficient (see also Cook 2022).

In addition to these processes, most recent digital developments have added another layer of 'mobility' in our lives – that of augmented reality experience through technologies such as the Metaverse. Beyond remote work such technologies promise a sensory experience that is similar to physical presence (Ma 2022). While this virtual mobility is not expected to supplant physical mobility, it certainly adds a layer of complexity as one is poised to ask whether this augmented reality can create some identity confusion.

Focusing on the virtual transnational or national space that new advanced digital technologies and internet algorithms can create, I wonder whether Riva Kastoryano's (2018) notion of transnational nationalism would be a good conceptual starting point. Kastoryano reflects on the phenomenon of nationalist exclusion through transnational exposure and openness. She notes that in a world of increased migration and interdependence, we witness the re-territorialisation of global identities through the back door. Communities and states, argues Kastoryano (2018: 7), strive to create new configurations of nations and nationalism that are relevant in a globalised context. One strategy for achieving this is to argue for transnational solidarity. Such transnational solidarity can be that of a global 'nation' – an irredentist nation, a global diaspora, such as, argues Kastoryano, a transnational European Muslim community. Kastoryano notes that this transnational nationalism can be aggressive and exclusionary as it reflects on the deficiencies of human rights and citizenship rights that are not fully actualised, and seeks to mobilise individuals against their territorial nation, in favour of a transnational virtual one. Kastoryano notes that this invented and imagined transnational national community, fuelled by external events such as wars, conflict in other countries and colonial relations, re-ethicises identities through its zero-sum, militant discourse.

Making sense of how people will develop their agency and negotiate their identities in this new environment, the conceptual reflections offered by theories of everyday nationhood can be useful (see, for instance, Skey and Antonsich 2017; Skey 2011; Antonsich 2016; Thompson 2001; Fox and Idriss 2008). These theories point to how nationalism and national identity become 'invisible' in everyday life because they are omnipresent. The question arises of whether people will transfer their national identity (and its complexities and ramifications) to their virtual reality and digital mobility or whether they will opt for creating new identities that are separate and autonomous from their 'real' identities. It would be necessary to engage in an analysis of how 'digital nomads' and diginauts will negotiate their identities in their remote work or digital citizenship communities and whether the identity processes activated there will (a) reformulate the interactive dynamics that I have tried to describe in my plural vs neo-tribal framework or that Tariq Modood has analysed in his multicultural nationalism approach, (b) whether these identities will develop alongside dimensions of transnational nationalism of the kind that Kastoryano has analysed, or (c) whether we should conceptualise these two 'realities' as intertwined only through the individual as the locus of these different identities and what this means for our concepts of identity, citizenship, polity and so on.

Concluding Remarks

This chapter is inspired by Tariq Modood's work in two fundamental ways. First, Modood's work has always been informed by his own context and positionality. Unlike other political theorists whose arguments have developed in abstract terms, Modood has always grounded his theoretical analysis in the specific historical context – notably Britain and more largely Europe or the West – and in the lives of the people concerned, notably members of minority groups. Thus, this chapter borrows this approach in seeking to make sense of recent developments in our societies, in migration and in identity formation and negotiation.

Second, this contribution also borrows from Tariq Modood's methodology of inquiry, as exemplified in his recent work on iterative contextualism (Modood and Thompson 2018), which points to the need of going back and forth between values, norms, theories and empirical realities to test the former and enrich our theoretical understandings. This is what I have tried to do here.

Last but not least, my contribution to this book aims to open up some new challenges for Tariq's thinking by pointing out how rapid and often disruptive technological transformation is shaping our social, economic and political realities and how we need to rethink our concepts of diversity and identity and our theories of nationalism, and particularly of multicultural nationalism, to make sense of these new realities that are transnational and that involve simultaneous physical and digital mobility and hence digital and physical modes of presence, participation, claiming and co-existence. Tariq is a political theorist with a very insightful sociological understanding eager to address new socio-political developments through his methodology of iterative contextualism (Thompson and Modood 2021), so I hope this chapter, rather than celebrating his past work, will offer an opportunity for future thinking and future collaboration.

References

Abel, G. J. and N. Sander (2014), 'Quantifying Global International Migration Flows', *Science*, 343 (6178), 1520–2.

Castles, S. (2010), 'Understanding Global Migration: A Social Transformation Perspective', *Journal of Ethnic and Migration Studies*, 36 (10), 1565–86.

Centeno, M. A., M. Nag., T. S. Patterson., A. Shaver and A. J. Windawi (2015), 'The Emergence of Global Systemic Risk', *Annual Review of Sociology*, 41, 65–85.

Chua, A. (2018), *Political Tribes*. London: Bloomsbury.

Cook, D. (2022), 'Digital Nomads Have Rejected the Office and Now Want to Replace the Nation State. But There is a Darker Dide to this Quest for Global Freedom'. Accessed at: <https://theconversation.com/digital-nomads-have-rejected-the-office-and-now-want-to-replace-the-nation-state-but-there-is-a-darker-side-to-this-quest-for-global-freedom-189835>

de Haas, H. (2021), 'A Theory of Migration: The Aspirations-Capabilities Framework', *Comparative Migration Studies*, 9 (1).

Dorries, H., D. Hugill and J. Tomiak (2022), 'Racial Capitalism and the Production of Settler Colonial Cities', *Geoforum*, 132, 263–70.

Florida, R. (2019 [2003]), *The Rise of the Creative Class*. NY: Basic Books.

Fox, J. E. and C. Miller-Idriss (2008), 'Everyday Nationhood', *Ethnicities*, 8 (4), 536–63.

Jubilut, L. L. and M. M. Casagrande (2019), 'Shortcomings and/or Missed Opportunities of the Global Compacts for the Protection of Forced Migrants', *International Migration*, 57 (6), 139–57.

Kastoryano, R. (2018), 'Transnational Politics of Integration and an "Imagined Global Diaspora"', *Diversity and Contestations over Nationalism in Europe and Canada*, 63–87. Accessed at: <https://link.springer.com/chapter/10.1057/978-1-137-58987-3_3>

Kent, J. (2021), 'Looking Back and Moving Forward: The Research Agenda on the Global Governance of Mixed Migration', *International Migration*, 59 (1), 89–104.

Kenwick, M. R. and B. A. Simmons (2020), 'Pandemic Response as Border Politics', *International Organization*, E36–E58.

Lemaine, G., J. Kastersztein, and B. Persononaz (1978), 'Social Differentiation', in H. Tajfel (ed.), *Differentiation Between Social Groups*. London: Academic Press.

Lock, S. (2021), 'Global Tourism Industry – Statistics and Facts'. Accessed at: <https://www.statista.com/topics/962/global-tourism/#dossierKeyfigures>

Ma, A. (2022), 'What is the Metaverse, and What Can We Do There?'. Accessed at: <https://theconversation.com/what-is-the-metaverse-and-what-can-we-do-there-179200>

Maru, N. (2020), 'A Relational View of Pastoral (Im)Mobilities', *Nomadic Peoples*, 24 (2), 209–27.

Maru, N., M. Nori, I. Scoones, G. Semplici and A. Triandafyllidou (2022), 'Embracing Uncertainty: Rethinking Migration Policy through Pastoralists' Experiences', *CMS*, 10, 5. Accessed at: <https://doi.org/10.1186/s40878-022-00277-1>

McAuliffe, M. and A. Triandafyllidou (eds) (2021), 'World Migration Report 2022'. Geneva: International Organization for Migration.

McAuliffe, M. and A. Triandafyllidou (2022), 'Report Overview: Technological, Geopolitical and Environmental Transformations Shaping Our Migration and Mobility Futures', *World Migration Report*. Geneva: International Organization for Migration.

McLeman, R. (2019), 'International Migration and Climate Adaptation in an Era of Hardening Borders', *Nature Climate Change*, 9, 911–18.

Mixed Migration Centre (2019), Mixed Migration in West Africa in 2030. Results from the Mixed Migration Scenario Building Workshop, October 2019, Abidjan, Ivory Coast.

Modood, T. (2003), 'New Forms of Britishness: Post-Immigration Ethnicity and Hybridity in Britain', in B. Peters and R. Sackman (eds), *Identity and Integration: Migrants in Western Europe*. London: Routledge, 77–90.

Modood, T. (2007), *Multiculturalism: A Civic Idea*. Cambridge: Polity.

Modood, T. (2018), 'A Multicultural Nationalism', *Brown Journal of World Affairs*, 25, 233.

Modood, T. (2019), *Essays on Secularism and Multiculturalism*. London: ECPR Rowman and Littlefield.

Modood, T. and S. Thompson (2021), 'Alienation, Othering, and Establishment', *Political Studies*, 70 (3), 780–96.

Modood, T. and S. Thompson (2018), 'Revisiting Contextualism in Political Theory: Putting Principles into Context', *Res Publica*, 24 (3), 339–57.

Polanyi, K. (2001), *The Great Transformation: The Political and Economic Origins of our Time*. Boston, MA: Beacon Press.

Recchi, E., E. Deutschmann and M. Vespe (2019), *Migration Research in a Digitized World*. Springer Cham.

Sassen, S. (2014), *Expulsions. Brutality and Complexity in the Global Economy*. Cambridge, MA: Harvard University Press.

Scoones, I. (2018.), 'What is Uncertainty and Why does it Matter?', STEPS Working Paper 105.

Skey, M. and M. Antonsich (eds) (2017), *Everyday Nationhood: Theorising Culture, Identity and Belonging after Banal Nationalism*. London: Palgrave Macmillan.

Stan, C. (2018), 'Identity in *The Unbearable Lightness of Being* by Milan Kundera', *Cultural Intertexts*, 8 (8), 148–55.

Triandafyllidou, A. (1998), 'National Identity and the "Other"', *Ethnic and Racial Studies*, 21 (4), 593–612.

Triandafyllidou, A. (2013), *Circular Migration between Europe and Its Neighbourhood: Choice or Necessity?*. Oxford: Oxford University Press.

Triandafyllidou, A. (2017), 'Beyond Irregular Migration Governance. Zooming in on Migrants' Agency', *European Journal of Migration and Law*, 19 (1), 1–11.

Triandafyllidou, A. (2020), 'Nationalism in the 21st Century: Neo-Tribal or Plural?', *Nations and Nationalism*, 26 (4), 792–806.

Triandafyllidou, A. (2022), 'Temporary Migration: Category of Analysis or Category of Practice?', *Journal of Ethnic and Migration Studies*, 48 (16), DOI: 10.1080/1369183X.2022.2028350.

Triandafyllidou, A. and M. Ambrosini (2011), 'Irregular Migration Control in Italy and Greece: Strong Fencing and Weak Gate-Keeping Strategies Serving the Labour Market', *European Journal of Migration and Law*, 13 (3), 251–73.

Triandafyllidou, A., M. B. Erdal, S. Marchetti, P. Raghuram, Z. S. Mencutek, J. Salamońska, P. Scholten and D. Vintila (2024), 'Rethinking Migration Studies for 2050', *Journal of Immigrant & Refugee Studies*, 22 (1), 1–21, DOI: 10.1080/15562948.2023.2289116.

Vertovec, S. (2021), 'The Social Organization of Difference', *Ethnic and Racial Studies*, 44 (8), 1273–95.

Part Four

Multiculturalism and Secularism

ELEVEN

Rethinking Race and Religion with Rawls and Modood

Cécile Laborde[1]

Given the spontaneous intersectionality of religious and racial identities, it is surprising that Western political theory has maintained an 'acoustical separation' (Stolzenberg 2011) between the two. In the work of John Rawls, for example, race and religion are distinct categories that pertain to different normative universes. The pioneering work of Tariq Modood offers a welcome corrective to this tendency. It draws on a distinctive European (and global) historical sociology, whereas much of Rawlsian and post-Rawlsian political philosophy remains more comfortable in the intellectual home of the US constitution and the specific trajectory of American law. In this chapter, I seek to explain what is at stake in these differing conceptualisations of race and religion. I first account for Rawls's bifurcated views of religion and race, before describing the rationale behind Modood's more integrated view. In the last section, I will offer some thoughts towards an interpretive framework that retrieves the gist of Rawls's insights while shedding light on the crucial normative dimensions of Modood's theory.

Rawls's Bifurcated View

Rawls gives a central place to religion in his political philosophy, and a marginal – almost inexistent – place to race. This replicates some key features of US historical and legal self-understandings. As Jerry Gaus pointed out, Rawls's theory is a 'distinctively American political theory', displaying a 'prepossession with the political implications of theistic religious disagreement' (Gaus 2003: 185). The USA is a country founded both on an idealised history of religious pluralism and toleration, and a shameful – often repressed – history of racial slavery and segregation. Consequently, religious freedom has its own special provision in the US constitution; whereas racial equality falls under the tortuous application of equal protection and anti-discrimination. Rawls's theory mirrors the respective place of race and religion in the US constitution, albeit in highly abstract fashion.

More specifically, in Rawls's theory, race and religion belong to two sociological and normative universes. Religion refers to individual beliefs, related to ethics and the good life, and worthy of respect in virtue of their tight connection with personal agency and subjectivity. The apt political response to the diversity of religious beliefs is one of toleration and the protection of freedom. Religions also have a dark face, connected as they are to uncompromising, totalising claims on political life. Rawls hoped that liberal states could accommodate religious disagreement, provided believers endorse 'reasonable' interpretations of their religion – those compatible with a shared, thin set of purely political principles affirming principles such as liberty, equality and fairness (Rawls 1996).

The concept of race pertains to a different universe, for Rawls. It receives much more schematic treatment than that of religion in his writings – a lacuna for which he has been much criticised. There is hardly any reference in his work to the history of racial oppression, the inequalities it has generated, and to the place of racial equality in the vision of liberal justice. This is because, for Rawls, 'race' only exists in the minds of unreasonable racists, those who grant ethical salience to morally arbitrary biological traits such as skin colour. Rawls recognised that racial injustice is a pervasive feature of US society and participated in campaigns for racial equality (Terry 2021). Yet as Rawls's philosophical work mostly focused on ideal theory, he himself had hardly anything to say about these.

Here's how Rawls explained (retrospectively) his lack of interest in racial issues, even as he was writing in a society deeply marked by slavery and segregation, and in the throes of controversies about civil rights, affirmative action and reparations for historical injustice. For him, questions of race raised acute *political* problems, but did not pose *philosophical* problems. That is the main difference between race and religion. Religious divisions are a permanent feature of the human condition and will have a place even in the ideal society, whereas racial conflict is a contingent, pathological feature of the non-ideal society.

Why is that? Religious beliefs hold a special place in Rawls's thinking because they are the natural product of the exercise of human reason (understood as the capacity to provide arguments and justifications to others). Rawls did not subscribe to the opposition David Hume (and many of today's anti-religious philosophers) draw between faith and reason. Even if the core of religion involves 'a leap of faith', religious beliefs are, like other cognitive beliefs, grounded in reason. Yet given their essential fallibility, human beings naturally reach different conclusions about religious and moral truths. Religious toleration is a response to the epistemic difficulty of interpersonal justification of the most fundamental truths (Bok 2017; Reidy 2010). It follows that ethical disagreement – what Rawls calls 'the fact of pluralism' – is to be accepted as a permanent feature of free societies. When human beings exercise their reason freely – even in well-ordered societies where most sources of oppression and injustice have been removed – there is no expectation that they will converge on the truth (or untruth) of religion. As Rawls put it, 'the diversity of reasonable comprehensive, philosophical and moral doctrines . . . is a permanent feature of the public culture of democracy' (Rawls 1996: 36). To be sure, unreasonable religions – religions incompatible with the public culture of liberal democracy – should be combated or contained. But reasonable religions are there to stay, even in the just society.

Race is entirely different, for Rawls. This is because racist beliefs are paradigmatically unreasonable beliefs, which can be discounted without loss in political justification. By contrast to religious belief, there is no such thing as reasonable racial belief. Rawls considers segregation and chattel slavery as so self-evidently wrong that he makes them exemplars in his expositions of reflective equilibrium (Rawls 1972: 19). Race, like gender, is morally arbitrary in a special sense, for Rawls. Both are 'natural characteristics' on the basis of which inequalities could never be justified, because such inequalities could never be to the advantage of people of colour or women. In the well-ordered society, there would be a total absence of race, as a socio-political system of subordination. Whatever residual discrimination would persist should be addressed by principles of equal opportunity. Generally, skin colour would be no more salient than, say, eye colour. It is only under non-ideal conditions that the pursuit of racial justice demands stronger egalitarian measures, such as rectification, compensation and reparations for historically disadvantaged groups. Rawls supported measures of affirmative action; and recent archival research has demonstrated that he saw the racial bias of the Vietnam draft as evidence of a deep, structural injustice suffered by African Americans (Terry 2021). However, Rawls did not write about such matters. Corrective racial justice belonged to non-ideal, not ideal theory (Rawls 2001: 66). And ideal theory was concerned with religious and ethical disagreement, not racial conflict.

Critics – Charles Mills most prominently among them (Mills 2005, 2017) – have argued that the very project of Rawlsian ideal theory is ideological (it masks existing racial inequalities), useless (it provides no guidance for social change) and illusory (Rawls underestimated the stickiness of the category of race in any remotely realistic utopia). Those critics have mainly focused on Rawls's ideal theory. In this chapter I explore a different criticism of Rawls – one that targets his *non-ideal* theory. I shall suggest that Rawls's primary interest in religion – and a very intellectualist, cognitivist concept of religion at that – was responsible for a number of sociological blind spots in his (rare) ventures into *non-ideal* theory. Because of Rawls's primarily philosophical interest in religion, he tended to interpret political life through the lens of religious toleration, disagreement and pluralism. This led him to miscast or exaggerate the relevance of religion, including in relation to other dimensions of social and political salience, such as race. There are three chief instances of this mistake in Rawls's writings.

First, Rawls tended to interpret political conflict as primarily a conflict between competing belief systems. As he wrote in *Political Liberalism*, 'the most intractable struggles are confessedly for the sake of the highest of things: for religion, for philosophical views of the world, and for different conceptions of the good' (Rawls 1996: 4). Rawls was drawn towards naively ideational explanations of socio-political conflict – a hasty generalisation from the early modern religious wars in Europe as involving competing political claims by comprehensive ethical philosophies. Unfortunately, Rawls transposed this ideational picture of politics to the fictional yet realistic example of the decent Muslim society that he fashions in his book on international toleration, the *Law of Peoples* (Idris 2021; El Amine 2021). Many have denounced Rawls's Orientalist view of non-Western societies; but few have drawn attention to the role played by Rawls's unhistorical, un-sociological, purely philosophical account of the role of ideas in history. This made him vulnerable to un-reflected-upon, essentialising ideas about Muslim societies. Rawls in fact 'religionised' the political – in non-Western as well as Western societies. In line with his own conception of religion, he construed Islam as a homogeneous comprehensive doctrine offering a systematic ethical world view tightly regulating the lives of its adherents. He had little sense of the diversity of Islam, of its multifaceted connection to politics, and of the plurality of ways of being a Muslim. In sum, it is (in part) because Rawls overemphasised the role of homogeneous religious doctrines in explaining politics – whether European seventeenth-century wars or contemporary politics – that he uncritically endorsed something close to a 'clash of civilisations' view of international politics.

The second consequence of Rawls's privileged focus on religion qua cognitive system of ethical beliefs in his non-ideal theory is that he idealised the power of public reasoning, including in unjust societies marked by deep racial inequalities. At Harvard, Rawls campaigned to denounce the racial injustice of the Vietnam draft, seeing it as symptomatic of a system of structural Black disadvantage and illicit white advantage (Terry 2021). Yet in his published writings, there is a gap between this deeply critical view of the injustice of the US basic structure and the sanitised process of social change that he recommends. He did not critically question his commitment to the power of public reason and speech. He held a faith that American institutions in principle approximated justice, and that it was possible to separate American values from its system of racial injustice (Forrester 2019). Rawls did not see that the operations of public reason, in racially unjust societies, would be inevitably distorted by the continuing prevalence of false ideas about race and the causes of racial inequality, and by the ideological hegemony secured by conservative construals of colour blindness (Boettcher 2009).

The third implication of Rawls's focus on religion over race is that he seemed to believe that the issues raised by the former could help with the latter: that his theory of religious toleration offered a paradigm that could be applied to the resolution of racial conflict. In a suggestive yet opaque passage in the original introduction to *Political Liberalism*, Rawls wrote: 'it may seem that my emphasis on the Reformation and the long controversy about toleration as the origin of liberalism is dated . . . Among our most basic problems are those of race, ethnicity and gender.' He then explained that he focused on key historical questions – like toleration – because 'once we get the conceptions and principles right for the basic historical questions, those conceptions and principles should be widely applicable to our own problems also' (Rawls 1996: xxix). In other words, racial and religious conflict have similar features that may demand similar solutions.

What did Rawls mean? We can hypothesise that racial resentment is analogous to religious conflict in the crucial sense that both stem from fear of difference. However, fear of religious difference is sometimes reasonable, for Rawls, because religions can be unreasonable, but fear of racial difference never can be. Yet both, he suggested, can be addressed via the system of collective assurance provided by political justice (Hertzberg 2017). This confirms, once again, that Rawls thought of religious pluralism as a paradigm for political theory. He may have hoped that racial divisions, at bottom, could be eased through something akin to interfaith reconciliation. Thus it was that, in Rawls's theory, race was brought into the highly ideational world view where he had already located religion – a world of beliefs, propositions, and matters of the mind.

Modood: A Unified View

The background for Tariq Modood's theories of race and religion is very different from that of Rawls. Modood initially trained in a philosophy department and was influenced by the Idealist philosophy of Michael Oakeshott and R. G. Collingwood. From the 1980s he began to study the British tradition of multiculturalism that began with the anti-racist ideas, activism and policies of the 1960s and 1970s. He wondered what the ideas, activism and policies of this tradition 'intimate' about how we should think about the claims of religious minorities (Modood 1994; Uberoi 2021). From the start, Modood was attuned to the multidimensionality and complexity of religious life, which should not be reduced to the cognitivist holding of beliefs or to homogeneous, self-contained systems of thought. His personal background as a British academic of Pakistani and Muslim descent connects him to a more expansive and more nuanced understanding of the 'religio-racial' complex, one rooted in the history of European Christianity, colonialism and multiculturalism. The immediate context for Modood's first interventions on the theme of race and religion was the heated UK debates about the scope of the Race Relations Act and its possible extension to religious minorities such as Muslims. The bifurcation between race and religion, so pregnant and intuitive in the US context, is less natural in the context within which Modood operates. After all, European identity has been framed, in large part, in opposition to its internal Others: Jews and Muslims. Within Christendom, both Jews and Muslims were castigated as theological heretics – the holders of incorrect or unreasonable beliefs – and, from the start, they were also seen as essentially different from Christians – in their customs, mores, bodies, skin colour and civilisational levels (Blijdenstein 2021).

This is to say that Jews and Muslims were, historically, the main victims of European racism. From the 1980s, anti-immigrant prejudice was 'religionised': groups and controversies defined in terms of race or foreignness came to be redefined in terms of religion, and the accommodation of Muslims became the dominant issue in what Sune Lægaard has called Euro-multiculturalism (Lægaard 2015). This is the dominant framework, on this side of the Atlantic, for dealing with religious diversity – thus bringing together the concerns underlying racial, cultural and religious diversity that are often kept separate in North America. This European context provides a crucial backdrop to the alternative to Rawls's bifurcated view that Modood has developed.

Over the course of several decades, Modood has made crucial contributions to rethinking the connections between race, religion and culture, thereby decisively breaking from the highly ideational strictures of US liberal philosophy. Religious identity, he has argued, is sometimes not that different from racial identity: it can suffer the same indignities and exclusions, and should benefit from the same rights and recognition. Racism can take a cultural, not only a biological form (Modood 1992: 69–78). Modood influentially argued that race relations protections should extend to Muslims. Jews and Sikhs are already protected as ethnic groups under English anti-discrimination law (another illustration of the porosity of the categories of race and religion in the English context). Muslims should be seen as not only a religious, but more broadly an ethno-religious group (Modood 1990, 2005).

In the aftermath of the publication of *The Satanic Verses*, Modood endeavoured to show how certain forms of speech amounted not to the 'cognitivist' critique of intellectual ideas but to racial-like attacks on vulnerable minorities. Islamophobia is not so different from antisemitism insofar as it signifies the hatred and rejection of racialised minorities (Modood 2013, 2020). And once we have a grip of the concept of Muslim-ness as a public ethnic identity, we can also show the limits of difference-blind liberalism, and suggest that public religious identities could take their rightful place alongside the plurality of cultural, gender and sexual identities (Modood 2021). Religious identities can be a basis for political agency (Modood 2014). This multiculturalism forces us to refashion secularism as well. Insofar as the secularity of the state is compatible with recognition by the state of religion, including via formal connections such as traditional establishment of religion, there is no reason why Muslims should not benefit from a kind of multifaith establishment (Modood 1994, 2010, 2016).

In Modood's stimulating and progressive vision, the category of 'Muslim-ness' is a pluralist, flexible, anti-essentialist category, one attuned to the complexity and multidimensionality of the lived experience of being a Muslim in the UK (Modood 1998). At times treated like a racial group, at times like an ethnic identity, at times like a set of conscientious practices, Muslim-ness takes a protean form. Modood has resisted the reduction of Muslim-ness both to a cognitivist belief and to an ascribed identity constructed from the outside as a form of Othering: he rightly insists they can be both (Modood 2020: 40, 46). There is much to recommend about this anti-essentialist view of religion: it substitutes a phenomenological description (what experience does this concept capture?) and a pragmatic question (what do we need this concept for?) for the essentialist semantics of definition.

I would like to take Modood's approach a step further. *When*, and *why*, should Muslim-ness be treated like a race, like a religion, like an ethnic identity? Why does it matter? What are the stakes of these conceptual choices? What does it mean to say that Muslims are 'racialised', or 'religionised' – is there anything to the difference? Do the concepts of race and religion stand for distinct phenomenologies, and do they have different normative import, or are they to be subsumed within a diffuse 'religio-ethnic-racial' complex? In the last section of the chapter, I seek to recover some of the normative concerns that underlay Rawls's bifurcation, without however collapsing these normative concerns onto the semantic categories of race and religion. I propose an interpretive, not a semantic, conception of the two categories (Laborde 2017).

A Proposal: First Person v. Third Person

Before I introduce my proposal, let me first set out a couple of popular frames commonly deployed for glossing the race–religion distinction. I assess each of them according to two desiderata: (i) are the frames empirically extensional of the relevant lived experiences? And (ii) do they single out a normatively relevant feature?

The first frame is what we could call the 'folk' understanding of race and religion, where the distinction tracks, roughly, a phenotype v. belief divide. It is commonly thought that religion is about the holding of beliefs, and race about the colour of one's skin. This, however, is too limiting, because the distinction fails to capture the phenomenology – the lived reality – of both religious and racial experiences. Religion is more than belief; race is more than skin colour; and under the folk understanding, ethnic identities (neither just beliefs nor phenotypes) fall out of the picture. In sum, even if (*pro arguendo*) there is normative salience to the belief/phenotype distinction, it fails to be empirically extensional.

Second, on an alternative understanding favoured by so-called 'luck egalitarian' philosophers, the race/religion distinction is a proxy for tracking a relevant normative distinction, that between involuntary and voluntary identities. That distinction is relevant to theories of justice as responsibility, according to which people should be deemed responsible (and therefore not accommodated or compensated) for burdens that they have chosen to bear. The problem with this framework is the opposite to the folk one: even if (that's a big if) we could sort out various empirical affiliations according to whether they have been voluntarily acquired or not, it is not clear why this should be normatively salient. The idea according to which people must be held responsible for their choices, but should be compensated for identities that they have been involuntarily burdened with, is ill-suited to account for our basic normative intuitions, for example about the special protection due to freedom of religion, irrespective of whether religious belief is a voluntary choice or not.

A third framework is that of Rawls-inspired philosophers who, as we saw above in our discussion of Rawls's theory, see religious disagreement as a permanent feature of the politics of the just society, and racial conflict as only a contingent and irrational product of non-ideal injustice. The problem with this Rawlsian bifurcation is twofold. Not only does it disarm philosophers' ability to theorise the complex identities prevalent in non-ideal societies. It also places a narrow, Protestant-biased and ethnocentric understanding of religion – as high-minded comprehensive cognitivist system – at the heart of political theorising, both in ideal and non-ideal theory.

Building on some insights from these various frameworks while addressing their limitations, I propose an alternative mapping. I propose that we identify two broad normative frames, what I have called *First-person* and *Third-person* frames (Laborde 2017). These do not map out perfectly onto the semantic distinction between race and religion as they are ordinarily used, yet they are extensionally inclusive of all their phenomenological manifestations – thus meeting our first desideratum. Moreover, the frames point to two distinct kinds of salient normative concerns, thereby offering an attractive interpretive theory of race and religion – thus meeting our second desideratum.

The *First-person* perspective points to the respect due to the specific ways in which people live their lives. It echoes what Rawls calls the second moral power: the ability that people have to frame, develop and revise the conception of the good that is theirs. The First-person perspective is not narrowly cognitivist or belief-based: it respects a broad range of practices, customs and traditions. Nor is the First-person perspective biased towards ways of life that are theistic, or otherwise oriented towards spiritual concerns. Religion is not uniquely special: it is only one of the ways in which people affirm their autonomy and integrity. Importantly, the First-person perspective protects commitment and projects regardless of how they were acquired (voluntarily or not): as long as they are endorsed by individuals from the inside: as long as individuals identify with them. Finally, the First-person standard is not an individualist standard: it recognises that many protection-worthy practices are collective practices. In sum, what I call First-person perspective is broader than standard liberal conceptions of religion, which are often suspected of harbouring a 'Protestant' (individualist, cognitivist, theistic) bias. Yet it shares the liberal commitment to show respect to people's own (and diverse) commitments, seen from their own *internal* perspective.

The First-person paradigm is primarily a liberty standard. It is not comparative: it is about what people are entitled to be able to do, or not do, regardless of how other people are treated. It does not simply equalise generic opportunities and capacities: it singles out the protection of agent-specific actions and activities. For example, some religious believers can be exempted from general laws out of respect for the special burdens they suffer. This does not mean, however, that the First-person standard does not aim at equality between citizens. It does – but this is a more abstract equality of respect of individuals as moral equals, which sometimes demands that specific attention be paid to the valuable set of commitments that some hold.

The *Third-person* perspective, for its part, invokes the respect due to individuals qua individuals, unburdened from the burdens and disadvantages that stem from their being reduced to the assumptions or stereotypes that others have formed about them. It is close to what Stephen Darwall has called recognition respect: the respect due to all as individuals, *irrespective* of their particular conceptions of the good, beliefs, origins and identities (Darwall 1977). While the First-person perspective shows appraisive respect for agent-specific actions and practices, the Third-person perspective protects people's generic set of opportunities and entitlements.

The Third-person perspective is the standard that animates the bulk of modern anti-discrimination law. It recognises that many of the burdens and disadvantages suffered by racial or religious minorities stem from how they are, or have been, treated by others, regardless of what they themselves are, do, or aspire to be and do. The Third-person standard seeks to rectify *that* treatment. By contrast to the First-person standard, it is a standard that is directly egalitarian, insofar as it seeks to ensure that some individuals are not unfairly disadvantaged, compared to others, in their access to broad opportunities, in virtue of their commitments or identity. It aims at equalising the opportunities and social standing of groups that have historically been subjected to discrimination and exclusion. Its paradigm is that of affirmative action, which aims at reserving specific opportunities – notably in higher education – for groups that have historically been dramatically under-represented.

My proposal draws on the insights of the other three I have briefly discussed. First, it remains quite close to ordinary language (a useful result on the broadly Wittgensteinian approach that I share with Modood). As we saw, folk conceptions explicate the race–religion difference by appeal to the distinction between belief and skin colour. My approach *explains* why we treat belief and skin colour differently, *when we do*: insofar as the first expresses the claimed (self-endorsed) identity of persons; whereas the other is a social marker of ascribed difference. Second, the distinction I draw between claimed (First-person) and ascribed (Third-person) identities echoes the normative worry of luck egalitarian philosophers (according to which people should not be penalised for burdens that are out of their control), without however relying on the dubious sociology and metaphysics of choice and voluntariness. Finally, my proposal, like Rawls's, operates with a distinction between what is permanent and valuable (First-person integrity and autonomy), and what is socially contingent and regrettable (Third-person stigmatisation and discrimination), yet it is not committed to his paralysing distinction between ideal and non-ideal theory.

As I pointed out earlier, the First- v. Third-person frame does not map out perfectly onto the semantic distinction between race and religion: lived religious identities are not only or always First-person; and lived racial identities are not only or always Third-person. This is a virtue of the approach, allowing it to capture both the depth of the phenomenological experience and the multiple normative demands involved in controversies about 'race' and 'religion'. To be sure, we can predict that the First-person standard will generally be the most apt to express respect for religious demands, and the Third-person standard is the most fitting to address inequalities of racial standing. Yet – as the work of Modood has extensively shown – religious individuals and groups are sometimes subject to the same process of racialisation, ethnicisation and otherisation as racial groups. When religion is experienced in this way, as a race, the Third-person standard is apt. Conversely, it is a well-known phenomenon that persons whose identities have been stigmatised, and who have been relegated to the margins of society, often build communal solidarities in their resistance to domination and reappropriate these identities through 'reversal of stigma'. African American identities, for example, are not only Third-person, but also First-person positive affirmations, seeking equality of recognition in societies that have privileged dominant – coded as 'white' – attitudes, norms and traits. Race can be a First-person identity too – something that Rawls's bifurcated vision blinded him to.

A similar approach to the one I advocate here is discernible in Modood's pluralist disaggregation of the different facets of 'Muslim-ness'. On Modood's approach, the normative salience of 'Muslim-ness' is articulated by appeal to whatever standard best helps the participation of Muslims as full and equal members of society. Muslim-ness can be construed as a race for purposes of anti-discrimination and (some) anti-religious speech; as a community-based culture for ethnic relations purposes; as a religion for purposes of exemptions; as a public identity for purposes of multifaith establishment. Tactically, it makes sense to opt for the legal or political strategy that is the most protective of Muslims – as the aim is to combat their historical stigmatisation and exclusion. The most reliable path to inclusive integration will often combine elements of the First- and the Third-person approaches. Advocating a combination of the two standards has been a key philosophical insight of multicultural political theory. Multicultural approaches have helped us see that, often, the best response to the persistent Third-person stigmatisation and otherisation of members of minorities is the positive First-person affirmation of their specific identities. As Modood has insisted, the point of multiculturalism, as a struggle for recognition, 'prioritises groups fighting negative outsider perceptions by giving normative and political weight to insider identifications in all their plurality' (Modood 2007). Modood has in recent years expressed misgivings about the uni-dimensional direction taken by some Islamophobia/Muslim studies, which insist only on the dynamics of Othering and the construction of identities from the outside, at the expense of fuller consideration of Muslims' own subjectivity and agency (Modood 2020). Modood's insistence on the relevance of the two standards is well taken.

In what follows, I suggest further that firmly keeping in mind the different normative stakes of the First- and Third-person perspectives can be helpful in thinking through the orientation of a number of identity-related controversies. I highlight three of them. The first concerns the *politics of presence* – referring to multicultural policies of recognition of diversity destined to increase the representation of minorities in positions of power and influence. My dual framework allows us to identify two rationales at play. The point of the politics of presence can be (i) to publicly recognise and value specific First-person identities and commitments (for example, women's voices, Muslim voices, LGBTQ voices) – especially when these have been historically silenced or marginalised, and/or (ii) to combat the persisting inegalitarian stereotypes regarding the legitimacy of minority citizens in positions of power and influence. The First-person standard informs the first rationale, and the Third-person standard informs the second.

While the two standards articulate important ideals, there is often a dialectical, sometimes conflicting relationship between the two. Feminist advocates of quotas for women in politics have long been aware of the tension between the recognition of the specificity of women's needs and voices and the dangers of essentialism associated with strong claims about what women qua women are and want (Phillips 1998). Advocates of affirmative action have alternated between the defence of a racially conscious 'diversity agenda' and the pursuit of egalitarian policies aimed at the broader 'de-racialisation' of the polity. The aim sometimes is to *recognise difference so as to mainstream it*, so that difference is no longer singled out, otherised and pathologised (Laborde 2008). Note that this should not be interpreted as the advocacy of a difference-blind or colour-blind liberal approach. Third-person defences of the politics of presence do not argue that difference should be privatised or invisibilised. Rather, they suggest there is a complex dialectical relationship between identity affirmation and identity mainstreaming.

To illustrate: consider Sadiq Khan, the Muslim mayor of London. Khan is a practising Muslim and has no qualms about making this fact about him a public fact. Yet his Muslim-ness is only one of the identities of the multifaceted individual that he is; and no one expects him to be an Islam-centred mayor, a mayor for Muslims. This means that his public identity as a Muslim is mainstreamed – that is, it is deemed as normal an identity as that of a public school-educated (or a Black or a mother or a gay) person – or all of them at once. Khan as Muslim can represent Londoners as well as (probably better than!) Boris Johnson as an Etonian white man.

The second area in which the distinction between First and Third person can illuminate the normative stakes of contested disputes is that of *religious accommodations*. On the view I favour, some religious accommodations are primarily about freedom of religion and integrity (First person); and others are also about Equality (Third person). To see how the two standards operate, consider a classic case where they are both at play. In South Carolina in the early 1960s, a member of the Seventh-Day Adventist Church, Adell Sherbert, was denied unemployment compensation on the grounds that no 'good cause' justified her unwillingness to comply with her employer's demand that she, like other employees, accept Saturday work. The US Supreme Court reversed the lower court's decision, and found that denying Sherbert's compensation claim violated her rights to religious freedom. *Sherbert v. Verner* (1963) became a landmark case in the constitutionalisation of religious freedom. Consider, however, two different ways in which Sherbert's religious freedom claim could be justified. On the one hand, one could say (as the Court in fact said) that to condition Sherbert's access to benefit on her willingness to violate a cardinal principle of her faith would unduly burden her rights of religious freedom. On this view, Sherbert has a liberty-based, First-person claim to practise her religion freely (absent a compelling state interest). On the other hand, one could say that denying compensation would entail unjustly discriminating against Sherbert who cannot, *by contrast to mainstream Christians*, enjoy the structural advantage of benefiting from an official workweek allowing her to combine her work with her religious practices. (For a UK case with the same structure, see *Ahmad*, concerning a Muslim teacher who sought to absent himself for Friday prayer.) On this view, Sherbert and Ahmad have an additional, Third-person egalitarian claim not to be denied entitlements that others have as a matter of invisible privilege.

For a religious claim to raise equality concerns, on my view, it has to be the case that dominant norms entrench the historical privilege of religious majorities. It is important to note that not all demands for religious accommodations have this egalitarian form. When religious believers or groups – Muslims, Christians or Jews – demand to be exempted from laws promoting gender and sexual equality, for example, they might have a (defeasible) religious claim as First-person claims, but it is not clear that they have a Third-person equality claim – there is no background inequality there.

There is a deep reason why – tactically as well as philosophically – we would do well to keep religious freedom and equality claims apart. The language of multicultural equality has recently been instrumentalised by Christian groups to complain that they are minoritised – stigmatised, treated as second-class citizens – whenever they are required to comply with secular laws of gender or sexuality equality. Yet religious groups should not always be treated like oppressed minorities such as racial groups. Religious believers can seek recognition of some of their First-person claims, but they should not claim to be disrespected as equal citizens just because their claims to depart from democratic norms are not acceded to (Laborde 2024).

A third area in which the First-person/Third-person distinction is useful is that of *anti-religious speech*. One of Modood's most influential arguments, in the aftermath of the Rushdie Affair, was that anti-religious speech was sometimes indistinguishable from racist speech. On this basis, he welcomed the introduction of a new legal prohibition in English law, that of religious offence. Critically, Modood has also insisted that we should draw a wedge between Islamophobia and reasonable criticism of Islam and Muslims (Modood 2020). The category of 'anti-religious' speech, therefore, is internally complex. There are cases where anti-religious speech will indeed be a Third-person affront – when it reproduces stereotypes that stigmatise, exclude and lower the social standing of vulnerable minorities. Some of the notorious Danish cartoons, which associated the Prophet Muhammad with terrorism, bestiality and vile antisemitic imagery, are clearly in that category. Yet other forms of contested speech – including, in my view, the contested pages in Rushdie's *The Satanic Verses* – may pertain to the First-person right of authors to play, mock and deride beliefs. Those lines are difficult to draw, of course, but it does not mean that they are not there. One last thought on speech. It is possible that these controversies also have to do neither with the First-person legal right of speakers to speak, nor with the Third-person legal right of targets to be protected from speech. Very often, they have to do with what we may call the *Second-person* moral point of view: the entitlement we have to be treated decently by our fellow citizens in our interpersonal, social interactions.

In this chapter, I have contrasted Rawls's bifurcated view of race and religion with Modood's more integrated view, which is more sensitive both to the complex phenomenology of lived experience and to the normative demands of democratic respect for different types of identities. We still need to know, however, when it is apt to treat a religious group 'like' a racial group. To that effect, I introduced an interpretive frame distinguishing between First-person and Third-person perspectives, showing them to articulate different types of normative concerns. The distinction allows us to maintain some of the normative insights behind Rawls's bifurcation, without endorsing the problematic sociology that underpinned his non-ideal theory. Modood's multicultural theory could adopt this interpretive frame without any loss of the enviable richness of its analyses.

Note

1. An earlier version of this chapter was presented at a conference in honour of Tariq Modood in Bristol on 29–30 September 2022. I am grateful to participants for their questions, and to the editors of this volume for their suggestions. Section 1 draws on my 'Rawls, Race, Religion' (forthcoming), in M. Schwartzman, L. Watson and B. Neufeld (eds), *A Theory of Justice in the 21st Century*. Oxford: Oxford University Press.

References

Blijdenstein, A. (2021), *Liberalism's Dangerous Religions. Enlightenment Legacies in Political Theory*. PhD thesis, University of Amsterdam.

Boettcher, J. (2009), 'Race, Ideology and Ideal Theory', *Metaphilosophy*, 40 (2), 237–58.

Bok, M. P. (2017), 'To the Mountaintop Again: The Early Rawls and Post-Protestant Ethics in Post-War America', *Modern Intellectual History*, 14 (1): 153–85.

Darwall, S. L. (1977), 'Two Kinds of Respect', *Ethics*, 88 (1): 36–49.

Dobbernack, J., N. Meer and T. Modood (2014), 'Misrecognition and Political Agency. The Case of Muslim Organisations in a General Election', *British Journal of Politics and International Relations*, 17 (2), 189–206.

El Amine, L. (2021), 'Political Liberalism, Western History and the Conjectural Non-West', *Political Theory*, 49 (2), 190–214.

Forrester, K. (2019), *In the Shadow of Justice. Post-war Liberalism and the Remaking of Political Philosophy*. Princeton, NJ: Princeton University Press.

Gaus, G. (2003), *Contemporary Theories of Liberalism*. London: Sage.

Hertzberg, B. (2017), 'John Rawls and the Race-Religion Analogy', Paper presented at the 'Historical Rawls' conference in Oxford, 26 May, unpublished, on file with author.

Idris, M. (2021), 'The Kazanistan Papers: Reading the Muslim Question in the John Rawls Archives', *Perspectives on Politics*, March, 19 (1), 110–30.

Laborde, C. (2008), *Critical Republicanism*. Oxford: Oxford University Press.

Laborde, C. (2017), *Liberalism's Religion*. Cambridge, MA: Harvard University Press.

Laborde, C. (2024), 'Secular Rules and Indirect Discrimination against Christians', in C. Laborde, M. Schwartzman and N. Tebbe (eds), *Discrimination By/Against Religion*. Oxford: Oxford University Press.

Laborde, C. (forthcoming), 'Rawls, Race, Religion', in M. Schwartzman, L. Watson and B. Neufeld (eds), *A Theory of Justice in the 21st Century*. Oxford: Oxford University Press.

Lægaard, S. (2015), 'Multiculturalism and Contextualism: How is Context Relevant for Political Theory?', *European Journal of Political Theory*, 14 (3), 259–76.

Mills, C. (2005), '"Ideal Theory" as Ideology', *Hypathia: A Journal of Feminist Philosophy*, 20 (3), 165–84.

Mills, C. (2017), *Black Rights/White Wrongs: The Critique of Racial Liberalism*. New York: Oxford University Press.

Modood, T. (1990), 'Muslims, Race and Equality in Britain: Some Post-Rushdie Affair Reflections', *Third Text*, 4 (11).

Modood, T. (1992), *Not Easy Being British*. Stoke on Trent: Runnymede Trust and Trentham Books.

Modood, T. (1994), 'Establishment, Multiculturalism and British Citizenship', *Political Quarterly*, 65 (1).

Modood, T. (1998), 'Anti-Essentialism, Multiculturalism and the "Recognition" of Religious Minorities', *Journal of Political Philosophy*, 6 (1).

Modood, T. (2005), 'British Asian Muslims and the Rushdie Affair', *The Political Quarterly*, 61 (2).

Modood, T. (2007), *Multiculturalism. A Civic Idea*. Polity.

Modood, T. (2010), 'Moderate Secularism, Religion as Identity and Respect for Religion', *Political Quarterly*, 81 (1).

Modood, T. (2013), 'Afterword: Islamophobia and the Struggle for Recognition', in N. Meer (ed.), *Racialization and Religion: Race, Culture and Difference in the Study of Anti-Semitism and Islamophobia*. London: Routledge.

Modood, T. (2016), 'State–Religion Connections and Multicultural Citizenship', in J. L. Cohen and C. Laborde (eds), *Religion, Secularism, and Constitutional Democracy*. Columbia University Press.

Modood, T. (2020), 'Islamophobia and Normative Sociology', *Journal of the British Academy*, 8, 29–49.

Modood, T. and T. Sealy (2021), 'Freedom of Religion and the Accommodation of Religious Diversity: Multiculturalising Secularism', *Religions*, 12 (10).

Phillips, A. (1998), *The Politics of Presence*. Oxford: Oxford University Press.

Rawls, J. (1972), *A Theory of Justice*. Oxford: Oxford University Press.

Rawls, J. (1996), *Political Liberalism*. New York: Columbia University Press.

Rawls, J. (2001), *Justice as Fairness: A Restatement*, ed. Erin Kelly. Cambridge, MA: Harvard University Press.

Reidy, D. A. (2010), 'Rawls's Religion and Justice as Fairness', *History of Political Thought*, 31 (2), 309–43.

Stolzenberg, N. (2011), 'Righting the Relationship between Race and Religion', *Oxford Journal of Legal Studies*, 31 (3), 583–602.

Terry, B. M. (2021), 'Conscription and the Color Line: Rawls, Race and Vietnam', *Modern Intellectual History*, 18 (4), 960–83.

Uberoi, V. (2021), 'Oakeshott and Parekh: The Influence of British Idealism on British Multiculturalism', *History of Political Thought*, 42 (4), 730–54.

TWELVE

On Modood's Moderate Secularism

Rajeev Bhargava

Introduction

Tariq Modood and I have been in dialogue on secularism for nearly two decades now. He was among the few who very early on recognised the main point of my 1998 book *Secularism and its Critics* (Bhargava 1998): that we need not an alternative to but an alternative conception of political secularism, one that is different from mainstream conceptions shaped by French laïcité and the American wall of separation variant.

Since we agree on much, I begin with identifying and stating six points where we do and how much. First, it is not enough that states be committed to liberal and democratic principles. They should, in addition, be committed to a normative perspective called political secularism. Second, there are many models or conceptions of political secularism. Third, most European states follow neither the French nor the American model. Virtually all European states have a stable regime of individual rights that includes the right to religious liberty. None could have managed to install such a regime without in the past weakening the power and privilege of their churches, and without installing some degree of state–church separation. Yet, unlike the French, there is less lingering hostility towards religion in other European state-structures. Virtually all of Europe developed an institutional arrangement that grants some privilege or public recognition to a given church. Indeed, some states still have an established church, a privileged arrangement that goes well beyond recognition. Like me, Modood finds the combination of separation of church and state and support for a given church compatible with secularism, this being a feature of what he calls moderate secularism. States that run in accordance with such a regime are secular states.

Fourth, Modood is also quite right that there is no effective challenge from the church or radical secularists to this moderate political secularism. This may not be the best of all possible worlds from their points of view, and currently it might even be tilted in favour of secularists, but it is an acceptable compromise.

Such is the context in which non-Christian migrants, the majority of whom are Muslims, have been arriving, settling, and making claims that 'relate to the place of religious identity in the public sphere' (Modood 2011). This leads to our fifth agreement. The migration from former colonies and an intensified globalisation has *thrown together in Western public spaces* pre-Christian faiths, Christianity and Islam (Turner 2011). The cumulative result is unprecedented religious diversity, the weakening of the public monopoly of single religions, and the generation of mutual suspicion, distrust, hostility and conflict. Modood says that it is here, if anywhere, that a sense of crisis of secularism can be found (for example, Modood 2011). So we both agree that the crisis of secularism is directly related to the arrival, predominantly, of Muslim immigrants in Europe.

We have another, sixth, agreement to report. It lies in our joint hope that European secularism will respond to these changes. Europe can't just go on with the same 'moderate secularism' and jettison the problem. As Modood puts it, this secularism needs to be multiculturalised (Modood and Sealy 2021). I take this to mean that the historical compromises between church and state have to be extended to other religions, particularly to Islam.

Here, however, is where we profoundly disagree. Moderate secularism, for me, was irretrievably flawed (that, I confess, was a polemical overstatement). Yet, I maintain that the multiculturalisation of this secularism is neither easy nor sufficient. It is not easy because it presupposes massive change in cultural background. Institutional adjustment is bound to be difficult because an internal link exists between the collective, secular self-understanding of European societies and deeply problematic institutional arrangements. This is so because current European institutions are deeply biased. They have accommodated Christians but will not be able to easily accommodate Muslims. It is not sufficient because simple accommodation without some accompanying 'hostility' may not work for all Muslim citizens. In my view, the required institutional adjustments are not possible without a theoretical revision in modest secularism. Let me elaborate on each of these points.

What is Political Secularism?

First, we both accept the necessity of political secularism. But what is it? Political secularism answers the question: what is the appropriate relation between state and religious institutions? Modood takes political secularism to be the view that political authority does not rest on religious authority and the latter does not dominate political authority; each has considerable, though not absolute, autonomy. He believes this is the generic idea common to all versions of liberal democratic states. Implicit in this statement is the judgement that it would be wrong for political authority (state) to be under the control of religious authority. The two should be independent of one another. But why? For the sake of which values? Modood does not clarify but clearly the values in question are liberal and democratic. I agree with this broad understanding but, apart from making my own formulation more specific, I wish to go beyond it. Secularism to me is constitutively tied to specific goals and values.

In an article published in 1994, I introduced the term 'political secularism', distinguishing it from what I called ethical secularism (Bhargava 1994: 7). Ethical secularism tells one how best to live in the only world and only life we have, this one, here and now, and what the goals of human flourishing are, conceived independently of God, gods or some other world. I distinguished this ethic from political secularism, a normative project that defends a certain kind of polity in which organised religious power is separated from organised political power for values such as freedom and equality of citizenship. One idea behind this distinction was to argue that both those who believe in ethical secularism and those who believe in or practice various religions can come to agree on the constitutive principles that underlie political secularism. Political secularism neither entails nor presupposes ethical secularism. To believe that in order to be a political secularist one had to be an ethical secularist is simply false.

Later I argued that the goal of secularism is to ensure that the social and political order is free from institutionalised religious domination so that there is religious freedom, freedom to exit from religion, inter-religious equality, equality between believers and non-believers, and solidarity that fosters principled co-existence between followers of religious and non-religious perspectives, and that this is forged when people are freed from religious sectarianism. Thus, religion defines the scope of secularism. The very point of secularism is lost either when religion disappears or if it purges itself from its oppressive, tyrannical, inegalitarian or exclusionary features. Because religion is a far more complex and ambivalent entity, has both negative features and is a positive good, a secularism which responds to religion must capture this ambivalence.

The broadest and perhaps vaguest answer provided by political secularism is that state and religion must be separated. Political secularism, however, does not come in one unique form but is open to many interpretations and conceptions depending on how the metaphor of separation is unpacked, which values separation is meant to promote, how these values are combined, and what weight is assigned to each of them. However, to grasp its structure, it is first important to contrast political secularism with doctrines to which it is in one sense related and opposed. This is particularly relevant given Modood's differences with me over establishment of religion. Such anti-secular, religion-centric doctrines favour not separation, but a union or alliance between religion and state. They advocate religion-centred rather than secular states.

Here, a further set of distinctions needs to be introduced. States may be strongly connected to religion at three distinct levels: (1) the level of ends, (2) the level of institutions and personnel, and (3) the level of public policy and, even more relevantly, law. A state that has union with a particular religious order, and is as such strongly connected to religion at each of the three levels, is a theocratic state, governed by divine laws directly administered by a priestly order claiming divine commission (Bhargava 2016: 159; Bhargava 2009). Historical examples of theocracies are ancient Israel, some Buddhist regimes of Japan and China, the Geneva of John Calvin and the papal states. The Islamic republic of Iran as Khomeini aspired to run it is an obvious example. These states are clearly not politically secular.

A theocratic state, however, must be distinguished from a state that establishes religion. Here, religion is granted official, legal recognition by the state and while both benefit from a formal alliance with one another, the sacerdotal order does not govern a state where religion is established. Because they do not unify church and state but install only a privileged alliance between them, states with an established church are in some ways disconnected from it. In states with established religions, there is personnel differentiation and state functionaries and church functionaries are largely different from one another. Yet, there is a more significant sense in which the state and the church are connected to one another: they share a common end largely defined by religion. The states grant privileged recognition to religion. Religion even partially defines the identity of the state. Thus, both benefit from this mutual alliance.

There is finally another level of connection between church and state at the level of policy and law. Such policies and laws flow from and are justified in terms of the union or alliance that exists between the state and the church. The institutional disconnection or separation of church and state – at the level of roles, functions and powers – goes hand in hand with the first- and third-level connection of ends with policies and laws.

Yet, a secular state goes beyond church–state separation, refusing to establish religion or, if religion is already established, disestablishing it.

It withdraws privileges that established religion had previously taken for granted. This it can do only when its primary ends or goals are defined independently of religion. Therefore, a secular state follows what can be called the principle of non-establishment. I see this as consistent with Modood's statement that political authority does not rest on religious authority but is autonomous of it. For example, it cannot be the constitutive objective of the state to ensure salvation, nirvana or moksha. Nor can the conversion of one individual or a group from one religion to another be the goal of the state. Official privileged status is not given to religion. This is largely what is meant when it is said that in a secular state, a formal or legal union or alliance between state and religion is impermissible. Thus, a crucial requirement of a secular state is that it has no constitutive links with religion, that the ends of any religion should not be installed as the ends of the state. No religious community in such a state can say that the state belongs exclusively to it. The identity of the state is defined independently of religion, and not just one but all religions.

To grasp this point at a more general theoretical level, let me distinguish three levels of disconnection to correspond with the already identified three levels of connection. A state may be disconnected from religion at the level of ends (first level), at the level of institutions (second level) and at the level of law and public policy (third level). A secular state is distinguished from theocracies and states with established religions by a primary, first-level disconnection. A secular state has freestanding ends, substantially, if not always completely, disconnected from the ends of religion. At the second level, disconnection ensues so that there is no mandatory or presumed presence of religious personnel in the structures of a state. No part of state power is automatically available to members of religious institutions. Finally, a secular state may be disconnected from religion even at the level of law and public policy. For many proponents or opponents of political secularism, all three levels of separation matter equally. In short, separation must be strict or perfect if states are to be fully secular. I believe the identification of this third level is important, but not because separation at this level is constitutive of political secularism; rather, differences at this level generate a variety of political secularisms (Bhargava 2009).

Until recently, however, the existence of multiple secularisms remained unacknowledged. Wittgenstein's warning that the hold of a particular picture is sometimes so strong that it prevents, even occludes, the awareness of other models of reality is probably more apt about secularism than about other related social and political doctrines. We have failed to recognise multiple secularisms because our imagination is severely controlled by particular conceptions of secularism developed in parts of the Western world. I have written elsewhere about what I have referred to as the idealised American or the mutual exclusion model, and the idealised French or the one-sided exclusion model, and observed that these have been hegemonic in theoretical discussions (Bhargava 2009). In this chapter I want to make the point of multiple and non-Western secularisms more emphatically because it has caused some confusion, even in Modood's writings. In what follows I therefore discuss two models. The first is Modood's theorisation based in how political secularism has developed in large parts of Western Europe, namely his moderate secularism. Then I go on to consider one of the two models developed in India, centred on principled distance and embodied in the Indian constitution. What then are the features of these two variants?

Moderate Secularism

Since I had made only cursory remarks about other European states in our early exchanges on political secularism, Modood raised some pertinent issues. He noted in particular my identification of the United States and French models as 'the most dominant and defensible Western versions of secularism' (Bhargava 2009: 93). This he believed was mistaken and argued that 'most of Western, especially north-western Europe, where France is the exception not the rule, is best understood in more . . . moderate terms . . . They have several important features to do with a more pragmatic politics; with a sense of history, tradition and identity; and, most importantly, there is an accommodative character which is an essential feature of some historical and contemporary secularisms in practice' (Modood 2019: 148).

In the first instance it is important to note that my argument was not about what was happening in Western polities as against Indian polity. The contrast that I wished to draw was between two or three idealised models, or theoretical conceptions. I wished to compare different theories or models of secularism, not the actual experience of different polities. My main focus was to identify the distinctiveness of the Indian model. Contrasting this with the idealised American and French was useful. I am a political theorist, not a sociologist. I did not have a good understanding of the British experience. In any case, British practice had not had the opportunity to express itself as a model, as theoretical formulation. At the time I wrote my initial pieces, scholars had not identified a theoretical model of European secularism. I could immediately relate to it once Modood did articulate his idea of moderate secularism and through conversations and dialogue with my writings with which he was familiar, at least since 2001.

I can honestly say that Modood did us a great service by theorising the actual practices of Western European states, particularly the British state. He showed us more clearly that when properly theorised, European secularism is different from the prevailing mainstream models. In my dialogues and arguments with Modood, I developed my own conception of the Western European experience and he, with his own vast experience and better understanding of British society, formulated what he later called moderate secularism.

My account of the European model (modest secularism)

Despite the entanglements of religion and state in Europe, and the criticisms I developed of them, I defended European states as secular on three grounds. First, the social and political power of churches has been largely restricted. Second, there has over time been a decline not only in church belonging but also in belief in Christianity. If there is one place where secular humanism or what Charles Taylor calls exclusive humanism is strong, even naively taken for granted as the only ontological and epistemological game in town, it is surely Western Europe. Both these points have had an impact on Europe's constitutional regimes and a fair degree of disconnection exists at level 2 (that of institutions and personnel). Third, and more importantly, the ends of state are delinked from religion to a significant degree (level 1 disconnection), and so the same basket of formal rights (to different kinds of liberty, and forms of equality, etc.) are offered to all individuals regardless of their church affiliation and regardless of whether they are or are not religious. In the dominant political discourse, the self-definition of these states is that they are not religious (Christian) but (purely) liberal democratic.

However, it is equally true that at both levels 1 and 2, some connection exists between state and religion. Several states continue to grant monopolistic privileges to one or the other branch of Christianity. Examples include the Presbyterian Church in Scotland, the Lutheran Church in all Nordic countries (except Sweden, where it was disestablished in 2000), the Orthodox Church in Greece, and the Anglican Church in England, where twenty-six bishops sit in the House of Lords with full voting rights, and where the monarch is also the Supreme Governor of the Church. Moreover, at level 3, at the level of law and public policy, state intervention exists in the form of support either for the dominant church or of Christian churches. Thus, most European states remain connected to religion (the dominant religion or church) at all three levels.

The connection at levels 1 and 2 means that they still have some form of establishment, perhaps elements of theocracy. At level 3, there is

neither mutual nor one-sided exclusion of religion, but positive entanglement with it. None of this entails that such states are confessional or
have strong establishment. Rather, such state–religion connections combined with a significant degree of disconnection mean that these states
are at best modestly secular by the standards set by the idealised American model or the French model. Indeed, this is what Tariq Modood has
called 'moderate secularism'. He has argued that this secularism is compatible with a more than symbolic but weak establishment. The moder-
ateness comes largely from the rejection of exclusion and the adoption
of some distance instead. The secularity comes largely from the ends for
which states have distanced themselves and which are largely defined
independently of religion.

On Modood's own account, moderate secularism can and should go
on more or less as it is, but, in order to accommodate Muslims, 'must
undergo some institutional adjustments'. But this account needs correc-
tion, because Modood, in fact, is more ambitious because he seeks not
just institutional adjustments but also theoretical revisions. One important shift that Modood seeks is from an individualist understanding of
'equality' that aims at cultural assimilation to a politics of recognition,
to equality 'as encompassing public ethnicity'. This perception of equality means not having to hide or apologise for one's origins, family or
community and requires others to show respect for them. Public attitudes and arrangements must adapt so that this heritage is encouraged,
not contemptuously expected to wither away. So apart from absence of
discrimination on grounds of religion and greater even-handedness in
support from the state for minority religions, he wishes to have positive inclusion of religious groups. The demand here is that religion in
general, or at least the category of 'Muslim' in particular, should be a
category by which the inclusiveness of social institutions may be judged,
as they increasingly are in relation to race and gender. For example,
employers should have to demonstrate that they do not discriminate
against Muslims by explicit monitoring of Muslims' position. Among
other things, this entails the recognition of collectivities and not just
individuals. Muslims and other religious groups utilise this kind of argument, claiming that religious identity, just like gay identity and just like
certain forms of racial identity, should not just be privatised or toler-
ated, but should be part of the public space.

In the case of Muslims, however, they come into conflict with a major
dimension of liberal secular citizenship: the view that religion is a feature, perhaps uniquely, of private and not public identity. Overall, the
key feature of moderate secularism is that it sees organised religion as
not just a private benefit but also as a potential public good or national

resource, and which the state can in some circumstances assist to realise – even through an 'established' church. These public benefits can be direct, such as a contribution to education and social care through autonomous church-based organisations funded by the taxpayer; or indirect, such as the production of attitudes that create economic equality (Modood 2019: 180). Multicultural equality, then, when applied to religious groups means that secularism simpliciter (that is equivalent as I see it to radical conceptions of secularism as strict separation for the sake of an exclusively individualist understanding of ends) appears to be an obstacle to pluralistic integration and equality. But secularism pure and simple is not what exists in the world. The country-by-country situation is more complex, and indeed, far less inhospitable to the accommodation of Muslims than the ideology of secularism – or, for that matter, the ideology of anti-secularism – might suggest (Modood and Kastoryano 2006). All actual practices of secularism consist of institutional compromises and these can, should be and are being extended to accommodate Muslims.

But these institutional adjustments need a theoretical vision. So, unlike what Modood himself suggests, what is required is not institutional adjustment but more wide-ranging theoretical reforms. Indeed, my own main claim in this chapter is that the crisis of secularism is due largely to the failure of Europe to make a conceptual shift from a secularism developed in and for single-religion societies to one that is far more sensitive and finely tuned to deep religious diversity. A further aspect of this is that although Modood says that 'state control and support of religion must not compromise the autonomy of politics and statecraft: it must be largely justifiable in political terms, not just religious reasons, and must not restrict (but may support) political authority and state action', he provides few examples where such interference would be legitimate. As far as I can tell, concrete discussions of where a secular state, in appropriate circumstances, might negatively intervene on grounds of gender, caste or other variables in churches or patriarchal Muslim groups are missing.

There are then two insufficiencies in moderate secularism that produce its 'crisis', one related to its capacity to accommodate non-Christian religious diversity, and one related to legitimate state interference. At its root the crisis of European secularism is conceptual. Europe must reconceptualise its secularism and, in order to do so, possibly learn from the experience of non-European, non-Western societies such as India. Modood has suggested that while my judgement is politically sound, it lacks theoretical rationale. I hope these points I made more than a decade ago demonstrate that I had a fairly sound theoretical justification too. I will return to this point later, but in order to do so let me offer a brief outline of two models of Indian secularism about which I have written, as these will form the basis of my subsequent normative evaluation of European moderate secularism.

Indian Secularisms

For a rich, complex and complete understanding of secularism, one must examine how the secular ideal has developed over time transnationally. In short, we must acknowledge that several Western and non-Western societies have developed their own variants of secular states and imagined multiple secularisms. Allow me to explicate them and then evaluate European secularism by the norms of one of these, in my view a richer, transcultural variant of secularism.

Perhaps the best way to begin articulating it is by sketching two broad and contrasting pictures of the socio-religious world. In the first, a persistent, deep and pervasive anxiety exists about the 'other', both the other outside one's religion and the other within. The other is viewed and felt as an existential threat: doctrinal differences are felt not as mere intellectual disagreements but are cast in a way that undermines basic trust in one another. The other cannot be lived with but simply has to be expelled or exterminated. This results in major wars and a consequent religious homogenisation. Though admittedly skewed, this picture approximates what happened in Europe in the sixteenth century (Cohen and Laborde 2015: 169). One might then add that this constitutes the hidden background condition of European ideas of toleration and even its political secularism.

Consider now an entirely different situation. Here different faiths, modes of worship, philosophical outlooks and ways of practising exist customarily. Deep diversity is accepted as part of the natural landscape: Syrian Christians, Zoroastrians, Jews, Muslims (Arab traders or Turks and Afghanis who came initially as conquerors but settled down), not to speak of a variety of South Asian faiths – all are at home. To feel and be secure is a basic psychosocial condition. All groups exhibit basic collective self-confidence, possible only when there is trust between communities. In short, the presence of the other is never questioned. There is no deep anxiety; the other does not present an existential threat. Instead, a basic level of comfort exists. This is not to say that there are no deep intellectual disagreements and conflicts, some of which even lead to violent skirmishes, but these do not result in major wars or religious persecution. There is no collective physical assault on the other on a major scale. This approximates the socio-religious world of the Indian subcontinent, at least until the advent of colonial modernity, and constitutes the background condition of civility and co-existence, perhaps even a different form of 'toleration', in India. Indeed, it is not entirely mistaken to say it was not until the advent of colonial modernity and the formation of Hindus and Muslims as national communities that this background condition was unsettled. Religious co-existence could now no longer be taken for granted, doubts about co-existence forced themselves upon the public arena, and conceptions in order to perform its primary function; that is, to promote a certain quality of sociability, to foster a certain quality of relations among religious communities, perhaps even inter-religious equality under conditions of deep religious diversity.

A second conception developed too, even more ambitious, that tried to combine the aim of fostering better quality of social relations with an emancipatory agenda, to not only respect all religions and philosophies but also protect individuals from the oppressive features of their own religions or religious communities – or to put it differently, to confront and fight both inter-religious and intra-religious domination simultaneously. This is the constitutional secularism of India. Several features of this model are worth mentioning. First, multiple religions are not optional extras added on as an afterthought but were present at Indian secularism's starting point as part of its foundation. Indian secularism is inextricably tied to deep religious diversity. Acknowledgement of deep diversity entails the acceptance that some religions are intrinsically public. So, and this is its second feature, it is not entirely averse to the public character of religions. Although the state is not identified with a particular religion or with religion more generally (disconnection at level 1), official and, therefore, public recognition is granted to religious communities (at level 3). The model admits a distinction between de-publicisation and de-politicisation, as well as between different kinds of de-politicisation. Because it is not hostile to the public presence of religion, it does not aim to de-publicise it. It accepts the importance of one form of de-politicisation of religion.

Third, this form of secularism has a commitment to multiple values, namely liberty, equality and fraternity – not conceived narrowly as pertaining only to individuals but interpreted broadly also to cover the relative autonomy of religious communities and, in limited and specific domains, their equality of status in society – as well as other more basic values such as peace, toleration, and mutual respect between communities. It has a place not only for the right of individuals to profess their religious beliefs but also for the right of religious communities to establish and maintain educational institutions crucial for the survival and sustenance of their distinctive religious traditions.

The acceptance of community-specific rights brings me to the fourth feature of this model. Because it was born in a deeply multireligious society, it is concerned as much with inter-religious domination as it is with intra-religious domination. Whereas the two Western conceptions of secularism have provided benefits to minority religious groups only incidentally (for example, Jews benefited in some European countries such as France not because their special needs and demands were met via public recognition but because of a more general restructuring of society guided by an individual-based emancipatory agenda), under the Indian conception some community-specific socio-cultural rights are granted. Common citizenship rights are not seen as incompatible with community-specific rights in limited domains such as education.

Fifth, this model does not erect a wall of separation between religion and state. There are boundaries, of course, but they are porous. This situation allows the state to intervene in religions in order to help or hinder them without the impulse to control or destroy them. This intervention can include granting aid to educational institutions of religious communities on a non-preferential basis and interfering in socio-religious institutions that deny equal dignity and status to members of their own religion or to those of others; for example, the ban on untouchability and the obligation to allow everyone, irrespective of their caste, to enter Hindu temples, as well as, potentially, other actions to correct gender inequalities.

In short, Indian secularism interprets separation to mean not strict exclusion or strict neutrality, but what I call principled distance, which is poles apart from one-sided exclusion or mutual exclusion. When I say that principled distance allows for both engagement with or disengagement from and does so by allowing differential treatment, what kind of treatment do I have in mind? Religious groups have sought exemptions when states have intervened in religious practices by promulgating laws designed to apply neutrally across society. This demand for non-interference is made on the grounds either that the law requires them to do things not permitted by their religion or that it prevents them from doing things mandated by their religion. For example, Sikhs demand exemptions from mandatory helmet laws and from police dress codes to accommodate religiously required turbans. Muslim women and girls demand that the state not interfere in the religious requirement that they wear the chador. Rightly or wrongly, religiously grounded personal laws may be exempted. Elsewhere, Jews and Muslims seek exemptions from Sunday closing laws on the grounds that such closing is not required by their religion. Principled distance allows a practice that is banned or regulated in the majority culture to be permitted in the minority culture because of the distinctive status and meaning it has for the minority culture's members. For other conceptions of secularism, this variability is a problem because of a simple and somewhat absolutist morality that attributes overwhelming importance to one value – particularly to equal treatment, equal liberty or equality of individual citizenship.

Religious groups may demand that the state refrain from interference in their practices, but they may equally demand that the state interfere in such a way as to give them special assistance so that they are able to secure what other groups are routinely able to acquire by virtue of their social dominance in the political community. The state may grant authority to religious officials to perform legally binding marriages or to have their own rules for or methods of obtaining a divorce. Principled distance allows the possibility of such policies on the grounds that holding people accountable to a law to which they have not consented might be unfair. Furthermore, it does not discourage public justification; that is, justification based on reasons endorsable by all. Indeed, it encourages people to pursue public justification. However, if the attempt to arrive at public justification fails, it enjoins religiously minded citizens to support coercive laws that, although based purely on religious reasons, are consistent with freedom and equality. Principled distance is not just a recipe for differential treatment in the form of special exemptions. It may even require state intervention and, moreover, in some religions more than in others in line with consideration of the historical and social condition of all relevant religions. State engagement then can also take a negative interventionist form. For the promotion of a particular value constitutive of secularism, some religions, relative to other religions, may require more interference from the state. For example, suppose that the value to be advanced is social equality. This requires in part undermining caste and gender hierarchies. Thus, there is a constitutional ban on untouchability: Hindu temples were thrown open to all, particularly to former untouchables should they choose to enter them. Child marriage was banned among Hindus and a right to divorce was introduced. Likewise, constitutionally it is possible to undertake gender-based reforms in Muslim personal law.

Other points must be noted. Sixth, this model shows that in responding to religion, we do not have to choose between active hostility and passive indifference or between disrespectful hostility and respectful indifference. We can combine the two, permitting the necessary hostility as long as there is also active respect. The state may intervene to inhibit some practices as long as it shows respect for other practices of the religious community and does so by publicly lending support to them. This is a complex dialectical attitude to religion that I have called critical respect. So, on the one hand, the state protects all religions, makes them feel equally at home, especially vulnerable religious communities, by granting them community-specific rights. For instance, the right to establish and maintain their own educational institutions and the provision of subsidies to schools run by religious communities. But the state also hits hard at religion-based oppression, exclusion and discrimination.

Seventh, by not fixing its commitment from the start exclusively to individual or community values and by not marking rigid boundaries between the public and the private, India's constitutional secularism allows decisions on these matters (all matters pertaining to religion at level 3) to be made by contextual reasoning in the courts and sometimes even within the open dynamics of democratic politics. Finally, the commitment to multiple values and principled distance means that the state tries to balance different, ambiguous, but equally important values. This makes its secular ideal more like a contextual, ethically sensitive, politically negotiated arrangement – which it really is – rather than a scientific doctrine conjured by ideologues and merely implemented by political agents.

A somewhat forced, formulaic articulation of Indian secularism goes something like this. The state must keep a principled distance from all public or private and individual-oriented or community-oriented religious institutions for the sake of the equally significant – and sometimes conflicting – values of peace, worldly goods, dignity, liberty, equality and fraternity in all of its complicated individualistic and non-individualist versions. I believe the norms of secularism have been fundamentally altered by this conception of Indian secularism as principled distance. In what follows I thus turn to evaluate European moderate secularisms against the norms of Indian secularism as principled distance.

Evaluating European Secularism

How then do European states fare when evaluated by these new norms? I think not all that well. By these new standards that require states to be sensitive to deep religious diversity and to both forms of institutionalised religious domination, European nation-states fail to be even modestly secular. Blind to the dimension of inter-religious domination, they do not even see that in this dimension they are not secular. Several phenomena that are clearly seen to be anti-secular in, say, India, are not seen to be so in Europe.

When judged by these new standards, all kinds of institutional biases begin to show up in European state–religion arrangements. Despite all changes, European states have continued to privilege Christianity in one form or another. The liberal democratisation and the consequent secularisation of many European states have helped citizens with non-Christian faiths to acquire most formal rights (Cohen and Laborde 2015: 174–5). But such a scheme of rights neither embodies a regime of inter-religious equality nor effectively prevents religion-based discrimination and exclusion. Indeed, it masks majoritarian, ethno-religious biases. Thus, to go back to the example of schools run by religious communities, one finds that as of 2019, only fourteen schools run by Muslims in England are provided state funding. In France there is at least one state-funded Muslim school (in Réunion), and about four or five new private Muslim schools that are in the process of signing 'contrats d'association' with the state. My impression is that in Germany there is not a single school run by Muslims that is funded by the state. Not that attempts to rectify this have not been made. Article 7, para 3 of the German constitution allows for the provision of religious education in public non-denominational schools. Religious education is made available not as the right of parents or students, but through religious societies that are given the right to offer religious instruction through public schools. While this is in theory open to newer religious minorities too, owing to requirements that must be met to be officially recognised (including conditions such as permanency in the territory and numbers), only a couple of Muslim organisations have been officially granted this status (Körs 2017, 2019), and so in practice Christian religious societies have had the advantage of availing this right. The state has attempted to temporarily solve this problem by setting up an advisory body (beirat) that includes Muslim public intellectuals and representatives of Muslim associations that can then offer Islamic education in government-maintained schools. This shows, as I have argued, that though governments attempt to face the issue of an increasingly religiously diverse population and their needs, institutional adjustments to install moderate secularism in European states are still facing hurdles precisely because these original institutions arose in predominantly single-religion societies.

Institutional biases are also evident in other difficulties faced by Muslims. For example, in the failure of many Western European states to deal with the issue of headscarves (most notably France), in unheeded demands by Muslims to build mosques and therefore to practice their own faith properly (Germany and Italy), in discrimination against ritual slaughter (Germany) and in unheeded demands by Muslims for proper burial grounds of their own (Denmark, among others). Given that in recent times Islamophobia has gripped the imagination of several Western societies – as exemplified by the cartoon controversy in Denmark and by the ban on new minarets in Switzerland – it is very likely that their Muslim citizens will continue to face disadvantages due only to membership in their religious community. All these are issues of inter-religious inequalities and therefore are part of what I call inter-religious domination.

I have so far been talking as if the initiative lies squarely with only one agent, the European state (and its supporters), and Muslims will respond enthusiastically to any initiative from this reformed (multiculturalised) state. But this is being too sanguine about the self-understanding of Muslims or their current condition in Europe. It underestimates their alienation and ghettoisation. Only after we attain a better, deeper understanding of Muslims in different parts of Europe can we learn about what should and should not be and what currently can and cannot be accommodated. Indeed, only in a more relaxed atmosphere can a plurality of voices – the more vulnerable voices included – emerge and be better heard, a change that will have a huge bearing on our collective judgement on what should and should not be accommodated. (As of now we hear two dominant voices – the ultra-orthodox and the lapsed Muslim, the latter a convert to radical secularism). Indeed, a hearing of these diverse voices may necessitate not just accommodation but more active fostering of some hitherto unnoticed Muslim beliefs and practices or more negative state intervention in others; it is entirely possible that the state may not only have to support some religious practices but also inhibit others. Now, European states may be only too happy to abort some Muslim practices, but such intervention will entail a massive shift in their conception of secularism – from that of separation followed by support of religion to one of separation followed sometimes by support and sometimes by an inhibition of religion, what I call *principled distance* (Bhargava 2019: 21–52). In short, the state may have to set aside its moderate (accommodative, not hostile to religion) stance. Currently, the practice of most European states towards Muslims is: offer little official support, no accommodation, and, with few exceptions, stay indifferent to massive societal intolerance. What might be required is more support to some Muslim practices, less to others, and active interference in societal intolerance – in short, an attempt by the state to tackle both inter- and intra-religious domination.

To sum up: the Indian model allows for positive entanglements with religion – with all religions. A secular state must show equal respect for all religions. Modood entirely agrees with this point, which is consistent with his claim that religion is a positive good. But in addition the state must also be ready for negative entanglements with religion. States must be prepared to interfere in religion for the sake of individualistically and non-individualistically construed values of freedom, equality and fraternity or, alternatively put, to reduce intra- and inter-religious domination. This is consistent with our mutually agreed view that in secular states religion has no special status. (Though in Europe, privileges for one church or one religion, no matter how few, are commonplace.) Indeed, Modood even agrees with this in principle. He says, 'It is consistent with some government control of religion, some interference in religion, some support for religion and some cooperation with (selected) religious organizations and religious purposes' (Modood 2019: 196).

Evaluating Modood's moderate secularism

To extend the above at a more theoretical level, Modood has argued that the presence of state–religion connections is not normatively problematic in itself and that in principle they are integral to a reasonable version of secularism because they do not constitute an unwarranted privileging of religion. He has argued that while I allow a great deal of flexibility at level 3 (policy and law), I take a more rigid view and work with dichotomous distinctions at levels 1 (ends) and 2 (institutions). Modood makes a case that even at these two levels, a greater degree of elasticity is required, which is exactly what a number of European states continue to do. In my view, and I believe evident in the examples above, the privileging of (one) religion is precisely what weak establishments and European moderate secularisms do and why they are not sufficiently secular.

For a start, my third level includes not only policies but also laws that are not easy to change with a change in government. Indeed, some of these laws may be part of written or unwritten constitutions and therefore may be even more difficult to amend. Given this, they can be legitimately seen as part of the state structure. Because I allow a great deal of interaction between religion and law, I can readily agree with Modood that even in states without a formal establishment, religion can be a part of a durable state structure. My own version of political secularism allows for this. However, I maintain that at levels 1 and 2, separation between religion and state should be fairly sharp. Unlike states with establishment of religion and theocratic states which have a strong connection with one religion, secular states must not have a constitutive connection with the ultimate goals of any religion or for that matter with any comprehensive non-religious doctrine. To have a constitutive connection is to bring the ends of religions and comprehensive non-religious doctrines definitionally into the state structure. Likewise, a stronger connection at level 2 makes it virtually mandatory for religious personnel to be present as officials in this structure of the state. A state loses its secularity if it is bound in this manner. Of course, a constitutionally democratic state may require that a certain number of people from a particular religious group, including a few religious personnel, may by law be present in (say) the parliament. But this may happen on grounds of removing inter-religious domination, which in my view is a more legitimate constitutive end of a secular state. Because the presence of members of a religious group, including religious clerics, is a result of a law and is done on grounds of inter-religious domination, I see this as happening at level 3 and not at level 2. Thus, in my perspective the greater flexibility required at level 3 presupposes a certain rigidity at levels 1 and 2. Without this somewhat inflexible separation, a state loses its secular character. All European states that continue to have constitutive connections at levels 1 and 2 compromise on their secularity.

In short, moderate secularism's secularity does not go deep enough. This is also the case in relation to state interference in religions. If a moderate secularism is moderate because it continues to be friendly to one religion and is indifferent or, worse, hostile to others, then this secularism must be abandoned in favour of a version that is equally hostile to inter-religious and intra-religious domination and critically respects all religious and non-religious perspectives. Extending moderate (that is, accommodative) secularism to Muslims under existing conditions will not be sufficient because the modern (that is, democratic) state must have the legitimacy to also negatively intervene in some socio-religious practices, if only to protect the interests of vulnerable internal minorities. This in part entails abandoning moderate secularism. It may even be very difficult, because not appreciating deep religious and cultural diversity is one of the central failures of modern Europe. To my knowledge, overcoming this issue is a bigger challenge than any other. Even the conceptual resources for such change appear to be missing.

To respond to the challenge of deep diversity, Europe might be better off with an altogether different conception of secularism (Bhargava 2006: 22; Bhargava 2014a; Bhargava 2019). While secularism continues to be a value everywhere in Europe, its transgression is not seen as a threat to it because the meaning of secularism has not shifted from the one developed in the nineteenth century to another more suited to conditions of deep religious diversity. That is also why European secularism is not that secular. As a result, it continues to see virtually all versions of Islam as a threat to secularism, not recognising that religious Muslims may be unsettling only one version of political secularism and providing in the process an opportunity to shift to the deeper, richer conception.

Evaluating Indian Secularism

I have been speaking of how European secular states are not secular enough when judged by standards of the principled distance model. But it might legitimately be asked: how about evaluating the Indian state by yardsticks developed in India? This must be done and by any reckoning, news on this count is very bad. For some time now, distance from religion has been maintained on opportunist not principled grounds. The word 'critical' from respect has been discarded and respect has come to mean making deals with the most orthodox or fanatical fringe of religious communities. This is a travesty of the principled distance model. Matters have become worse. Since 2014, the Indian state has failed even by the standards of moderate secularism. Not only is there, by virtue of violation of the rights of individuals within communities, a marked decline in intra-religious equality but a dramatic increase in inter-religious domination. On this second dimension, the Indian state today is barely secular. Since it came to power in 2014, the BJP's majoritarianism has done much to undermine the democratic and institutional conditions of secularism. With the abrogation of the Kashmir-related article 370, the introduction of the severely discriminatory Citizenship Amendment Act that adds a religious test to the procedure of granting citizenship, the bewildering court judgement on the Ayodhya dispute and the brazenly partisan handling of the Delhi communal riots following the Shaheen Bagh protests, Indian constitutional secularism has been forced to go on the ventilator. Though none of this divests Indian secularism of its inspirational value, today, as conditions for maintaining principle distance of the state from religion disappear, I would give my left arm to steal, borrow and keep Modood's moderate secularism!

References

Bhargava, R. (1994), 'Giving Secularism Its Due', *Economic and Political Weekly*, (29), 28.

Bhargava, R. (1998), *Secularism and Its Critics*. Delhi: Oxford University Press.

Bhargava, R. (2009), 'Political Secularism: Why It Is Needed and What Can Be Learnt from Its Indian Version', in G. B. Levey and T. Modood (eds), *Secularism, Religion and Multicultural Citizenship*. Cambridge: Cambridge University Press, 82–110.

Bhargava, R. (2011), 'States, Religious Diversity and the Crisis of Secularism', *Open Democracy*, 22 March. Accessed at: <http://www.opendemocracy.net/rajeev-bhargava/statesreligious-diversity-and-crisis-of-secularism-0>

Bhargava, R. (2013), 'Reimagining Secularism: Respect, Domination and Principled Distance', *Economic and Political Weekly*, (48) 50.

Bhargava, R. (2013), 'Can Secularism be Rehabilitated?', in B. J. Berman, R. Bhargava and A. Lalliberte (eds), *Secular States and Religious Diversity*. Vancouver: University of British Columbia Press, 69–97.

Bhargava, R. (2014a), 'How Secular is European Secularism?', *European Societies*, 16 (3), 329–36.

Bhargava, R. (2014b), 'Should Europe Learn from Indian Secularism?', in B. Black, G. Hyman and G. M. Smith (eds), *Confronting Secularism in Europe and India*. London: Bloomsbury, 39–58.

Bhargava, R. (2019), 'Reimagining Secularism: Respect, Domination and Principled Distance', in N. Bhuta (ed.), *Freedom of Religion, Secularism and Human Rights*. Oxford: Oxford University Press, 21–52.

Cohen, J. L. and C. Laborde (2016), *Religion, Secularism and Constitutional Democracy*. New York: Columbia University Press.

Körs, A. (2017), 'The Plurality of Peter Berger's "Two Pluralisms" in Germany', *Society*, 54 (5), 445–53.

Körs, A. (2019), 'Contract Governance of Religious Diversity in a German City-State and Its Ambivalences', *Religion, State and Society*, 47 (4–5), 456–73.

Modood, T. (2004a), 'Multiculturalism, Muslims and the British State', in S. J. Sutcliffe (ed.), *Religion: Empirical Studies*. Farnham: Ashgate, 245–58.

Modood, T. (2004b), 'Britishness out of Immigration and Anti-Racism', in R. Phillips and H. Brocklehurst (eds), *History, Nationhood and the Question of Britain*. Basingstoke: Palgrave.

Modood, T. (2005), 'Foreword', in T. Abbas (ed.), *Muslim Britain: Communities under Pressure*. London: Zed Books.

Modood, T. (2011a), 'Multiculturalism, Ethnicity and Integration: Some Contemporary Challenges', in T. Modood and J. Salt (eds), *Global Migration, Ethnicity and Britishness*. Basingstoke: Palgrave, 40–62.

Modood, T. (2011b), 'Is there a Crisis of Secularism in Europe?'. Accessed at: <https://tif.ssrc.org/2011/08/24/is-there-a-crisis-of-secularism-in-western-europe/

Modood, T. (2019), *Essays on Secularism and Multiculturalism*. London: ECPR and Rowman and Littlefield International.

Modood, T. and R. Kastoryano (2006), 'Secularism and the Accommodation of Muslims in Europe', in T. Modood, A. Triandafyllidou and R. Zapata-Barrero (eds), *Multiculturalism, Muslims and Citizenship: A European Approach*. London: Routledge.

Modood, T. and T. Sealy (2021), 'Freedom of Religion and the Accommodation of Religious Diversity: Multiculturalising Secularism', *Religions*, 12 (10), 868.

Turner, B. (2011), *Religion in Modern Society: Citizenship, Secularization and the Modern State*. Cambridge: Cambridge University Press.

THIRTEEN

Secular State:
Its Importance and Limits

Bhikhu Parekh

The relation between state and religion has proved almost as contentious as that between it and the economy, to which it bears some resemblance. It is argued that the identification of the two or even close relation between them is damaging to both. They should therefore be separated and assigned their own spheres of activity. This will protect the state against religion, and religion against the state, safeguard the moral integrity of both and secure the best results their combination is capable of giving. The state enjoys sovereignty, a supreme power over a particular territory and its people, and God enjoys even greater power over the entire universe or at least a dedicated area of it. Concentration of these two powers in the same pair of hands could cause the greatest danger to human dignity and well-being. They can be separated in several ways, of which secularism is one of the most important.

While it is easy to talk of separating religion and the state, it is most difficult to do so in practice. The state cannot be wholly indifferent to or detached from religion. It is concerned with public order, morality, respect for the law, justice and social harmony, and is necessarily interested in religious beliefs and practices that impinge on these. If a religion advocates killing people of other religions, hating them or stealing their property, no state would tolerate such a belief. Even as the state cannot be detached from religion, the latter too cannot be separated from the state. At its best it is concerned with peace, human brotherhood, social justice and human stewardship of nature, and is inevitably drawn into the sphere of the state. Indeed, there is no area of the state's activities in which religion does not have a keen interest, be it its economic policy, foreign policy, social welfare or education. In these and related areas, religious people bring to political life a distinct humanist and universalist perspective and sensibility.

Since state and religion, or rather the activities associated with them, cannot be separated neatly and beyond a certain point, we need to undertake a nuanced inquiry into what kind of separation is possible and desirable. Separation should be both possible and valuable, and neither alone will do. Possibility is a matter of determining the areas or activities that can be separated or demarcated with a reasonable degree of clarity and precision. Desirability is a matter of determining what kind of separation is essential for the good life that the citizen should be able to live and its contribution to the common good. This can only be decided on the basis of values we consider central to human life. They are subject to much dispute but generally include liberty, equality and common belonging, to mention the most important of them. Briefly, liberty is the basis of individual autonomy and human dignity. In its absence the individual is at the mercy of others and an instrument of their will. Equality is important because in its absence some exercise arbitrary power over others, dominate and control them and restrict their opportunities. A state composed of such free and equal individuals needs a united community to hold them together and to have the required degree of stability and cooperative energy to generate and sustain a common sense of belonging.

These values can be achieved only when state and religion are separated. If the state had an established religion, its citizens would lack religious as well as other related liberties. Those belonging to other religions than the established one, or to none, would be discriminated against in the religious and related areas of life and denied equal treatment. Being marginalised and denied both liberty and equality, they would remain deeply dissatisfied members of society and a permanent source of disaffection and disunity. Not any kind of separation between state and religion will do. As we saw, religious people have much to contribute to public good, and our collective life would be the poorer without it. The separation should be fully alert to this, and largely apply to areas where it is consistent with, and conducive to, liberty, equality and common belonging.

Although I cannot argue the point here, it would seem that such separation minimally requires the following. First, the state should not institutionalise or establish a religion and require its citizens to belong to it as a condition of their citizenship. They are all its equal citizens, irrespective of their religion or none.

Second, the state should not pursue religious goals but only those its citizens can understand and share, irrespective of whether or not they are religious. Its goals should be capable of being debated and defended in terms of public reason or more accurately on secular grounds, that is, those that fall within the experience of all, or at least the majority, of its citizens. The goals pursued by the state can sometimes be defended on both secular and religious grounds. Although for the secular state only the former matter, some of the citizens might share its goals only for religious reasons. This kind of double justification occurs in many other areas of life as well. The state needs to be particularly careful that its secular reasons are clearly stated and not mixed up with the religious.

Third, the state should take its decisions itself and not be subject to a religious body. It should be free to take its decisions on its own and not in deference to the wishes or commands of a religious authority.

A state that meets these requirements is secular: one that fails in one or more of them is not. The heart, the core, of the secular state lies here and it should be guarded with the greatest care. A state might not be secular in some other area, but so long as it is so in these areas its secular integrity remains undiminished.

Take a state whose constitution formally acknowledges the existence of God, but says no more. The reference to God is largely symbolic, intended to reassure the religious people, and to locate the state within a transcendental framework and give it a spiritual basis. The state is not run by the clergy. Its laws are not expected to meet scriptural require-ments. It does not impose any burden on, or discriminate against, non-believers. For all practical purposes the state is secular. Even if it declared God or Allah to be the ultimate source of all authority, its secular char-acter would not be undermined. God wields authority in principle, but in practice it is the people who exercise it and autonomously decide how to use it. God or the religious text doesn't tell them what to do and remains a distant presence. The basic spirit of democracy or popular sov-ereignty is effectively maintained, albeit within a religious framework. It is true that such a state privileges the believers and might one day use its constitutional authority to pursue religious policies. However, like 'In God We Trust' inscribed on the US dollar bill, the practical effect of the formal acknowledgement of the existence of God is negligible so far as the state's relations with its citizens are concerned. Such a state is a religious but not a theological state. The constitution of Malaysia, for example, describes itself as belonging to this type. It is Islamic but has no commitment to follow the Quran or the mullahs.

Let us take another slightly different case. The head of a state might take an oath of office on the scripture of a particular religion but this might not have any effect on the citizen's rights and relation to the state. The same is broadly the case when a legislative assembly begins its daily sessions with a prayer, or when the head of state ends his speeches by invoking divine blessings. God is mentioned, even taken seriously, but exercises no influence and has no or little practical relevance. In all these cases the formal secular character of the state is compromised, but the constitutional functioning of the state and its relations with its citizens are not. We may seek to remove all such religious references but that is not always easy. It could also deeply hurt and alienate the majority, impose unacceptable constraints on citizens, and even then not succeed in creating a wholly secular or religion-free state. Even if it did, there would be no significant positive gains to compensate for the damage this might do. It makes far more sense to allow religious references and practices, so long as they do not affect the core secular character of the state and the citizens' rights and liberties (Modood 2019; Copson 2017).

Such questions also arise in that nebulous area where religion is not easily distinguishable from culture. Indians debate whether *yoga* is secular or religious in nature and should be taught in state-supported secular institutions. They also debate whether supporting Indian classical dances, with their religious origins and themes, is a secular activity that the state may legitimately undertake or a religious activity it should refrain from supporting. Such disputes also arise in relation to activities that once had a religious origin but are now continued for almost entirely cultural reasons. Lighting a lamp or breaking a coconut at the inauguration of a public event in India has religious origins and rationale, but it is now largely a custom or at best a cultural practice. Some see even the necktie as a cultural residue of the Christian Cross. Even such obviously secular activities as eating, sleeping and making love are religious activities for deeply religious persons who undertake them in obedience to God's command, and in a form approved by the scriptures. It is difficult to say whether these practices should be seen as 'essentially' or 'primarily' secular or religious. What is a secular way of making love and how is it different from the religious? Or of helping a neighbour? They could be either, depending on the meaning and significance assigned to them by the individuals or the communities involved. This is, however, not easy to ascertain, lacks objectivity, and can involve unfair discrimination. Given the ambiguity about whether an activity is secular, religious or both, it is important not to be too dogmatic in one's views and to be guided instead by the importance of the practice to the institution or individual concerned and how deeply it implicates the state in religious matters.

It is sometimes argued that secularism misdiagnoses an important problem and seeks to solve it in an irrelevant idiom. It is basically about ensuring religious tolerance and respect, and such an attitude is best cultivated by appealing to people's religious sensibility. Rather than ask people to turn their back on religion and become secular, we should purify their religion of misconceptions and hateful implications, and make them appreciate the importance of tolerance and respect rather than try to cultivate a new and artificial virtue of secularity. We should rely on the traditional and well-tested religious sources of tolerance rather than seek to create an entirely new and untried way of getting people to behave in secularly tolerant ways (Nandy 2016).

This argument is unconvincing. It assumes that secularism is only about tolerance or respect for other religions, and that is not the case. Secularism is also about creating a particular kind of political culture in which citizens relate to each other in a respectful and responsible manner. Its purpose is to reduce the hold of religion on the state, and that surely cannot be achieved by giving it the kind of importance this argument gives. Furthermore, every religion has resources for tolerance as well as intolerance. To emphasise only the former is to rely on a half-truth. And since every religion can be intolerant, the answer lies not in remaining confined to religion but in seeking the help of the state. Tolerance further is of several different kinds depending on its basis or source. Tolerance on religious grounds generally covers one class of objects or actions arbitrarily and on secular grounds a different one. Limiting tolerance to religious grounds alone limits its scope.

In determining whether or not a state is secular, it is important to consider not only the religious aspect of the state's activities but also the countervailing forces that regulate it. The state might, for example, use religious symbols as part of its identity but possess enough institutional and other resources to guard against their misuse, or it might use religious rhetoric in its political discourse but possess the mechanism to counter its impact. England, for example, has an established church, but it also has a sufficiently strong secular culture to counter its impact, with the result that the British state is basically secular. By contrast, the United States has built a 'Wall of Separation' between the state and the church that however offers little protection against the domination by religious groups. The important thing therefore is not to look at a particular practice in isolation and judge the state on that basis, but rather to examine the political system as a whole, including its overall ethos and the ease with which its citizens are able to speak on religious matters.

I argued earlier that a secular state should treat its citizens equally and grant them equal rights. Granting equal rights to religions or, more precisely, to religious groups or communities, however, is not as easy as sometimes suggested. Religions differ greatly. Some, such as Christianity and Islam, are belief-centred, while others such as Hinduism and Buddhism give primacy to practice. Some are individually oriented, others communally. Some are seen by their adherents as a matter of choice, others as a kind of birthmark one must carry until one's death. Abrahamic religions are all *theistic; dharmic* religions take little account of God or draw the boundary between the human and the divine quite differently or not at all. For some religions, diet, dress and so on are markers of their identity, while others treat them as matters of personal choice. For some, such as the Hindus, temples or public places of worship are not central to their religious identity; for others, such as the Muslims, mosques are; Christians take a view that falls between the two. Different religions make different kinds of impact on society and these are rarely equal. What is more, a majority religion exercises a silent and largely imperceptible influence that minority religions do not and which often passes as culture.

Since religions are not all alike, treating them equally does not mean treating them the same. Their treatment is necessarily different, diverse, appropriate to each religion, discriminating without being discriminatory. The principle of equality would require, for example, that those for whom a particular dress is a mandatory marker of their religious identity should have a right to wear it whereas those for whom it is not should not, or that practice-based religions could be subjected to greater restraints than the belief-based ones. Similarly, seeing secularism as involving a wall of separation between the state and religion makes sense in relation to the individualistically oriented Protestantism but not many other religions. To define secularism in this way, as is often done in several states including the USA, is to Protestantise it and to universalise a parochial historical practice. All this calls for a highly nuanced and context-sensitive interpretation and application of the principle of equality, and ensuring that in order to avoid mechanical and unfair uniformity we do not fall prey to subtle and stealthy discrimination.

To a large extent, secularism is about maintaining the boundary between the state and religion, or more generally between political life and religion. The boundary can be subverted from either side. The state might transgress and interfere in the religious life of a community by, say, taxing only the Catholics or denying state honours to atheists. Conversely, religious organisations might do the same by refusing to recognise state-registered marriages or excommunicating a prime minister or a president for voting for a particular party or supporting euthanasia. Both compromise secularism, the former far more so because of the state's greater coercive power and reach. One can appeal to the state against the policies of a religious organisation but there is none against the state with its sovereignty over its territory.

Symbols are an important part of religious life and raise the question of their equivalence across religions. In the French debate on the Muslim girl's right to wear the hijab in school, it was argued that since a Christian girl was free to wear a cross and even a crucifix, her Muslim counterpart should be free to wear the hijab. This implied that the hijab was broadly equivalent to and had the same religious weight and significance for a Muslim as the cross had for a Christian. At one level this view is correct because both the cross and the hijab have a religious meaning for the wearer, are markers of their religious identity, are considered mandatory by them, and so on. At a different level it is not. Unlike the cross, the hijab is a dress and can be worn by non-Muslims as well without suggesting that they have converted to Islam. The Quran prescribes a modest dress but not a hijab, which has never been worn by Muslims in many parts of the world.

Some secularists, particularly those influenced by the French model, strongly plead for the avoidance of almost all institutional contact between the state and religion, especially in the delivery of public services and goods. In their view, it entangles the state in religious matters, compromises its secular character, and gives undeserved legitimacy to religion. This view makes an important point but overstates it. Cooperation between the state and religious organisations does reduce the institutional distance between the two, and makes the state complicit in their appeal to religious motivations and language. However, this does not detract from its secular character if the state's reasons for cooperation are secular and intended to pursue valuable public goods.

Some of the problems every state faces are too intractable to be tackled by it on its own, and need the support of other kinds of organisations, including the religious. The latter appeal to different motives, speak in a different language and mobilise moral resources. They also provide non-bureaucratic networks and support groups and inspire imaginative ways of resolving conflicts, as was evident in the various Truth and Reconciliation Commissions in South Africa and Latin America. Religious organisations could be of great help in healing broken selves, rehabilitating prisoners and addicts, restoring fractured relations, creating mutual trust and building a sense of community. This is not to say that they alone can do these things or that they might not cause divisions and complicate the matter further, but rather that they have the potential to do good and, when suitably steered, can produce results of great public value which it would be wrong to reject in the name of arbitrarily restrictive secularism.

It is of course important that collaboration with religious organisations should not put non-believers at a disadvantage or place them in situations they cannot accept. There is no reason why it should. In Germany, for example, 80 per cent of its publicly funded nursery schools are run by churches on behalf of the state, and this is also broadly the case with some of its hospitals. There is no evidence that this has adversely affected the secular character of the German state or generated a widespread sense of discrimination and discontent among non-believers. The experiences of some other countries, such as Northern Ireland, however, have not been so happy. The structure of the secular state should be adjusted to the local culture and ethos.

When defined in unrealistic terms, secularism can easily become a source of widespread alienation from the state. During the early decades of Indian independence, secularism was taken to mean a more or less total separation between the state and religion. This raised a number of disturbing and pointless questions. Should government ministers inaugurate religious buildings, offer prayers, join in the celebration of religious events or holy days? Should Mahatma Gandhi be given a state funeral? Yes, because he was the Father of the Nation. Should it be Hindu or secular? The former because he was a religious person. The latter because a secular state such as India cannot be a party to a religious event. In short, whatever action the government took provoked a controversy and satisfied nobody. The charges of crypto-religiosity and hypocrisy that came to be made against the government received convoluted and unconvincing explanations. Not surprisingly, the large Hindu majority felt stifled, inhibited, even oppressed, and began to mount vigorous complaints. Even some government officers and diplomats felt deeply troubled at not being able to express their religious feelings in an innocent manner. Over time the Hindutva-based BJP gained popular supremacy and power, and posed a serious threat to the security and identity of the minorities, especially the Muslims. Secularism is a valuable goal but it can cause havoc if it is defined and applied without sensitivity to its context, the prevailing political culture and its likely long-term consequences. To argue that a secular state should not in any way be associated with religious organisations and activities is to take an unacceptably dogmatic and ultimately untenable approach. To go further and insist that this is what secular means and that the state disregarding it is not secular is to engage in definitional dictatorship. Everything depends on the nature, reach and depth of state–religion cooperation and the way in which it affects the citizens' basic rights and liberties.

While sharing in common the minimum preconditions of secularity discussed earlier, secular states can accommodate religious differences in different ways and devise different modes of collaboration. Some have established churches, others do not. Some fund religious schools, others do not or do so partially. Some sacralise their secularism, clothe it in a quasi-religious imagery, and even talk of civil religion; others seek to squeeze out all traces of religious elements from their practice of secularism. Some allow religiously based political parties and reduce the functional distance between the state and religion; others ban them or subject them to severe constraints. Some secular states grant their minorities certain privileges, and provide them with resources to over-come their numerical and other disadvantages; others find this unfair, discriminatory against the majority, and dismiss it as selective or pseudo-secularism. These and other differences arise from the country's culture, history, values, and the kinds of challenges it faced in the past from its religious organisations and the compromises it reached.

Indian secularism is in a class by itself and raises unusual and com-plex questions with no analogues elsewhere. Born in the trauma of the Partition and the enormous bloodshed that it caused, its Hindu majority leaders reached a broad consensus on how to deal with their society. They were convinced that both the Hindu majority and the non-Hindu minorities had developed ugly social practices and needed reform. For principled and prudential reasons they decided to start the reform with the Hindus. The reasons were clearly stated. This would reassure the minorities, give them a long start and make sure that they were fully convinced of the reasons of reform. This was seen very differently by the Hindus. They saw it as discriminatory against them, making them targets of reform and even of the government's whims on what prac-tices to reform. Both sides had a point. The Hindus felt aggrieved and began to build up grudges against the government and its policies. Similar misunderstandings occurred at other levels as well. The consti-tution-makers felt that the Hindus being a majority had an obligation to treat the minorities with generosity. This was taken to mean offering them privileges they otherwise would not have, giving them resources they didn't have, and so on. All this again was taken by the Hindu major-ity to mean an attempt to pamper minorities and give them preferential treatment. The minorities took a very different view. They saw this as a just recompense for their poverty and backwardness, and represent-ing their share in the national wealth. While the majority favoured the minorities in these and other ways and opened up itself to the charge of pseudo-secularism or giving them preferential treatment, many of its members also saw it as an act of sacrifice, a gift that deserved a reward in the shape of gratitude, compliance with Hindu wishes and obedience to the law. Their expectations were naturally not shared by the minorities and the result was an obvious impasse.

There were also other difficulties in applying the idea of secularism to India. It talked about separating religion and the state. But what is religion? Hindus had great difficulty understanding religion in the widely accepted sense of a systematic body of beliefs generated by a set of doctrines in terms of which the religion is defined. Hinduism is not a religion in that sense and the state could not possibly be separated from it. At a different level, where religion was taken to mean *dharma* a different difficulty arose. *Dharma* means righteousness, and separating the state from it implied an immoral state free from all kinds of ethical constraints. Such a notion simply could not be accepted by a large body of Hindus. Even now, Hindus have difficulty talking about secularism in Indian languages.

Yet another difficulty arising in the Indian context was created by the caste. Religion is largely an ascribed identity, one inherited at birth and not a matter of conscious choice. Caste seems very similar. Naturally, therefore, caste and religion came to overlap in their meanings. Both were considered non-secular and treated as an obstacle to progress. Caste was seen as standing in the way of India's unity. It was argued that Indians should be Indians, 'First and Last', and nothing more or less. This was basically a way of saying that India could and should be a nation of equals, moulding all Indians in a liberal individualist fashion. This is an interesting way of equating secularism with liberalism, and filling an important gap caused by the absence of a liberal vocabulary.

Secularism in India, unlike in other countries, is hospitable to religion, not hostile to it. It recognises the positive contribution religion makes to society's moral and spiritual enrichment. This attitude to secularism permeates society and shapes its approaches to contentious issues. This is evident most clearly in the way in which the term has come be used in recent times. Thanks to the enormous influence of Gandhi and India's religious tradition, secularism is understood as equal respect for all religions, being well disposed to all of them, not offending any of them or instigating hatred against them. Secularism is increasingly translated as Sarva Dharma Samabhava. This is quite a contrast to the way in which the term is used in most of the world, especially the West. Indian secularism is born not out of fear of religion but rather out of respect for it. This shows further how the discourse on secularism takes different forms in different countries and cannot and should not be homogenised.

There can be and are multiple secularisms, each with its unique story, each respecting the core beliefs of secularism but taking small or large liberties with them and embedding them in different political systems. And although they can be fruitfully compared in particular respects and judged better or worse, they cannot be assessed on a single axis and graded overall. And although they can learn from each other, the history of each secular state is unique and cannot be replicated in or be a model for another. Take the case of India. The term secular began its life there meaning broadly the same as it did in Europe. Increasingly its meaning began to expand and it came to mean the denial of not just religious but all kinds of ascriptive identities, including those based on religion, ethnicity, caste and creed. These identities were deemed to stand in the way of national unity and equal citizenship, which was supposed to require free, liberated or secular individuals. National integration or unity was taken to require Indians to see themselves 'first and last' as Indians whose political identity was not questioned or circumscribed by regional, religious or linguistic considerations. The discussion of secularism came to centre on creating citizens in a liberal, individualist mould. The term secular is contrasted in India not with religion alone, but with communal or narrow group affiliations and equated with liberal, an ingenious way of filling the gap left by the absence of a liberal vocabulary.

Strictly speaking, secularity is not a primary or first-order value like liberty or equality, but largely an instrumental value whose significance lies in facilitating the realisation of others. Take a society all of whose members belong to a single religion and are agreed on a broadly liberal interpretation of its basic doctrines. If it decides to organise its political life along religious lines it is difficult to see why it should not. Its liberal and open-minded religiosity virtually achieves all that a secular state does, including guaranteeing basic rights and equal treatment. Indeed, it may be seen to represent not only a different form of secularism but an alternative to it. There is nothing inherently virtuous about being secular.

As one value among several, secularity might sometimes come into conflict with other values and then a balance needs to be struck. A secular state should resist the temptation to become a secularist state in which secularity is absolutised and dogmatically used to push religion out of every area of political life. Religion has a long history and deep roots in almost every culture. Rather than declare an open war on it and encourage its dark forces, we should assign it a respectable but non-hegemonic place in political life and make it a responsible and disciplined partner in a generously designed secular political order. Such an order in which religious and non-religious voices are heard at all levels offers an ideal basis for a creative and mutually beneficial engagement between the two. The state here is neither so frightened of religion as to feel nervous about any kind of association with it, nor so awed by it as to surrender to its uncritical zeal. Achieving this kind of mature, self-limiting and relaxed state should be the goal of any kind of well-considered secularism.

References

Copson, A. (2017), *Secularism: Politics, Religion, and Freedom*. Oxford: Oxford University Press.

Modood, T. (2019), *Essays on Secularism and Multiculturalism*. London: Rowman and Littlefield.

Nandy, A. (2016), *Talking India. Ashis Nandy in conversation with Ramin Jahanbegloo*. Oxford: Oxford University Press.

FOURTEEN

From Then to Now: Some Friendly Responses

Tariq Modood

Orientations and Underpinnings

It is most fitting that the substantive chapters of this volume begin with one by David Boucher. Dai is one of, if not the very oldest of my academic friends. I don't mean by age, I mean in terms of length of friendship. We met when we were unemployed political theorists, waiting to be interviewed for a temporary lectureship – which neither of us got – at Bristol Polytechnic (more than a decade later it was renamed the University of the West of England or UWE, which we Bristolians treat as a word not as initials). This was some years before I had any scholarly interest in race or ethnicity. Of course, this was to become, as my family call it, an obsession, and it has certainly given me a most rewarding career, of which this book and the conference from which it derives are among the high points. It is therefore perhaps a bit embarrassing and ungrateful to say that the interest in these themes and their sociological study was due to existential circumstances: a combination of a disappearance of jobs in political theory in Thatcherite Britain, the prospect of becoming an unemployed father, and being of Pakistani descent in Britain and so being able to talk about certain things in the first person that others were prognosticating on in the third person. A feature of my subsequent work that Gurpreet Mahajan notes.

In the postgraduate days that David reminds me of, I had another obsession. It was about how to come up with a convincing theory on the relationship between philosophy and politics. It was driven by the fact that my intellectual heroes of those days, Ludwig Wittgenstein and Michael Oakeshott, had very uncompromisingly negative views on the possibility of a connexion. Wittgenstein famously declared that 'philosophy leaves everything as it is' and Oakeshott insisted that any academic inquiry and practical life were categorially different worlds such that an argument beginning in one could not validly lead to a conclusion in the other, at best it might offer some rhetorical flourish. Such a view was at odds with my sense that politics was an important activity, that one was incomplete if one did not take one's membership in the polis seriously. This did not convince me that Wittgenstein and Oakeshott were mistaken – for a long time I thought they were compelling on the point; rather, I thought that we needed to elaborate a theory to establish the point. In pursuing that task, I came to the view that they were wrong. I did so with the help of R. G. Collingwood. After floundering around for a couple of years I chose to make my PhD topic the comparative study of Oakeshott and Collingwood on the theory–practice distinction. I matched the two because on the one hand they belonged to a similar late English Idealist intellectual universe and on the other hand they took opposing views on my obsessive interest. The idea was that in studying the two together I could show that the source of Oakeshott's erroneous view lay in his philosophical logic as elaborated in his *Experience and its Modes* (1933). The fundamental feature of this logic was the idea that once an activity of understanding or doing had achieved its own high level of internal coherence, as in the case of science, history or politics, what was valid within the activity was of no significance in another activity, that is, outside the logical structure that gave it significance, its own distinctive way of looking at the world or 'mode of experience'. Collingwood, on the other hand, while also seeing such activities and modes of inquiry as having their own distinctive character, deployed a more dialectical logic which enabled one to see how one mode could have a legitimate, not merely accidental or superficial, impact on another; he expressed such relationships differently in different phases of his career, but one which expresses it well was 'rapprochement'. He thought that philosophy and history, or political theory and politics, were distinct activities but distinct did not mean absolutely separate (Modood 1984). I am then a dualist (actually I prefer the term pluralist), not a monist (using the terms deployed by Abbot 2018). I do not hold that theory and practice, inquiry and action, are the same thing or different phases within a single process or system of thought, but dualism or pluralism does not mean the impossibility of rapprochement or bridging or connecting across distinctness. Such bridging has ever since been an important feature of my thought and ambition. As David Boucher insightfully observes, my thesis, which otherwise does not, or at least seems not to, feature in my subsequent academic career, is the ground of my wish for public intellectual engagement (see also Uberoi 2021: 752; reflected upon in Modood 2017). More recently, it has led me to attempt to articulate the grounds of a political theory – sociology interdisciplinarity, both from the side of political theory

(Modood and Thompson 2018) and from the side of sociology, designating my approach 'normative sociology' (Modood 2022a; Becker 2022; Hammersley 2023; Laegaard forthcoming).

While I managed to satisfy my PhD examiners, I should record here that I did not satisfy Oakeshott. He very generously read my thesis after it was complete and wrote me a long hand-written letter pointing out how I had misunderstood him. David too thinks that I misunderstand Oakeshott in some ways, especially that Oakeshott is not so much prohibiting certain activities, for example, appealing to philosophy or history or art in the process of a political argument, simply pointing out that such an appeal is different from a philosophical or historical argument or a work of art. It seems to me, however, that such a purist logic is undermining the appeal to philosophy, etc. What I am arguing for, for instance, in the idea of public intellectual engagement, is that ideas that one brings to bear on contemporary public discussion and controversies can be, will be, the result of theoretical inquiry – even if at the point that one adapts them and makes them suitable for a public and a polity of a particular time and place involves for that moment stepping outside theoretical inquiry. The point is that one could not engage in that second stage, the joining of a public controversy, without having done the first, namely the theorising or the historical research or the sociological inquiry; and so it is not a self-delusion to think that one's public engagement is indebted to the inquiry. David also thinks that an Oakeshottian would not, as I do, criticise Stuart Hall for describing 'the black subject' as a 'necessary fiction' because Oakeshott thought all politics was a 'fiction', that is, not ultimately a perfectly coherent set of ideas. I think there is some misunderstanding here as Hall certainly did not think that all political ideas were 'fictions', only that some that were fictions were also politically efficacious and so one should not reject them, that is, he made the un-Oakeshottian distinction between theoretically grounded political ideas and theoretically flawed political ideas, and only the latter were 'fictions', albeit that some of them were of political value. In general, I do think that David does a good job in bringing out how some ideas that characterise my work, such as an anti-foundationalism, anti-essentialism and conventionalism, emphasis on contingency and historical or national specificity rather than seeing history as the working out of an inevitable logic of an 'ism', such as capitalism or racism or 'modernity', and a scepticism of such sweeping, ideological thinking shows the long-term influence of Oakeshott (and one should add, Wittgenstein) on me.

Moving on, I am pleased and impressed by how over so many years and through an expanding focus of questioning Sune Lægaard has offered critical observations and posed various challenges for me. The clarity and analytical incisiveness with which he probes into what I have said; typically finding that a certain lack of precision means I could be saying several different things; and he helpfully explores those possibilities, pointing to the difficulties that each separately or jointly pose for me in reaching my desired conclusion. While such critiques are full of insights and I always learn something from them, I do not always know how to answer the difficulties he poses. He may remember that my response to his very first of what is now quite a long series of critical engagements was to say – in print (Modood 2009) as well as in person – well, ok, if that's the problem, tell me how to find the solution! While we did not proceed collaboratively, we have continued in close dialogue. I mention all this to thank Sune but also because it describes part of my response to his chapter in this book. He tests my claim to be following a methodological contextualism, which I have articulated with Simon Thompson (Modood and Thompson 2018), noting that it owes something, at least in self-description, to the Oakeshottian idea of 'the pursuit of intimations', in relation to my intervention in relation to the Danish Cartoons affair. He finds that in general what I have to say on the matter – admittedly not very much, even if quite assertive – is not very contextualist. Sometimes there are factual errors, sometimes I am appealing to a precedent that does not exist, sometimes ignoring a precedent, failing to take all relevant points of view into consideration and in general more attention to context and explication of the choices made in the characterisation of the context are required. I can only say 'mea culpa'. Luckily, he does allow that my normative arguments about how Muslims are being racialised and deserve protection in law may be good ones (or not) and may even apply to the case of the Danish cartoons but that they do not do so because I have followed the 'iterative contextualism' recommended in Modood and Thompson (2018). Nor does he dismiss (or commend) the method. His conclusion is that his critique 'does not necessarily invalidate [Modood's] more general arguments or his contextualist views. Rather, this shows how a contextualist defence and development of these arguments is a continuous work in progress'. Not only do I accept his general conclusion, but I think the exercise is a typically Lægaardian one: your argument may be right but not on the grounds that you have supplied in the study in question.

The last chapter in Part One is by Simon Thompson, who is, as will have been noted, a political theory and methodology collaborator. He appreciates the central place of the idea of recognition to my multiculturalism and that I make it do a number of different things. He notes that my point of departure is a distinction which I, perhaps not wholly accurately, attribute to Charles Taylor between 'equal dignity' or the 'politics of universalism' and 'equal respect' or the 'politics of difference'. I insist that both are essential to multiculturalism and the latter grows out of the universalism of the former; that political equality is incomplete without equal respect is the distinctive claim of multiculturalism and critique of liberal or classical citizenship. As Simon further notes, this linkage means that I insist that 'individuals always stand in need of recognition both for what they have in common, and for what makes them distinct' (p. 62, Thompson, this volume). He unpacks my uses of the concept of recognition around four themes denoted by four single words: equality, identity, struggle and inclusion. This way of structuring what I have written on the subject is most helpful – not least to me, as I learnt from this way of packaging what I have said. Simon then goes on to make a number of criticisms or suggestions under each theme. The criticisms are very gently made and tend to be about the need for more clarity or development of an existing feature, on the one hand, or about going beyond its existing features to include important matters that are omitted. There are far too many good criticisms for me to respond to all of them here but let me respond to one of each of these two kinds.

As an example of internal development – though actually it is a development of a limitation that Simon does not mention – is how I have in recent years started asking myself whether majorities (in addition to minorities) can be misrecognised or under-recognised or may have legitimate concerns about the status of their identities, especially in the context of multiculturalist minority assertiveness and contestations about the nature of the national identity. If majorities can have legitimate recognition anxieties, then should not multiculturalists think about that and what recognition should be due to majorities? This has led to two kinds of developments. One actually was present before but I have come to give it much more importance, and that is that the institutions and cultures of the majority, such as say the English language, probably already entwined with the polity and national identity, should be given normative status. What I mean here is that it should be valued and supported by the state for more than just functional reasons to do with the economy or for the sake of civic efficiency. French language and literature should be taught in state schools not just because it may be useful for finding employment in adult life but because it is a constitutive feature of national life (a reason that may be given by a minority nation such as Quebec, but which I now think can also be given by a country like France). I say that this was actually present in the work that Simon discusses (Modood 2013 [2007]). There I was thinking in terms of the status of the Church of England as an 'established' church. I realised later that I was inexplicit in specifying the conditions on the recognition of majority or national institutions. I have gone on to argue explicitly that even in the context of multifaith recognition of a multiculturalist sort, the Church of England should continue to enjoy a rightful precedence in religious representation in the House of Lords and in the coronation of the monarch. Such precedence makes sense because of, on the one hand, the Anglican church's historical contribution to the development of Britain as a country, but also if it exercises a leading role in the evolution of a multiculturalist national identity, society and state, as I believe it is doing (Modood 2019: 14). The important point is that the second condition is as essential as the first. Simon and I have actually gone on to develop this argument further in relation to the multidimensional recognition of religion, though Simon does not refer to it in his discussion (Thompson and Modood 2022). A related way of approaching the question of majority recognition is to ask whether recognition should understood as uni-directional or dialogical. That is to say, whether some groups are givers and others just recipients only or whether all groups are givers and recipients of recognition. I have come to the view that the kind of aspirational citizenship I am working with must have dialogical, not just uni-directional recognition. Which means that multiculturalism is not just about majority recognition of minorities but the mutual recognition of all groups of citizens and their right to belong to the body of citizens. I believe that these developments only strengthen the importance I have always placed on national identity in a theory of multiculturalism.

As a response to one of the omissions in my theory that Simon identifies, I will say that I am disappointed that despite extensive work I have done on the socio-economic profiles of the minorities compared to the white British and in relation to the 'ethnic penalty', and the hidden capacities for social mobility that I have conceptualised as 'ethnic capital' (Modood 2004), that I have been unable to theoretically connect that body of work with my political theory of multiculturalism. It is not a theme that has been a focus of much work and what there is seems to have failed to stimulate me sufficiently to work on the theme. Simon mentions the case of Fraser (2003) as an integrated theory of recognition and redistribution. I think, however, it has too restricted an understanding of recognition. Fraser's recognition is tied to an idea of status, that is, to what society thinks of your group, how it treats you, the status or identity it confers on you (Fraser 2003). It is thus designed to identify a cultural status as a form of inequality (which in effect is her understanding of misrecognition) and to connect it to a wider political project of reducing inequalities. My problem with this is that it is too 'external' an understanding of recognition. It can proceed and end without an understanding of what the cultural practice in question means. Or, to put it another way, it makes the meaning of a cultural practice what the majority thinks it is. For example, if a police force does not allow its officers to wear a turban as part of its uniform, then it is clear that Sikh culture has not been valued. But it may be that no one else's culture or religion is incorporated into the police uniform either, so there is not a cultural status inequality. Or, we may say that a police uniform already reflects the dress norms of the majority culture but fails to incorporate those of the Sikh minority and that is a form of cultural inequality or misrecognition. So, what would recognition be here? On a status view, all we need to do is to give Sikh dress requirements the same consideration as that of the majority (and go on to connect this status [in]equality with other [in]equalities). The multiculturalist, however, begins with the meaning of the turban, not for the police force or the majority society but for the minority. Recognition consists of understanding the minority and the place the turban has for Sikhs. A status argument is – theoretically, even if not always in practice – indifferent to minority intersubjectivity and agency, and to the minority culture, attending only to what standing it is or is not given in the wider society. Fraser's theory may connect such minority status to other forms of inequality – including those shared by many groups – but it is not a recognition of Sikh identity and distinctiveness and so falls short of a multiculturalism which seeks to weave minority meanings and respect for those meanings into the larger public culture (Taylor 1994 as interpreted by Modood 2013 [2007]: 47–52 [51–6]). If this is so, then Fraser's theory of social justice has no space for my understanding of recognition (cf. Lewicki 2014). A more promising place to start might be Parekh (2004). It is not a systematic theory but nicely brings out the multiple ways that issues of recognition and redistribution are entwined in practice. I am grateful to Simon for all his useful suggestions and am pleased that his conclusion is that my theory of recognition does do some good work, it is not flawed but is limited and could be developed across the important themes it engages with.

The Inclusion of Diversity

Charles Taylor is surely one of the leading living philosophers and so I am really honoured that he wished to be in this volume and has found the time to make it happen. I have been influenced by his philosophical interpretivism, especially in relation to the social sciences and political theory, and found it coheres well with some of the things that I have taken from Wittgenstein, Collingwood and Oakeshott. Most specifically, my multiculturalism is based on his concept of recognition (or as Simon Thompson tells me, based on a misreading of it), which I have continued to work with and apply to the accommodation of religious minorities, even though I observe that he does not do so himself, especially in relation to the case of his native Quebec, and prefers to restrict the application of recognition to linguistic culture.

I very much agree with the emphasis that Charles gives to rethinking the national stories as part of the larger project of challenging majority fears and minority exclusion and alienation. He rightly emphasises that the issues of racism, of 'hierarchies of precedence' and of accommodating (post-)immigrant groups and recognition of actual differences is strongly intertwined with the larger story a country tells about itself and of remaking the national identity. It was part of my response to *The Satanic Verses* affair with essays jointly entitled *Not Easy Being British* (Modood 1992) and it was a key, controversial theme of the Commission on Multi-Ethnic Britain (CMEB 2000). As is apparent from various chapters in this book, this is a question which tends to be given a different amount of prominence in different kinds of multiculturalism. Charles points out that it, together with the majority's sense of nationhood, is one of the distinguishing features of Quebecan interculturalism in contrast to Canadian multiculturalism, and he thinks it might be appropriate for European states. Indeed, I partly came to see the importance of the majority through Quebecan interculturalism, though I think that in at least some of its versions it is too majoritarian (Bouchard 2011; Modood 2014) and too supportive of Islamophobic restrictions on Muslims. In relation to the latter, I am thinking of the Commission Charles co-led with Gérard Bouchard (Bouchard and Taylor 2008), and was pleased that Charles withdrew his support for a ban on public sector employees not being able to wear the hijab when he saw where that sentiment was going. Yet, it has to be said that European interculturalism is quite different from the Quebecan one: it explicitly does not emphasise the national, rather its focus is on the local, 'the everyday', of mixing and rubbing along (Cantle 2012; Zapata-Barrero 2016). This exclusive focus on the micro detached from the macro and the larger national story, favoured among social and migration researchers, cuts off the possibility of theorising it with a national story; or if a connection is made, as in France, they connect it in the Quebecan style, namely with laïcité, thus undermining the inclusion of new religious minorities into a reformed national identity. And yet the emphasis on the local and mixing – if not based on an abandonment of macro-multiculturalism – is also compatible with the Bristol School (Antonsich 2016), indeed it is a welcome complementarity (Mansouri and Modood 2022), though, as I say, this is not how the local or the micro is typically theorised in European interculturalism, where the possibility of it connecting to the national is systematically absent.

Gurpreet Mahajan and I have only got to know each other recently; this relative novelty perhaps explaining her flattering portrait of my work for which, while blushing, I thank her. We have worked together on the recent GREASE project, in which period and since, we have had a number of discussions, both within and outwith the project, getting used to our different vocabularies and conceptualisations and working out to what extent we agree or disagree and extending our perspective through dialogue. In Gurpreet's chapter here, the agreement considerably outweighs any disagreement, and that includes the four challenges she identifies for me and multiculturalists in general, including I suspect for herself as well. She starts, however, by insightfully noting how I have tried to weave together my positionality as a British Asian Muslim, my optimistic sense of the potentials of British society, its political culture, dynamic civil society and its moderate secularism with a larger idea of multiculturalism, which is not the possession of any one country and yet which in my rendering has a British inflection. I have sought 'intimations' of multiculturalism in the Britain of my experience and my imagination and sought a theory of multiculturalism that speaks to Britain; prioritising getting that fit right before considering its multinational application. The four challenges she raises are: the role of religion in public life, its place and its limits; secondly, the limits of diversity, including unacceptable demands from some parts of the minorities; thirdly, of the oppression and discrimination of minorities within minorities; and fourthly, taking the family resemblance argument further to not just highlight the diversity among the minorities but also the presence of diverse voices within any minority.

There is not space or ability on my part to discuss them all here. In relation to the place of religion and of the limits of multiculturalism I will have to refer the reader to my latest writings on that with Thomas Sealy, which Gurpreet will be pleased to know included engaging with India and her characterisation of it in terms of a 'deep diversity' that eludes most, even Indian, conceptions of secularism (Modood and Sealy 2024). So, here I will briefly say something relating to the last two challenges and by taking them together. I tried to address the problem of how should a state or civil society recognise and accommodate a minority like British Muslims, when they clearly do not speak with a single voice and when some minorities within the minority, like young women, very much want to be heard and engaged as Muslims, but want to speak for themselves and not be subsumed by a male, elderly leadership that they may be critical of, that does not understand them or even may be marginalising them. Writing in the 2000s I was aware that British Muslim civil society had spawned a myriad of religious, welfare, political (domestic and international) solidarity and campaigning organisations and despite – or because of – the backlash from 9/11 and 7/7 there was a ferment of activism and assertiveness. They were asking themselves and giving expression to what it was to be Muslim, to be British and to be a British Muslim – and unsurprisingly coming up with various, sometimes overlapping answers, usually but not in all respects consistent with each other. I wanted to find a way of giving expression to this which did not endorse internal hierarchies nor denote a reductive homogenisation and yet not suppress that there was a recognisable relation between all the organisations and their varied and contested way to being Muslim and representing Muslims. I came up with the image of a 'democratic constellation' (Modood 2013 [2007]: 139–46). 'Democratic' because it was allowed to speak for itself and in its own way, agreeing and disagreeing with the others and by doing so becoming part of a larger democratic landscape. A 'constellation' because it is not a random set of lights in the sky but a pattern with a unity, albeit an irregular unity which conformed to no template and which to an undiscerning eye could not be seen as a something – British Muslims – and distinguishable from other dots in the sky. I was able with co-researchers to utilise it to understand how British Muslims could be understood to be an electoral constituency without homogenising or delegitimising ('the Muslim vote' or as inherently inward-looking) (Dobbernack, Meer and Modood 2015) and am pleased that Jan Dobbernack has continued to develop its use (Dobbernack 2018, 2019). I appreciate this only partially and perhaps only indirectly addresses Gurpreet's challenge, but it may be a framework that can be taken further to do so.

I first met Maleiha Malik when she was a student at Oxford and she happened to turn up uninvited at a party at my house – and I am so glad she did. She was an important ally in a British Muslim email group formed after 9/11, called Brighton Beach, as it was a place where Mod(erate)s and (off their) Rockers met to do battle. She has gone on to be one of the leading analysts of racial discrimination legislation in Britain. Accordingly, she has provided a very useful historical overview of Britain's racial discrimination legislation, placing it within a legacy of the British Empire and emphasising racist ideas and sense of being British rather than just a matter of economic competition or violent behaviour as the appropriate context. A story marked by a very slow recognition that the core issue was not of discrimination but of what it was to be British. However, while I agree that 'racism is consistently understood within the paradigm of placating the white working class, rather than a structural challenge for the whole population on how to adjust their national identity after the end of the British Empire', I am not sure I would go so far as to say that debates about disadvantage 'from the 1950s all the way to Brexit prioritised the white working class' (p. 135, Malik, this volume). I think we have to see the rise of racial equality movements, agendas, laws, policies and its growing prominence in public consciousness and debates during this period, at least from the 1980s onwards, as coinciding within – but not causing – the decline of the white working class by many measures including employment, relative access to higher education, welfare state supports including housing, trades unions, representation by and in the Labour Party and the political process more generally and as an object of political concern, either in relative terms (comparatively to the middle classes, let alone to the very rich, but also to the ethnic minorities) or absolutely or both (Evans and Tilley 2017). This is also reflected in terms of a decline in the status of their collective identifiers, whether that be community or national, as argued by one of my PhD graduates (Taylor Hill 2023). I have been of the view for some time now this is data multiculturalists need to consider as part of rectifying the neglect of the normative status of the majority (Modood 2014). In any case, I appreciate the centrality that Maleiha has given to the remaking of the national identity to engaging with racial equality, which, as I said earlier, was one of the central messages of the report of the Commission on Multi-Ethnic Britain, on which it was a privilege for me to work with Bhikhu Parekh as Chair and who, together with Stuart Hall, Robin Richardson and I took on the responsibility for the chapters with this message (CMEB 2000). Maleiha rightly points to how the progressive remaking of British identity has been set back or at least complicated by Brexit and the ideas of racialised nationhood that drove it (though perhaps not for the third of ethnic minorities who voted to Leave the EU (Begum 2023)). I would go further than she does in noting that, in or out, Britain continues to have the most developed multiculturalist legislation and sense of multiculturalist nationhood in Europe (Modood 2022c, Kundnani 2023). Brexit is not an unqualified triumph for the neo-imperialists, whose motto might be 'Make Britain Great Again', as the work of making an inclusive, post-imperial nation seems to have more salience in Britain than in any part of the EU (and at times is capable of bipartisan support: Uberoi and Modood 2013). Some younger people, who have only known the good times, think that I tend to only see that the glass is half full and not also half empty, so for a more careful measure of the water level, see Meer 2022.

Multiculturalism, Nationalism and Transnationalism

As Will Kymlicka says, we have over the years elaborated versions of multiculturalism in which we offer different accounts of and give different normative significance to liberalism and political secularism. As Will is the biggest thing there is in the political theory of multiculturalism, this has largely taken the form of me questioning his take on these matters and offering an alternative approach. In his chapter in this book, however, as Will notes, he addresses one of our core agreements, namely multiculturalism as a conception of membership, specifically as an ethic of citizenship and of remaking national identities. Will addresses these issues admirably and by developing the theory of democratic citizenship offered by T. H. Marshall. He makes a number of insightful comments, historical and normative, from which I both learn and find my views reinforced – a most pleasing combination, not unique to his chapter. For me the difficulty here is not a disagreement but the query why Will does not relate this understanding of multiculturalism, which as he rightly says is a core commitment of his, to the liberal multiculturalism that he is most famous for. I refer to the foundational justification for the valuing of culture and of differential or group rights, namely that liberal autonomy depends on contexts of choice, specifically 'societal cultures', and so liberal states should actively support and promote (some) minority cultures so that individuals within them achieve individual autonomy (Kymlicka 1995). I have argued a number of times that this argument is not necessary for a multiculturalism, like mine and most Europeans', focused on the accommodation of post-immigration ethno-racial and ethno-religious groups and – relevantly here – not necessary for a multiculturalism based on an ethic of citizenship as opposed to individual autonomy. The issue of what is the normative or logical relationship between these two foundations, liberal autonomy and ethical citizenship, remains unaddressed (Modood 2022b). It is thus a lacuna in the theory of multiculturalism and I look forward to it being further discussed by us all.

The second half of Will's chapter reports on some surveys, first carried out in Canada and then replicated in parts of Western Europe, which very nicely show that how minorities are perceived by majorities is not simply based on stereotypes about minorities, for example, they are lazy or disposed to be criminals or are disproportionately claiming welfare benefits without contributing to the pot. Rather, such attitudes are determined by perceptions as to whether a minority is perceived to be committed to the country, say, to Canada. For example, in relation to the right to wear religious symbols in public, there is a hierarchy of support, with Christians at the top, Muslims at the bottom and other minorities, such as Jews and Sikhs, in the middle. This hierarchy correlates strongly with how committed those religious groups are perceived to be to Canada. However, 'where minorities are perceived as committed to Canada, there is actually higher levels of support for their right to wear religious symbols than for Christians' (p. 158, Kymlicka, this volume). Based on a Canadian template, these are very important surveys as they test the idea whether perceptions of commitment to a country, to a national citizenship is relevant to determining attitudes to the minority and attitudes to how it should be treated, for example, whether it is 'deserving' of social rights, but also where we are with this development. The survey shows that minorities typically but not uniformly are perceived as less committed to the country, sometimes by a wide margin, and this is less likely to be the case where a country has some form of inclusive multiculturalism, as with Canada and, to some extent, the UK. Theoretically, these are important findings for a multiculturalism based on valuing (rather than devaluing) citizenship, and politically they provide support for such a multiculturalism. So, I feel vindicated for the kind of multiculturalism I have developed, namely one based on citizenship and not on the primacy of liberal autonomy.

Geoff Levey and I started conversing on multiculturalism in 1994 and were able to do so face to face (or side by side, as one of our favoured modes of conversing is while strolling) as we were in Oxford at the time, but have continued to do so at least on an electronic basis on a regular and sometimes very frequent basis, despite only occasionally meeting, given that he left Oxford to return to Sydney quite early on in our friendship. I always learn something from Geoff's astute assessments of different positions, and sometimes have to adjust my own position accordingly. Additionally, his discussions on multiculturalism and the national have been very helpful to me. On the other hand, he has had to put up for many years with my telling him why I am not a liberal multiculturalist and correcting his interpretations of my position such that he is not only an expert on that but has gone on to identify a non-liberal Bristol School of Multiculturalism, greatly aiding some of us in terms of our self-reflection as a group and in our profile (Levey 2018; Uberoi and Modood 2019). This is the backdrop to his chapter where he carefully weighs the competing claims of whether the Bristol School is anything other than a version of the liberal multiculturalism à la Will Kymlicka.

At the heart of this assessment is the role of the national identity or national culture and to what extent it is taken up as a component of a political programme of multiculturalism. He detects some differences between Will and I, for instance: where Kymlicka seeks to arrest majority cultural dominance and extend solidarity by means of minority cultural rights, Modood seeks to arrest majority cultural dominance and extend belongingness through an inclusive national identity (p. 172, Levey, this volume). He offers a very interesting analytical grid for how national membership and identity may be remade and to what extent specific ways are state interventions or society driven (p. 173, Levey, this volume). Furthermore, by looking at the recurring examples I use, Geoff comes to the view that I see the state as the major actor and am more likely to want to broaden or reinterpret existing national traditions and cultural practices in order to make them more inclusive rather than demote them from their national standing. He characterises this approach as 'top-down' but this is misleading because the culmination of state action is in my account often the product of 'bottom-up' political mobilisation; in this way I contrast the lobbying by an independently formed Muslim Council of Britain from peak Muslim organisations in, say, France and Germany, which are formed by the state and so are truly 'top-down'. In any case, Geoff thinks that Will has always favoured or has come to favour or could favour within his conception of polyethnic rights all of the measures that I usually hold up as forms of multiculturalising the national identity. The main difference that he sees between the two multiculturalisms, and it is both theoretically based and has different practical implications, is that he sees liberal nationalism as requiring minorities to change their cultural practices to both be accommodated and to be accepted by the cultural majority as fully part of the nation. While multicultural nationalism is not simply focused on getting cultural practices accommodated but in changing everybody's understanding of the national imaginary too. Geoff sees that, if successful, this makes the accommodation of minority practices easier but he cautions that this is a slow process and so the liberal offer of cultural rights meanwhile will be essential and may have a lot of work to do. He concludes by cautioning against expecting too much from national identity, which is too amorphous and organic, to be an object of a political project and so it is best to see liberal nationalism and multicultural nationalism as complementing each other in practice, despite their differences in theory. I think Geoff's chapter thus offers both a careful probing into the similarities and differences between Will's position and mine, judiciously weighing our claims to be distinct and not distinct, as well as a balanced assessment and constructive approach to create a successful multicultural society and polity.

Riva Kastoryano and I first met at a conference soon after I had transitioned from racial equality policy work to research. Many years later we came together on several multiteams European projects, the most recent being of our own devising. She is from Turkey and has spent nearly all her adult life in Paris. We quip that she has a French way of seeing everything and I a British way. It means that our collaborations are lively but have their limits. We once decided to write a book chapter together on the political accommodation of Muslims, she presenting the French case, I the British one, offering not just a comparison but a joint framing. One way or another we managed to agree on much of the latter but Riva insisted that while migrants and minorities did not have to individually assimilate, they must assimilate into the existing template of the institutions of the state as these must have a uniform or symmetrical character in relation to all groups, while I, on the other hand, was of the view that institutional innovation was to be expected and justifiable in minority accommodation and differing minority needs and ways of being would create a 'variable geometry'. However much we argued about this and offered rephrasings, we simply could not agree. We published the joint piece in which we stated that the authors did not agree on this important question (Modood and Kastoryano 2006: 172–3). In recent years our disagreement has tended to be on the relationship between multiculturalism and transnationalism. She has come to be a leading theorist of political transnationalism and says that my multiculturalism does not take account of the phenomena she has highlighted. Indeed, I do have some reservations about her position: she makes no distinction between the politics that she approves of and that she does not; more fundamentally, she offers no suggestions for evaluating transnationalism. When one discusses nationalism, one assumes that there are aspects or versions of it that one (conditionally) approves and those not. However, Riva (and she is by no means alone in this among transnationalists) does not offer a corresponding discussion about transnationalism (or indeed about nationalism, which tends to be swept aside in some essentialised notion of 'methodological nationalism'). There are some versions of transnationalism that have been argued for as desirable and compatible with multiculturalism, which I find persuasive. Erdem Dikici, a PhD graduate of mine and in the mould of the Bristol School, has shown a certain 'three-way integration' at work among some Turkish-origin people in London, in which the minority and the majority mutually adjust, but this can be facilitated with the activity of transnational actors involved in this process of multicultural national integration (indeed who, in the case of The Dialogue Society, insist on a duty to integrate and identify with the country of settlement, with a new nationalised citizenship) (Dikici 2021). This is compatible with hyphenated identities, dual citizenship, with transnational families and residence and generally some sort of lived connexion with a country of familial origin or associated diaspora, including with the pan-international Muslim ummah, but not with some of the things that Riva describes (and endorses?).

I refer here to what she suggests as the novel feature of transnationalism, namely 'its organisational aspect' (p. 191, Kastoryano, this volume), which leads to the creation of new 'nationalist' or transnational communities without reference to one territory but several territories (which she calls 'non-territorial'). Riva says that transnationalism, on the one hand, uses citizenship in the country of settlement to gain rights but its main collective, affective and imaginative identification remains with the country of origin in terms of roots and ethnicity. So, on the one hand there is an instrumentalisation of multicultural citizenship so that citizens of migrant origins see the citizenship in the country of settlement as merely a legal status and claim rights without having, indeed withholding, a sense of belonging to the country. On the other hand, transnationalism is used by states such as Turkey and Morocco as strategies to extend their power and sovereignty beyond borders (pp. 199–200, Kastoryano, this volume) as they try to influence a diaspora and to intervene in other countries or use their diaspora to negotiate advantages over another country. Riva does not try to persuade me that this double-aspected, strong transnationalism is compatible with my multicultural nationalism (or even with an ethic of democratic citizenship), indeed she says that it challenges it (p. 201, Kastoryano, this volume). That is how it appears to me too. I am too committed to multiculturalism to give up on it in the drastic ways that this transnationalism requires. I am, however, willing to see if a) transnationalism has any real empirical existence in Western Europe and if so in what form and to what extent and b) to include transnationalism, together with cosmopolitan-universalism and interculturalism as well as multiculturalism in thinking about a multilevel, multiphilosophical normative analysis of the possible and feasible approaches to the governance of diversity in Western Europe today. This was exactly the ambition of the project, Plurispace, that Riva and I, together with John-Erik Fossum and Ricard Zapata-Barrero, recently undertook (Fossum et al. 2023). Our main finding, currently being written up for publication, was that strong transnationalism is largely absent from discussion and practice in Western Europe today, not just in policymaking, national and local, but also among the leaders of ethnic minority associations. So, while the transnationalism that Riva has brought into our discussions has to be approached cautiously, it is not necessarily very potent in Western Europe. In any case, Riva has said to me that she is grateful for making her think normatively and not just empirically about transnationalism and indeed Plurispace has given us a vehicle for doing so collaboratively and I hope we will continue to do so.

While I have had some kind of an intellectual and research relationship with just about every contributor and editor of this book, I must mention my relationship with Anna Triandafyllidou. My most international and European Union funded projects have been ones on which she has been the Principal Investigator – and I doubt if we could have got them funded without her grantsmanship and track record in funding success – and in which she has enabled me to play a leading role. To the extent that I have gradually developed from being a Britain-focused researcher and theorist to a comparativist, I owe mainly to my collaboration with Anna. The projects would never have been achieved without an intellectual understanding between us and the synergies between our two skill sets. This has been not just a productive partnership but an enriching experience. It has worked not just because of some intellectual alignment but despite our having some important interests we have not shared. Anna has led pioneering and extensive research into many diverse aspects of migration and mobility and in varied geographical locations. This is a significant part of her CV but it's an interest I have not shared and it has not got in the way of our joint work. Her contribution in this book is an example of her cutting-edge work on mobilities and given my lack of expertise in this area I will not comment on it in general. She usefully raises an issue I have not considered: the identity-making and identity-fragmenting quality of connexions of people via the Internet, especially connections with people within and outside your nation-state; especially in connexion with national identity and national belonging; and what resources do some existing theories offer in understanding the phenomena under study. Part of Anna's explanatory approach to understanding the new forms of mobility and migration and the ensuing identity dichotomies that arise is her conceptualisation of some of the current developments of nations and nationalisms in terms of the proposed notion of plural v. neo-tribal nationalism (Triandafyllidou 2020). As she notes, her concept of 'plural nationalism' is very close to my 'multicultural nationalism' (Modood 2018), though she is more attentive than me to minority nations like Quebec in Canada and Scotland in Britain, and on the transnational currents, while my focus is on thinking about what normative understanding of membership is desirable and feasible, at least in certain countries. For me, this normative understanding centres on citizenship and national identity and their capacity to be rethought and remade from versions which centre on cultural homogeneity and interclass cooperation – basically the social democratic conception of citizenship of Western Europe from the late 1940s into the 1980s – to those centred on recognition of ethno-religious and ethno-racial difference within a multilayered, complex sense of common, inclusive national belonging. As I noted earlier, this is a conception of multicultural citizenship that Will Kymlicka and I share and while Anna works with some aspects of current globalisation and mobilities that are missing in my conception, she leaves unclear, certainly unelaborated, the normative underpinnings of her plural nationalism. So, we both face certain, albeit different, challenges here and I agree with Anna that the promise of some future collaboration beckons. It may even be that we might find some productive reconciliation between her suggestion of the imperative to look to the everyday, and mine that we first work out what normativity is needed at the macro level.

Multiculturalism and Secularism

Cécile Laborde and I were briefly at Nuffield College, Oxford at the same time but did not really interact and she really first came to my attention some years later when she developed a 'critical republicanism' and applied it to the case of the accommodation of Muslims in Europe. It was 'critical' in the sense that it was a critique of what was actually being practised in France but it was 'republican' in that it was an interpretation of some of the ideals of republicanism. It was a republicanism that was not being and should be practised. Cécile has gone on to achieve considerable prominence through a systematic, elegant reworking of liberal egalitarianism in relation to the place of religion (Laborde 2017). She has achieved this through continuous adaptations, a feature of which for me is that on each iteration she has come closer to multiculturalism and further from republican or liberal church–state separationism. Her chapter offers a penetrating discussion of the connexions between race and religion. She has a number of kind things to say about aspects of my work, specifically, in my insisting that the position of Muslims in a country like Britain cannot be understood simply as members of a faith nor simply as a set of racially disadvantaged groups (like Pakistanis, Arabs, etc.) or defined by skin colour. So, the remedy for the vulnerabilities they suffer from cannot be to do with the goals of religious pluralism such as freedom of belief and toleration only nor simply in opposing the racism they are subjected to. Cécile flatters me considerably in pairing me with John Rawls, who is an exemplar of the bifurcations I oppose, in a discussion of the relationship and contrasts between race and religion. Her incisive comments on Rawls were new to me and most stimulating. She went on to present a proposal of her own which would retain the valuable intuitions of luck egalitarianism in Rawls, without entailing some of the difficulties she points to in those positions. The proposal goes beyond her earlier work, in which she has recognised how minorities, including religious minorities, are othered or stigmatised, and has presented an egalitarian approach almost completely focused on reducing or eliminating such liabilities. At more than one seminar, I have put my hand up to say that this represents a truncated and one-sided understanding of equality; it misses the identity and group subjectivity of the racialised persons, which it should be the goal of multicultural equality to allow to be present and respected as part of our shared public lives. In her chapter, Cécile has taken this point seriously and has offered a dual framework of holding together a First Person perspective of how people think of themselves and their identity-aspirations and a Third Person perspective of how others see them, including, all too often, in terms of demeaning stereotypes and distorting group slurs. She recognises that sometimes both these perspectives can be present and so, even when we are just talking about a religious group, the normative goals associated with racial equality have to be part of the analysis of the group's vulnerability and its removal. My initial response to this development of her thought is that, as she claims, it captures the thrust of the egalitarian aspects of multiculturalism; she may even be right in thinking that it is an addition to multiculturalism without any problematic implications but for the moment it may be best for me to reserve judgement on that.

Rajeev Bhargava and I first came to the topic of political secularism as we strongly felt that our countries, respectively India and Britain, were moving towards a hostility to some or all religions, and doing so in the name of a misconceived secularism (Bhargava 1999; Modood 1994). In theorising Indian secularism, Rajeev argued that a different theoretical conception was at work from what he formulated as the mainstream Western conceptions: a freedom of religion model, as in the US, and a freedom from religion model, as in France (Bhargava 2009). As I had already begun to engage with British controversies about secularism, Muslim militancy and the rightful place of religion, I could see that Britain and indeed Western Europe (with the exception of France) did not fit into Rajeev's two Western models (Modood 2010). Thus began a fairly intense dialogue between us about the nature of political secularism, and specifically how to characterise Britain and Western Europe. As Rajeev notes, I conceptualised the latter in terms of 'moderate secularism' and Rajeev came to accept that in due course. On the other hand, he has persuaded me that we should not be too squeamish about characterising our times as a crisis of secularism. I had protested that we were not headed for any kind of breakdown, that the scale of the challenges was quite manageable within our available resources (at least in Britain), but Rajeev pointed out that while that was a possible interpretation of 'crisis', it was an extreme one and surely I would not deny that we were at a moment of critical juncture, even if it varies in intensity between countries. Once we were able to agree on these two points: that moderate secularism was a good way to understand Western Europe and that existing political secular arrangements were being stress-tested and needed to be rethought; it laid bare what we continue to disagree about. Reading his chapter, I believe Rajeev points to three areas of disagreement. Firstly, he argues that political secularism is always geared to some values, to liberal democracy in fact, and I omit these in my account. The purpose of my minimalist definition of secularism as the autonomy of politics, specifically from religious authority and control, is so as to be able to include the full range of cases. These include the former USSR and the People's Republic of China, for instance, who are evidently and militantly secularist and so it would be odd to say they are not secularist because they reject liberal democracy. Of course, I think moderate secularisms – but not all versions of political secularism – sit within and have a historically symbiotic relationship with liberal democracy, as also with nationalism, and social democratic welfarism, but I don't want to distort the concept of political secularism by privileging moderate secularism or liberal democracy.

Secondly, Rajeev believes that the accommodation of Muslims in Western Europe will not occur through institutional adjustments but requires also fundamental change in how Europeans view Muslims and Islam. I have also argued that for me recognition is fundamental but that it should not be understood as merely about perceptions or social imaginaries but also institutional accommodation, so I don't think we differ. Thirdly, he says, I do not cite examples of where the state may legitimately interfere with Muslims, for example, in relation to gender or sectarianism, such interventionism being a critical feature of the Indian secularism that Rajeev theorises and justifies. It's true that I have not been as exercised about this as Rajeev or the Indian state has. Yet, as my advocacy of the multiculturalising of moderate secularism is based on and includes a robust framework of individual rights, which should be enforced to protect individuals and minorities, including if necessary from their own religious organisations as well as from anyone else, and I am clearly committed to laws on religious discrimination and incitement to religious hatred, I don't think my position could be construed as non-interventionist in relation to regulation of religions and protection against victimisation. An instance is my support for sharia councils in Britain, which are mainly resorted to by Muslim women in relation to their (usually, ex-) husbands, as supplements to and within the laws of the land based on the councils being a voluntary institution, open to public scrutiny and the women petitioners being explained their rights in law, by social workers or solicitors if necessary (Modood 2019: 140–3; see also the work of my PhD graduate, Azzouz 2022). Rajeev's general point in relation to the second and third differences he sees between us is that each requires some modification of moderate secularism, in fact, he says, a new theoretical conception. Well, yes, I have been arguing for a multiculturalising of moderate secularism (2013 [2007]: 72–8 [78–86]). The difference between us has been that I thought and he denied this could be done without abandoning it, including weak establishment; specifically I argued that moderate secularism lends itself to being multiculturalised in the way that liberal neutrality and laïcité do not; and moreover, such adaptation was already taking place in Britain, though needed to be taken much further. That continues to be, as Rajeev, says, 'where we profoundly disagree' (p. 241, Bhargava, this volume).

Rajeev's chapter also discusses Indian secularism, which I think is indeed in a state of crisis that goes way beyond that in Europe, given what has been happening in relation to the violence that the ruling party has brought upon Muslims and where they are being made not just de facto but de jure second-class citizens. India now seems to be a leader in the Islamophobia that Rajeev feels is an obstacle to reforming moderate secularism in Europe (Sikka 2022). Together with Thomas Sealy I have been giving some thought to the place of Indian secularism within a conceptual framework of secularism that is not confined to Western cases, and to how Indian secularism relates to multiculturalism or deep diversity (Modood and Sealy 2024).

Bhikhu Parekh, like Charles Taylor, was already a prominent political philosopher when I was a student, and has come to be rightly recognised as one of the seventeen leading British political theorists of the twentieth century (Kelly 2010). I initially was interested in his writings on philosophical method and Michael Oakeshott, who had been like a PhD supervisor to him without actually being one. Later, I devoured his work on multiculturalism. Bhikhu has been a personal mentor to me but more fundamentally I would say that through his theoretical originality, courageous public intellectual engagement and long public service, and as part of the pioneering generation of South Asians in Britain, he has been not just a model and an inspiration to me but that he opened up intellectual and political space in Britain into which I and many others could step. In this way, without ever being at Bristol University, he is foundational to what in the fullness of time came to be the Bristol School of Multiculturalism (Levey 2018). As with David Boucher, I first met Bhikhu at a job interview: not for a political theory position but for a policy post at the Commission of Racial Equality in London in 1989, where Bhikhu was Deputy Chairman and led the panel that interviewed me (this time I got the job!). We have actually worked on relatively few things together, the main one being on the Commission on Multi-Ethnic Britain (1998–2000), which Bhikhu chaired and to which I was formally an academic advisor but Bhikhu encouraged me to play a much more active role.

Bhikhu's chapter in this book is on the secular state. The thrust of it in general is one I largely agree with and Bhikhu does cite my collection of essays on the theme (Modood 2019), so perhaps here I might focus on some subtle differences between us and caution against some possible overstatements of our shared position. Interestingly, we approach our common ground from different sides. Bhikhu assumes or starts with an understanding of political secularism in terms of 'separation' of religion and the state, which he then goes on to highly qualify. I work on the assumption that there is some degree – more or less – of autonomy, mutual or one-sided, and then ask myself what kinds of connexions exist. Looking at the variety of possible connexions, actual and possible, allows me to avoid the position that the values of liberty, equality and common belonging 'can be achieved only when state and religion are separated' (p. 261, Parekh, this volume) and to appreciate the value of certain aspects of that kind of connexion. Bhikhu argues that 'the state should not pursue religious goals' (p. 261, Parekh, this volume) whereas I leave this open: the state may pursue religious goals as long as there are good state reasons for them, and the relevant state institutions and policies have requisite popular support. The state should not pursue religious goals without due consideration of the good of the polity as a whole and with popular support – ideally, in a liberal, democratic, constitutional manner. This may considerably restrict what religious goals it may pursue, but it does not rule it out a priori. Just as I would wish to allow for more variation in religion–state connexions within the rubric of secularism, I would also like to see the shared characteristics as well as differences between different religious traditions and their capacity to change, converge as well as diverge over time. 'Religions differ greatly. Some, such as Christianity and Islam, are belief-centred, others such as Hinduism and Buddhism, give primacy to practice' (pp. 264–5, Parekh, this volume). I would nudge this so as to turn these differences in kinds of religion into a spectrum, that is, a belief–practice–identity spectral complex, not just a binary or a triad. True, some religions are more at one end than others and though this can depend on time and place, it is widely acknowledged that Protestantism is towards the belief end.

Moreover, within any religion there is a spectrum: for some Muslims, Islam is about belief, believing in the shahada, or at least in not denying it; for others, it is very much about some observance of rules; and for others, it is participation in a Muslim heritage, encompassing the ideational and the aesthetic. My response then to Bhikhu's chapter is to soften some of his binaries into a spectrum of possibilities, the extreme ends of which should not exclusively characterise concepts such as secular and the differences between religions. Bhikhu rightly emphasises our shared 'multiple secularisms' approach but the nature of secularism could be expressed in a less categorical and more anti-essentialist way. One way to do so, as I said in my response to Rajeev, is to have a more minimalist conception of secularism (Modood 2019), not one that necessarily meets the requirements of liberty, equality and common belonging, and then see how these and other values can or should come into play in relation to the governance of religious diversity in different societal contexts, the comparative, anti-essentialist approach I have recently developed with Thomas Sealy (Modood and Sealy 2024).

In concluding, I would like to note that at the Festschrift conference from which this book is derived there were a number of other presentations. While practical issues have prevented them from being included here, I would like those presenters to know that I have not forgotten their generosity in finding time and taking the effort to prepare and present their papers and I thank them no less than the contributors here. Understandably, my biggest thanks go to my mentees and friends, Nasar Meer, Varun Uberoi and Thomas Sealy (in the order of the length of time I have known them, from about twenty to about ten years), who conceived of, raised funding for, organised and brought into existence the Festschrift conference and this book.

References

Abbott, A. (2018), 'Varieties of Normative Inquiry: Moral Alternatives to Politicization in Sociology', *The American Sociologist*, 49, 158–80.

Antonsich, M. (2016), 'Interculturalism versus Multiculturalism – The Cantle–Modood Debate', *Ethnicities*, 16 (3), 470–93.

Azzouz, F. (2022), *Muslim Marriage and Divorce Practices in Britain: Avenues for Regulation*. Doctoral dissertation, University of Bristol.

Bhargava, R. (ed.) (1999), *Secularism and Its Critics*. New Delhi: Oxford University Press.

Bhargava, R. (2009), 'Political Secularism: Why It Is Needed and What Can Be Learnt from Its Indian Version', in G. B. Levey and T. Modood (eds), *Secularism, Religion and Multicultural Citizenship*. Cambridge: Cambridge University Press.

Bouchard, G. (2011), 'What Is Interculturalism?', *McGill Law Journal / Revue de droit de McGill*, 56 (2), 435–46.

Bouchard, G. and C. Taylor (2008), *Building the Future: A Time for Reconciliation*. Toronto: Canadian Scholars.

Begum, N. (2023), '"The European family? Wouldn't that be the white people?": Brexit and British Ethnic Minority Attitudes towards Europe', *Ethnic and Racial Studies*, 46 (15), 1–23.

Cantle, T. (2012), *Interculturalism: The New Era of Cohesion and Diversity*. Basingstoke: Palgrave Macmillan.

Commission on Multi-Ethnic Britain (CMEB) (2000), *The Future of Multi-Ethnic Britain*. London: Profile Books.

Dobbernack, J. (2018), 'The Missing Politics of Muscular Liberalism', *Identities*, 25 (4), 377–96.

Dobbernack, J. (2019), 'Making a Presence: Images of Polity and Constituency in British Muslim Representative Politics', *Ethnicities*, 19 (2), 292–310.

Dobbernack, J., N. Meer and T. Modood (2015), 'Misrecognition and Political Agency. The Case of Muslim Organisations in a General Election', *The British Journal of Politics and International Relations*, 17 (2), 189–206.

Dikici, E. (2021), *Transnational Islam and the Integration of Turks in Great Britain*. Springer International Publishing.

Evans, G. and J. Tilley (2017), *The New Politics of Class: The Political Exclusion of the British Working Class*. Oxford: Oxford University Press.

Fossum, J. E., R. Kastoryano, T. Modood and R. Zapata-Barrero (2023), 'Governing Diversity in the Multilevel European Public Space', *Ethnicities*, 24 (1), 3–30.

Fraser, N. (2003), 'Social Justice in the Age of Identity Politics: Redistribution, Recognition and Participation', in N. Fraser and A. Honneth, *Redistribution or Recognition: A Political–Philosophical Exchange*. London: Verso, 7–109.

Hammersley, M. (2023), 'Should Sociology be Normative?', *The American Sociologist*, 1–14.

Kelly, P. (ed.) (2010), *British Political Theory in the Twentieth Century*. Wiley-Blackwell.

Kundnani, H. (2023), *Eurowhiteness: Culture, Empire and Race in the European Project*. Hurst Publishers.

Kymlicka, W. (1995), *Multicultural Citizenship: A Liberal Theory of Minority Rights*. Oxford: Clarendon Press.

Laborde, C. (2017), *Liberalism's Religion*. Cambridge, MA: Harvard University Press.

Lægaard, S. (forthcoming), 'Normative Sociology and Normative Behaviorism: Recent Discussions of How Empirical Social Science and Normative Political Theory Can Inform Each Other', [update information at page proof stage].

Lewicki, A. (2014), *Social Justice through Citizenship?: The Politics of Muslim Integration in Germany and Great Britain*. Springer.

Mansouri, F. and T. Modood (2021), 'The Complementarity of Multiculturalism and Interculturalism: Theory Backed by Australian Evidence', *Ethnic and Racial Studies*, 44 (16), 1–20.

Meer, N. (2022), *The Cruel Optimism of Racial Justice*. Bristol: Policy Press.

Modood, T. (1984), 'R. G. Collingwood, M. J. Oakeshott and the Idea of a Philosophical Culture', PhD Thesis, University College, Swansea, University of Wales.

Modood, T. (1992), *Not Easy Being British: Colour, Culture and Citizenship*. London: Runnymede Trust and Trentham Books.

Modood, T. (2004), 'Capitals, Ethnic Identity and Educational Qualifications'. *Cultural Trends*, 13 (2), 87–105.

Modood, T. (2009), 'Moderate Secularism and Multiculturalism', *Politics*, 29 (1), 71–6.

Modood, T. (2010), 'Moderate Secularism, Religion as Identity and Respect for Religion', *The Political Quarterly*, 81 (1), 4–14.

Modood, T. (2013 [2007]), *Multiculturalism: A Civic Idea*. 2nd edn. Cambridge: Polity Press.

Modood, T. (2014), 'Multiculturalism, Interculturalisms and the Majority', *Journal of Moral Education*, 43 (3), 302–15.

Modood, T. (2017), 'Intercultural Public Intellectual Engagement', *Journal of Citizenship and Globalisation Studies*, 1 (1), 36–47.

Modood, T. (2018), 'A Multicultural Nationalism', *Brown Journal of World Affairs*, 25, 233–46.

Modood, T. (2019), *Essays on Secularism and Multiculturalism*. United Kingdom: ECPR Press/Rowman & Littlefield International Limited.

Modood, T. (2022a), 'Bristol School of Multiculturalism as Normative Sociology', *Civic Sociology*, 3 (1), 573–9.

Modood, T. (2022b), 'Is Multicultural Nationalism Possible? If it is, what benefits follow?', Is Multiculturalism Compatible with Nationalism?, Symposium, CERC, Toronto Metropolitan University, 26 May.

Modood, T. (2022c), 'Brexit Means Less Hope for Multiculturalism in the EU', OpenDemocracy, 22 November. Accessed at: <https://www.opendemocracy.net/en/podcasts/podcast-borders-belonging/brexit-migration-white-uk-european-union/>

Modood, T. and E. Becker (2022), 'Normative Sociology in the Bristol School of Multiculturalism: An Interview with Tariq Modood', *Civic Sociology*, 3 (1), 574–98.

Modood, T. and R. Kastoryano (2006), 'Secularism and the Accommodation of Muslims in Europe', in A. Triandafyllidou, T. Modood and R. Zapata-Barrero (eds), *Multiculturalism, Muslims and Citizenship*. London: Routledge.

Modood, T. and T. Sealy (2024), *The New Governance of Religious Diversity*. Cambridge: Polity Press.

Modood, T. and S. Thompson (2018), 'Revisiting Contextualism in Political Theory: Putting Principles into Context', *Res Publica*, 24, 339–57.

Oakeshott, M. (1933), *Experience and its Modes*. Cambridge: Cambridge University Press.

Parekh, B. (2004), 'Redistribution or Recognition? A Misguided Debate', in S. May, T. Modood and J. Squires (eds), *Ethnicity, Nationalism and Minority Rights*. Cambridge: Cambridge University Press.

Taylor, C. (1994), *Multiculturalism*. Expanded paperback edn. Germany: Princeton University Press.

Taylor Hill, S. (2023), 'Building a Community of Equals: Challenging Alienation in the British Working Class', PhD Thesis, University of Bristol.

Thompson, S. and T. Modood (2022), 'The Multidimensional Recognition of Religion', *Critical Review of International Social and Political Philosophy*, 1–22.

Triandafyllidou, A. (2020), 'Nationalism in the 21st Century: Neo-tribal or Plural?', *Nations and Nationalism*, 26 (4), 792–806.

Uberoi, V. and T. Modood (2013), 'Inclusive Britishness: A Multiculturalist Advance', *Political Studies*, 61 (1), 23–41.

Uberoi, V. (2021), 'Oakeshott and Parekh: The Influence of British Idealism on British Multiculturalism', *History of Political Thought*, 42 (4), 730–54.

Uberoi, V. and T. Modood (2019), 'The Emergence of the Bristol School of Multiculturalism', *Ethnicities*, 19 (6), 955–70.

INDEX

EU representative:
Easy Access System Europe
Mustamäe tee 50, 10621 Tallinn, Estonia
Gpsr.requests@easproject.com

www.ingramcontent.com/pod-product-compliance
Lightning Source LLC
Chambersburg PA
CBHW071731270326
41928CB00013B/2636